Tradition
and
Change in
Three
Generations
of
Japanese
Americans

John W. Connor

Nelson-Hall [nh] Chicago

Library of Congress Cataloging in Publication Data

Connor, John W
    Tradition and change in Three Generations of Japanese
Americans.

    Bibliography: p.
    Includes index.
      1. Japanese Americans—California—Sacramento.
2. Acculturation. 3. Sacramento, Calif.—Social conditions. I.   Title.
F869.S12C68   301.45'19'56079454   76-46942
ISBN 0-88229-288-9

To my wife,
Minako,
of course.

Contents

List of Tables   ix
List of Figures   xii
Introduction   xiii
Chapter 1   **Statement of the Problem**   1
Chapter 2   **Methodology and Theoretical Issues**   7
Chapter 3   **Japanese Psychological
                 and Behavioral Characteristics**   15
Chapter 4   **American Psychological
                 and Behavioral Characteristica**   45
Chapter 5   **Contrasting Japanese and American
                 Patterns of Individuation and
                 Conformity**   67
Chapter 6   **The Issei Interview Schedule**   81
Chapter 7   **The Nisei Interview Schedule**   101
Chapter 8   **The Sansei Interview Schedule**   117
Chapter 9   **The Incomplete Sentence Test**   137
Chapter 10   **The Ethnic Identity Questionnaire**   193
Chapter 11   **The Contrasting Values Survey**   223
Chapter 12   **The Edwards Personal Preference
                 Schedule**   271
Chapter 13   **Summary and Conclusions**   295
Appendix A   **Issei Interview Questionnaire**   321
Appendix B   **Nisei Interview Schedule**   325
Appendix C   **Sansei Interview Schedule**   329
Appendix D   **The Ethnic Identity Questionnaire**   333
Appendix E   **The Contrasting Values Survey**   337
References   341
Index   351

List of Tables

Table 1   Percentage Distribution on
             Identification of Japanese Words   108
Table 2   Percentage Distribution on
             Observation of Holidays   110
Table 3   Percentage Distribution on Attitude
             Expressed Toward Sansei Dating
             Non-Japanese   123
Table 4   Percentage Distribution on Attitude
             Expressed Toward Sansei Marrying
             Non-Japanese   124
Table 5   Number of Recorded Marriages Involving
             Individuals of Japanese and Non-Japanese
             Surnames in Sacramento County
             for the Years 1961-1970   126
Table 6   Percentage Distribution of Nisei and
             Sansei Reporting Parental Stress on
             Certain Principles   129
Table 7   Arithmetic Mean Distribution on
             Subjective Self-Evaluation of
             Degree of Acculturation   132
Table 8   The Assimilation Variables   134
Table 9.1   Percentage Distribution on Incomplete
             Sentence 1, All Children Should. . . .,
             for Total Sample   149
Table 9.2   Percentage Distribution on Incomplete
             Sentence 2, The Most Important Lesson
             Parents Can Teach. . . ., for Total
             Sample   ᕁ   152
Table 9.3   Percentage Distribution on Incomplete
             Sentence 3, The Best Time of Life. . . .,
             for Total Sample   155
Table 9.4   Percentage Distribution on Incomplete
             Sentence 4, A Person Is Better Off If
             He Depends. . . ., for Total Sample   156
Table 9.5   Percentage Distribution on Incomplete
             Sentence 8, When Someone Does Him A
             Favor. . . ., for Total Sample   159

Table 9.6   Percentage Distribution on Incomplete
Sentence 9, A Man's Strongest
Obligation. . . ., for Total Sample   163

Table 9.7   Percentage Distribution on Incomplete
Sentence 12, When His Boss Asked Him
to Work. . . ., for Total Sample   165

Table 9.8   Percentage Distribution on Incomplete
Sentence 15, When An Elected Official
Recommends A Policy. . . ., for
Total Sample   169

Table 9.9   Percentage Distribution on Incomplete
Sentence 16, The Deepest Emotional
Relationship. . . ., for Total Sample   171

Table 9.10   Percentage Distribution on Incomplete
Sentence 17, When A Neighbor Reported
Her Child Misbehaving. . . ., for
Total Sample   175

Table 9.11   Percentage Distribution on Incomplete
Sentence 20, When He Thinks of His
Mother. . . ., for Total Sample   177

Table 9.12   Percentage Distribution on Incomplete
Sentence 21, If A Person Finds Himself
in Difficulty. . . ., for Total Sample   180

Table 9.13   Percentage Distribution on Incomplete
Sentence 22, When Seated on A Crowded
Bus. . . ., for Total Sample   182

Table 9.14   Percentage Distribution on Incomplete
Sentence 23, When He Heard That His
Child Had Been Threatened. . . .,
for Total Sample   185

Table 9.15   Percentage Distribution on Incomplete
Sentence 24, When He Thinks of His
Father. . . ., for Total Sample   186

Table 9.16   Percentage Distribution on Incomplete
Sentence 25, When His Superior Gave Him
an Order. . . ., for Total Sample   189

Table 9.17   Percentage Distribution on Incomplete
Sentence 28, What He Is Really Afraid
Of. . . ., for Total Sample   191

Table 10.1   Significant Differences Between Sexes
Within Generations   197

Table 10.2	**Items Showing Hypothesized Generation Differences**	200
Table 10.3	**Items Not Showing Hypothesized Generation Differences**	202
Table 10.4	**Items Scored Positively by the Issei Generation**	206
Table 10.5	**Comparison of Sacramento and Seattle Issei Scores on Ten Items**	209
Table 10.6	**Items Scored Negatively by the Issei Generation**	212
Table 10.7	**Items Scored Positively by the Nisei Generation**	213
Table 10.8	**Items Scored Negatively by the Nisei Generation**	215
Table 10.9	**Items Scored Positively by the Sansei Generation**	218
Table 10.10	**Items Scored Negatively by the Sansei Generation**	220
Table 11.1	**Significant Differences Between Sexes Within Groups**	227
Table 11.2	**Items Showing Hypothesized Group Differences**	234
Table 11.3	**Items Not Showing Hypothesized Group Differences**	238
Table 11.4	**Items Scored Positively by the Issei Group**	246
Table 11.5	**Items Scored Negatively by the Issei Group**	250
Table 11.6	**Items Scored Positively by the Nisei Group**	251
Table 11.7	**Items Scored Negatively by the Nisei Group**	253
Table 11.8	**Items Scored Positively by the Sansei Group**	255
Table 11.9	**Items Scored Negatively by the Sansei Group**	256
Table 11.10	**Items Scored Positively by the Caucasian Group**	258
Table 11.11	**Items Scored Negatively by the Caucasian Group**	259
Table 11.12	**Total Mean Dominance Scores**	261

Table 11.13	Total Mean Deference Scores	262
Table 11.14	Male Mean Dominance Scores	264
Table 11.15	Female Mean Dominance Scores	265
Table 11.16	Male Mean Deference Scores	266
Table 11.17	Female Mean Deference Scores	268
Table 12.1	Mean Scores of the EPPS Variables for All Groups	277
Table 12.2	Mean Scores of EPPS Variables for Male Groups	279
Table 12.3	Mean Scores of EPPS Variables for Female Groups	281
Table 12.4	Mean Scores of EPPS Variables for Males and Females in Six Groups	288

List of Figures

Figure 1.	Individuation Model	70
Figure 2.	Individualization Dominant	73
Figure 3.	Democratization Dominant	73
Figure 4.	Privatization Dominant	75
Figure 5.	Atomization Dominant	75

Introduction

In recent years there has been considerable interest in the Japanese Americans and in their experience in this country, both from the larger American society and within the Japanese community itself. Ironically, this revival of interest in the Japanese Americans on the part of the larger American society is now prompted by a somewhat belated recognition that the Japanese Americans are in many respects "model citizens," who exemplify a number of middle-class virtues such as a strong achievement motivation, long-range goals, the importance of keeping up appearances, and a respect for law and order. This last virtue is present in the Japanese Americans to such an extent that they now have the lowest crime and delinquency rate of any group (Kitano 1969:118).

The interest within the Japanese American community, on the other hand, is in part a reflection of the outside interest, but it is also motivated by a retrospective nostalgia and a growing sense of pride in the accomplishments of the first-generation immigrants (Issei) and their second-generation offspring, the Nisei. It is further motivated by an increasing concern in the extent of acculturation and a concomitant desire for the preservation of a Japanese identity in the third generation, the Sansei.

On a more theoretical level, the Japanese Americans are of interest both for the rapidity of their advancement and the means by which they attained it. More than twenty years ago Caudill (1952) was able to demonstrate that the successful and rapid advancement to middle-class status by the Japanese Americans in the Chicago area was due to values and adaptive mechanisms that were similar to, but by no means identical with, those of the American middle class. Moreover, for the past two decades there has been considerable speculation as to the extent or even desirability of further acculturation. Members of the community have repeatedly emphasized that the rapid advancement of the Japanese Americans was due to their attributes as Japanese Americans; therefore, the preservation of these attributes would result in even greater advancement. Furthermore, there was a commonly voiced fear that with increased acculturation would come an increase in the crime and delinquency rate, especially in the younger generation.

The subject of the present study incorporates many of the above interests. The principle focus is one of acculturation, with an emphasis on the psychological and behavioral changes that have occurred in the three generations. Additionally, it is appropriate to mention at this point that the study was also prompted by a personal interest on the part of the author and his family, who have resided in the Sacramento area for the last sixteen years. During that time we have come to know and share the interests of a large number of Japanese Americans, many of whom were of considerable assistance during this study. It was through our association with these people that we came to understand the concerns and problems facing the Japanese American community today.

Finally, apart from its general and theoretical interest, the most important consideration in doing this study at the present is one of time. We know now that the average age of Issei is about 72, of the Nisei 47, and of the Sansei 23.

Soon it will no longer be possible to study the three generations together. Moreover, this will be our last opportunity to study all three generations using the same testing protocols. Indeed, during the last stage of our research a note of urgency came in when we attempted to obtain some supplementary information on two Issei individuals who had been most helpful. When we attempted to contact them, we were sadly informed by relatives that they had died a few weeks before.

Chapter 1

Statement of the Problem

A number of observers (Caudill and DeVos 1956, Iga 1966, Kitano 1969, Peterson 1966) have remarked on the rapid advancement of Japanese Americans to middle-class status as measured by such criteria as income, education, and occupation. Their conclusions have been substantiated in a report issued in 1965 by the California Fair Employment Practices Commission entitled *Californians of Japanese, Chinese, and Filipino Ancestry*. The report indicated that the level of education was higher and the unemployment level lower than the corresponding levels for the overall white population. Of the attempts to explain this high level of achievement and rapid advancement, one of the earliest was an interdisciplinary study conducted by William Caudill, George DeVos, Lee Rainwater, and others.

In 1952, William Caudill advanced the thesis that the rapid adjustment of first- and second-generation Japanese Americans in the Chicago area after World War II was due to a compatibility of the value systems and adaptive mechanisms of the Japanese Americans and the American middle class. The thesis further states that these values and adaptive mechanisms are only compatible and are not identical (1952:10).

Caudill's discussion leaves open the question of the degree of acculturation and assimilation. Once having arrived at middle-class status, is the next step complete assimilation into the larger American culture with the concomitant loss of ethnic identity or will there be a retention of Japanese characteristics? Another question arises. If the observed success is due to the utilization of

1

adaptive mechanisms and values that are essentially Japanese in nature, will there then be a tendency to retain those characteristics and inculcate them in the oncoming generation or will they ultimately be replaced with values that are more characteristic of the larger American society?

The literature on the subject is by no means unanimous. There are those such as Kitano who state that the Sansei "are, on most measurements of acculturation, completely identical to the Caucasian group. Their test results, achievement and interest preferences, and social values are typically American" (1969:141-142). In somewhat the same vein, Iga states of the Sansei: "Their desire to be assimilated appears to be so complete and their knowledge of Japanese culture so marginal that we cannot anticipate their return to traditional Japanese interests" (1966).

On the other hand, other observers such as Arkoff (1959), Fenz and Arkoff (1962), Berrien, Arkoff, and Iwahara (1967), Arkoff, Meredith, and Dong (1963), and Masuda, Matsumoto, and Meredith (1970) have found both considerable acculturation of the Issei generation and an appreciable residue of ethnic identity in the third generation.

Similarly, the literature on acculturation records numerous instances in which groups were able to preserve a high degree of ethnic identity. For example, Dozier found that the Hopi Tewa were able to maintain a "cultural, linguistic, and personality distinction from a numerically larger group" (1951:56). In another study, Hallowell discovered personality traits among the Ojibwa that were similar to those reported by missionaries some three centuries before (1967).

It may be justifiably argued, however, that the interaction of the Japanese Americans with the larger society has been quite different from that of the isolated reservation Indian. In this sense, perhaps, the experience of American Jews could better be used as a paradigm of acculturation and assimilation. Like the Japanese Americans, the American Jews have also risen in status, as Milton Gordon has indicated:

> The rise in socio-economic status of the Eastern European Jews and their descendants is, in fact, the greatest collective Horatio Alger story in American immigration history . . . . Numerous surveys of Jews in medium-sized communi-

ties show them to be bunched overwhelmingly in middle-class occupations, especially as managers and proprietors in retail and wholesale trade and manufacturing, and increasingly in the professions. (Gordon 1964:185-86)

As with the Japanese Americans, these Jews arrived at about the time of the turn of the century (Gordon 1964:185). And, again like the Japanese Americans, they were in a sense "preadapted" to middle-class values as Gordon indicated:

The reasons for this phenomenal rise in occupational status are complex, but in essence they pertain to the cultural history of the Jews before they came to America. The learning was easily transferred under new conditions to a desire for secular education, if not for the parent generation, at least for the children. The restrictions of Jewish occupational choice in medieval and post-medieval Europe had placed them in the traditional role of traders, self-employed artisans, and scholars. Thus the Jews arrived in America with the middle-class values of thrift, sobriety, ambition, desire for education, ability to postpone immediate gratifications for the sake of long range goals, and aversion to violence already internalized. (Gordon 1964:186)

What, then, can we learn from the Jewish experience that may help us to understand the direction of Japanese American acculturation and assimilation? Again, Gordon indicates that, while there have been numerous adaptations to the American middle class, there remains a desire to retain a Jewish ethnic identity:

In fact, the trend among native-born Jews in middle-class and suburban areas away from Orthodox cultural patterns (and one must remember that in Orthodox Judaism, religion and culture are hardly distinguishable) accompanied, simultaneously, by a strong desire for the preservation of ethnic identity as Jews, has led to the development of what Herbert Gans, in a perceptive discussion, has called "symbolic Judaism." By this he means a kind of minimal adherence to specifically Jewish cultural values or patterns, in which emphasis is placed on a selection of nostalgic items of "Yiddish culinary delicacies or Yiddish phrases," and possession in the home of tangible objects denoting Jewishness (for example, books, records, or pictures with Jewish themes), a concern with "Jewish" problems, and a selection of festive religious traditions which help socialize the children into an awareness of and affection for their Jewish identity. . . . The acculturation process, thus, has drastically modified American Jewish life in the direction of adaptation to American middle-class values, while it has not by any means dissolved the group in a structural sense. (Gordon 1964:194)

The implication of the above material is that the conflict between the two opposing views of acculturation or retention may be resolved in part by the understanding that acculturation need not be a unitary process whereby all of the culture traits, beliefs, and values of one group are completely replaced by those of another. In 1960, for example, Sol Tax was able to demonstrate that complete acculturation need not be inevitable. Frequently a core of meanings, beliefs, and practices would be retained so that it was often possible to maintain a culturally distinct group in the midst of a culturally different larger society (Tax 1960). Additional aid in resolving the conflict may be found in the concept of "psychological lag" as formulated by George DeVos (1973:13-60). From evidence obtained by projective tests in rural Japan, DeVos was able to deduce that although individuals may express a desire for a love marriage, it was psychologically easier for them to have an arranged marriage because of internalized sanctions. There was, therefore, a lag between expressed desire and actual behavior.

Similarly, such a concept may be of aid in understanding the behavior of Japanese Americans who are considered to be a "model minority" by such authors as Peterson, who writes: "By any criterion of good citizenship that we choose, the Japanese Americans are better than any other groups in our society, including native-born white" (1966:20). Moreover, the concept of "psychological lag" permits us to examine the values of the Sansei by utilizing Caudill and DeVos' (1956) theory that the good citizenship and observed success of the first two generations of Japanese Americans were due to adaptive mechanisms and values which, because of internalized sanctions or "psychological lag," were essentially Japanese in nature.

It may be objected, however, that the term "psychological lag" implies ultimate acculturation to the larger society. This is not the intent. As utilized here the concept merely refers to the continuation (and attenuation) in the three generations of Japanese Americans of certain values which are found to be characteristic of the more traditional Japanese culture.

The problem, then, is to investigate certain psychological and behavioral characteristics of three generations of Japanese Americans in order to determine the degree to which the various generations have retained certain characteristics which are distinctively Japanese or have replaced them with those which are distinctively American.

Chapter 2

Methodology and Theoretical Issues

Since the study is basically one of acculturation, the first step is to identify clearly those psychological and behavioral characteristics that are distinctively Japanese. These, in turn, are to be contrasted with distinctively American psychological and behavioral characteristics. This approach is in accord with the conclusions of the 1953 Social Science Research Council Summer Seminar on Acculturation:

> For the purposes of the formulation under consideration, acculturation may be defined as culture change that is initiated by the conjunction of two or more autonomous cultural systems . . . . Its dynamics can be seen as the selective adaptation of value systems, the processes of integration and differentiation, the generation of developmental sequences, and the operation of role determinants and personality factors. (Broom et al. 1967:156-57)

The psychological dimension is given additional emphasis in an appendix to the above formulation:

> As far as acculturation is concerned, the psychological problem is to determine the depth of commitment to certain shared patterns and values and consequently to assess the difficulties of accepting changes. For what is important in this connection is not the structure of the orientation of personality itself but the extent to which certain basic values are internalized or rejected and the extent to which they function as selective mechanisms in acculturation. (Broom et al. 1967:283-84)

In identifying these characteristics, several factors are to be kept in mind. One, in order to study acculturation it is necessary to establish a base line.

The concept of a zero point or base line from which change can be measured is attributed to Lucy Mair by Ralph Beals in his article "Acculturation," which appeared in *Anthropology Today*. In the article, Beals notes that the initial objection to the term came from Malinowski, who thought of the zero point as a point from which change began, the implication being that before contact no change took place. Yet, according to Beals, "Mair . . . proposed establishing a zero point on the best and most convenient base line with respect to a specified series of changes permitted by the data and the situation. The most historical-minded would ask no more" (Beals 1962:386). With respect to the Japanese American experience the base line is established by first identifying those distinctively Japanese characteristics that the first generation brought with them when they emigrated from Japan.

The second factor is that the lists of Japanese and American characteristics should be so constructed that they clearly and distinctly contrast with each other. That is, the lists should contain not only those characteristics that are clearly dominant in each of the cultures, but they should also omit those areas in which the two cultures share characteristics. For example, Caudill notes that both:

> Japanese and American middle-class cultures share in common the values of: politeness, respect for authority and parental wishes, duty and community, diligence, cleanliness and neatness, emphasis on personal achievement of long-range goals, shame (more than guilt) concerning nonsanctioned behavior, importance of keeping up appearances, and others. (1952:9)

He does go on to say, however, that these are only compatible and not identical (1952:10).

With these factors in mind, the following compilation of psychological and behavioral characteristics was made. Research indicated that the distinctively Japanese characteristics could be grouped under five major headings. These were an emphasis on collectivity, duty and obligation, hierarchy, deference, and dependence. The contrasting American characteristics were also grouped under major headings: individualism, equality, rights and privileges, self-reliance, and self-assertion. In turn, these major areas were elaborated into the following lists of twenty characteristics:

Japanese	American
1. Reliance on the group.	1. Individualism.
2. Children trained to be docile, obedient, and dependent.	2. Children trained to be independent.
3. Mother-son bond.	3. Husband-wife bond.
4. Emphasis on hierarchy.	4. Emphasis on equality.
5. Emphasis on duty.	5. Emphasis on rights.
6. Dependency need.	6. Independence, fear of dependence.
7. Passivity (nonagressiveness).	7. Aggressiveness or active mastery.
8. Submissive attitude toward authority.	8. Grudging acceptance of those in authority.
9. Emphasis on collaterality.	9. Emphasis on individual autonomy.
10. Achievement of goals set by others.	10. Achievement of individual goals.
11. Emphasis on ascribed status.	11. Emphasis on achieved status.
12. Compulsive obedience to rules and controls.	12. Resentment and dislike of rules and controls.
13. Obligation to the family.	13. Obligation to oneself.
14. Emphasis on self-effacement.	14. Emphasis on self-assertiveness.
15. Restriction of personal relations to a small group.	15. Openness and accessibility to others.
16. A sense of responsibility to others.	16. Responsibility to oneself.
17. Deference and politeness to superiors at all times.	17. Tendency to mask or play down the superiority of others.
18. A sense of fatalism.	18. A sense of optimism.
19. Success through self-discipline.	19. Success through pragmatism and the exploitation of opportunities.

| 20. Emphasis on compromise, precise rules of conduct, and a situational ethic. | 20. Emphasis on moral righteousness, generalized rules of conduct, and a universal ethic. |

The Japanese characteristics are derived from the works of Benedict (1946), Beardsley, Hall, and Ward (1959), Caudill (1952), (1956), (1962), (1969), (1970), DeVos (1965), (1967), Doi (1962), Nakamura (1964), Norbeck (1961), Reischauer (1965), Sansom (1943), Silberman (1964), and Vogel (1967).

The American characteristics are derived from the works of Coleman (1964), De Tocqueville (1964), Du Bois (1964), Fischer (1966), Hsu (1961), Kluckhohn (1949), Lerner (1964), Lipset (1964), Minturn and Lambert (1964), Potter (1964), and especially Williams (1969). A more thorough presentation of both the Japanese and American characteristics will be made in subsequent chapters.

In attempting to measure the amount of change from those characteristics that are distinctively Japanese to those that are distinctively American, we felt that the best approach would be to utilize several research instruments rather than to rely on one alone. In particular, we attempted to obtain copies of research instruments that had been used in Japan. For example, F. K. Berrien administered a Japanese version of the Edwards Personal Preference Schedule to some eighteen hundred Japanese students (1965).

We finally decided that the investigation could best be conducted by utilizing two main categories of instruments. One type of instrument would be used for gathering biographical information and data on the more overt forms of acculturation (e.g., changes in language use, attitudes toward intermarriage, etc.). The other type of instrument was to measure the more covert forms of acculturation (e.g., changes in values, belief systems, and personality characteristics). In all, there were four instruments in the second category: (1) An Incomplete Sentence Test, (2) The Edwards Personal Preference Schedule, (3) An Ethnic Identity Questionnaire, and (4) A Survey of Contrasting Values. Copies of these instruments appear in the Appendices.

The basic methodology has been to test all three generations with the same instruments where possible. In addition, the data so compiled were compared with the results of similar studies of Japanese, Japanese Americans, and Caucasian Americans.

The method of gathering data has been by means of personal interviews supplemented by mailed questionnaires. Greater emphasis has been placed on the personal interviews to provide the basic biographic information and the data on psychological and behavioral characteristics. Each informant was required to complete both the basic interview form and an additional questionnaire or schedule.

The author and his wife, who is a native speaker of Japanese, began to interview members of the Japanese American community in the spring of 1970. We began by interviewing those who were known to us personally. The next step was to ask those whom we had already interviewed to help us find others who would be willing to cooperate in the study.

We soon discovered, however, that there were a number of limitations on this approach. The basic limitation was one of time. For the most part, the informants were available only in the evenings or on weekends. Completion of the interview form itself usually required about one and a half to two hours. Moreover, since we also wished to administer either the Incomplete Sentence Test or the Edwards Personal Preference Schedule in addition to the basic interview form, we usually found it necessary to return for an hour or so on a subsequent evening.

Given the above limitations, we soon realized that at our rate of two or three interviews a week we would need several years in order to obtain a sizable sample. It was at this time that we arrived at a solution. At California State University, Sacramento, a number of Sansei (third-generation Japanese Americans) had expressed an interest in having courses that would explore the Japanese American experience in California. Classes had been established in both Sociology and History, and there was a request to involve the Anthropology Department.

After talking to a few of the Sansei, I soon realized that their interests were much the same as ours. They wanted to know more about the community and especially about the Nisei (second-generation Japanese Americans) and Issei (first-generation Japanese Americans). At a personal level the Sansei themselves were very much aware of some of the problems touched upon in this study. They wanted to know if their heritage would be lost or, contrarily, if because of their race they would even be allowed to assimilate into American society if they so desired.

We then proceeded to establish a Japanese American Community Study Class. Enrollment was limited to fifteen or twenty students who had been previously screened by the author. The students were required to read a number of books and articles in the initial few weeks of the course. During this time we discussed the forms we were to use and the rationale used in their construction. Further, in order that they might better understand the instruments they were using, the students were also required to take the Edwards Personal Preference Schedule, the Ethnic Identity Questionnaire, the Contrasting Values Survey, and the Incomplete Sentence Test.

In the last week prior to beginning their interviewing, the students were instructed in interviewing techniques. Most of the Sansei began their interviewing with other Sansei. As they became more confident, they next interviewed the Nisei. Finally, with the aid of the Nisei as interpreters, they interviewed the Issei.

During the period of interviewing, the students were required to meet with the instructor every week. At that time we would review the week's work, check the accuracy of the forms, and discuss the findings in relation to our own interviewing.

Near the end of the semester we met again as a group to discuss the data and any uniformities that had emerged from our study. The students then wrote a term paper based on their data and, finally, the material was filed under their names.

By this method we were able to increase our sample to include 177 male and 195 female Sansei, 110 male and 131 female Nisei, and 124 male and 110 female Issei. In addition, to further broaden our sample, both the Ethnic Identity Questionnaire and the Contrasting Values Survey were mailed to over 1,200 members of the Japanese American community in Sacramento. More detailed information on the procedures used in obtaining data will be given in subsequent chapters as the various instruments and forms are discussed.

In the course of this study no effort was made to obtain a strictly random sample of the community. Interviews were conducted and tests were administered only to those who expressed a willingness to cooperate. Nonetheless, as will be demonstrated in later chapters, it is believed that our sample size is sufficiently large enough to be representative of the Sacramento Japanese American community and, indeed, of Japanese Americans in general. The U. S. Bureau of the Census (1973) reveals that as of 1970 there were approximately 12,000 Japanese Americans living in the Sacramento metropolitan area.

Chapter 3

Japanese Psychological and Behavioral Characteristics

The Historical Basis: The Tokugawa Legacy

After nearly three centuries of intermittent civil war, Japan became unified in the sixteenth century under the leadership of Nobunaga and Hideyoshi. The process of unification was completed in the early seventeenth century by Tokugawa Ieyasu, one of the most remarkable figures in Japanese history.

Following the battle of Sekigahara in 1600, Ieyasu was named Shogun by the emperor and initiated the Tokugawa period which was to last for some two-and-one-half centuries until the Meiji restoration of 1868. The guiding philosophy and chief object of the Tokugawa government was to stop political change. In order to accomplish this, Japan must isolate itself from outside interference and preserve the feudal system for centuries after it had begun to disappear in Europe.

The first steps were taken in the early seventeenth century when Christian missionaries were ordered to leave the country. The persecution which accompanied the outlawing of Christianity intensified following the ill-fated Shimabara rebellion of 1638 in which 37,000 people were killed. The Portuguese were then expelled because of a belief in their complicity in the rebellion, and the English left soon after because trade was unprofitable. This left the Dutch, who were confined to a small island in Nagasaki harbor, as Japan's only effective window on the West.

The peace and order so highly desired by the Tokugawa could be achieved only by creating a rigidly hierarchical social order, freezing the social system, and then preserving the status quo for centuries. This was accomplished by organizing the populace into four main classes: the samurai, the farmers, the artisans, and the merchants. The samurai, who were at the top of the social pyramid, constituted only 5 or 6 per cent of the population. As a privileged warrior class they alone were permitted to carry swords and had the right of *kirisute*, the right to cut down and leave anyone who offered them an insult. They were not permitted to marry outside their class, and their code of conduct was cold, austere, and uncompromising. The samurai were expected to live spartan lives marked by frugality, enormous self-discipline, and absolute obedience and loyalty to their lords. They were trained to a life of self-sacrifice and enormous dedication to the task at hand. In time they became the administrators of the Tokugawa, and their code of ethics permeated the whole of Japanese society.

The economic base of the Tokugawa government was rice. Surveys were made of all land at the beginning of the Tokugawa period and estimates were made of potential yields. The tax was usually between 40 to 50 per cent of total production. Rice also formed the basis for establishing one's status as a *daimyo*, or great lord.

According to Tokugawa policy, Japan was divided into about 265 *han*. A *han* by definition was the realm of a *daimyo*. In order to be a *daimyo*, a lord must have a *han* that produced at least 10,000 *koku* of rice, or about 50,000 bushels. Each *han* was an autonomous unit with its own local rules and government.

The *daimyo*, in turn, were divided into three main categories: the *shimpan* or related *han*, that is, those who were related to the Tokugawa by blood or marriage; the *fudai*, or "hereditary" *daimyo*, whose ancestors had recognized Ieyasu as their lord before the battle of Sekigahara; and the *tozama*, or outer lords, whose ancestors were enemies, allies, or neutrals before the battle of Sekigahara. Of the three categories, the greatest lords were the *tozama*, but because they were under the most suspicion, they were treated harshly, and by the end of the Tokugawa period they were outnumbered by the *fudai*.

A major problem in such a feudal system was the maintenance of control over the various *han*. The Tokugawa government solved this by an ingenious arrangement which combined actual central control with theoretical local autonomy. To begin with, each *daimyo* was an autocrat in his own realm and could establish his own rules and laws. In practice, however, his government was only a miniature of the house rules of the Tokugawa, and he could not transgress the Tokugawa's laws, which were many. The *daimyo* paid no taxes to the Tokugawa, which had its own income of over 3 million *koku* of rice; however, they were required to make ritual tribute and were responsible for the maintenance of roads and other facilities in the *han*, and also its defense.

In order to prevent coalitions, the *fudai daimyo* were scattered among the *tozama* lords. There was to be no intermarriage between *daimyo* families without permission, and no *daimyo* could improve or repair their fortifications without approval.

To enforce these rules the Tokugawa employed a system of *metsuke*, or spies who kept a close watch on the *daimyo*. Another effective means of control was the *sankin kotai* system and the use of hostages.

The holding of hostages, which had long been practiced, became mandatory in 1634. The major provision of this rule was that the *daimyo* must leave their wives and children in Edo. The most important device, though, was the *sankin kotai* system, or attendance by turns, which became a requirement in 1642. Under this system each of the various categories of *daimyo* was divided into two groups which alternated annually. This requirement meant that periodically, usually every other year, each *daimyo* was expected to make the journey to Edo and remain in attendance. While at Edo the ceremonial and other duties of the *daimyo* were prescribed in great detail. This, together with the expense of travelling and maintaining separate residences, placed an enormous economic burden on the *daimyo*, a burden that was soon shifted to the already impoverished samurai retainers and the increasingly desperate farmers, who represented some 80 per cent of the population (Reischauer and Fairbank 1960:590-631).

Given the agrarian economic base, it is natural that local *daimyo* and the Tokugawa government would develop an active interest in agriculture and especially rice production. The

Tokugawa government's policy was to encourage agriculture and increase the rice yields. New farming techniques were developed, new irrigation systems were established, and new land was brought under production.

The new techniques brought both an increase in production and an increase in population, which ultimately resulted in a shortage of land for cultivation. It was at this time (1673) that the central government issued a law prohibiting the subdivision of any holding producing less than 10 *koku* of rice to prevent increasing the ratio of people to the land. Moreover, because of the *sankin kotai* system taxes were raised in some villages to nearly 60 per cent. In turn, the burden of even heavier taxes forced many of the marginal peasants to the wall and greatly increased the number of tenant farmers. By 1730 the carrying capacity of the land was reached and the population had to be limited. This was achieved by various folk contraceptive methods and by the use of more drastic measures such as selling daughters and infanticide.

Villages at this time became closed corporate units. Each village was an autonomous administrative and economic unit that was represented by a headman and administered by a village council. The village was self-sufficient and self-supporting and represented a fairly closed economic and political social unit. Each village was responsible for its own law and for the repair of its roads, bridges, and irrigation system. It could make contracts and be sued. Villagers were collectively responsible for tax payments and accountable for crimes committed by any village member (Beardsley et al. 1959:50).

Land holdings were small, on the average about 2½ acres, and wet rice agriculture required a great deal of cooperative labor. At the time of rice transplanting, for example, a larger labor force was needed than could be mustered by any one household. Moreover, irrigation networks required a great deal of cooperative labor in order to keep them functioning, and such activities as roof rethatching, weeding, and road repair were also done on a cooperative basis.

If such a closed corporate community is allowed to simmer for several centuries, it is obvious that there will be an enormous emphasis on the importance of the collectivity or group and there would be little or no place for what we would call the rugged individualist. Given the closed corporate nature of the community and the necessity for cooperative activity in order to survive, it is obvious that most social controls would be in the form of gossip, shaming, or ridicule. Given the absolute necessity for cooperation, it would also seem reasonable that one of the most effective sanctions would be the denial of all but emergency aid.

Such an extreme sanction was known as *mura hachibu*, or "village eight-parts," which signified that with the exception of aid in the case of fire or funerals, all other interaction and aid would be discontinued. In extreme cases the village would practice *mura harai*, or "village cleansing," in which case the offending party would be expelled from the village (Smith 1966:36-64).

It can be seen, then, that for more than two-and-one-half centuries, life in Japan, in many respects, resembled life in a police state. The social order was authoritarian and rigidly hierarchical; one could not easily move from one class to another, or even from one occupation to another. Protocol and etiquette were highly formalized and were extended to such areas as language use and even to the style of clothing to be worn by members of the various classes.

Nor can it be said that the Tokugawa ethical system disappeared with the modernization of Japan. While it is true that there was an initial wave of enthusiasm for all things Western, the enthusiasm was soon replaced by a return to the samurai virtues and Neo-Confucian doctrines of the Tokugawa period. In 1880 the Ministry of Education made the *shūshin* or "morals" course a required part of the curriculum. Schools were forbidden to use texts that contained material that would be detrimental to the national peace or to public morals (Hall 1965:400). The *shūshin* course was highly moralistic and often frankly chauvinistic. In essense it marked a return to the Tokugawa heritage with its emphasis on superior-inferior relationships, an enormous feeling of duty and obligation, and a heightened sense of loyalty to one's superiors. The stories in the texts were not entirely Japanese. Frequently, moralistic tales were adapted from Aesop's fables, the maxims of Benjamin Franklin, and stories from the European and American classics. The life of Abraham Lincoln, for example, was used as an illustration of the importance of a tireless thirst for knowledge, absolute honesty, and the determination to succeed against all odds. Almost every Japanese elementary schoolyard contained a statue of Ninomiya Sontaku, the peasant sage, who was self-educated and who was usually depicted as reading a book while carrying a bundle of firewood on his back. The samurai type of family system, with its hierarchical and authoritarian structure, was formally created as the key legal institution in the 1898 civil code (Yoshino 1968:25). With such a family system as its base, the entire Japanese nation was thought of as being one large family with the emperor at its head. All loyalties, then, led up to the emperor, and the principle responsibility of the family was to develop loyal and obedient subjects. There was at this time a great emphasis placed on duties and obligations; there was little place for the concept of individual rights and privileges. As Sansom states, "There was nothing in the Japanese language that stood for 'popular rights' and a term had to be invented" (1973:311).

The Tokugawa legacy, with its highly authoritarian and feudalistic ethical system, endured long after most such systems had disappeared elsewhere simply because these very beliefs and values were most adaptive and useful in the creation of a modern state. Indeed, in retrospect, given the samurai background and feudalistic mentality of the creators of modern Japan it could hardly be otherwise. The extraordinary pervasiveness of the system is noted by Sansom (1973:239), who records the experiences of Fukuzawa Yukichi, who was one of the strongest advocates of Western liberal learning in the early Meiji period. He had strong equalitarian views, yet often found himself addressing the peasants in the authoritarian tones of the samurai. Unless he deliberately softened his voice, he was treated by them in a deferential and cringing fashion.

It was this legacy, then, with its feudalistic ethical system and uncompromising moral code, that was so deeply inculcated into the Issei and brought with them from Japan. It is from this legacy that we have identified the major Japanese characteristics of duty and obligation, hierarchy, deference, collectivity, and dependence. Some indication of the degree to which these values were inculcated into the prewar Japanese population is readily apparent in the behavior of Japanese soldiers during the Pacific war.

The sense of duty and obligation was so strongly internalized that thousands chose to die rather than surrender, while a few, such as Lt. Onoda, continued to fight by carrying on guerrilla warfare for some thirty years after the war ended.

The Structural Basis:
The Individual and the Household System (Ie)

Of the major Japanese characteristics of collectivity, hierarchy, duty and obligation, deference, and dependence, there are two from which the others are derived. These are collectivity and hierarchy. In turn, both collectivity and hierarchy are derived from the very strong emphasis on the household, or *ie*, which is the primary unit of social organization in Japan.

The concept of *ie* is so strong that it overshadows the importance of the individual. Both Beardsley (1959) and Nakane (1967) have written extensively on the importance of the *ie* in understanding Japanese social structure. As Beardsley states:

> The household is the fundamental social unit of the community. There is no enduring group of small size. It is the elemental unit in situations within the *buraku* (hamlet) or outside of it, for activities usually are undertaken either by single households or by larger units made up of households. Almost every larger group of the community is regarded as an assembly of households. Thus when a meeting of a larger group is held, usually only a single person from each of the several households attends. But this person is a delegate. The household rather than the person is the participant. (Beardsley et al. 1959:216)

The emphasis on the household rather than on the individual is to be seen not only in terms of its effect on individual identity, but is also reflected in the manner in which the government itself stresses the importance of the household over the individual:

> Seldom does any man, woman, or child think of himself or another person apart from his role as a member of his house (*ie*). The *ie* looms above the individual identities of its members to a degree that is hard to overstress . . . . Virtually all personal records are filed by household, vital statistics among them; no separate birth or death register is kept for individuals. In the eyes of the government, a man's birth, marriage, or death are

events not so much in his own life as in the career of his household. (Beardsley et al. 1959:216)

It is apparent from the above that, given the structural importance of the household, there would be a corresponding emphasis on collectivity and a de-emphasis on the importance of the individual. Indeed, Nakane supports Beardsley's remarks by noting:

This basic sociological unit of co-residential members of a house is called *ie* in Japanese. The term *ie* is often used in sociological literature as an equivalent of family, but the English term household is close to the conception since it includes all co-residents and is not necessarily restricted only to the members of a family. . . . Further, the *ie* is not simply a contemporary household as its English counterpart suggests, but is conceptualized in the time continuum from past to future, including not only the actual residential members but also dead members, with some projection also towards those yet unborn. The *ie* is always conceived as persisting through time by the succession of the members. Hence succession to the headship is of great functional importance, and the line of succession is the axis of the structure of the *ie*, while the house gives the material and social frame of the *ie*. (Nakane 1967:2-3)

It is the principle of continuity through time and the resultant emphasis on succession that in turn lead to the vertical structuring of the *ie* and the consequent importance of hierarchy. Once more, as Nakane notes:

There are two important rules of succession to the headship common throughout Japan. One is that the head should be succeeded by the "son," not by any other kind of kinsman. However, the successor is not necessarily the real son: any male (whether he be kin to the head or not) can be "the son" provided that the necessary legal procedure has taken place for him to become a member of the household *(ie)* by the relationship commonly expressed as "adopted son" or "adopted son-in-law". . . . Another important rule of succession to headship of the household is that it should be by one son only; never by two or more sons jointly. Whatever the composition of a household may be its basic structure is always in terms of this principle. Hence in Japan, theoretically there has been no joint family structure like that of the Chinese or the Hindus. (Nakane 1967:5-6)

In turn, this emphasis on succession usually entails an

impartible inheritance and single succession. The nonsuccessors must leave and establish their own households:

> The principle of father-son succession is combined with the principle of the one-son succession, and produces a residential pattern in which married siblings are expected to have separate households. Non-successors are supposed to leave the father's household on marriage, whether or not they may be given a share of the property. Once they have established their own independent households, each forms a distinctive property unit in which again the same principle operates. (Nakane 1967:5-6)

Nakane further notes that, because of the small size of land holdings among average farm households in rural Japan, it would be unwise continually to fragment the land by dividing the holdings equally among all of the heirs. It was therefore the custom of the successor to obtain all of the property intact. The sons, in turn, left without receiving a share to obtain their fortunes elsewhere. In time they would establish their own households (Nakane 1967:6-7).

What is important to remember here, however, is that the emphasis on patrilineal succession in the household is not based on the ideal of actual genetic continuity, but rather on the great importance placed on the continuance of the corporate unit of the household. In this regard, succession to the family headship may be accomplished in a variety of ways other than primogeniture.

Befu (1962:34-41) notes that there may be a number of reasons why the eldest son does not succeed to the headship. He may be physically too weak or incompetent, he may die before maturity, or he may decide to establish an independent family elsewhere. In these events, the headship would pass to another son. However, there are also those cases in which the eldest son is too young at the time of his father's death to succeed him and the mother may decide to adopt a male substitute, known as a *mukoyoshi*, who then marries a woman of his adopter's choice. Futhermore, he takes the name and Buddhist sect of his adopters and worships their ancestors. If the family has only a daughter and no male heir, it is likely she will become the bride of an adopted son (Befu 1962:35).

In commenting on these deviations from the ideal of patrilineal succession by means of primogeniture, Befu reemphasizes the

great importance placed on the continuance of the corporate
unity of the family:

> It should be clear by now that what lies behind these varied
> practices of descent in Japan is the primary emphasis placed on
> the perpetuity of the family as a corporate unit, compared with
> which, continuity of the blood line is of only secondary impor-
> tance. Thus the "unbroken line of descent," of which old
> Japanese families are so proud, refers not to the genetic conti-
> nuity but rather to the succession of the family name and
> occupation. (Befu 1962:38)

With regard to the problem of succession, Nakane elaborates
upon her previous discussion on the practice of establishing
separate households by stating:

> In the above discussion it is clear that there are two kinds of
> households in terms of sociological history: One is that of a
> successor, and the other is that of a nonsuccessor. The former
> includes the successor's elementary family and his parents (or
> parents-in-law) with their unmarried sons and daughters, while
> the latter is formed normally by one elementary family. How-
> ever, in the next generation this small household also will grow
> into a larger one, and may again produce a new household by
> its extra members. . . . This is also in accordance with the
> weak relationship of siblings as compared with the strong
> functional relationship of father and successor son. Social
> organization in rural Japan is indeed structured by this out-
> standing principle, which regards the vertical line as of supreme
> importance against the collateral line. The well-known Japa-
> nese proverb, "The sibling is the beginning of the stranger"
> may well reflect this structural process. (Nakane 1967:7)

Nakane also notes that , while most frequently it is the father
who is also the household head, the legitimate authority of the
father is more a result of his being the head of the household:

> In most cases, the office of headship is occupied by the father
> of the family residing in the household. However, it should be
> noted that his authority over the household members is vali-
> dated by his office as the head of the household, not by his being
> the father: the authority of the head resides primarily in the
> office rather than the person. (Nakane 1967:17-18)

The authority of the father as household head was enormous
and was supported by the civil law in the pre-World War II years.
Nakane mentions that the head of the household had a special

place at the center of the dining room reserved for his exclusive use; no one else was allowed to occupy it. In addition, he was served first at meals and no one could take a hot bath before him.

> The father, as head of the household, was often regarded as a figure to be much feared by other members of the household. As the proverb has it: "The things that one has most to fear are *jishin, kaminari, kaji, oyaji* (earthquake, thunder, fire, and father)." The household with a firmly authoritarian father was highly regarded, and treated as an ideal model for the majority, and indeed this was enforced and influenced by the legal (and ethical) pattern established by the old Civil Code . . . which reflected the feudal ideology of the preceding period. In these households, every activity of the individual member was regulated under the leadership of the father. The father was the sole figure to make final decisions, and he often made them unilaterally. (Nakane 1967:19)

In the above discussions by Beardsley, Befu, and Nakane, it can be seen that not only is the household the basic unit of Japanese society, but that from its structure and the resultant influence exerted on its members can be derived the basis for the major Japanese characteristics of collectivity and hierarchy. This is not to imply that all of our major and minor characteristics are reducible to the experiences one might have had as a member of a household. Rather, we are attempting to illustrate that the household is the social unit wherein the five major characteristics are inculcated, maintained, and transmitted to the next generation. Further, in our subsequent discussion of each of the major characteristics we will demonstrate that there is a definite continuation of the household model with its role expectations to other social institutions.

We have seen that the basis for the emphasis on collectivity and hierarchy is initially established in the household. The household member is not thought of as an entity apart from his role of household member and, indeed, is thought to have no existence apart from the household. Further, the emphasis on collectivity in the household leads to an emphasis on dependence, since the household member is not a free agent but is dependent upon the household both for identity and support. In turn, one's position as a representative of the household leads to an emphasis on duty and obligation since one must cooperate with others and avoid bringing shame to the household. Moreover, the emphasis placed on succession leads to hierarchy, which in turn implies a vertical stress upon superior-inferior relationships and, by extension, implies deference.

The emphasis on succession leads also to the emphasis on dependence or the inculcation of dependency needs. For instance, it has been frequently observed that the strongest emotional tie in Japan is between the mother and the child rather than between the husband and wife as in the United States. There are a number of reasons for this. For example, it was once a rather widespread custom in rural areas not to record the marriage of the bride until she became pregnant. Another reason is that the bride usually lived with the husband's family and was under the supervision of the mother-in-law. She was constantly watched to see if she would prove to be a good wife. Relationships were quite formal and, with the mother-in-law, often strained.

Because of her loneliness, the greatest ties of affection of the young wife are with her children. Children are extremely important to the young wife; once she has children everything seems to change. She is now accepted into the family, there is little chance she will be sent home, and the formality is largely dropped (Beardsley et al. 1959:292).

For a number of reasons, then, the strongest emotional bond in the family is between the mother and the child, usually between the mother and the *chōnan*, or successor son. This bond is initially established by giving the child an enormous amount of oral and other gratification, which create in him strong dependency needs. This emotional attachment subsequently can be manipulated by the mother to motivate the child to achieve or to do what the mother believes is proper or necessary.

As DeVos (1973) has so clearly indicated, socialization consists largely of shaming the child, that is, telling the child that others will laugh at him for his behavior. The ideal child, then, is one who is *sunao*, or docile, quiet, and obedient. The end result of the socialization process, with its gratifications and the use of shaming and teasing, is development in the child not only strong dependency needs but also a heightened sensitivity to the opinions of significant others. There is, therefore, no place in the Japanese household for the rugged individualist, and few Japanese achieve a sense of self that would be independent of the attitudes of significant others. Moreover, there is frequently found in the Japanese, both male and female, an all-pervasive sense of guilt or abasedness, which is the result of the great need to justify oneself to society and the acute awareness that one has failed to realize one's own internalized high standards of role performance. Such feelings of guilt and abasedness frequently give rise to an extremely high degree of role dedication or "role narcissism" as DeVos has so aptly described it (1973:474). DeVos (1973) has used the concepts of role dedication, dependency needs, and a heightened sensitivity to the opinions of others as key concepts for understanding Japanese achievement motivation; it is little wonder, then, that the emotional tie to the mother and the resultant dependency needs have proved to be so highly adaptive, both within the family itself and in Japanese society in general.

One might also add that the inculcation of dependency insures that the offspring will have a strong emotional tie to the household. Therefore, the child will supply aid when needed and provide for the wants of the retired parents if necessary. By extension, it would seem likely that the behavior of the parents toward the successor would be somewhat different than it would be toward other offspring, who would ultimately be required to leave and establish their own households. And, indeed, this does appear to be the case. As Johnson notes:

> The eldest son is singled out as the heir of the headship of the house. He is referred to as the *chōnan* (principal son) and distinguished from the succeeding ones, the *jisannan* (literally second and third sons, but actually referring to the category "all but the eldest son"). As the heir apparent, the *chōnan* receives special treatment because he is the one who will remain in the household and also because he is the eldest of the brothers. The succeeding sons are distinguished by birth order, and their respective ages will affect the way in which they are treated, but the distinction among them is much less than that between the eldest and the rest. There is, then, in the structure of the family itself, a mechanism for producing heterogeneous attitudes in each generation. This heterogeneity may involve only the immediacy of the values learned—for example, the eldest son knows he must fit into the same community as his father; he knows his future peers in the present and can apply any learning to a real, not merely a possible, situation, whereas the

younger sons, not knowing their future, cannot. For as long as the special position of the *chōnan* existed, we assume there was some regular heterogeneity in family socialization. (Johnson 1962:91-92)

Johnson then goes on to suggest that the differential socialization of the *jisannan* produces an orientation toward achievement and self-sufficiency which can be quickly converted into an entrepreneurial attitude (1962:92). This last remark is most interesting in light of the Japanese-American experience in the United States. The mere fact of their presence in the United States would indicate that the vast majority of Issei were not household successors, or *chōnan*, but *jisannan*. As such, they were undoubtedly subjected to the differential socialization described above and were perhaps more self-reliant and achievement oriented than their siblings in Japan.

At the same time it should also be remembered that, while the Issei were nonsuccessors to the headship of their households in Japan, they nonetheless brought with them the *ie* concept. In time, when they established their own households, it would seem reasonable to expect that they would attempt to preserve as much as possible of the *ie* ideal as they could in a new country. In turn, their success in preserving the *ie* ideal would result at least in the inculcation of the Japanese characteristics in their offspring, the Nisei. The Nisei, as they matured, would retain at least a feeling for the *ie* ideal which they, in turn, would transmit to the Sansei, albeit in a somewhat attenuated form.

The Major Japanese Psychological and Behavioral Characteristics

As previously stated, an examination of the literature disclosed that the Japanese characteristics could be grouped under the five major headings of collectivity, duty and obligation, hierarchy, deference, and dependence. Again it should be emphasized that there has been no attempt to make the list exhaustive. Rather, the approach was to list those characteristics that clearly and distinctly contrast with American ones. There is, for example, no extended discussion of educational achievement although this is one area that has received a great deal of attention. A number of Japanese and foreign observers have frequently commented on the high degree of academic achievement, the literacy rate, and the respect for learning in Japan. While one may argue that academic achievement, literacy, and respect for learning are not so highly regarded overall in American society, they are rather highly regarded in the middle class, the one segment of American society with which the Japanese Americans have been most frequently compared.

Collectivity. The Japanese emphasis on relying upon the group is related to a strong group orientation or collectivity. The evidence for the great emphasis on collectivity as opposed to individualism is given by a number of authors. For example, in *Twelve Doors to Japan* Richard Beardsley notes:

> Social life throughout Japan is noted for the solidarity of group associations. To be Japanese is to be involved in close, complex, and enduring relationships with one's family, one's neighbors, and other specific associates. Even persons who, in recent terminology, are "dry," meaning that they have shed emotional attachments to past traditions cherished by the "wets," nevertheless accept close-knit group ties to family, office clique, schoolmates, or business and professional athletes . . . . Tradition has stabilized such groups by expecting each member to subordinate his personal wants to the requirements of the group. (Beardsley 1965:361-65)

Moreover, this subordination of personal wants to the requirements of the group is so strong that what may be thought of as an act of extreme self-sacrifice in another society is seen simply as an expected act of group loyalty in Japan:

> . . . The closeness of group affiliation, we suggest, may have a significant bearing on youthful suicide, for it may drastically curtail alternative solutions to personal problems. Provided that a person can get along without family or other group attachments, he may run away from otherwise intolerable situations; provided that he can rely on his internal standards to judge his capacity and accomplishments rather than needing reassurance from others, he can bear up under difficulties without even running away. But evidence suggests that neither provision holds true for many Japanese. Living alone without group support is subjectively as well as objectively difficult for persons deeply conditioned to putting group needs ahead of their own wants, and the same conditioning makes persons emotionally dependent on external reinforcement of their self-

images. Hence, one cannot ease the guilt of failure to meet group expectations by running away for one carries one's guilt along and at the same time removes the support for one's superego. In a personally intolerable situation, such as is created by unpleasant marriage prospects, one is torn between self-love and love of family; if damage to the family is unthinkable, aggression has to be turned not outward upon others but inwards upon oneself. (Beardsley 1965:361-65)

The collectivity orientation is supported by the work of Caudill and Scarr. In 1954-55, they conducted a study of value orientations among rural and urban populations in Japan (Caudill and Scarr 1962:53-91). In commenting on this study, Caudill has stated:

From the results of this study, I wish to indicate here only that on those schedule items which measure value orientations in the area of the relations among men, and particularly in the sphere of family life there was a strong emphasis on Collaterality. Collaterality stresses the welfare of the group, and consensus among its members as primary goals. As such, in terms of the theory behind the schedule, Collaterality is distinct from Lineality or Individualism—the former emphasizing superior and subordinate relationships, the latter focusing on the relative autonomy of person. (Caudill 1962:29)

In a later report with Helen Weinstein, Caudill remarks that the Japanese are more group oriented than the Americans. The difference in behavior is especially pronounced in the area of family life. The Japanese are more interdependent in interpersonal behavior while the Americans are more "individual" oriented and have a greater emphasis on independence (Caudill and Weinstein 1969:13).

Charles A. Moore, in an editorial supplement to the book *The Japanese Mind*, concludes:

The status of the individual in Japan is a problem that leaves one bewildered because of the widely varying interpretations available. The emphasis has always seemed to be on the group rather than on the individual, on duties rather than rights, on loyalty to group or hierarchical superior, and this emphasis has seemed to be stronger in Japan than in any other major tradition. (1967:299)

Matsumoto's findings are also in accord with the above. In

his monograph entitled *Contemporary Japan: The Individual and the Group,* he finds a great emphasis on collectivity:

> The collectivity orientation in Japan subordinates individual goals and interests and thus places a great emphasis on group membership. . . . The membership in a group is critically important to the individual in Japan. The individual tends to be seen as having no existence outside his group identifications. (1960:61)

The importance of the group over the individual receives additional emphasis from Nakamura:

> Due to the stress on social proprieties in Japan another characteristic of its culture appears—the tendency of social relationships to supersede or take precedence over the individual. To lay stress upon human relationships is to place heavy stress upon the relations among many individuals rather than upon the individual as an independent entity. (1964:409)

Ezra Vogel reports that the emphasis on the group is still quite strong even among urban white-collar families:

> Perhaps the most striking characteristic of Japanese society is the existence of a series of tightly-knit groups connected by a controlled and limited amount of movement. . . . Because the Mamachi resident ordinarily belongs to only one or two intimate groups to which he is absolutely devoted, these groups tend to absorb his total personality. He has no clear conception of himself apart from the group. (1967:118)

The last statement is amplified by David Plath, who remarks:

> To overstate the case, Western ideals honor the rugged individualist who sticks to his rights no matter what; Japanese ideals shame him as one of the worst of malefactors. He is guilty, as one modern Japanese phrase has it, of "nihilistic" selfishness. . . . In the words of George DeVos, "certain types of psychological security found in a relationship to a personal God in the West are found only in relation to the actual family in Japan." (1964:74)

And finally, as Reischauer states:

> In theory, the individual does not even exist as an individual but only as a member of certain larger groupings—family, school, community, or nation. There are no individuals but only sons and fathers, students and teachers, citizens and

officials, subjects and rulers. . . . The Japanese whenever possible avoid individual decisions and individual responsibility. Group decisions and group responsibility seem to him the only way to achieve group interests. (1965:150)

Duty and obligation. The Japanese emphasis on duty and obligation has been remarked upon by a number of observers. Ruth Benedict, for example, attached great importance to the concepts of *on, gimu,* and *giri.* As defined by her, an *on* is an obligation that is passively incurred. A person receives an *on* from another. *On,* then, is obligation from the standpoint of the passive recipient. A person receives an *on* from his parents, from his teachers, or from anyone who has done something for him (1946:116).

There are also reciprocals of *on.* These are debts or obligations that must be repaid. Benedict classifies these into two major groupings: *gimu,* which are obligations that can never really be repaid and take the form of various duties, such as *chū*—a duty to the Emperor, the law, Japan; *kō*—duty to parents and ancestors; and *nimmu*—duty to one's work. *Giri,* on the other hand, are debts that must be repaid with mathematical equivalence within a certain time. Thus one has duties to one's family, to those from whom one has received a favor, and so on (Benedict 1946:116).

The pervasiveness of the above system is illustrated in the case of Ishikawa Takuboku cited by Thomas C. Smith:

Takuboku wrote a novel in which the hero, who is surely Takuboku himself, thinks existing society utterly corrupt and worthy only of destruction. While writing this novel, Takuboku wrote to a friend that he badly needed the money from its publication to discharge a long-neglected duty to his elder brother. What this duty was he did not say, but the term he used for it was *giri*—one of the central concepts of the ethics taught in the schools; and Takuboku was at this time a village school teacher, and his story's hero was the principal of a village elementary school. (1959:207)

In the foregoing discussion it is important to distinguish the concept of duty and obligation from that of a right. As Kawashima remarks:

The Japanese traditionally expect that, in principle, social obligations will be fulfilled by a voluntary act on the part of the person under obligation, usually with particular friendliness or benevolence. They consider it unproper for the other party (beneficiary) of an obligation to demand or claim that the obligated person fulfill his obligation. An obligation is considered valueless, if although it is fulfilled by the obligated person, he does not fulfill it in addition with a special friendliness or favor toward the other party. In other words, the actual value of social obligations depends upon the good will and favor of the obligated person, and there is no place for the existence of the notion of "right." . . . In a concept of social obligations which does not have the counterbalancing notion of "right," the interest of the individual is not made distinct and fixed. Here, an individual is not considered to be an independent entity. Rather, his interest is absorbed in the interest of the collectivity to which he belongs, and the interest of the collectivity is recognized as having primary importance, while the interest of the individual has merely a secondary importance. Under this notion of the individual, there has been no place for the concept of "human rights." (Kawashima 1967:263-64)

An additional comment on both the importance and pervasiveness of the sense of duty and obligation is given by Reischauer:

There are myriad obligations which must be meticulously fulfilled, if self-respect is to be maintained. Among the most burdensome is the obligation to one's family. The child inevitably becomes heavily indebted to his parents and his family in general, and a life of selfless service to family interests is not too much repayment. In feudal times there was also the primary obligation to one's lord, which necessitated unwavering and unquestioning loyalty at all times. This obligation has been transformed in modern times into unlimited loyalty to the Emperor, serving as the personification of the state. The individual, as the recipient of the heritage of a long civilization, is unendingly indebted to society, usually thought of as the state and symbolized by the Emperor. No sacrifice, however great, can be more than partial payment of this debt. Absolute fanatical devotion to the service of the state is thus built into the foundations of Japan's ethical code. (Reischauer 1965:148-49)

Reischauer goes on to say that the great emphasis placed on duty and obligation led to both a determination to repay a favor and to a great sense of loyalty:

Such obligations to family and state are unlimited, and the individual Japanese is willing to bear a very heavy burden in their name, but in addition there are many other specific obligations which differ from individual to individual. Any benefit received from another carries with it obligations which should, if possible, be repaid. One's teachers deserve unending loyalty. Once a disciple always a disciple, and the disciple never doubts or corrects his master. One's employer or supervisor is due his share of loyal service, if he in turn has lived up to his obligations. The bond between master and servant is likely to develop into a lifelong exchange of patronage for loyalty. In fact this is the pattern for all relationships between superiors and inferiors. Between equals a careful balance of favors must be maintained. Gifts are not to be received with casual thanks. They must be paid in kind if one is to maintain self-respect. A present for a present is the inflexible rule in Japan. . . . Nowhere in the world are people more determined to repay casual favors as well as real indebtedness, and nowhere else are they more capable of devoted loyalty to those who have aided or befriended them. (Reischauer 1965:149)

Finally, George Sansom, in his survey of Japanese history, has this to say:

. . . throughout Japanese history . . . the whole trend of social ethics . . . has been to emphasize the duties of the individual and to neglect his right. The group came first. Loyalty to the family, the community, the tribe or state transcended all other obligations. (1943:vi)

Hierarchy. The Japanese characteristic that appears to have been noticed by all observers has been the persistent emphasis on hierarchy. Ruth Benedict devotes an entire chapter to the subject and makes repeated reference to it throughout her book. As she states in the chapter entitled "Taking One's Proper Station":

Any attempt to understand the Japanese must begin with their version of what it means to "take one's proper station." Their reliance upon order and hierarchy and our faith in freedom and equality are poles apart and it is hard for us to give hierarchy its just due as a possible social mechanism. Japan's confidence in hierarchy is basic in her whole notion of man's relation to his fellow man and of man's relation to the State and it is only by describing some of their national institutions like the family, the State, religious and economic life that it is possible for us to understand their view of life. (1946:43)

Yamamoto, in his article on Japanese national character, analyzed the literature and was able to list some seventeen traits on the subject. Of these, two (10 and 11) have to do with hierarchy. They are listed as follows:

> Paternalistic benevolence in social contracts, boss-and-follower relations fictitiously identified with father and son, submission and non-resistance to authority, devoted service to lord annihilating private concerns—sometimes connected with the ascetic practice of Zen Buddhism, self-immolation on the death of the lord.
>
> Having proper place in the graded social system, importance of honorifics and self-abasing expressions in the language. . . . (1965:96-97)

From his long residence in Japan, Douglas Haring adds this information:

> . . . status continues to involve anxiety. The ubiquitous calling cards shed light on this situation. . . . These cards invariably provide status clues, however subtle. . . . Verbs, for example, differ in form according to the relative status of the speaker and the person addressed. . . . These linguistic formalities are obsolescent in contemporary Japan. Nevertheless, status anxiety persists; the average Japanese needs to know the status of everyone with whom he deals before he can act with confidence. . . . As always when a Japanese discovers that he has overestimated his standing vis-a-vis another person, he "submits to the powerful" instantly.(1967:136)

Again, however, it is Reischauer who provides the most comprehensive treatment of the subject. As he states:

> With obedience to authority so stressed throughout Japanese society, a primary problem is that of hierarchy among the different types of authority. No major people in the world places greater emphasis on hierarchy than do the Japanese. *Nippon-ichi*, "the first in Japan," is a uniquitous phrase applied to anything or anyone from the nation's leading poet down to the biggest eater of raw fish. Proficiency in judo wrestling or the minor arts is graded and regulated like our masonic orders. Almost anyone can tell you the order of prestige of the Japanese universities. Each person, each thing, fits into an accepted order of prestige and power. Position on this scale must be clear so that one can distinguish the superior from the inferior and know where authority lies. A committee without its chairman, a delegation without its chief makes the Japanese uneasy and unhappy. They, like the Germans, love titles and use them wherever possible, not only on the calling cards they

exchange on every conceivable occasion but also in direct address, for titles take the place of pronouns in polite conversation. Their whole language, with its precise gradations of politeness, implies a hierarchical society. . . . (1965:163)

One very important aspect of hierarchy is the *oyabun-kobun* relationship, which is quite prevalent in Japanese society. The individual in a position of authority becomes the *oyabun*, or one who assumes the father role in a relationship. In the father role the *oyabun* is expected to act as a father should. That is, he will assume obligations and in general act toward his subordinates as though he were a foster father interested in their welfare. The *kobun*, or child part, is complementary to the *oyabun*, and in this role the subordinates, or *kobun*, behave as dutiful children and have great loyalty toward their superiors. As Herbert Passin writes:

> It is important, however, to make it clear that *oyabun-kobun* can refer to a specific form of organization as well as to a specific principle of organization. Even when the specific form is lacking, one often finds that the spirit or ethos is present. . . . The *oyabun-kobun* relation has shown a remarkable tenacity in spite of the growth of modern institutions. When the form cannot be directly realized, either for ideological or organizational reasons it is covertly expressed in the form of cliques and patron-client relations. . . . Whatever the reason, *oyabun-kobun* relations can be found in a wide variety of organizations. Characteristically, the head is the benevolent father, the subordinates are loyal and obedient children; and the relation between them is not only functional, specific, and economic, but personal and diffuse as well. The relationship may last for the duration of specific tasks, over the lifetime of individuals, or even over many generations. Some well known Tokyo gangs can boast an ancestry of over three hundred years and enumerate fourteen or sixteen generations, just as would a great family of artists, actors, or craftsmen. Generation after generation the same family provides the *oyabun*, and the same subordinate families provide the *kobun*. (1968:243-44)

Nakane amplifies Passin's discussion by emphasizing that the basis of the structural principle in Japanese society is the relationship between two individuals of upper and lower status which is often expressed in the traditional *oyabun-kobun* relationship:

The essential elements in the relationship are that the *kobun* receives benefits or help from his *oyabun*. . . . The *kobun*, in turn, is ready to offer his services whenever the *oyabun* requires them. . . . Most Japanese, whatever their status or occupation, are involved in *oyabun-kobun* relationships. (1970:42-43)

Deference. In contrasting the Japanese form of government with that of Western Europe, Ruth Benedict drew attention to:

The true difference between the Japanese form of government and such cases in Western Europe lies not in form but in functioning. The Japanese rely on an old habit of deference set up in their past experience and formalized in their ethical system and in their etiquette. (1946:86)

While it is true that the deference Benedict spoke of was more typical of prewar Japan, it is interesting to note that Vogel found present-day urban Japanese were also quite deferent to officials:

The ability of present-day residents of Mamachi to laugh at their fear of officialdom before 1945 indicates that they now feel greater freedom and confidence in facing government officials. Yet, in comparison with American standards, they still are very humble before officials and still regard encounters with them as trying experiences. . . . Most Mamachi residents are uncertain about the rights of a citizen vis-a-vis the government and think that it is rude or senseless to try to oppose an official on the basis of regulations. They believe that it is not might or law that makes right, but position. A person in a position of authority is always right and can ensure that his wishes are carried out. (1967:95-96)

In an article on "Japanese vs. American Values," F. K. Berrien reports on a then-unpublished study by Whitehall and Takezawa, who asked some two thousand Japanese and American blue-collar workers thirty questions, one of which was the following: "If my immediate supervisor enters a crowded bus on which I am riding, I should": The replies were most interesting. To the answer, "remain seated and offer to hold any package he may have," some 41 per cent of the Japanese and 33 per cent of the Americans agreed. Yet to the answer "always offer him my seat since he is my superior," some 10 per cent of the Japanese and 2 per cent of the Americans agreed. A truly significant difference was found on the last two answers. To the answer "offer him my seat unless I am not feeling well," 44 per cent of the Japanese agreed while only 2 per cent of the Americans agreed. The last answer, "remain seated: since the fair rule is first come, first served," was agreed to by 63 per cent of the Americans while only 5 per cent of the Japanese agreed (Berrien 1965:184). In concluding his article, Berrien stated:

> The studies reviewed in this article portray the Japanese in comparison with Americans as being more deferent, more respectful of and dependent upon high status persons, more self-abasing, and more willing to work long hours. Individual aspirations appear to be less important than the achievements of work groups. The boundaries of their interests and concerns are more limited than seems to be true of Americans, but their loyalty to family and work is greater. (1965:190)

Reischauer's findings are in agreement with all of the foregoing, especially the remarks of Benedict and Vogel:

> Even the poor policeman, post office employee, or stationmaster on the government railways derives considerable prestige and authority from his uniform and connections with the government. The Japanese show a respect—one might almost say reverence—for the government and its officials, both high and low, which, though known in many parts of Europe, is entirely foreign to the United States. The prestige and power of the official and the meek subservience of the common citizen make a psychological soil which is not congenial to the growth of democracy. (1965:168)

With the value placed upon deference there is a concomitant emphasis placed upon passivity, and nonaggressiveness begins in childhood. As Ezra Vogel reports on a middle-class urban household:

> When a child reaches the age of three or four, he is taught to withhold his aggression. When a child below that age hits an older sibling the mother may regard this simply as a form of play, but she may say that it will not do (ikenai) for the older child to hit the younger one. If she hears that the child has been in a fight with a neighbor, she will tell him that will not do, regardless of whether he started the fight or not. To hit in self-defense is considered about as bad as to start a fight. While the mother may sympathize with her child when he has been wronged by others, there is virtually no situation in which returning aggression is condoned. (1963:247)

Dependency. In recent years there have appeared a number of articles in reference to the strong dependency needs of the Japanese. In particular, Caudill and Doi have devoted much time in an attempt to explain the importance of dependency needs in understanding Japanese behavior. The Japanese psychiatrist, Doi, in a brilliant article has related the permissiveness of Japanese child-rearing practices and the closeness of the mother-child bond to the widespread Japanese use of the word *amaeru,* an intransitive verb which has no exact equivalent in English but means to depend and presume upon another's benevolence. It implies a desire to be pampered and has the same root as *amai,* an adjective meaning "sweet." The verb *amaeru* is used to describe the relationship between a child and his mother or a very close relationship between two adults (1962:132).

Doi believes that the need to *amaeru* lies at the root of many neurotic symptoms. In a later article, written in collaboration with Caudill, he states:

> Patients would frequently say to the doctor, *"Watashi o omakase shite imasu,"* meaning "I am completely in your hands." In saying this, the patient is indicating that he wants to be cared for, and is asking to be allowed to take a passive and dependent position with reference to the doctor, and the doctor accepts and fosters this wish. (1963:381)

It is also interesting to note that in Japanese hospitals there will be found a type of subprofessional nurse called a *tsukisoi.* The *tsukisoi* are women who sleep in the same room as the patient and care for him on a twenty-four-hour-a-day basis. Although hospitals consider these women largely in terms of their domestic services, the *tsukisoi* frequently think of their role in relation to the patient as being analogous to that of mother or elder sister (Caudill and Doi 1963:386).

Later in the article, the authors summarize what they believe to be the major emphasis on character formation in Japan:

> In the early stages of infancy (in the traditional oral stage) there is a great deal of gratification given to the Japanese infant in almost all spheres of behavior. This would encourage the development of a very close attachment to the mother, and sense of trust in others, but this would also tend to lay the ground for

the future "never fully satisfied desire to *amaeru* (to be loved passively)," and for a chronic mild longing in later life for the state of childhood gratification. (Caudill and Doi 1963:412)

The close mother-son bond is fostered by the mother in order to keep the child dependent on her. Vogel, for example, states that a common practice is to provoke anxiety about the outside world and reward intimacy:

> The process of encouraging this dependency begins in earliest infancy. While the American baby who cries learns that at times he must deal with his internal tensions, the Japanese infant learns that whatever tensions he has will be relieved by the nearby mother who offers physical comfort, and at a later age, candy or some other sweet. It is not surprising that so many children are anxious about the mother's leaving and that so many mothers are frightened of the child's reaction if they were to go out and leave the child with someone else.
>
> While curious, the Mamachi child is frightened of the strange outside world. We never heard of a child talking about running away from home, and the Mamachi mother has little worry about a child not sticking close by in public. While in America one sees mothers chasing down the street after a child, in Mamachi one is more apt to see a child frantically chasing after a mother who is encouraging her child to hurry by running slightly ahead. We have never heard of a mother punishing a child by forbidding him to go outside, but we have on several occasions heard children frantically yelling for their mother because they had been placed out of the house and not permitted to come in again until they repented their behavior. (1963:234-35)

In a more recent study comparing thirty first-born, three-to-four-month-old Japanese infants with a similar group in the United States, Caudill and Weinstein reached the following conclusions:

> On the basis of our previous work in Japan over the past fourteen years coupled with a study of the literature, we have come to feel that the following different emphases on what is valued in behavior are important when life in Japan is compared with life in America. These differing emphases seem to be particularly sharp in the areas of family life and general interpersonal relations with which we are most directly concerned here, and perhaps to be somewhat less evident in other areas of life such as business, the professions, or politics.

Japanese are more "group" oriented and interdependent in their relations with others, while Americans are more "individual" oriented and independent. Going along . . . Japanese are more self-effacing and passive in contrast to Americans, who appear more self-assertive and aggressive. . . . In summary, in normal family life in Japan there is an emphasis on interdependence and reliance on others, while in America the emphasis is on independence and self-assertion. The conception of the infant would appear to be somewhat different in the two cultures. In Japan the infant is seen more as a separate biological organism who from the beginning, in order to develop, needs to be drawn into increasingly interdependent relations with others. In America, the infant is seen more as a dependent biological organism who, in order to develop, needs to be made increasingly independent of others. (1969:14-15)

It is interesting to note that others have come to a similar conclusion, although for different reasons. In an article written a few years after the war, Fredrick Hulse took issue with Ruth Benedict's contention that women were subjugated and inferior to males. In the article, Hulse attempted to show that the Japanese female was in reality quite strong. However, it is interesting to read that in refuting the notion of male superiority he reinforces the preceding statements by Vogel and Caudill on the nature of the mother-son bond and the dependency behavior it induces:

Anyone who has observed the Japanese family functioning will agree that the strength of the Japanese mother is far from fictional alone; and the diaries kept by so many Japanese during the war provide still further evidence to support this point. It is surprising to an American to see expressed, so often, nostalgia for the mother and so rarely, nostalgia for the wife. (1962:305-6)

Finally, in an article summarizing personality psychology in Japan, Beardsley refers to the institutionalized hierarchical male roles in adult life as fostering the continuance of dependency needs inculcated in childhood:

Studying ordinary families and communities rather than patients at clinics, as Doi has done, several have identified dependency as most characteristic among men, which at first seems to be in conflict with the Japanese use of the term *amae* more often in reference to women. Caudill, DeVos, and others conjecture that personal relationships within the family foster dependency in the first instance, while outside relationships also can be structured to preserve dependency well beyond the age at which American males begin to resist and repress the urge. Any child is inevitably dependent on his mother in infancy; she may unconsciously preserve psychological dominance over a male child merely by punctiliously following tradition, treating him with tender concern that befits her social subservience to him . . . his dependency then is transferable, also unconsciously to others in adulthood. The last is possible because institutionalized male roles in Japanese society tolerate self-centered, juvenile dependency as one way of performing the role. (1965:377)

Summary

In review, the five major Japanese characteristics considered were an emphasis on collectivity, duty and obligation, hierarchy, deference, and dependency. Related to these major orientations and implicit in many of them are a number of subsidiary psychological and behavioral characteristics which may be listed as follows:

1. A reliance on the group.
2. Children are trained to be docile, obedient, and dependent.
3. The strongest emotional bond is between mother and son.
4. An overriding emphasis on hierarchical relationships.
5. A great emphasis on duty and obligations.
6. Relatively strong dependency needs.
7. An emphasis on passivity or non-aggressiveness.
8. A submissive attitude towards authority.
9. An emphasis on collaterality or "we" against "they."
10. Achievement is largely seen in terms of goals set by others.
11. An emphasis on ascribed status.
12. A compulsive obedience to rules and controls.
13. A great obligation to the family with deference to parental wishes.
14. An emphasis on self-effacement.
15. A restriction of personal relationships to a small group.
16. A great feeling of responsibility towards those with whom he has a tie.
17. Deference and politeness to superiors at all times.
18. A sense of fatalism.
19. Success is achieved through self-discipline and will power.

20. An emphasis on compromise, precise rules of conduct, and a "situational ethic."

Of the characteristics just listed, there are several which need additional comment for clarification. Number 18, "a sense of fatalism," was not mentioned explicitly in the preceding discussion, yet is implicit in several of the characteristics listed. For example, given the emphasis on collectivity, hierarchy, deference, and especially on duty and obligation, it would be somewhat difficult for an individual to believe that he was solely in command of his own destiny. With such a system it would be understandable that a person would frequently believe that he was the pawn of forces over which he had little control.

Listings 19 and 20 also require some amplification. As stated, number 19 implies that the individual is not complete—that is, in order to succeed he must change himself into something he is not. As such, success implies a manipulation of the self rather than a manipulation of others.

The "situational ethic" of number 20 needs some explanation. A "situational ethic" is one that allows behavior to be guided by the rules of a given situation. As such it is related to number 12, "a compulsive obedience to rules and controls." Given such a compulsive adherence to rules, it would seem that behavior would be very rigid and quite inflexible. And indeed it is, within a given situation for which rules of conduct are prescribed. Predictably, once the situation changes, so do the rules—and so does the behavior.

There is, however, one great weakness in the system as Reischauer and others have pointed out. That is, once an individual finds himself in a situation not covered by the rules, he is more completely lost than Americans or others who live by less exact rules and a more generalized ethic. As Reischauer remarks:

> The unaccustomed human relationships created by war mean a clearer break with all past experience for the modern Japanese soldier than for our G.I.'s. Our peacetime virtues may seem to lose some of their validity in battle, but his more meticulous code of conduct becomes clearly inapplicable in many of the situations he meets and consequently he may disregard it completely. Whereas at home he is far less given to physical violence than are we in the United States, on the battlefield

brutality comes as less of a shock to him than to us. Torture in war and meticulous politeness in peace seem less of a contradiction to him than organized mass murder and simple friendliness under our more universalistic ethic. The loyal Japanese soldier, who was never prepared for the possibility of capture, had nothing to guide him, if, by any chance, he did fall into our hands. The prisoner who had participated willingly in the suicide charge of the night before saw nothing inconsistent in volunteering his services to aid the Americans the next day. The unforeseen had happened, and obviously none of the old rules were any longer applicable. (1965:139-40)

Yet, as Reischauer also notes, such a situational ethic does provide a flexibility of response that Americans often lack. At various times in their history the Japanese have been able to reverse their attitudes quickly once they realized that the situation had clearly changed and the old approach was no longer viable. Thus the insularity, exclusiveness, and hostility to foreigners that marked the Tokugawa period rapidly gave way to an enthusiasm for Western learning once it appeared that social and commercial interaction was inevitable. The behavior of the Japanese following their defeat in the Pacific War is also another dramatic example of their ability to change. The millions who were prepared to oppose the American invasion with nothing more than sharpened sticks now felt it their duty to greet the conquerors not with guerrilla warfare or even sullen hostility but with a friendliness and wholehearted cooperation that astounded many Americans. (Reischauer 1965:140-41)

Chapter 4

American Psychological and Behavioral Characteristics

Again, as stated in the presentation of Japanese characteristics, the following discussion of American characteristics is not intended to be exhaustive. Rather, it is an attempt to list characteristics that contrast with those already given for the Japanese.

For that reason there is no discussion of such oft-mentioned American attributes as an orientation toward success and a desire for material goods. Nor is there mention of either the pragmatic or anti-intellectualist elements in American society. On the other hand, there has been an attempt to give a full presentation and justification for the choice of individualism, equality, concern for rights and privileges, self-reliance, and self-assertion.

The Historical Basis:
The Frontier Heritage

It is not the intent of this section to recapitulate Turner's famous frontier thesis (1893:199-227), or to present an elaborate discourse of the development of the American character; rather, the function is more to utilize the concept of an expanding frontier and the availability of seemingly endless tracts of rich and fertile land, virtually free for the asking, as a significant factor in the formation of the major American values. It is therefore most essential to note that at a time when the Japanese had already expanded to the limits of their agricultural land, and the population had so increased as to force the Tokugawa government to enact laws limiting the size of plots that could be subdivided and sold, the Americans were only just beginning their westward expansion.

Land for the American, then, was not the setting for the development of the inbred, tightly knit, closed, corporate communities of Japan, but was treated as an inexhaustible commodity which could be ruthlessly exploited and carelessly wasted. There was little need to work in harmony with nature or adopt the more modern caretaker attitude toward the land. Compared to the ecologically minded Tokugawa peasant, with his carefully husbanded and immaculately manicured fields, the American farmer saw nature more as an adversary to be conquered: fields were roughly cleared and as easily abandoned, and the landscape was rapidly transformed into a gullied, soil-depleted wasteland.

In this regard, the settlement patterns of American farms are most informative. Far from resembling the densely packed agricultural villages of Europe and Asia, with their closely clustered houses, communally owned land, and outlying fields, the typical American farm consisted of a single farm family living alone and isolated on land holdings that could only be described as immense by European and Asian standards. What came to be called "villages" by European and other observers were really market towns that provided the necessary goods and services and were utilized by the farmers mostly on weekends. This distinction was well known in the early nineteenth century when Albert Gallatin, who had been secretary of the treasury during Jefferson's administration, reminded the Frenchman Alexis de Tocqueville in 1831: "We have no villages, that is to say centers peopled by farmers. The landowner lives on the land and the houses are all scattered throughout the countryside. What you call villages (here) deserves rather the name of town, since the population is composed of merchants, artisans, and lawyers" (Tunnard and Read 1956:34).

The effect of an expanding frontier was such that while there had been a few early attempts to transplant the European feudal or manorial system by the Dutch in New York, by Lord Baltimore in Maryland, and by the aristocratic founders of the Carolinas, the availability and easy access to vast tracts of virgin land made it theoretically possible, at least, for even the common man to become as wealthy as European landed gentry, and all of the early feudal experiments withered on the vine. It was, therefore, not impossible, and indeed it was thought to be only natural, for a man to make the jump from indentured servant to freeman, from freeman to freeholder, and from freeholder to wealthy speculator in lands on the western frontier.

In short, the prospect of easily available land on an expanding frontier not only provided a safety valve for the urban proletariat, but also made virtually impossible the maintenance of anything that even approximated European class distinctions, let alone the more authoritarian feudal ethic of Tokugawa Japan. Americans had become an independent, restless, and highly mobile people, with little of the European or Asian peasant's attachment to the soil. Even today land is thought of primarily as an investment, and the house trailer is considered a typically American invention.

Nor was it easily possible for the isolated American farmer to achieve the sense of community that was so characteristic of the Tokugawa peasant villages. Throughout rural America, and especially on the frontier, one of the most commonly expressed emotions was that of loneliness often bordering on despair. From James Fenimore Cooper to Willa Cather, American writers have brooded over the loneliness and isolation of rural life, and the search for community remains a dominant theme in American literature down to the present.

It was not until the first quarter of this century, with the invention of the automobile and the construction of hard-surfaced, all-weather highways, that the isolation of rural America finally came to a close. Until that time, roads were axle-breaking, often muddy morasses. To travel the dozen or more miles into town was an exhausting journey that took on many of the aspects of a minor expedition. In reflecting on the transformations made by the automobile in the last half century, it is one of the ironies of American history that Henry Ford, who had wanted so desperately to preserve the virtues of rural America, was to become the one man most instrumental in changing them.

It was the nature of the American experience, then, that both the philosophy of government and the easy availability of land were to favor the development of some uniquely American characteristics. To this day, Americans like to think of themselves as staunchly individualistic, self-reliant, and self-assertive people, who are as proud of their egalitarianism as they are defensive about their rights and privileges. Such characteristics could hardly be planted, let alone matured, in the more restricted soil and highly authoritarian climate of feudal Japan. And while it is true that the Jeffersonian ideal of a nation composed of independent, self-reliant, and self-sufficient yeoman farmers was never to be realized, it has remained a potent ideal, and one that has exerted a powerful influence on the character of Americans down to the present.

The Major American Psychological and Behavioral Characteristics

Individualism. The American emphasis on individualism is one on which a large number of observers agree. In 1941, Coleman made a listing of American traits upon which there was relative agreement. Foremost among these· was individualism (1934:28). In his chapter on "Major Value Orientations in America " Williams quotes many sources and devotes several pages to an explication of the importance of individualism as a value in itself and as a necessary basic assumption for the functioning of a democracy. Thus he quotes Becker:

> Its (modern liberal democracy's) fundamental assumption is the worth and dignity and creative capacity of the individual, so that the chief aim of government is the maximum of individual self-direction, the chief means to that end the minimum of compulsion by the state. Ideally considered means and ends are conjoined in the concept of freedom; freedom of thought, so that the truth may prevail; freedom of self-government, so that no one may be compelled against his will. (Becker 1941:27)

Individualism can be said to be a part of an overall emphasis or cult of individual personality. Williams makes use of this concept as it has been developed in Western civilization in his discussion of individualism. As he states:

> Basically this cult sets a high value on the unique development of each individual personality and is correspondingly averse to invasion of individual integrity; to be a person is to be independent, responsible, and self-respecting, and thereby to be worthy of concern and respect in one's own right. To be a person, in this sense, is to be an autonomous and responsible agent, not merely a reflection of external pressures, and to have an internal center of gravity, a set of standards, and a conviction

of personal worth. Above all, the individual is not considered to be released from all sociocultural controls. As Parsons has put it: "This is not a matter simply of freeing the individual from ethical restraints imposed by society, it is the matter of the imposition of a different *kind* of restraint. Individuality is a product of a certain social state. . . ." Not the unrestrained biologic human being, but the ethical decision making, unitary social personality is the object of this cult of the individual. (1970:495)

In subsequent paragraphs, Williams explores the "cult of the individual" as it has come to permeate American life. He states that it is manifest in such areas of law wherein an individual is forbidden to take his own life and suicide is defined as a crime. It is also manifest in the prohibition of slavery and peonage and on the very basic level of individual worth. On the religious level it is manifest in our belief in the immortality of the soul and our repugnance towards the cremation of the dead. Further, on the psychological level it is manifest in the area of unconscious assumptions.

By way of personal observation it can be added that these assumptions are basically a reflection of the emphasis on the belief in the integrity and uniqueness of the individual human being. As such, they are usually so ingrained that an instructor frequently encounters resistance in students when discussing the influence of social or group pressure on individual behavior. Indeed, even when they can recognize such influence on their own behavior, a commonly voiced complaint is that somehow it just isn't right.

As Watts notes:

> Now one of the most important Christian conventions is the view of man as what I have called the "skin-encapsulated ego," the separate soul and its fleshy vehicle together constituting a personality which is unique and ultimately valuable in the sight of God. This view is undoubtedly the historical basis of the Western style of individuality, giving us the sensation of ourselves as isolated islands of consciousness confronted with objective experiences which are quite "other." We have developed this sensation to a particularly high degree. (1963:18)

This unconscious assumption on the value of the individual person as an individual begins at birth. Lee, in an article that complements Caudill's and Weinstein's study of Japanese and American child rearing notes the following:

> In our own culture, the value of individualism is axiomatically assumed. How else would it be possible for us to pluck twenty infants, newly severed from complete unity with their mothers, out of all social and emotional context and classify them as twenty atoms on the basis of a similarity of age? On this assumption of individualism, a mother has need for individual self-expression. She has to have time for and by herself; and since she values individualism, the mother in our culture usually does have this need for a private life.
>
> We also believe that a newborn infant must become individuated, must be taught physical and emotional self-dependence; we assume, in fact, that he has a separate identity which he must be helped to recognize. We believe that he has distinct rights and sociologists urge us to reconcile the needs of the child to those of the adults in the family. . . . Now the child grows up needing time to himself, a room of his own, freedom of choice, freedom to plan his own time and his own life. . . . This need for privacy is an imperative one in our society, recognized by official bodies of our government. (1959:74-75)

Again, with reference to the area of unconscious assumptions, it can be demonstrated that even the methodology and end result of psychotherapy are based upon different views of the individual in American culture and in Japan. For example, Freudian psychoanalysis has as its greatest concern the well-being of the individual as contrasted with that of society. In speaking of Freud's emphasis on the individual, Rieff has noted:

> His interest in the social constantly mirrors his concern with the individual. It is because he is first of all a student of the individual that Freud could entertain the notion of individual and society in active and prolonged conflict with each other, in a theory that supports at different analytical points the claims of both. . . .
>
> Freud's own sentiments were formed by an ascendant doctrine of individuality, according to which "society" meant the sacrifice of individuality, not, as in earlier notions of organic community, its fulfillment . . . .
>
> Psychoanalysis is the private man defending himself against public encroachment. He cultivates the private life and its pleasures, and if he does take part in public affairs it is for consciously private motives. . . .

It is fair to accuse him [Freud] of a medical egoism, allied to that of other nineteenth-century defenders of the individual against society—Nietzsche and Stirner for example. Individual health, not the perfection of society, is the psychological measure. (1961:276-79)

Rieff's remarks on individualism might be compared with the conclusions reached by Moloney in his comments on the goals of Japanese psychoanalysis:

Kosawa . . . quotes some material from a Japanese analysand who, as he approached the successful (by Japanese standards) conclusions of his treatment said, "During my vacation my mother told me on one occasion that I was now pleasing my father better again." This, of course, means that the analysand was performing *ko* (filial piety) toward his father. Kosawa, in reviewing the changes in the patient's personality, says, "His psychic state is now as harmonious a one as can be reached by human beings." But this does not mean that he is developing individualism; he may be feeling more comfortable because he no longer assails his super-ego (emperor) with his individual strivings. What Kosawa actually describes here is an individual who is now performing *giri* (duty) in accordance with the national entity program. . . . A system so foreign to the national entity program as western psychoanalysis—stressing as it does the importance of adult stability, maturity, and especially individualism—would have to be drastically overhauled to render it compatible with Japanese political requirements. (1954:200-201)

Because of the Japanese emphasis on collectivity as opposed to individualism, Moloney was very pessimistic about the future of Japanese psychoanalysis:

I predict that psychoanalysis (by Western definition) will be a failure in the sense that Christianity has been a failure in Japan. . . . The culture of Japan, I feel certain, will not in the near future permit other than isolated examples of anything resembling occidental psychoanalysis. . . . (1954:211)

The contrast between a valuation of the individual as an individual and the opposing view of the individual as a member of society is reflected in the comparison of nineteenth-century European and American literature as given by Parkes:

The European novel during the nineteenth century was largely concerned with sociological analysis. Society was portrayed on a broad canvas, and individual characters were presented as specimens of social classes and types. The central theme was usually the struggle of a young man to establish himself in the social organism, often through a process of successful climbing culminating in a good marriage. Novelists displayed varying attitudes toward the values of bourgeois society, but they rarely suggested that it was possible for individuals to repudiate them. The heroes of American fiction, on the other hand, have mostly been divorced from all social ties and obligations except those of loyalty to personal friends and comrades. Of obscure origin and background, they have represented the ideal of natural virtue and integrity, which owed nothing to external discipline, and would in fact, be endangered by social pressure. American novelists have been relatively uninterested in describing and analyzing social types, and have generally regarded organized society as corrupt or oppressive, so that the hero can preserve his virtue only through rebellion or escape. (1954:193-94)

Equality. At this point, however, it may be objected that, far from being rugged individualists, Americans are just as frequently seen as blind conformists. There is, of course, a considerable body of literature supporting the latter view. As Potter remarks:

> Almost every trait, good or bad, has been attributed to the American people by someone. . . . But it is probably safe to say that at bottom there have been only two primary ways of explaining the American. . . . One depicts the American primarily as an individual and an idealist, while the other makes him out as a conformist and a materialist. (1964:233)

Potter relates these two contrasting views to the overall American value of equality:

> For more than a century we have lived with the contrasting images of the American character which Thomas Jefferson and Alexis de Tocqueville visualized. Both of these images presented the American as an equalitarian and therefore as a democrat, but one was an agrarian democrat while the other was a majoritarian democrat; one an independent individualist, the other a mass-dominated conformist; one an idealist, the other a materialist. (1964:237)

The equalitarian basis for the divergent views is summarized in the closing paragraphs of the essay:

There is one common factor conspicuous in the extreme—
namely equality, so dear both to Jefferson's American and to de
Tocqueville. . . . Tocqueville . . . observed that the ideal of
equality was the fundamental fact from which all others seem to
be derived. . . .

[Has] the belief that all men are of equal worth . . . contributed to a feature so much deplored as American conformity? . . . [It] has done both, for the same respect of the American
for his fellow citizens . . . has also made many another American think that he has no business to question the opinion which
his neighbors have sanctioned. True, he says, if all men are
equal, each ought to think for himself, but on the other hand,
no man should consider himself better than his neighbors, and
if the majority have adopted an opinion on a matter, how can
one man question their opinion, without setting himself up as
being better than they. Moreover, it is understood that the
majority are pledged not to force him to adopt their opinion.
But it is also understood that in return for this immunity he will
voluntarily accept the will of the majority in most things. The
absence of a formal compulsion to conform seemingly increases
the obligation to conform voluntarily. Thus, the other directed
man is seen to be derived as much from the American tradition
of equalitarianism as the rugged individualist. . . . (1964:242-
44)

The equalitarian ideal that Potter discerned as being at the
root of conformity has also been noticed by others. Lipset, in his
essay entitled "A Changing American Character?," takes issue
with Riesman's contention that there has been a discernible shift
from "inner directed" to "other directed" personality types.
Lipset states that the "inner" and "other" types are a reflection of
periodic shifts between the ethics of equality and achievement.
When the ethic of equality is dominant, achievement with its
stress on individualism and competitiveness is played down. On
the other hand, when achievement is being emphasized then the
"other directed" type will be played down:

Complete commitment to equality involves rejecting some of
the implications of valuing achievement; and the opposite is
also true. Thus, when the equalitarianism of left or liberal
politics is dominant, there is a reaction against achievement,
and when the values of achievement prevail in a conservative
political and economic atmosphere, men tend to depreciate
some of the consequences of equality, such as the influence of
popular taste on culture. (1967:144)

Lipset further argues that if social character and values are dependent upon a certain type of economy and its concomitant technology, social organization, and value structure, then we should expect to find somewhat the same type of social character in countries having similar economies:

The occupational profiles of Sweden, Germany, and the United States have been similar for decades. If the causal connection between technology and social character were direct, then the patterns described as typical of "other-direction" or the "organization man" should have occurred in Great Britain prior to their occurrence in the United States and should now be found to predominate in other European nations. Yet "other-direction" and the "social ethic" appear to be preeminently American traits. In Europe, one sees the continued, even though declining, strength of deferential norms, enjoining conformity to class standards of behavior.

Thus comparative analysis strikingly suggests that the derivation of social character almost exclusively from the traits associated with occupational or population profiles is invalid. So important an element in a social system as social character must be deeply affected by the dominant value system. For the value system is perhaps the most enduring part of what we think of as society, or a social system. (1967:140-41)

A more convincing argument, however, is that to be found in the writings of Alexis de Tocqueville, who visited the United States in the 1830's before industrialism and at a time when Jacksonian democracy and a belief in equality were very high. Far from finding a nation of discrete individuals, each going his own way, he was much impressed by the tendency toward conformity:

I know of no country where there is so little independence of mind and freedom of discussion as in America. . . . In America, the majority raises very formidable barriers to write whatever he pleases, but he will repent it if he ever steps beyond them. Not that he is exposed to the terrors of an auto-da-fé, but he is tormented by the sights and persecutions of daily obloquy. His political career is closed forever, since he has offended the only authority which is able to promote his success. (1964:51-52)

The last sentence is revealing because, as Tocqueville recognized, if authority is made to reside in the majority, then the majority can at times· be as tyrannic as any despot. Again, however, Tocqueville is able to trace this tyranny of the majority back to the principle of equality:

When the ranks of society are unequal, and men unlike each other in condition, there are some individuals invested with all the power of superior intelligence, learning, and enlightenment, while the multitude is sunk in ignorance and prejudice. Men living at these aristocratic periods are therefore naturally induced to shape their opinions by the superior standard of a person or a class of persons, while they are averse to recognize the infallibility of the mass of the people. The contrary takes place in ages of equality. The nearer the citizens are drawn to the common level of an equal and similar condition, the less prone does each man become to place implicit faith in a certain man or a certain class of men. But his readiness to believe the multitude increases, and opinion is more than ever mistress of the world. Not only is common opinion the only guide which private judgement retains among a democratic people, but among such a people it possesses a power infinitely beyond what it has elsewhere. . . . When the inhabitant of a democratic country compares himself individually with all those about him, he feels with pride that he is the equal of any one of them; but when he comes to survey the totality of his fellows . . . he is instantly overwhelmed by the sense of his own insignificance and weakness. The same equality which renders him independent of each of his fellow-citizens taken severally exposes him alone and unprotected to the influence of the greater number. (1964:55-56)

Williams's discussion of external conformity is in accord with that of Tocqueville. Williams states that American "individualism" has not tended to set an autonomous individual against the group, rather it has been characterized by an impatience with restraints on economic activity and a rejection of the state. Further, individualism tends to be a matter of group individualism:

. . . an emphasis upon external conformity early develops out of the premise of basic human equality: if all are equal, then all have an equal right to judge their fellows and to regulate their conduct according to commonly accepted standards. . . . Interestingly enough, the very heterogeneity of American culture tends to produce a stress upon external conformity. Given the varied cultural backgrounds of the population and the desire that the various groups should continue to live together in the same society, conformity in externals becomes a sort of "social currency" making it possible to continue the society in spite of many clashes of interests and basic values. (1970:485-86)

Williams's statement, in turn, seems remarkably similar to that of Kluckhohn, who concluded:

> Today's kind of "conformity" may actually be a step toward more genuine individuality in the United States. "Conformity" is less of a personal and psychological problem—less tinged with anxiety and guilt. . . . If someone accepts outwardly the convention of one's group, one may have greater psychic energy to develop and fulfill one's private potentialities as a unique person. I have encountered no substantial evidence that this "conformity" is thoroughgoingly "inward." (1958:187)

Yet even the importance placed on the value of equality may be attacked. It is common observation that, in America, people are not equal in that there are wide differences in wealth, education, etc. These differences may be explained in terms of the often conflicting values of achievement and equality. Equality in relation to achievement has meant equality of opportunity.

Potter notes that equality of opportunity of access to undeveloped resources was the best economic benefit the government could give. In turn, this form of equality became the most highly sanctioned form of equalitarianism in the United States.

It is because of this sanction that Americans have tolerated great discrepancies in wealth—especially if they believed the wealth was earned and not acquired by special privilege. Yet, as Potter clearly indicates, to say that the ideal of equality refers only to equality of opportunity is to tell only half the story:

> The American faith has also held, with intense conviction, the belief that all men are equal in the sense that they share a common humanity—that all are alike in the eyes of God—and that every person has a certain dignity, no matter how low his circumstances, which no one else, no matter how high *his* circumstances, is entitled to disregard. When this concept of the nature of man was translated into a system of social arrangements, the crucial point on which it came to focus was the question of rank. For the concept of rank essentially denies that all men are equally worthy and argues that some are better than others—that some are born to serve and others born to command. The American creed not only denied this view but even condemned it and placed a taboo upon it. Some people, according to the American creed, might be more fortunate than others, but they must never regard themselves as better than others. Pulling one's rank has therefore been the unforgivable

sin against American democracy, and the American people have, accordingly, reserved their heartiest dislike for the officer class in the military, for people with upstage or condescending manners, and for anyone who tries to convert power or wealth (which are not resented) into overt rank or privilege (which are). Thus it is permissible for an American to have servants (which is a matter of function), but he must not put them in livery (which is a matter of rank); permissible to attend expensive schools, but not to speak with a cultivated accent; permissible to rise in the world, but never to repudiate the origins from which he rose. The most palpable and overt possible claim of rank is, of course, the effort of one individual to assert authority, in a personal sense, over others, and accordingly the rejection of authority is the most pronounced of all the concrete expressions of American beliefs in equality. (1964:241)

Somewhat the same distinction is made by Williams in his discussion of intrinsic and extrinsic valuations. Extrinsic valuation has to do with external symbols such as occupation, income, nationality, race, or other social category. Intrinsic valuation has to do with the personal qualities of the individual and is manifest in the obligation to treat others as ends in themselves rather than as means:

> Extrinsic valuations focus upon what a person *has;* intrinsic valuation concerns what the person is as an individual. It is obvious that the two imputations of value do not coincide, as when we say that a man "doesn't deserve his rank" or "he may have a million dollars but he isn't worth two cents as a man." (1970:475)

Rights and privileges. The American emphasis on rights and privileges as opposed to an emphasis on duty and obligations has already been mentioned. It will be recalled that in their cross-national study Gillespie and Allport stated:

> We have previously remarked upon the striking contrast that exists between Japanese and American cultures in this regard. Our American students . . . emphasized their rights rather than their duties, and all in all presented a picture of individuality, separation from the social context of living, and privatism of values and personal plans. (1955:29)

Williams relates the concern with rights and privileges to the pervasive American value of freedom. He points out that the American conception of freedom is derived from the European

historical experience in emancipating area after area of life from
feudalistic control. In the American colonies, the trend toward
emancipation became intensified:

> Always the demand was for freedom *from* some existing
> restraint. That the major American freedoms were in this sense
> negative does not mean, of course, that they were not also
> positive: they were rights to *do*, by the same token that they were
> rights to be protected from restraint. Nevertheless, the historical
> process left its mark in a culturally standardized way of thought
> and evaluation—a tendency to think of rights rather than
> duties, a suspicion of established (especially personal) author-
> ity, a distrust of central government, a deep aversion to accep-
> tance of obviously coercive restraint through visible social
> organization. (1970:480)

Williams's comments are echoed by other observers. Parkes,
for example, traces the American valuation of individual rights to
the English liberal tradition, especially that of John Locke:

> The American belief in individual rights was initially derived
> from the liberal tradition of England, and was strengthened by
> the colonizing and pioneering experience; but its more specific
> formulation was provided by European theorists of the social-
> contract school, and particularly by John Locke. That men
> were endowed by nature with rights to life, liberty, and private
> property; that the state was based on a contract freely entered
> into by its citizens; that the only true function of government
> was to protect the rights of the citizens; and that a government
> might be changed or overthrown whenever it ceased to maintain
> these rights—these doctrines were in harmony with American
> attitudes and were corroborated to a remarkable degree by actual
> American experience. (1959:58-59)

Kluckhohn's observations are similar to those of Parkes. In
Mirror For Man he associates the American valuation on personal
rights with a comparable dislike of authority:

> To this day Americans hate "being told what to do." They
> have always distrusted strong government. The social roles
> most frequently jibed at in comic strips are those that interfere
> with the freedom of others: the dog catcher, the truant officer,
> the female social climber (Mrs. Jiggs) who forces her husband
> and family to give up their habitual satisfactions. "My rights" is
> one of the commonest phrases in the American language. This
> historically conditioned attitude toward authority is constantly

reinforced by child-training patterns. The son must "go farther" than his father, and revolt against the father in adolescence is expected. (1960:179)

The concern for rights and privileges has, of course, both political and historical antecedents. The Declaration of Independence of the United States states: "We hold these truths to be self-evident: That all men are created equal; that they are endowed by their Creator with certain inalienable rights; that among these are life, liberty, and the pursuit of happiness. . . . "

The high valuation placed on individual rights is reflected in American child-rearing practices. In a report on Orchard Town, a pseudonym for a New England community, Minturn and Lambert report:

> Mothers want their children to be independent; a necessary goal in a society that requires it of adults. They also consider principle to be sometimes more important than group solidarity. As part of their child training they encourage children to "stand up for their rights" and, if necessary, fight back when attacked by other children. (1964:198)

Self-reliance. Self-reliance is related to equality and individualism in that it is the counterpart of independence and the antithesis of dependency. As one of the major value orientations of America it has been the subject of considerable comment, and indeed provided the title of one of the major articles by Ralph Waldo Emerson in the nineteenth century. In his essay, "Self-Reliance," Emerson is also emphasizing self-realization or self-actualization:

> Society everywhere is in conspiracy against the manhood of every one of its members. Society is a joint-stock company, in which members agree, for the better securing of his bread to each shareholder, to surrender the liberty and culture of the eater. The virtue in most request is conformity. Self-reliance is its aversion. It loves not realities and creators, but names and customs.
>
> Whoso would be a man, must be a nonconformist. He who would gather immortal palms must not be hindered by the name of goodness, but must explore if it be goodness. Nothing at last is sacred but the integrity of your own mind. . . . A man is to carry himself in the presence of all opposition as if

every hing were titular and ephemeral but he. I am ashamed to think how easily we capitulate to badges and names, to large societies and dead institutions. (1957:149-50)

Yet, Hsu believes that it is just this faith in self-reliance that is responsible for the many tensions and contradictions in American life. Self-reliance, Hsu states, is the value most responsible for American conformity:

. . . the contradictory American "values" noted by the sociologists, psychologists, and historians are but manifestations of one core value. . . .

The American core value in question is *self-reliance,* the most persistent psychological expression of which is the fear of dependence. . . .

This self-reliance is also very different from self-sufficiency. Any Chinese or European village can achieve self-sufficiency as a matter of fact. . . . But American self-reliance is a militant ideal which parents inculcate in their children and by which they judge the worth of all mankind. . . .

In American society the fear of dependence is so great that an individual who is not self-reliant is an object of hostility and called a misfit. "Dependent Character" is a highly derogatory term, and a person so described is thought to be in need of psychiatric help. (1961:216-18)

In his study of major American value orientations, Williams comes to somewhat the same conclusion:

. . . American culture has tended to identify a very great variety of forms of personal dependence as lack of freedom. To "work under a boss" was not so long ago regarded as a loss of freedom. The widespread reluctance to take employment as a domestic servant and the low evaluation attached to this type of occupation appear to reflect in part the same complex. One of the earliest and most persistent criticisms of American society by aristocratically minded foreign observers has concerned the absence of a docile serving-class and the impertinence of the "lower orders." (1970:481-82)

There are those, however, who would object to the stress that both Hsu and Williams place on self-reliance. They would point out that self-reliance is a virtue more easily realized in an agrarian society than in a modern industrial society marked by a high degree of specialization and mutual interdependence. In answering such objections, Hsu indicates that not only is self-reliance a continuing value but it is also responsible for the often-observed American tendency toward conformity and prejudice:

> What has actually happened is that the American orientation remains one of self-reliance; as self-reliance gains momentum, however, it forces the individual to be even more conformist than if he was not oriented toward self-reliance in the first place. According to our analysis conformity is the extremely self-reliant man's defense against the fear of inferiority. . . . In the Chinese and Hindu situations the fear of the individual of inferiority is alleviated by the basic psychological factor of dependence. . . . With its aid the individual need have no qualms about seeking shelter behind human walls. In the American situation not only is the fear of inferiority greater because ambition is more generalized among the population but the individual must rely largely upon himself to deal with the pressures which threaten him. . . .
>
> What is not usually seen is the psychological connection between intensified conformity and prejudice as well as extreme bigotry. . . . In his fear of inferiority the self-reliant man envies those who have climbed above him and dreads the encroachment of those struggling below him. The greater the envy of those above, the more serious is his apprehension of encroachment from below. These sources of perpetual insecurity generate not only the passion for conformity but also the impulse for persecution. (1964:217-18)

Hsu's remarks in turn are supported by the work of Fischer and Fischer. In *The New Englanders of Orchard Town*, the Fischers focused on child-rearing practices and related these to the finding of child-rearing practices investigated in the five other cultures studied in the Six Cultures. project. In the epilogue to their study the Fischers state:

> In our chapter on the nature of the child, we said in a different way that the core of Orchard Town values, surpassing in importance the value of service to God, or the political community, is perhaps what Hsu calls self-reliance. If we add to self-reliance *self-realization*, the aim in the development of Orchard Town character is perhaps largely complete. Hsu (1961:p. 217) regards self-reliance as the American core value and considers the other values take on color from it. The Orchard Town belief in developing the inner potential of the child may be regarded as a manifestation of self-reliance. (Fischer and Fischer 1966:147)

Self-assertion. The American value orientation of self-assertion is in keeping with the previously discussed value of self-reliance. That is, if a person is self-reliant, he must stand up for himself and assert himself in order to protect his own rights. On a somewhat superficial level, this aspect of individualism and self-reliance is found in such expressions as "God helps them who help themselves," "If you don't look out for yourself, no one else will," and "You have to blow your own horn."

Undoubtedly, self-assertion is related not only to the American spirit of competition but also to the oft-remarked view of the American as being aggressive. There is some empirical evidence of the American tolerance of aggressive behavior as compared to other societies. In their study of maternal attitudes and behavior in six cultures, Minturn and Lambert reported:

> As part of their child training they encourage children to "stand up for their rights" and if necessary, fight back when attacked by other children. The extent to which these parents encourage such aggression is unusual, compared to other samples. The training is accompanied by rules for "fair fighting" that are rigidly enforced, so children are seldom injured in a fight.
>
> It is perhaps this same concern for the right of individuals as well as a desire to be democratic and not suppress their children's emotional development that makes these mothers lenient about obedience and permissive about aggression to themselves. They hesitate to nag their children or interfere too much with their activities. Many also feel that it is healthier to let children "blow off steam" than harbor suppressed hostility. (1964:198)

Somewhat the same findings are reported by Sears, Maccoby, and Levin in *Patterns of Child Rearing.* In attempting to measure attitudes toward aggression, they asked: "Some people feel it is very important for a child to learn not to fight with other children; and others feel there are times when a child has to learn to fight. How do you feel about this?" In answer to the question, 4 per cent did not want the child to fight others ever, 9 per cent said that it should always be discouraged, 27 per cent said the child should defend himself if bullied, 51 per cent said a child should defend himself but not start a fight, 6 per cent said a child should never take anything from anyone, and for 3 per cent the answer was not ascertained (1957:246).

Again, support for self-assertion is given in Williams' study of American value orientations. In a summarizing paragraph he lists eight major propositions, of which the first is:

> American culture is organized around the attempt at *active mastery* rather than *passive acceptance*. Into this dimension falls the low toleration of frustration; the refusal to accept ascetic renunciation; the positive encouragement of desire; the stress on power; the approval of ego assertion, and so on. (1970:501-2)

Finally, indirect evidence of the importance of self-assertion and its relationship to self-reliance can be found in an article by Caudill and Doi in which they contrast patterns of emotions in Japan and in the United States:

> It would be very difficult for a person in Japan to act independently and to disregard his collateral ties. Equally, in the United States, it would be very difficult for a person, particularly a man, to act in a dependent fashion and to neglect attention to the sanctions in his culture which call for independent behavior and judgement.
>
> One way, admittedly too shorthand a way, of summarizing this comparison between Japan and the United States, is to suggest that tenderness is handled well and adaptively in Japan, but that aggression is a source of great trouble since it has remained psychologically primitive and is less utilized and reworked for adaptive purposes during the course of childhood development. . . . On the other hand, aggression is handled more adaptively in the United States, since its use has been emphasized since childhood, and difficulties for Americans arise more in the adequate communication and expression of tenderness, which for them, in contrast to the Japanese, has remained on a psychologically primitive level. (1963:415-16)

Summary

The major American value orientations discussed in this chapter were individualism, equality, a concern for rights and privileges, self-reliance, and self-assertion. In addition to these, there are a number of related psychological and behavioral characteristics which are listed as follows:

1. A reliance on one's own resources rather than on others.
2. Children are trained to be assertive, self-reliant, and independent.

3. The strongest emotional bond is between the husband and the wife.
4. An emphasis on egalitarianism and horizontal rather than vertical relationships.
5. A strong emphasis on individual rights.
6. A need to feel independent of others, together with a strong fear of dependency.
7. Aggressiveness associated with self-assertion and active mastery.
8. A grudging acceptance of those in authority.
9. An emphasis on individual autonomy.
10. Achievement is seen in terms of individual goals.
11. A strong emphasis on achieved status.
12. A feeling of resentment and active dislike of rules and controls.
13. A primary obligation towards self-fulfillment.
14. An emphasis on dominance and self-assertiveness.
15. An openness and accessibility to others.
16. A primary responsibility to be true to one's self.
17. A tendency to play down or mask the superiority of others.
18. A sense of optimism.
19. Success is largely achieved through pragmatism and the exploitation of opportunities.
20. An emphasis on moral righteousness, generalized rules of conduct, and a "universal ethic."

Most of the above characteristics are implicit or even mentioned explicitly in the previous discussion of the major value orientations. Again, however, as in the case of the Japanese values, there are those which require additional discussion. For example, number 18, "a sense of optimism," follows naturally from the values of individualism and self-reliance. But perhaps of equal importance has been the nature of the American experience. Throughout most of American history, hard work, diligence, and ambition were rewarded and it was relatively easy for an individual to feel that he had a certain amount of control over his own destiny. This last, of course, is subject to considerable modification based on class differences. Several studies (Jessor, Graves et al., 1968) (Kohn 1970) indicate that the degree of belief in internal control (one's destiny is due to one's volition) as opposed to external control (one's destiny is due to control by outside forces—e.g., luck, fate, etc.) is directly related to parental values. As Kohn mentions in his study of Italian and American middle- and working-class families:

> Even though there are impressive differences between Italian and American parental values, the relationship of social class to parental values is much the same in both countries. In Italy and in the United States, middle-class parents put greater emphasis on children's self-direction, working-class parents on their conformity to external standards. There is something intrinsic to social stratification that yields similar results in the two countries. (1970:46)

The last characteristic, moreover, also requires some explanation. Number 20 states that there is "an emphasis on moral righteousness, generalized rules of conduct, and a 'universal ethic.' " With reference to the moral orientation, Williams notes that "authoritative observers from abroad from Tocqueville, through Bryce, Siegfried, and others, down to recent studies, have agreed on one point: Americans tend to 'see the world in moral terms' " (1970:461).

Kluckhohn reached somewhat similar conclusions. With regard to the generalized rules of conduct, he reported that while he was in Japan students complained to him that "it was difficult to understand American democracy because Americans seemed to . lack an explicit ideology that they could communicate" (1960:117). Again, however, with respect to the universalistic ethic, it is Williams who states: "With conspicuous deviations a main theme is a *universalistic* rather than a *particularistic* ethic" (1970:502).

Chapter 5

Contrasting Japanese and American Patterns of Individuation and Conformity

Patterns of Individuation

In the preceding discussion of American and Japanese psychological and behavioral characteristics an attempt was made to list those characteristics that clearly and distinctly contrasted with each other. Thus the Japanese emphasis on duties and obligation was seen to be in contrast to the American emphasis on rights and privileges. Similarly, the American emphasis on equality was contrasted with the Japanese emphasis on hierarchy, individualism was contrasted with collectivity, and so on.

The intent throughout has not been to suggest that the Japanese characteristics are unknown or even little valued in the United States, but rather to indicate that the American character-istics are more dominant. Therefore it is to be expected that in the larger American society there would be a greater probability that the American characteristics would be found more frequently than the Japanese ones.

By the same logic one might reasonably assume that the major American characteristics of individualism, equality, a concern for rights and privileges, self-reliance, and self-assertion could also be found in Japan, with correspondingly lesser fre-quency. Of these, the one that apparently provides the greatest contrast with the overall orientation of Japanese society is that of individualism. It is from the value placed on individualism that the major American characteristics of a concern for rights and privileges, self-reliance, and self-assertion are derived.

One might also assume that, given the stress placed on duty and obligation, deference, collectivity, dependence, and hierarchy, individualism in Japanese society would be quite different from that found in American society. Such, indeed, appears to be the case.

The most useful conceptual model for understanding the contrasting patterns of individuation in Japan and the United States is that given by Maruyama (1965). In his article, Maruyama begins his discussion of individuation by noting that "everywhere the process of 'modernization' has been *in some sense* disruptive for the individual living in 'traditional' society. He is 'emancipated,' willingly, or unwillingly, from the communal ties which have bound him. . . .For the sake of convenience, I shall call this general phenomenon 'individuation,' as distinguished from the term 'individualization'. . ." (1965:493-94).

Maruyama goes on to identify four possible patterns of the individuation process. These are: individualization, democratization, privatization, and atomization. These, in turn, may be grouped in two main categories depending upon the degree to which the individual associates voluntarily with others in order to attain a particular purpose. For example, both the individualized and democratized individuals are marked by a high degree of association with others. On the other hand, the privatized and atomized individuals are characterized by a lack of voluntary association with others.

A further dimension is added by Maruyama in separating the individualized from the democratized individual and the privatized from the atomized individual. This separation relates to the individual's distance from the focus of political authority. That is, it is dependent upon the degree to which the individual is interested in identifying himself with the center of decision-making. On this dimension both the democratized and atomized individuals are involved with political activity, but for different reasons. As Maruyama explains, the atomized individual is one characterized by a feeling of anomie; he is uprooted, lonely, and suffers from fear and anxiety. Although he is usually apathetic towards public affairs, he may turn into a fanatic participant in order to escape from his loneliness and insecurity. The democratized individual, on the other hand, is more interested in public goals, abolishing special privilege, and broadening the base of political participation (1965:496-97).

In the other direction there is a moving away from the center of decision-making or focus of political authority. On this dimension we find both the individualized and privatized individuals. These individuals are more interested in personal rather than public goals, but there are major differences. Because of his greater degree of association with others, the individualized person is more prone to emphasize personal rights and local autonomy than is the privatized individual. On the other hand, the privatized individual is more interested in the achievement of self-gratification than in public affairs. Although politically apathetic because of his lack of associations for larger public goals, his characterization is more of withdrawal than an escape from his inner self. As such, he is psychologically more stable than the atomized individual.

Maruyama has expressed graphically the various dimensions in a model which is duplicated in Figure 1.

In the model it can readily be seen that, as we go up the axis from dissociation to association, we find individuals who will associate with their neighbors to accomplish public ends. As we go down the axis, we find more whose sense of solidarity with their neighbors or fellow men is relatively weak. This will result in privatized or atomized individuals. It can also be seen that democratization is both associative and centripetal, in that there is an association with others for public ends and a movement towards the center of political authority or decision-making. Individualization, on the other hand, although associative for the purpose of public goals, is more characterized by an interest in personal rights and local autonomy and less in a centralized political authority.

On the lower end of the axis we find greater dissociation. The atomized individual feels a need to belong and may therefore lose himself in mass movements, in that he is driven toward a centralized political authority. The privatized individual, however, while also dissociative and politically apathetic, is more stable than the atomized individual. The significant difference between the individualized and privatized person is that the privatized individual is solely preoccupied with his private

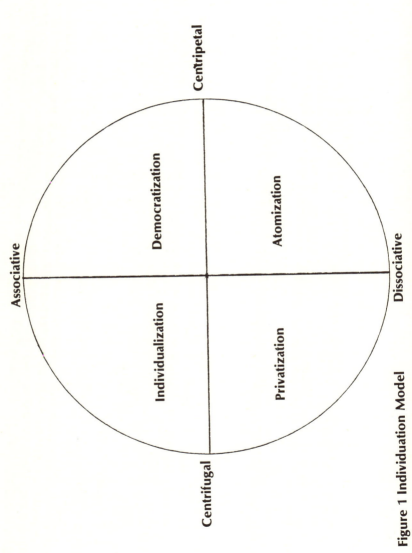

Figure 1 Individuation Model

affairs, while the individualized person is always ready to participate in political affairs because of his concern for his private interest (Maruyama 1965:498).

Maruyama explains the differences in the following:

> The INDIVIDUALIZED individual . . . is centrifugal and associative. He is self-made and independent minded. The personality of the rising bourgeoisie originated in the English yeomanry, or the colonial puritans who founded the United States, represents this type. He may roughly be equated to Professor Riesman's inner-directed personality. . . .
>
> Diametrically opposed to this type is the ATOMIZED individual, who is centripetal and dissociative. He is *other*-directed. He is the person who bitterly suffers from the actual or imagined state of uprootedness and the loss of norms of conduct (anomie). The feeling of loneliness, anxiety, fear, and frustration brought about by the precipitous change of his environment characterizes his psychology. The atomized individual is usually apathetic to public affairs, but sometimes this very apathy will turn abruptly into fanatic participation in politics. Just because he is concerned with escaping from loneliness and insecurity, he is inclined to identify himself totally with authoritarian leadership or to submerge himself into the mystical "whole" expressed in such ideas, culture, and so on. . . .
>
> The DEMOCRATIZED individual occupies the middle position between the individualized type and the atomized type. Like the individualized individual, the democratized individual is associative; i.e., prone to form voluntary groups and associations. They are both rational in their individual choice between alternative courses of social action, and relatively free from a compulsive submission to authority. The democratized individual, however, is more centripetal and is oriented toward innovations by the central government, while the individualized type is more centrifugal and is concerned with local autonomy. While the latter is more interested in institutional guarantees of civil liberties, the former is more inclined to go farther in abolishing privileges or of broadening the base of political participation to include the largest number of people dealing with the widest range of public affairs. Thus the democratized is more prone to mass movements—in this sense he comes closer to the atomized person—than the individualized. Where democratization predominates, the emphasis is likely to be on the ideal of equality rather than on that of liberty, to which the individualized person commits himself. . . .
>
> The exact opposite of the democratized type is the PRIVATIZED individual. Like the atomized individual, the privatized one is also oriented toward the achievement of self-gratification rather

than public goals. Both are dissociative in the sense that they
shun taking the initiative in associating themselves with their
neighbors. But in the case of privatization, the scope of interest
is rather confined to one's "private" affairs and is not as floating
as that of atomization. (1965:496-98)

In relating the four types of individuation to the historical
experience of Japan in modernization, Maruyama concludes that
individuation was usually in the form of privatization or atomization:

> Furthermore, what is noteworthy is that around the time of
> the Russo-Japanese War such expressions as "modern" ideas or
> "modern" women came to be used, instead of the more conven-
> tional adjective "Western." Yet, the question is whether and to
> what extent this new vogue of "individualism" or the emer-
> gence of labor unions reflected INDIVIDUALIZATION or DEMOCRA-
> TIZATION in terms of the attitudes prevalent among youths and
> industrial workers. The present author's conclusion is that the
> individuation of this stage meant the predominance of the
> PRIVATIZED and ATOMIZED type. (1965:507)

Again, in discussing the growth of individuation in postwar
Japan, Maruyama reaches the same conclusion:

> Whoever takes the trouble to examine the complicated score
> of the symphonic development of modern Japan, whose coda
> was the Second World War, will recognize the recurrence of
> certain characteristic features. . . . Whenever the phenomenon
> of individuation came to the surface and attracted the attention
> of the general public, the behavior patterns of either PRIVITI-
> ZATION or ATOMIZATION prevailed, usually outshining the
> faint flickering of INDIVIDUALIZATION and DEMOCRATIZATION.
> (1965:524)

With respect to the American and Japanese characteristics
previously mentioned, it can be readily seen that Maruyama's
model is a most useful one in explaining not only the emerging
patterns of individuation in Japan but also the previously mentioned periodic shifts in the emphasis Americans have placed on
individualism or equality. It will be recalled that the oft-observed
paradox in American society—that is, the contrasting values
placed on both individualism and conformity—were seen by
Lipset (1967:144) to be related to periodic shifts between the ethics
of equality and achievement. He notes that both the "inner" and
"other" directed types have always existed in American society.

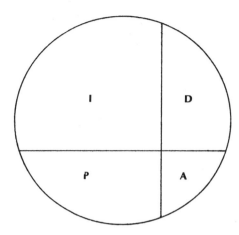

**Figure 2
Individualization
Dominant**

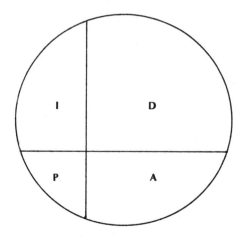

**Figure 3
• Democratization
Dominant**

However, when the ethic of equality is dominant, achievement—with its stress on competition, the "inner" directed man, and individualism—will be played down. Similarly, when achievement is being emphasized, then the "other" directed type, with its associative equalitarianism, will be played down:

> Complete commitment to equality involves rejecting some of the implications of valuing achievement; and the opposite is also true. Thus, when the equalitarianism of left or liberal politics is dominant, there is a reaction against conservative political and economic atmosphere, men tend to depreciate some of the consequences of equality, such as the influence of popular taste on culture. (1967:144)

Thus, according to Maruyama's model, the shift toward achievement and competition would be marked by a movement toward individualization, with its emphasis on personal rights and local autonomy. A shift in the other direction, on the other hand, would lead to a rise of democratization with its related stress on equality, abolishing special privilege, and broadening the base of political participation.

These two patterns of individuation are shown in Figures 2 and 3 below. In Figure 2 the dominant emphasis is on individuation, while in Figure 3 democratization is dominant.

The remaining two patterns of atomization and privatization become dominant when individuals feel apathetic, alienated, and helpless with regard to public affairs. Both types of individuals are more concerned with the achievement of personal rather than public ends. They shun taking the initiative in associating with their neighbors and their very apathy and helplessness lead more to a compulsive submission to authority. In the case of the atomized individual, the submissiveness will sometimes take the form of active participation in an attempt to escape from inner loneliness or insecurity by identifying totally with the authoritarian leadership and thereby losing himself in a mystical "whole."

The privatized individual, while also dissociative and little interested in public affairs, differs from the atomized individual in that his private affairs are more engrossing and he is not so normless or so "free floating" as the atomized. Further, the privatized would be more apt to lose himself in his work rather than in a "mystical" identification with others. Both types are depicted in Figures 4 and 5 below:

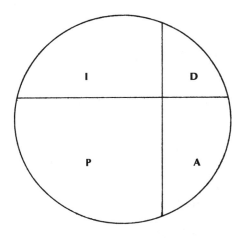

Figure 4
Privatization
Dominant

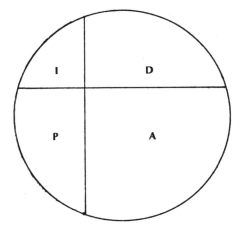

Figure 5
Atomization
Dominant

Patterns of Conformity

It will be recalled from Maruyama's definition that the distinguishing characteristics of the individualized and democratized types were not only their ability to enter into voluntary associations for public goals but also that such association should be an individual choice relatively free from a compulsive submission to authority. As such, the separation may prove useful in understanding the difference between American and Japanese styles of conformity. Given the American emphasis on rights and privileges, conformity is usually seen either in terms of a grudging relinquishing of one's personal autonomy or interests in order to promote the common good, or a willingness to recognize that others also have a claim to certain rights. The latter type of conformity is to be found in such expressions as a willingness to go along with the majority, or "your right to swing your fist ends where my nose begins." In all cases, as previously mentioned in the chapter on American characteristics, the pressure for conformity is a result of the value placed on equality and individualism. As such, as Williams has noted, these lead to an emphasis on external conformity:

> . . . an emphasis on external conformity early develops out of the premise of basic human equality: if all are equal, then all have an equal right to judge their fellows and to regulate their conduct according to commonly accepted standards. (1970:485)

Williams goes on to state that external conformity is also a result of the heterogeneity of American culture. Because of their varied backgrounds and desire to live together, external conformity makes it possible for the various groups to remain together in spite of conflicting interests and values.

Beardsley, moreover, sees important differences between the American and Japanese styles of group conformity in what he calls "antagonistic cooperation":

> A major premise on which the functioning of many American institutions is based is the supposition that the common welfare may be attained through adversary relationships, which might equally well be styled "antagonistic cooperation." This supposition runs through government, law, and business in ways that need be mentioned only briefly to be recognized. It is implicit in the confrontation between political parties before

elections and in the legislative debates that follow them. In law, litigation presupposes adversary action to such an extent that it is difficult to substitute conciliation, compromise, or other procedures even when their merit is recognized, as in divorces and other family cases. . . .
Modern Japanese are not unaware of these methods as applied to government, law and business. . . . Notwithstanding the fact that this pattern is recognized and advocated, it is by no means yet easily applied. . . . Adversaryship conflicts with presuppositions of self-effacement and harmony. . . . In sum, antagonistic cooperation is not an established premise in Japanese culture. (1965:65-66)

Nakane (1970) reached similar conclusions about the nature of conformity in Japan. In discussing the Japanese usage of the word democracy, she states that "what the Japanese mean by 'democracy' is a system that should take the side of, or give consideration to, the weaker or lower; in practice, any decision should be made on the basis of a consensus which includes those located lower in the hierarchy" (1970:144).

Nakane further quotes Riesman that "democracy" in Japan does not mean social equality since the consideration shown to one's equals and official superiors is not extended to those below. "Democracy" seems to indicate a way of doing business without factionalism or conflict. Organizations are said to be "undemocratic" if there is a lack of harmony and consensus (1970:143).

The emphasis on harmony as a source of conformity does not derive from a sense of equality but rather from the strong value placed on collectivity. Again, as Beardsley relates:

Patterns of Japanese behavior that catch the eye as accounting for differences in function often are derived from the tradition of commitment to collectivities, to group solidarity, to particular ways of maintaining or restoring harmony. The collectivities are often hierarchical and authoritarian, with gradations of privilege, but they are not necessarily so. Their members are bound by indefinitely enduring attachments. Conformity and efficiency on the part of members are valued for group solidarity and welfare; initiative is more often the prerogative of leaders. The individual is expected to give precedence to group welfare over his own interests; it is the group that acts, while its members seek anonymity. . . . All such groups seek power, but they also seek harmony, internally and externally, rather than abstract justice. (1965:64)

The essential difference between the Japanese and American styles of conformity, then, is the degree of self-commitment. That is, the degree to which the individual feels obligated to conform or has a need to conform. In this sense, then, although the justification for conformity may be culturally different, the difference is one of degree rather than kind.

The point to be made is that, from a psychological standpoint, group pressure can be just as intense, and perhaps almost as effective, in American society as it is in Japan. Numerous experiments such as those conducted by Asch (1955) and Bales (1955) testify as to the effectiveness of the influence of a group upon the individual. Similarly, our literature is full of references to the "organization man" and the "other-directed" character.

What is important to remember in all of these studies and typologies, however, is that the sentiments aroused in their discussion are almost always negative; very seldom are they reported in favorable terms. Indeed, the value placed on individualism is so strong in American society that even Asch felt it necessary to conclude his report on "Opinions and Social Pressure" with the following comment:

> That we have found the tendency to conformity in our society so strong that reasonably intelligent and well-meaning young people are willing to call white black is a matter of concern. It raises questions about our ways of education and about the values that guide our conduct.
> Yet anyone inclined to draw too pessimistic conclusions from this report would do well to remind himself that capacities for independence are not to be underestimated. He may also draw some consolation from a further observation: those who participated in this challenging experiment agreed nearly without exception that independence was preferable to conformity. (1955:6)

The American attitude toward conformity is better seen as a paraphrase of Beardsley's "antagonistic cooperation." That is, it is a form of "antagonistic" or at best "reluctant" conformity. As such, it differs greatly from the Japanese ideal of "democratic" conformity reported by Nakane:

> It seems from these and similar considerations that Japanese "democracy" is a kind of communitarian sentiment, with, as a

major premise, a high degree of cohesion and consensus within the group. Liberalism with respect to opinion is not part of the concept, for "democracy" may well be interpreted in terms of freedom of speech, by which is meant the freedom of the lower or the under-privileged to speak out; there is, however, no wish for opposition or realization of the function of opposition. In Japan it is extremely difficult to engage in a truly democratic discussion (of the type that I know from experience is common in India or in, for instance, Italy, England or America), in the course of which the statements of the opposition are taken by the other party and then form an important element in the development of the discussion. (1970:147)

And again:

Obedience in Japan takes the form of total submission. Any criticism of or opposition to authority tends to be seen as heroism (and some of the leading intellectuals are always inclined to take the side of the visionary hero who seldom succeeds in attaining his goal). And, interestingly enough, such deeds are today labelled as democratic action. Often it is merely opposition for opposition's sake; it is nearer in essence to emotional contradiction, than to the rational resistance from which further reasonable development might be expected. (1970:103)

This last comment by Nakane is most interesting. Given the great emphasis on duty and obligation, hierarchy, collectivity, dependence, and deference, it would seem that individuation, when expressed, would be most frequently seen in the form of either rebellion or negativism. In other words, far from having been trained for independence and personal autonomy, whereby the individual feels that he is a free agent with such complete mastery over his own affairs that he is able to choose from a wide range of alternatives, the privatized individual, especially in Japan, has far fewer options, a very limited range of alternatives, and frequently can express his independence only by negation. Like a small child with limited control over his affairs, he is able to express his disapproval only by being stubborn and refusing to cooperate. In this sense, then, those whose individualism rests upon negativism, rebellion, or stubborn opposition to authority are not truly independent or autonomous since they have limited their alternatives to a simple negative response to authority. Far from being able to influence or direct the course of events, they have power only to oppose it. From an existentialist point of view they are reduced to the one basic freedom that all men have: the freedom to say no.

In turn, this leads to another phenomenon. That is, where one may have little power to influence or manipulate others, one always has great power to manipulate oneself. In other words, the anger, hostility, or aggressiveness that is felt but cannot be directed toward others is reflected back upon the self. Such a privatized person is much more abasive, less dominant, more deferent, and has a weaker sense of personal autonomy than does the person who has greater control over his own affairs and is under less compulsion to conform.

Chapter 6

The Issei
Interview Schedule

Since the guiding principle of the study was to measure the changing psychological and behavioral characteristics of Japanese Americans, the purpose of the basic interview schedules was not only to gather data of a general biographical nature but also to include questions that would provide an index of the more overt forms of acculturation. In general, these indicated the amount of interaction with the larger community and the retention of such Japanese characteristics as the celebration of traditional holidays. In addition, a number of questions were included in order to relate this study to earlier ones. Caudill and DeVos (1956), Daniels (1962), Modell (1968), and Kitano (1969) have all indicated that the majority of the Issei emigrated from southwestern Japan and were largely of rural agricultural backgrounds. These sources further indicated that it was not the original intent of the Issei to settle permanently in the United States but rather to seek their fortunes and return to Japan. Of the various sources used, the greatest reliance was placed on Modell's, largely because of the size of his sample (1,047 Issei, male and female) and the nature of the questions asked.

In constructing the form it was felt that the best approach would be to arrange the initial section chronologically. That is, one would begin with the date and place of birth, followed by questions on the occupations of father and brothers, early schooling, childhood training, reasons for leaving Japan, initial impressions of the United States, first jobs, and subsequent occupations. Once rapport had been established, questions of a more revealing and personal nature would be asked, such as relations with other groups, opinions on Sansei intermarriage, and the relative success of Japanese in the United States. In all instances an attempt was made to avoid asking leading questions. For example, item number 32, relating to the experiencing of prejudice, was phrased: "Some Issei state that they experienced a great deal of prejudice; others state that it wasn't too bad. What do you think?"

In all, two hundred thirty-four Issei—one hundred twenty-four males and one hundred ten females—were interviewed. Where possible, an attempt was made to interview both husband and wife. This was not always possible because, as Modell (1968:70) indicates, the Issei females were on the average much younger than their husbands and have survived them. Indeed, our initial interviews were mostly with widows.

The sex ratio is now about two female Issei for every male. However, because previous research by Caudill (1952), Daniels (1962), Kitano (1969), and others had indicated that the Issei female had been much more sheltered and had experienced less interaction with the larger American community, it was decided to concentrate more on males than females. The data, then, do not necessarily reflect husbands and wives. This is readily apparent in our sample in comparing the mean age of Issei males (76.2) with that of the Issei females (73.9). By contrast, Daniels notes:

> Those Issei males able to marry generally did so rather late in life, and took wives much younger than themselves. Statistical verification can be found in the data compiled when the West Coast Japanese were incarcerated during the Second World War. At that time most of the Issei males were between fifty and sixty-four years of age, and most of the Issei females were between forty and fifty-four. (1962:14)

Again, it should be emphasized that the guiding criterion throughout the study was one of simple availability. No attempt was made in the interviews to obtain a random sample. Another limiting factor was the advanced age of the Issei—the oldest male was eighty-nine and the youngest fifty-eight, while the oldest and youngest females were eighty-seven and sixty respectively. The advanced age of some made it difficult to obtain complete answers to all questions as there were both a tendency for the mind to wander and a frequent desire to elaborate on some questions to the neglect of others. On the other hand, we were frequently amazed at the degree and detail of recall of some of the informants. Other limiting factors were our reluctance to tire our informants, and—as the study continued—our gradual awareness that the majority of Issei have remained quite active and are still in the habit of retiring early and rising early in the morning. For that reason we were unwilling to impose too much on their time and strength late in the evenings.

Despite the shortcomings listed above, it is believed that the sample is generally representative of the larger Issei population and is not unusual or aberrant to any degree. This is supported by the fact that our findings on such questions as the area from which the Issei emigrated, occupation of fathers, amount of education, age at time of emigration, intent to settle permanently, and so on, agree very closely with those of Modell (1968).

Issei Males

The mean average age of the 124 Issei males was 76.2 years, the oldest was 89 and the youngest 58. In general, the places of birth are in accordance with previous studies by Caudill (1952), Daniels (1962), and McWilliams (1944), which state that the heaviest emigration came from four prefectures in southwestern Japan. Our data give the following breakdown: Hiroshima (30 per cent), Yamaguchi (15 per cent), Wakayama (14 per cent), Okayama (6 per cent), other southern Japan—Kumamoto, Kochi, Kagawa (23 per cent), central Japan—Yamanashi, Aichi, Shizuoka (8 per cent), and Tokyo, Chiba area (4 per cent). In all, some 88 per cent came from the prefectures of Hiroshima, Yamaguchi, Wakayama, Okayama and others in southwestern and west-central Japan.

The occupation given for the fathers of the Issei was largely agriculture (74 per cent), followed by skilled labor (12 per cent), small business (10 per cent), clerical (2 per cent), and professional (2 per cent). Somewhat the same breakdown was given for the occupation of the brother. Of those who had brothers the occupation listed most frequently was that of farmer (58 per cent), followed by skilled labor (20 per cent), small business (12 per cent), clerical (6 per cent), and professional (4 per cent). Moreover, 64 per cent of the Issei were *jisannan* or nonsuccessor sons.

The schooling received by the Issei in Japan was an average of 9.4 years. The school subjects they remember most were arithmetic (28 per cent), history (32 per cent), reading (22 per cent), and *shūshin* or ethics (10 per cent); other subjects mentioned were writing, religion, and art.

When asked what part of their early training or schooling was of most value to them in later years, a surprisingly large number said home discipline (30 per cent) and the *shūshin* or ethics course (27 per cent). Other subjects mentioned were the language training in reading and writing (30 per cent), arithmetic (7 per cent), and apprentice or other training (6 per cent)

The age at which emigration occurred was quite young. The mean age given was 19.3 years. The reasons for leaving were by no means unanimous. While it is obvious from the answers given that almost all of them expected to prosper (in Japan they had heard almost no negative reports about the United States), only 41 per cent responded that their sole reason for emigrating was to seek a fortune. Other responses were to join a father or uncle who was already here (39 per cent), to study (8 per cent), there were no jobs in Japan (2 per cent), the eldest brother would get everything (3 per cent), to avoid the draft (2 per cent), and to join friends who were already here (5 per cent).

In other words, our data indicate that 44 per cent of the male Issei were *yobiyose*, or summoned migrants, and not the original or "pioneer" Issei. Of course, the present average age of 76.2 compared with that of the age at which emigration had occurred (19.3) would indicate that our average immigrant arrived here at about 1916, or some forty years after the initial immigration had taken place. Or, according to Daniels, after some 150,000 Japanese had already migrated to the United States (1962:1).

By 1916, Japanese communities had already been established on the West Coast and it was to these communities that our respondents first arrived. When one considers that 39 per cent came because their fathers or uncles called them, and another 5 per cent arrived because friends were here, it is surprising that only 20 per cent intended to leave Japan permanently. Of our total sample, 80 per cent had intended to return to their families. Frequently, even those whose fathers were here did not expect to remain in the United States permanently, but only to help their fathers to make a fortune and then return to Japan to set up a business. At the time of immigration, only 14 per cent had jobs promised them. By and large, these were the *yobiyose* or summoned immigrants whose relatives were already here. Again, of those who migrated, only 16 per cent paid for their fares through loans or other means. The vast majority, or 84 per cent, had their fares paid by the father or the family. Almost none of the Issei had received negative reports of America and were quite eager to see for themselves if the country was indeed as huge and wealthy as they had been told.

For most of the young men, leaving Japan was a time of mixed emotions. They were both sad at parting and eager for the adventure. One Issei remarked that his last memory was that of his mother crying. After a pause he added that he never saw her again.

The trip was long, often a month or longer, and most reported that they were seasick. For many it was their first experience in being away from home. Usually, however, there were many other young men their age and there was a great deal of joking and speculation as to what their new life would be like. Several remarked that they tried to learn English from phrase books but were not too successful. Others mentioned that they were looking forward to seeing their parents, relatives, or friends who already immigrated.

Upon arriving in the United States they were examined by immigration officials and later met by friends or other Japanese. Some indication of the extent of the Japanese community already in existence is to be found in the comments of several who stated that they were surprised to find so many Japanese in the United States.

In the same manner, their comments on their first impressions of the United States, its people, and customs, give an indication of the rural background and insularity of most of the immigrants. The most uniform initial impression of the United States was its great size—especially the vast expanse of empty land. Some expressed surprise at the modernity of the wooden sidewalks in San Francisco and elsewhere, others were amazed at the good quality of the soil, the heat and dryness of the central valley, and a few who had arrived earlier recalled the tremendous destruction of the 1906 San Francisco earthquake.

Many also registered surprise at the size of Americans; others were impressed by their loudness and informality. A few felt everything was backwards to what they had learned in Japan. One remembers laughing at the first kissing scene he saw in a movie, while another recalled his surprise at meeting a black man.

The first job for many was farm labor (58 per cent) or common labor (15 per cent). Others reported occupations such as school boy (17 per cent) or working as dishwashers, janitors, or laundrymen. Almost all of the Issei report a number of subsequent occupations. The most commonly reported were farmer (44 per cent), farm labor (10 per cent), small business (21 per cent), skilled trades (12 per cent), gardener (10 per cent), and professional (3 per cent).

When asked if their ideas or ambitions had changed in any way, 62 per cent stated that they had. The most common reply was that it was far more difficult to make money than they had supposed. This was especially true during the depression years, which were almost uniformly reported as being a very difficult time. Most reported receiving very low wages—10 or 15 cents an hour; others who were living on farms were thankful that they had enough to eat. Many found that their dreams had faded when they discovered that they could not afford to go to school, and some reported that as their families began to grow they gradually gave up the idea of returning to Japan with a fortune and starting a business. For most, however, as a later question indicates, the final decision to stay came during World War II and its aftermath. In all, a number of reasons were given, chief among them being the financial loss suffered by the Issei during relocation, along with the discouraging reports from Japan of the destruction and destitution caused by the war. As time progressed and their children matured, their own advancing years and the knowledge that they were no longer in their prime became factors to be considered.

The interaction of Issei with the larger Caucasian community before the war can be seen in the responses to several questions. When asked what were their relationship or dealings with

Caucasians, 34 per cent stated that they were fair to good, 41 per cent said that they were casual, usually in the form of a client-customer relationship, 16 per cent said they had no relationship with Caucasians, and 8 per cent said the encounters were hostile or prejudiced.

When the above is seen in relation to the fact that 68 per cent reported that at the time they were living in a Japanese community, and is compared to the question as to the experiencing of prejudice, some interesting figures emerge. For example, in answer to the question, " Some Issei state that they experienced a great deal of prejudice; others state that it wasn't too bad. What do you think?" a total of 26 per cent responded that it was quite bad, 14 per cent reported that it was moderate while some 54 per cent stated that it was not bad and some 5 per cent that stated they did not experience any at all. Given the documented cases of prejudice at the time, it would seem that the remarks are in error. However, closer examination reveals that in terms of their background and the type of interaction the Issei did not interpret the prejudice as being severe. For one thing, 68 per cent were living in the Japanese community and were somewhat insulated from the full effect of prejudice. This is substantiated by the data on Issei females, who were even more effectively isolated from the larger community in that 45 per cent of them indicated that they had little or no contact with Caucasians. This lack of contact is reflected in the amount of prejudice perceived. Some 60 per cent of the female Issei said that they were exposed to little or no prejudice, while 39 per cent said that it was moderate to heavy. Both males and females reported that it was not bad if they stayed in the Japanese community. Others stated that they were foreigners and had expected it.

The Issei reported that the Japanese community was in many respects self-contained. The large ones such as Sacramento's Japanese community, which extended for some twelve square blocks, provided food and services. There were doctors, dentists, Japanese food stores, banks, churches, boarding houses, theaters, hotels, Japanese language schools, and in some communities even Japanese baths; Sacramento, for example, at one time had four Japanese baths. The communities provided recreation, social and religious activities, midwives, the *kenjinkai* or prefectural associations, which organized the annual community picnics, and also arranged funerals, the *fujinkai* or women's association, and the *nihonjin kai* or Japanese Association. It was the Japanese Association that provided translation and interpreter service, legal assistance, and served as an intermediary with the larger society. Several mentioned that it would work to keep people from being drafted into the Japanese Army. One Issei also mentioned that at one time his cow was stolen by Caucasian kids, so he went to the Japanese Association, and they in turn went to the sheriff and got it back for him.

These communities changed somewhat before the war in that the Nisei were becoming older and were beginning to move into positions of leadership. The greatest change, however, came after the war. The Issei were practically unanimous in stating that after relocation the community became more widely dispersed. This is partly reflected in the finding that 88 per cent report having Caucasian or other non-Japanese neighbors at the present time.

Another factor is deducible from the information previously discussed. That is, given the initial intent not to settle permanently, the marginal use of English, and the insulating effect of the Japanese community, the Issei were not interpreting the prejudice shown against them in the same manner as were their offspring, the Nisei, who were becoming more directly involved in the larger society.

In their relations with other minority groups, the main experience of the Issei was as co-workers. By and large, the relationships with Mexican Americans were quite good, but those with the Chinese and Filipino workers were marred by the anti-Japanese prejudice during and after World War II.

A further measure of the strong ties maintained by the Issei to Japan can be seen in the amount of contact that was maintained with the family in Japan. It would seem that for almost no Issei was the trip to America a clear and ultimate break with his family in Japan. When asked if they maintained contact with relatives in Japan, 90 per cent said that they had. Usually these relatives would be the parents while alive and then brothers and sisters. At first many of the Issei wrote every few weeks, then gradually once or twice a year.

A surprising 84 per cent have been back to Japan, a figure that agrees closely with Modell's finding of 75 per cent for both male and female (1968:78). Of these, 54 per cent have been back more than once, 36 per cent have been back more than three times, and some have made the journey more than five times.

A further indication of the intent to preserve Japanese tradition can be seen in the marriage patterns. Some 42 per cent went back to Japan to obtain brides, while 26 per cent relied on picture brides or had their marriage arranged here (12 per cent). In addition, some 20 per cent stated that they picked their own wife here.

On the other hand, a change can be seen in the marriages of the offspring of the Issei. When asked if the marriages of their sons and daughters were any different, 80 per cent stated that they were. By this they usually meant that they had chosen their own spouse.

The direction of change is also apparent in child-rearing practices. The Issei report that they were more lenient or gave more freedom than they were given in Japan (47 per cent), while some 53 per cent reported that they had raised their children about the same. On the other hand, 88 per cent of the Issei reported that they believe that the Nisei are raising the Sansei with too much freedom, are too lenient, or are giving them too much of everything. Some change is also indicated in the religious preference of the respondents. While 74 per cent reported that they were Buddhists, 21 per cent listed themselves as Christians, and 5 per cent reported that they belonged to such Japanese religious sects as *Seicho no ie*.

Again, however, the retention of Japanese characteristics can be seen in the use of English. Some 52 per cent of the Issei state that they speak to the Nisei in Japanese, another 33 per cent in mixed Japanese and English, and 15 per cent in English only. With regard to the Sansei, 65 per cent say they communicate in broken English, 20 per cent say just English, and 15 per cent say that they use Japanese or that they cannot speak to them at all.

Further, the Issei have attempted to retain family ties with their offspring. Some 40 per cent stated that they see their children and grandchildren daily, another 26 per cent see their offspring several times a week, 11 per cent reported that they see them monthly, and the remainder mentioned several times a year. The frequency of contact is not surprising in view of the fact that 40 per cent of the Issei males report that they live with their relatives. Again, this finding is in close accord with Modell's (1968) finding that two-fifths of Issei live with their offspring. Of those that do live with their offspring, a total of 67 per cent live with their sons and the remainder live with their daughters.

In attempting to understand the differences separating the three generations, the Issei were asked to compare the Sansei with their own generation. By and large, 42 per cent of the Issei felt that the Sansei were completely Americanized. Other responses were that the Sansei were selfish or more independent (14 per cent). A few Issei mentioned that the Sansei show less respect (16 per cent) or that they did not know shame (8 per cent), and some 8 per cent went so far as to say that they did not understand the Sansei at all.

Indeed, the conservatism of the Issei was nowhere better expressed than in their responses to questions relating to Sansei dating practices. When asked what they thought about Sansei dating non-Japanese, 39 per cent were definitely against it; 26 per cent expressed reluctance, as illustrated by the phrase "*Shikata ga nai*" (nothing can be done about it); 16 per cent assented with reservations by stating that a Chinese or Causasian partner would be acceptable, but not a black; and only 18 per cent assented unreservedly.

However, when the Issei were asked their opinion on Sansei marrying non-Japanese, the number of those with reservations increased, while those who gave outright approval decreased. Again, those who were definitely against dating were also definitely against marriage—that is, 49 per cent. Those who expressed reluctance increased from 26 to 41 per cent, while those who agreed with reservations increased from 9 to 10 per cent. Once again, Chinese and Caucasians were accepted but strong reservations were expressed against Filipinos and blacks and, to a lesser extent, against Mexican Americans. The number who expressed approval declined from 18 per cent for dating to 10 per cent for marriage. Here again, however, there was just a tinge of qualification. Expressions of approval were usually accompanied by such comments as, "The Sansei are completely Americanized anyhow," or, "It is a natural trend," and, "All Americans are mixed."

A final question applying to the Sansei asked the Issei what Japanese characteristics they would like to see retained by the Sansei. The most frequent response (21 per cent) was that they should understand *on*, an obligation that is passively incurred, hence one is indebted for what others have done for him; *giri*, to return a favor, or pay back someone for what he has done for one; *haji*, a sense of shame for not doing what is expected of one; and *ninjō*, or human feelings and compassion. Others mentioned were respect for parents, elders, and others (22 per cent), hard work (17 per cent), Japanese values in general (17 per cent), the Japanese language (7 per cent), and others such as studying hard (16 per cent).

The retention of Japanese characteristics was readily apparent in the question relating to the disciplining of children. Most Issei reported that they used a variety of methods, including physical punishment as a last resort. However, 33 per cent mentioned that they told the children not to bring shame to the family, 30 per cent said that they would talk to the children, 28 per cent reported physical punishment, and 8 per cent said that they would isolate them.

There were other areas in which it was felt that the retention of Japanese characteristics would be rather strong. These were in the identification of certain words that are not easily translatable and which embody uniquely Japanese concepts or characteristics. The other area was in the observation of both American and the more traditional Japanese holidays.

It was expected, of course, since the Issei were native speakers of Japanese that there would be little difficulty in recognizing the Japanese words, and indeed such was the case. The real difficulty came in giving a definition or example of the word. Our purpose here was not to achieve a dictionary definition of a word but, rather, to find out if the word was a part of the recognition or working vocabulary of the person. The assumption was that, if the concept had been sufficiently important, the individual should be able to give some definition of it. A rather poor comparison in English might be the distinction between capital-

ism anc mercantilism, which is given in all high school history
courses While almost everyone would recognize capitalism and
could give an example of it, far fewer would be able to define
mercantilism.

The intent in utilizing both the word list and the traditional
holidays was to establish a base line against which the responses
of the Nisei and Sansei could be measured. It was expected that
there would be a reduction in both the words recognized and the
holidays observed. This proved to be as expected but the reduction was by no means a uniform one. As we shall demonstrate in
our discussion of the Nisei and Sansei data, there is still a
considerable retention of Japanese characteristics in certain areas.

The words used were as follows: *On*, an obligation that is
passively incurred. *Giri*, a reciprocal of *on*, one must pay back or
return a favor, usually with mathematical equivalence and within
a 'certain time. *Gimu*, also a reciprocal of *on*, but the idea is more
of one of indebtedness or obligation, or duty to do one's best
because of what others have done for you. A form of *gimu* is *chū*,
a duty or loyalty to the Emperor, to the law, and to the country.
Ninjō is defined as human feelings or compassion, as seen in the
ability to feel empathy for another. The distinction between *giri*
and *ninjō* can be illustrated by the saying that duty *(giri)* should
be tempered by human emotion *(ninjō)*. *Amaeru* has no exact
equivalent in English but means a desire to be placed in a
dependent relationship, to be pampered, or cared for by others.
Makenki is the will not to give up, not to give in, or not to lose. It
epitomizes a strong competitive spirit. Other words used were
seikō which can be literally translated as success; *gaman*, to
endure or suppress emotion; and *enryo*, to be reserved.

Again, it should be emphasized that the intent of the study
was not to determine if the Issei could give precise definitions but
rather if they could recognize a word or could identify it by
example or rough definition. By this method it was determined
that *on* was understood by 95 per cent of the respondents, *giri* by
98 per cent, *gimu* by 94 per cent, *chū* by 85 per cent, *ninjō* by 92
per cent, *amaeru* by 86 per cent, *seikō* by 99 per cent, *makenki* by
93 per cent, and *gaman* and *enryo* by 90 per cent.

One interesting finding was by way of correcting Benedict's
definition of the word *on*. In *The Chrysanthemum and the Sword*
(1946:99), she states:

On is in all its uses a load, an indebtedness, a burden, which one carries as best one may. A man receives an *on* from a superior and the act of accepting an *on* from any man not definitely one's superior or at least one's equal gives one an uncomfortable sense of inferiority. When they say, "I wear an *on* to him" they are saying, "I carry a load of obligations to him," and they call this creditor, this benefactor, their *on* man.

By contrast, more than one-third of the Issei used such expressions as "gratitude," "kindness," "appreciation," or "deep thanks" in defining *on*. In other words, when viewed from their personal perspective it would seem that a large number of the Issei do not consider an *on* a burden at all.

The observation of holidays was equally revealing. In all, sixteen holidays were listed, six of them American and ten of them Japanese. The tabulation of data revealed that both American and Japanese holidays are observed, although there is a considerable variation in frequency. For example, Table 2 discloses the following percentages: Easter (53 per cent), Memorial Day (76 per cent), Fourth of July (72 per cent), Labor Day (51 per cent), Thanksgiving (97 per cent), Christmas (92 per cent), *O-Shogatsu* (New Years) (95 per cent), *O-Dhohsydu* (New Years) Visiting (72 per cent), *Hinamatsuri* (Dolls' Festival) (57 per cent), Girls' Day (32 per cent), Boys' Day (47 per cent), *O-Bon* (Buddhist Festival of the Dead) (75 per cent), *Kigensetsu* (First Emperor's Birthday) (10 per cent), *O-Higan* (Buddhist equinox ceremony) (39 per cent), *Kiku-no-sekku* (Chrysanthemum Day) (7 per cent), and *Tenchōsetsu* (Emperor's Birthday) (none).

A number of respondents stated that the last time they observed the more obscure holidays such as *Kigensetsu* or *Tenchōsetsu* was either in Japan or before the war. On the other hand, the number still observing Boys' Day and Girls' Day is at first glance surprising, since these holidays are reserved for children. A number of Issei, however, make it a point to be with their grandchildren on those days.

A final measure of acculturation was devised to obtain an account of the individual respondent's own evaluation of how acculturated he had become. The question was asked: "On a scale ranging from one to ten, do you now consider yourself more American than Japanese or more Japanese than American?" The numerical placement was left to the individual. A few placed themselves more toward the American side of the scale (10) because they felt they had demonstrated their loyalty to the United States. On the other hand, a considerable number placed themselves at the extreme Japanese end of the scale (1) or just one or two units removed from it. The overall self-evaluation of the Issei male group was 3.9 on a ten-point scale. The change in identity is in part due to the fact that many of the Issei have obtained American citizenship. Also, for most, the decision to stay in the United States after the war and remain with their children has brought about a greater identification with the American society.

The final questions to be considered here are related to the impressions of the Issei on modern Japan and their evaluation of the success of Japanese Americans in the United States. Those who have been back to Japan are usually amazed at the changes, even though the Japanese publications they read may have prepared them somewhat beforehand. Those who returned in the early 1950s and again in the late 1960s could hardly believe the transformation. The changes in village Japan were most frequently commented upon, especially the large number of homes with television, refrigerators, and even washers.

Their evaluation of this increasing affluence is predictably ambivalent. As Issei they are proud of Japan's accomplishment and the spectacular economic recovery since the war. On the other hand, there were those who felt that it was "just like America," "too Westernized," or "they have all forgotten *on* and *giri.*"

When asked if they believe that Japanese Americans have been successful in the United States, 91 per cent answered "yes" while 8 per cent felt that complete success had not yet arrived. By far the most frequent reason given for success was "hard work," although a few added such attributes as a drive for education, and several went so far as to say that the Japanese are more intelligent than other immigrant groups.

Overall, the Issei are proud of their accomplishments. Many are seeing their dreams fulfilled in their children and grandchildren. Life is now easier as most are retired. Materially, it may seem that most have comparatively little to show for a lifetime of labor, but, as one Nisei has noted, their mark is everywhere, and perhaps most of all in their children.

Issei Females

As previously indicated, the intent of the survey was to interview more male than female Issei. Further, the guiding criterion was one of simple availability rather than one of obtaining a statistically valid random sample. Nonetheless, it is felt that individuals interviewed are representative of the total Issei population. We have no reason for believing that our sample differs from the total Issei population to any marked degree. This is further supported in the data for Issei males, which closely parallel the findings of Modell (1968).

The 110 Issei females were, on average, 73.9 years old. The oldest was 87 and the youngest 62. As with the male Issei, a large majority (72 per cent) came from southwestern Japan. Of these, the prefecture of Hiroshima alone accounted for 31 per cent. The other prefectures such as Okayama, Wakayama, Yamaguchi, Kumamoto, Osaka, Aichi, and Mie accounted for 45 per cent and the remaining 24 per cent came from Yamanashi, Kanagawa, and Miyagi in central Japan.

Again, the occupation given for the father paralleled that of the male Issei. Farmer was listed by 75 per cent; craftsman or skilled labor, 12 per cent; small business, 10 per cent; and professional, such as teacher, 3 per cent. The occupation of the brother was listed as farmer, 43 per cent; craftsman or skilled labor, 31 per cent; small business, 16 per cent; and professional, such as architect or lawyer, 10 per cent.

The number of years of schooling in Japan was an average of 7.5 years. The span was from twelve years to no formal schooling at all for one who was born in 1884. When asked what they remembered of their early schooling, 40 per cent answered history or *shūshin* (ethics); others answered sewing (37 per cent) and reading (24 per cent). When asked what of their early training or schooling had been of most benefit to them, 30 per cent answered sewing and cooking, 26 per cent said home discipline, 16 per cent said *shūshin* (ethics), and 24 per cent answered reading, writing, and mathematics.

The age at which they left Japan was twenty-two years. Some 97 per cent stated their reason for leaving was to join or accompany their husbands, and of these 30 per cent volunteered that they were picture brides. The average date at which they arrived was 1919. Yet, while almost all came to the United States to be with their husbands, only 30 per cent had expected to leave Japan permanently. The other 70 per cent had thought that they would be able to make enough money with their husbands to enable them to return to Japan and establish a small business. This is supported by their comments on what they had heard of the United States before leaving Japan. Again, as with the Issei males, there were no recorded negative reports. Almost all stated that they had heard of the prosperity, the wealth, and the size of the country. Most expected that they would remain a few years and return to Japan with their fortune.

Almost all reported mixed emotions on leaving Japan, and their comments on the trip itself and their first impressions of the United States were much like those of the males. On their arrival they were much impressed by the amount of empty land and by the size of both the country and the people. Of the customs of the country they had much less to say. Several mentioned that they were much too busy with household chores and helping their husbands as farmers' wives to have the time to meet other people.

When asked if their ideas or ambitions changed in any way after they arrived, 62 per cent reported they still wanted to return to Japan; however, they also realized that it was much more difficult for them to make money than they expected. Many remarked how lonely and homesick they were for the first two or three years. For most, the dream of returning began to fade as their children grew up. All of the females reported maintaining contact with relatives in Japan. At first they wrote almost every week but this declined as time went on, although in recent years 81 per cent have made at least one trip back to Japan.

Their comparative isolation is reflected in the fact that 45 per cent reported very little or no contact with Caucasians, 30 per cent reported occasional contact, and 25 per cent stated that they had a friendly or good relationship with them. With Chinese and other minority groups there was less contact. Seventy-five per cent reported that they had little or no contact with them, and the remainder mentioned having a good or average relationship with them. Again, as with the males, some 67 per cent reported having lived in a Japanese community before the war. The services provided by the community were much as those previously mentioned, although the females placed more emphasis on the various types of assistance available. Frequently mentioned were midwife service, help for those Issei who did not speak English, providing contact with Japan, and the usefulness of the prefectural associations in arranging for picnics or funerals.

All of the females reported that their marriages were arranged. However, 86 per cent mentioned that the marriages of their sons and daughters were different in that they picked their own spouse. One-half believed that they had not raised their children in any way differently from the way in which they were raised in Japan. On the other hand, all of them felt that their children were raising the Sansei in a different manner. The most frequent comments were that the Nisei were more lenient and consequently the Sansei had more freedom and were spoiled.

Other indices of insularity and low acculturation can be seen in the many who reported little or no contact with Caucasians and are reflected in the 60 per cent who stated that they experienced little or no prejudice. Further, it was noted that the language spoken to the Nisei was mostly Japanese, while to the Sansei they spoke some Japanese or broken English. A total of 79 per cent stated that they were Buddhist, and the remainder Protestant.

The amount of contact with their relatives was about the same as for the males. In all, 34 per cent stated that they saw their relatives daily, 27 per cent mentioned several times a week, and 22 per cent said monthly. A larger number (51 per cent) said they were living with relatives. Of these, 64 per cent reported that they were living with the son, while the remainder lived with a daughter and her family. Moreover, many of those who do not live with their children, live near them. The larger percentage of females living with their children is undoubtedly a reflection of the Issei male-female age discrepancy mentioned previously, the younger wives now having survived their husbands.

The dispersal of the Japanese community since the war is also apparent in the comments on non-Japanese friends. While 36 per cent said they had few or no non-Japanese friends, 64 per cent said that they had some such friends and most of these were neighbors. Of these, 84 per cent were Caucasian and 16 per cent Chinese or others.

When asked in what ways the Sansei differed from the Issei, the most common reply was that the Sansei were all Americanized (43 per cent), more independent (18 per cent), more selfish and less respectful (16 per cent), do not know their obligations (8 per cent), and others (15 per cent), including such responses as they don't understand the Sansei at all, or cannot speak to them.

The Issei females also felt that the Sansei were much different from the Nisei in that the Sansei had more freedom, were more independent, more American, and did not know hard times as the Nisei had.

The attitude of the Issei female towards the Sansei dating non-Japanese was much the same as for the Issei male. Some 36 per cent were definitely against it, another 30 per cent disliked the idea but felt it was beyond their power to control, 14 per cent assented with reservations, and 20 per cent approved.

Again, as with the Issei males, there were far more negative feelings expressed on the question of Sansei marrying non-Japanese. The number of those who were definitely against it increased to 70 per cent, those expressing reluctance increased to 13 per cent, those assenting with reservations decreased to 7 per cent, and those approving decreased to 9 per cent.

With respect to the identification of the Japanese words mentioned in the previous section on Issei males, the percentages remained about the same. The only significant difference was in the identification of *chū* (patriotism or loyalty), which was identified by 85 per cent of the males and 97 per cent of the females.

Somewhat the same findings were reported for the American and Japanese holidays observed. Table 2 indicates the following frequency of observance: Easter (58 per cent), Memorial Day (59 per cent), Fourth of July (61 per cent), Labor Day (38 per cent), Thanksgiving (94 per cent), Christmas (91 per cent), *O-Shōgatsu* (New Years) (93 per cent), *O-Dhohsydu* (New Years) Visiting (55 per cent), *Hinamatsuri* (Dolls' Festival) (77 per cent), Girls' Day (56 per cent), Boys' Day (54 per cent), *O-Bon* (Buddhist Festival of the Dead) (85 per cent), *Kigensetsu* (First Emperor's Birthday) (none), *O-Higan* (Buddhist equinox ceremony) (55 per cent), *Kiku-no-sekku* (Chrysanthemum Day) (none), and *Tenchōsetsu* (Emperor's Birthday) (none).

In all, when compared with the Issei males there were fewer observances of American holidays and a greater observance of Japanese holidays. The larger percentage observing Girls' Day (56 vs 32 per cent) and Boys' Day (54 vs 47 per cent) may be attributed to the larger percentage of females (51 vs 40 per cent) living with their children and hence being near grandchildren.

When asked what Japanese characteristics they would like to see retained by the Sansei, the most frequent response was to have respect for parents and elders (45 per cent), hard work (26 per cent), know the Japanese language (19 per cent), and know *on*, *giri*, and *ninjō* (11 per cent).

Two final measures of acculturation were to be seen in child training practices and in self-evaluation. While most stated that they had used a variety of methods in disciplining a child, the most commonly reported method was to tell the children that they would bring shame to the family (52 per cent). Others reported that they also resorted to physical punishment (23 per cent), or a combination of both (25 per cent).

The final measure of acculturation was one of self-evaluation. This is a subjective account of how acculturated the individual believes herself to have become. On a scale from one to ten, the individual was asked to rate herself, ranging from a completely Japanese identity (1) to a completely American identity (10). Again, as reported for the Issei males, the placement was left entirely to the individual. As compared with the arithmetic mean of 3.9 for the males, the mean rating for the females was 3.3.

When asked if they believed the Japanese had been successful in the United States, the answer was overwhelmingly affirmative. This success they attributed to hard work and perseverance. Education was also mentioned as having been critically important.

Like the Issei males, the females too take pride in their accomplishments, and especially in those of their children. One family in particular is very proud of the number of children who have entered the professions. For most, it has been a very busy and a rather full lifetime. In reflecting back over a half-century of frequent setbacks and struggle in this country, the Issei feel that they have accomplished much and have much to be proud of. Very few ever realized the dream of making a fortune that first drove them to a foreign shore. And, in the end, it is not really so much the homes or the material possessions that give them pride. For most see it as a triumph of the will, the drive to succeed, the courage and determination and raw stubbornness of *yamato damashii*, the Japanese spirit, that has won out over all. This they feel, and this they would like to see preserved in their children and grandchildren.

And indeed it is true that the Issei have succeeded as a result of the retention of some uniquely Japanese characteristics. Moreover, as this chapter so clearly indicates it could hardly be otherwise. Given the intention of the Issei not to settle permanently in this country, their continued ties with Japan, their protracted residence in more or less self-contained Japanese communities, their lack of fluency in English, and their continued attempt to preserve as much as possible of the *ie* ideal, it is understandable that so many would be only marginally acculturated. This fact is clearly evident not only in the celebration of Japanese holidays and their comments on Sansei dating and marriage practices, but is also reflected in their own subjective evaluation of their low degree of acculturation. Further, it was the preservation of these uniquely Japanese characteristics and their transmission to their offspring that enabled the Nisei to make such striking contributions to American society. Indeed, as the next and subsequent chapters will disclose, it was largely through the retention and application of these characteristics and values by the Nisei that the success story of the Japanese Americans finally came to be realized.

Chapter 7

The Nisei
Interview Schedule

The Nisei Interview Schedule contains far fewer questions than the Issei Interview Schedule. Fewer questions of a historical nature were asked. The basic orientation was to continue not only the questions on Japanese words and the observation of holidays but also those that measured the attitudes toward dating and marriage, and the subjective rating of acculturation.

In addition, questions were asked which related to other indices of acculturation such as attendance at Japanese schools, food preferences, and number of non-Japanese friends. Further questions were designed to assess the differences between Nisei and Sansei and to discern the retention of Japanese characteristics in the Nisei.

In contrast to the differences in exposure to the larger community which characterized the male-female experience in the Issei generation, the responses given by both male and female Nisei were very much the same in many areas. For that reason, and in the interest of conciseness, both were considered together in the same section rather than separately.

In all, 101 Nisei males and 131 Nisei females were interviewed. Initially, far more females than males were interviewed. There were a number of reasons for this, including their greater availability during the day and, to a lesser extent, their greater willingness to cooperate as they apparently had fewer outside commitments, such as bowling clubs or other meetings, during week nights. Therefore, in order to increase the male sample size to that of the females, individual male Nisei were contacted later in the survey on the basis of availability and willingness to cooperate. For that reason, the male-female sample does not necessarily reflect husbands and wives. The overall similarity of responses, however, would seem to indicate that, for our purpose, the difference was not crucial.

The mean average age of the Nisei males was 48.2. The oldest was 66 and the youngest 31. The vast majority, however, were in their middle and late forties. The mean average age of the females was a little younger at 45.3 years. Again, however, the age range was much the same, the youngest being 30 and the oldest 64, with the vast majority falling into the early and middle forties.

The occupations listed for the males were farmer (8 per cent), gardener (10 per cent), skilled labor or trades (23 per cent), small business (12 per cent), clerical (27 per cent), and professional (19 per cent). The occupations listed for the females were housewife (50 per cent), clerical (44 per cent), and professional, such as teaching and nursing (6 per cent).

On the other hand, the occupations listed for the fathers of the Nisei were much the same as that given for the Issei, with some slight differences in percentages reported. The male Nisei listed the occupations of their fathers as farmer (62 per cent), gardener (8 per cent), small business (21 per cent), skilled labor or craftsman (5 per cent), common labor (3 per cent), and clerical (1 per cent). The female Nisei reported a slightly higher number in small business (25 per cent), but essentially the percentages were much the same. As with the male Nisei, the females indicated that the largest occupation of their fathers was farmer (62 per cent), followed by skilled labor or craftsman (8 per cent), gardener (3 per cent), and other (2 per cent).

The education of the males was an average of one-half year more of college than the females. The arithmetic mean for the males was 13.4 years and for the females 12.6. These figures agree rather closely with the findings of Caudill (1952) and Kitano (1969), who indicate that the educational achievement of the Nisei generation was above the average for Americans in general. Kitano (1969:171) further indicates in data derived from a publication of the Division of Fair Employment Practices, State of California, that in the Sacramento area the median school years completed by persons 14 years old and older was 12.0 for the total male population. The median school years completed for all Japanese 14 years and older was 12.3 for the males and 12.2 for the females. Our figures are larger, of course, because they do not include the Sansei and Issei generations. The majority of the Nisei also attended Japanese school while they were attending elementary and high school. Surprisingly, slightly fewer males than females attended. A total of 89 per cent of the females and 85 per cent of the males stated that they had attended such schools. In retrospect, many of the Nisei indicated that the schools were not too effective in teaching them Japanese. Usually they were held for an hour or so in the late afternoon after the regular school day, and frequently also on Saturday. Several Nisei said that stern moral lectures were often incorporated into the language class. The subject matter was apparently derived from the *shūshin* or ethics courses their fathers had attended. Many of the Nisei said that, while they picked up some vocabulary, the ability to read and write the Japanese language was at best marginal. Indeed, many were satisfied if they mastered just the *katakana* and *hiragana* syllabaries. In their replies, especially when they compare their generation with that of the Sansei, one frequently detects a small note of resentment at being forced to attend the language school in addition to their regular school and the endless farm and household chores they were required to perform. In this regard the schools were probably serving another function. Kitano indicates:

> Another value of Japanese Language School, not often mentioned, was its baby-sitting function. Many of the Japanese families were large, and busy parents were much relieved to have the children spend time in such approved surroundings out of the house. Japanese Language School kept children off the streets, it kept them busy, and it may have been one of the factors responsible for the low rates of crime and delinquency among this group during the pre-World War II decade. (1969:25)

Over half of the Nisei (58 per cent of the females, 64 per cent of the males) indicated that they watch Japanese movies. Attendance is not too frequent, however. Both males and females indicated that they watched the movies on the average of only once every three to four months.

With regard to food habits there were some differences between males and females. The males reported having Japanese food more frequently. Forty-four per cent eat it every day as compared with 35 per cent of the females. On the other hand, 34 per cent of the females mentioned eating Japanese food four or five times a week as compared to 30 per cent of the males. Again, however, 26 per cent of the males mentioned once or twice a week as compared to 31 per cent of the females.

About the same number indicated there is Japanese food that they dislike. A total of 37 per cent of the males and 40 per cent of the females listed strong dislikes. Almost all of the disliked food was seafood, with raw fish leading the list. Others were raw or boiled squid, sea cucumbers, and fish eggs.

The direction of change toward increased interaction with the larger community is seen in the responses given to several questions. A little more than half of the Nisei reported having lived in a Japanese community before the war. The males report a slightly higher percentage (65 per cent) than the females (63 per cent). Most report somewhat the same services as did the Issei, although perhaps more Nisei would be inclined now to remark on how ingrown and insulated it was. All of the Nisei agree that the communities changed dramatically after the war. This was especially true in Sacramento when redevelopment began in the late 1950s and many Japanese businesses and households were dispersed from the Second and Fourth streets area to the Tenth Street area and other parts of Sacramento.

Some indication of the degree of interaction with the larger community is to be seen in the replies given to the questions pertaining to the percentages of friends who were non-Japanese. In all, 46 per cent of the females and 48 per cent of the males indicated that 50 per cent or more of their friends were Caucasian. With regard to Chinese, the number decreased greatly. A total of 83 per cent of the females and 87 per cent of the males stated that fewer than 10 per cent of their friends were Chinese. Interaction with other minority groups was even less. Over 90 per cent of both males and females reported that fewer than 10 per cent of their friends are Filipino, Mexican American, or black.

Again, however, there are indications that, although the overall direction is one of acculturation, there has been no wholesale abandonment of Japanese organizations for American ones. Thus, while 91 per cent of the Nisei, male and female, report that their courtships and marriages were different from those of their parents in that they largely chose their own spouse, almost all of the organizations that they belong to are basically Japanese American. For example, the most frequently listed organizations for both male and female were the Japanese American Citizens League and the Buddhist Church. These were followed by Nisei bowling clubs, veteran's clubs, and prefectural associations for the males and various women's clubs, the P.T.A., and auxiliary organizations for the females. By and large, membership in these organizations is a carry-over from the prewar and postwar period.

The religious faith of the Nisei can be listed as being predominantly Buddhist, although there are slightly more female (66 per cent) than male (64 per cent) adherents. The remainder list themselves as Christian Protestants.

The percentage of male and female Nisei reporting that their parents were deceased was the same (37 per cent), while the number reporting frequency of visits with their parents differed somewhat by sex. The frequency of visits reported by males was more. Daily contact was reported by 23 per cent of the males and 17 per cent of the females. Several visits a week were reported by 31 per cent of the females and 41 per cent of males. Several visits a month were reported by 21 per cent of the females and 16 per cent of the males. Also, 20 per cent of the males indicated that they saw their parents only once or twice a year. With both males and females there was a report of parents who had returned to Japan.

With regard to the differences between the Issei and Nisei generations, the males were inclined to stress their greater Americanization, better education, greater independence and outspokenness. The females were more apt to mention that the Nisei were more lenient with children, more outgoing in their behavior, and had no language barrier.

On the other hand, their comments on the differences between their generation and the Sansei generation were much the same. By and large, the Nisei remarked that the Sansei were very independent, very outspoken and frank, much more liberal, and—what was the most frequent response—"completely Americanized."

Considering that the Nisei regarded themselves as much more Americanized than their parents, it is interesting to hear the responses of the Nisei to the question that asked, "What behavior by the Sansei would be most likely to anger or upset you?" The most frequent reply, by 40 per cent of the males and 45 per cent of the females, was "lack of respect to parents or elders." The next most frequent answer was that of breaking the law or defying authority, which was given by 26 per cent of females and 17 per cent of the males. Other opinions given centered upon such subjects as drug taking, demonstrating against the government, and radicalism.

There was little significant male-female difference apparent in attitudes toward the Sansei dating or marrying non-Japanese. When asked their opinion about the Sansei dating non-Japanese, 32 per cent of the females and 31 per cent of the males were definitely against it. Yet only 25 per cent of the females and 32 per cent of the males assented with reservations, such as that approval depended upon whom they were dating, or that it would be acceptable as long as they did not become serious. The number giving outright approval without reservation, on the other hand, was somewhat stronger in the female (43 per cent) than in the male (37 per cent). Apparently the females are less prone to believe that dating must necessarily lead to marriage.

There was, however, a slight change when the Nisei were asked their opinion on the desirability of Sansei marrying non-Japanese. This time, slightly more of the females (42 per cent) than the males (39 per cent) expressed definite disapproval. Further, a change occurred in the number of males and females assenting with reservations. Only 17 per cent of the females gave a qualified assent, while 21 per cent of the males did so. Finally, 40 per cent of both males and females gave approval to Sansei marrying non-Japanese. Here again, though, approval ranged from a mild reluctance, such as "It is inevitable in America," to such enthusiastic expressions as "Great idea! Both of my children have married Caucasians."

Some indication of the conservatism of many Nisei can be found in their replies to the question, "What Japanese characteristics would you like to see retained in the Sansei generation?" Here again the male-female responses were quite close. The most common response was "respect for parents, elders, and authority," which was given by 54 per cent of the males and 51 per cent of the females. The achievement orientation of the male Nisei is seen in the reply, "hard work," which was given by 22 per cent of the males and 9 per cent of the females. A male-female difference was also seen in the response, "humility, endurance, and patience," which was reported by 19 per cent of the females and 6 per cent of the males. Other responses emphasized the retention of the Japanese language, good manners, and the Buddhist faith.

A definite generation difference was seen in the reporting of prejudice. When compared to 59 per cent of the Issei males and 60 per cent of the Issei females who reported little or no prejudice, 90 per cent of the Nisei males and 75 per cent of the Nisei females reported moderate to severe prejudice. The Nisei males were also more prone to list the relocation of Japanese Americans during World War II as the ultimate example of prejudice. The most frequently mentioned forms of prejudice reported by both males and females were name calling and the denial of service in restaurants or stores. Others also frequently mentioned were job and housing discrimination.

The direction and degree of acculturation were quite apparent when the Nisei were asked to identify the list of Japanese words. As indicated in Table 1, there was not only the predictable overall decline in correct identification but also a rather interesting shift in the type of words correctly identified.

On (an obligation passively incurred) was correctly identified by 49 per cent of the males and 50 per cent of the females. *Giri* (duty to pay back) was identified by 40 per cent of the males and 51 per cent of the females. *Gimu* (an obligation to do one's duty) was identified by 39 per cent of both males and females. *Chū* (loyalty to one's superior) was identified by 23 per cent of the males and 18 per cent of the females. *Ninjō* (human feelings) was identified by 31 per cent of the males and 32 per cent of the females. *Amaeru* (a desire to be pampered) was identified by 62 per cent of the males and 73 per cent of the females. *Makenki* (a desire not to lose) was identified by 74 per cent of the males and 84 per cent of the females. *Seikō* (success) was identified by 67 per cent of the males and 62 per cent of the females. *Gaman* (endurance or suppression of emotion) was identified by 75 per cent of the males and 84 per cent of the females. And, finally, *enryo* (to be reserved) was identified by 74 per cent of the males and 80 per cent of the females.

It is obvious from the above that there has been a shift away

from the identification of such words as *on, giri, gimu, chū,* and
ninjō. On the other hand, *amaeru, seikō, gaman, makenki,* and
enryo were still correctly identified by over half of the Nisei. It is
further apparent that there are rather clear male-female differences in the number of identifications. What, then, are the implications of these distinctions?

Table 1
Percentage Distribution on Identification
of Japanese Words

	Issei		Nisei		Sansei	
Japanese word identified	M.	F.	M.	F.	M.	F.
On	95	98	49	50	4	9
Giri	98	93	46	51	4	9
Gimu	94	96	39	39	2	5
Chū	85	97	23	18	0	0
Ninjō	92	99	31	32	3	2
Amaeru	86	91	62	73	10	25
Makenki	93	98	74	84	9	14
Seikō	99	99	67	62	5	6
Gaman	95	97	75	84	17	23
Enryo	95	96	74	80	25	36
Number of respondents	110	124	101	131	177	195

It is difficult to make an overall generalization. Initially, one
might be tempted to attribute the male-female difference to the
greater number of females (89 vs 85 per cent) who attended
Japanese language school. A closer examination of the data,
however, does not entirely support such a conclusion. For example, *seikō* (success), which was correctly identified by 99 per cent
of the Issei was identified by approximately the same number of
Nisei males (67 per cent) as Nisei females (62 per cent).

Likewise, the word *gimu* (an obligation to do one's duty) was
identified by 95 per cent of the Issei and only 39 per cent of male
and female Nisei. By the same token, the more obscure *chū*
(loyalty to one's superior), which was identified by 85 per cent of
the male Issei, was correctly identified by only 18 per cent of the
female Nisei and 23 per cent of the males.

It would seem, therefore, that other factors are involved. A closer examination of the words reveals that the greatest difference appears in the following list:

1. *Amaeru* (desire to be pampered), identified by 62 per cent of the males and 73 per cent of the females.
2. *Gaman* (endurance of suppression of emotion), identified by 75 per cent of the males and 84 per cent of the females.
3. *Enryo* (to be reserved), identified by 74 per cent of the males and 80 per cent of the females.

The difference, while not a great one, still exists. Moreover, the words apparently reflect male-female role differences. For example, the female is expected to be more reserved (*enryo*) and to be more actively involved in child rearing *(amaeru)*. Further, the word *gaman* implies more than simple physical endurance. It also connotes putting up with something and not complaining. As one housewife explained it: "You have to bite your tongue and keep quiet."

From the descriptions given for *on* (an obligation passively incurred), *giri* (a duty to pay back), *gimu* (an obligation to do one's duty), *chū* (loyalty to one's superior), and *ninjō* (human feelings), it is apparent, as Benedict (1946) indicates, that the principles associated with these words would best be suited for the feudalistic and authoritarian society that was typical of prewar Japan. This is not to say that the Issei did not attempt to inculcate and maintain these principles in their offspring. Indeed, as subsequent chapters will indicate, our instruments disclose that the Nisei still register at least verbal approval of the principles enumerated above. However, these principles were not so frequently articulated, or perhaps even so immediately adaptable to American society as were the principles and behavior associated with *makenki* (a desire not to lose), *seikō* (success), *gaman* (endurance or suppression of emotion), *enryo* (to be reserved), or even *amaeru* (a desire to be pampered), which was most often associated with children.

Overall, the change in the identification of Japanese words would seem to imply a change towards a more open, less constrictive social environment. There is much less of an emphasis on external duties and obligations that are owed to superiors. On the other hand, it would appear that there is a considerable retention of some Japanese characteristics such as endurance and a competitive spirit. The data further indicate a greater retention of Japanese characteristics in the female. Additional support for this is to be found in the self-evaluations. The Nisei were asked to rank themselves on a scale from one to ten, ranging from a completely Japanese identity (1) to a completely American identity (10). As depicted on Table 7, the arithmetic mean average for the Nisei males was 5.35. The arithmetic mean for females, 5.20, was slightly lower.

Again, with regard to the observation of Japanese and American holidays there was a definite tendency to place greater emphasis on American holidays, but not necessarily to the exclusion of the Japanese holidays. For example, as Table 2 indicates, four of the holidays listed for the Issei were discontinued on the Nisei survey form after a preliminary survey of the Nisei revealed that no one observed them. These were *Kigensetsu*, *O-Higan*, *Kiku-no-sekku*, and *Tenchōsetsu*.

Table 2
Percentage Distribution on Observation of Holidays

Holiday observed	Issei		Nisei		Sansei	
	M.	F.	M.	F.	M.	F.
Easter	53	58	84	85	82	85
Memorial Day	76	59	82	79	55	80
Fourth of July	72	61	85	87	87	95
Labor Day	51	38	74	68	71	74
Thanksgiving	97	94	97	97	96	96
Christmas	92	91	98	98	96	100
O-Shōgatsu	95	93	96	98	52	63
O-Shōgatsu visiting	72	55	72	74	27	50
Hinamatsuri	57	77	47	62	24	38
Girls' Day	32	56	22	47	15	35
Boys' Day	47	54	22	44	22	25
O-Bon	75	85	62	66	67	72
O-Higan†	39	55	0	0	0	0
Kigensetsu†	10	0	0	0	0	0
Kiku-no-Sekku†	7	0	0	0	0	0
Tenchōsetsu†	0	0	0	0	0	0
Number of respondents	124	110	101	131	177	195

†Discontinued in Nisei and Sansei survey.

The findings on the observation of the various holidays by the Nisei were much the same for males and females, although there was a tendency on the part of the females to observe the more traditional Japanese holidays. The findings are as follows: Easter (males, 84 per cent; females, 85 per cent), Memorial Day (males, 82 per cent; females, 79 per cent), Fourth of July (males, 85 per cent; females, 87 per cent), Labor Day (males, 74 per cent; females, 68 per cent), Thanksgiving (males, 97 per cent; females, 97 per cent), Christmas (males, 98 per cent; females, 98 per cent), O-Shōgatsu (males, 96 per cent; females, 98 per cent), O-Shōgatsu visiting (males, 72 per cent; females, 74 per cent), Hinamatsuri (males, 47 per cent; females, 62 per cent), Girls' Day (males 22 per cent; females, 47 per cent), Boys' Day (males, 22 per cent; females, 44 per cent), and O-Bon (males, 58 per cent; females, 66).

The male-female difference may be explained in part by the greater involvement with their children by the females, as in the case of Boys' Day and Girls' Day. Or it may be due to the fact that they are at home more often (50 per cent gave their occupation as housewife) and are thus able to participate more fully in activities organized by the Buddhist Church or other Japanese American organizations.

One further measure of acculturation was that of socialization or child-rearing practices. Given the age of the Nisei, one limitation was immediately apparent, and that was the necessity of relying on retrospective accounts. We attempted to overcome this by asking the Nisei *not* what they had stressed in raising their children but, rather, what had been stressed by their parents in raising them. Specifically, we wished to relate their accounts to what we had already learned from the disciplining habits of the Issei. In particular, we felt that the threat of bringing shame to the family, so frequently reported by the Issei, would prove to be a valuable indicator of change. That is, we could not only ask the Nisei if it had been stressed in their childhood, we could also discover the degree to which they had changed by asking the same questions of the Sansei.

When asked to state if their parents had stressed that they should behave properly and avoid bringing shame to the family, 90 per cent of Nisei males and 97 per cent of the females, reported that it had been stressed. Again, 92 per cent of both males and females, indicated that the principle that one make returns for kindness received was also strongly stressed. And further, the principle that one must act so as not to bring dishonor to the Japanese American community was stressed by 84 per cent of the parents of the male Nisei and 85 per cent of the females. It was reported not stressed by 10 per cent of the parents of both males and females, while 6 per cent of the males and 5 per cent of the females simply could not recall.

A final question asked of the Nisei was their evaluation of the success of Japanese Americans in the United States. In reply, 95 per cent answered that they believed the Japanese Americans were successful. Again, as in the case of the Issei, the reason most frequently given was "hard work" or "we try harder." Others noted that they took good care of their property and that they were home owners. Still others mentioned their drive for educa tion, their endurance, competitive spirit, and perseverance, and even that their success could be seen in that they have no one on welfare

In um, like the Issei the Nisei are relatively content. Most are now in the prime of life and it is they who occupy the positions of power and authority in the ethnic community. While considered conservative or even reactionary by some of the younger Sansei, the Nisei are truly and justifiably proud of their accomplishments. As time goes on, the Nisei generation grows more and more to resemble that of one of the age grades reported by Norbeck (1953) for rural Japan. They are set off from the Issei, the Sansei, and the larger American society by a unique set of shared experiences. They were, after all, the generation that grew up together during the Great Depression. They shared the common experience of trying to live in two dramatically different cultures. They shared the prejudice of the prewar and wartime period. As model citizens with an enviable record in education and a reputation for being scrupulously law-abiding, they shared the irony and keenly felt the humility of being declared undesirables and imprisoned in relocation centers.

Forced to prove their loyalty, many joined the army and fought together in the 442nd Regimental Combat Team, the most highly decorated unit of its size in American military history. Others served as translators and interpreters in risky intelligence operations in the Pacific, and most of them felt the poignancy of returning to the West Coast and attempting to salvage whatever they could of their shattered prewar lives.

With their shared experiences the Nisei have a further collective distinction—their facility in the Japanese language. It is an uneven facility and very few would pass muster in Tokyo, but it is nevertheless a common denominator that is increasingly separating them from the Sansei.

There is, then, a common identity, an understanding, an awareness of having participated in some rather remarkable historical events that gives to the Nisei generation a distinctiveness and feeling of uniqueness that can often transcend the petty bickering that usually marks the ethnic community.

And, in part, it is this consciousness of their uniqueness and their difficulty in understanding the world of their children that has widened the generation gap into a chasm. For in one highly ironic sense it is the Nisei who are becoming the victims of their own success. Like the Oriental proverb which admonishes one to be careful of what is wished for—because it might someday come true—the Nisei are watching the fruits of their labor being harvested by their children, some of whom now appear to have enjoyed sufficient affluence to be able to rebel against it. Along with the success of the parents came the cars, the increased allowances of the children, and the accompanying leisure to enjoy them. And with the leisure came trouble. In 1964, a number of Sansei in the Sacramento area were involved in handling stolen goods. The affair was quickly settled by means of probation and suspended sentences and was largely kept from the general public. Nevertheless, for most of the Nisei it was a shocking testimonial to the widening difference between the two generations.

And to a certain extent it could also be said that it is the awareness of their own distinctiveness as a generation that is in part responsible for the ambivalence that many Nisei feel towards their Sansei offspring. On the other hand, they are proud of the increasing independence displayed by the Sansei because they see it as a continuation of their own efforts. On the other hand, they are, more often than not, repelled by the defiance that frequently accompanies the growing independence. It is this latter feeling that is apparent in the comments by the Sansei that the Nisei are conservative and authoritarian. This observation is partly supported by the response of almost half the Nisei that the type of behavior most likely to anger or upset them would be a lack of respect by the Sansei.

And, in a broader sense, perhaps they both are right. Along with their sense of uniqueness, and perhaps also influenced by their middle position in the three-generation span, is a concomitant feeling that the Nisei combine the best of both cultures, a feeling brought to light not only in their own personal comments but also in their self-evaluations of slightly over 5 on the 10-point scale.

It is the experience of having been raised in the two cultures that gives the Nisei a capacity for bifocal vision. Perhaps it is this background, along with their awareness of their minority group status, that is responsible for often apparent contradictions. Most Nisei are registered Democrats who are rather liberal in some areas such as civil rights but are quite conservative on others such as welfare, foreign policy, and student demonstrations on campus.

A distinction should be made, however. The conservatism of the middle-class Nisei is really not so much a result of their having a long and vested interest in the status quo as it is a reflection of the price they had to pay to achieve it. Underneath all their complaints about the "pushy" minorities and their own ungrateful offspring is a common thread of resentment, with perhaps even a tinge of regret, for having had to make it the hard way.

But there is also the pride of accomplishment, and it is this pride, more than anything else, that illuminates their success and contributes so much to their self-satisfaction. And, indeed, while relatively modest by Sansei standards, when seen in terms of their own aspirations and the odds they faced in attaining them, they did in fact succeed.

Perhaps therein is the source of their final satisfaction. For the Nisei know that, if their children aspire higher and their visions are greater, it is only because they are standing on the accomplishment of others.

And yet, in retrospect, it cannot be said that for all their self-satisfaction the Nisei epitomize the major values of the larger American society. Despite their oft-acclaimed rise to middle-class respectability and their enviable achievements as a "model minority," it must be remembered that their attainments were more often than not the result of their utilization of ideals and values that were essentially Japanese in nature. As the Sansei so correctly recognize, there is a starkness, a rigidity, an uncompromisingly conservative, and basically authoritarian, if not completely puritanical aspect to the Nisei personality. This aspect, while not entirely foreign to the American character, has usually been manifested in the backwaters rather than in the mainstream of the American experience. We shall explore this aspect of the Nisei personality in a later chapter.

Chapter 8

The Sansei
Interview Schedule

As with the Nisei Interview Schedule, the Sansei Schedule has fewer questions than were asked for the Issei. Again the basic approach was to continue the questions pertaining to the observations of various holidays and the identification of Japanese words. In addition, of course, both the subjective evaluation of acculturation and the attitudes toward dating and marriage were also continued.

Other questions pertaining to movie viewing, food preferences, and the number of non-Japanese friends were also continued for the purpose of comparison with the Nisei generation.

Certain questions were specifically designed for the Sansei group. Generally these were intended not only to relate the study to previous research but also to provide additional information on acculturation. In particular, we wanted to know if the Sansei were becoming more active in school activities and perhaps concentrating a little less on grades than did their parents.

In all, 177 Sansei males and 195 Sansei females were interviewed. The larger number of those interviewed in comparison with the Issei and Nisei generations was the result of greater accessibility. Approximately 65 per cent were students at California State University, Sacramento. The remainder were scattered throughout the community and were contacted usually on the basis of their being personally known to the interviewer. For example, several of those interviewed by the author were students in various classes; others were personal friends of the family. Again, as was the experience in the Nisei interviews, we were initially more successful in contacting the females than the males. Once those who were readily accessible had been interviewed we attempted to concentrate on the males in order to balance the survey.

The mean average age of the Sansei was 23.2 for the males and 22.9 for the females. The oldest male was 32 and the youngest 17. The oldest female was 34 and the youngest 17. The average education was 13.9 years for males and 13.6 for the females. The figures, of course, are not too meaningful since many of those interviewed were still in the process of completing their education.

We asked the questions pertaining to school activities and academic achievement in order to provide an index of acculturation, and also to relate the survey to a previous study by Kitano (1962). In that study he demonstrated, by the use of the school records of Nisei and Sansei over a two-decade period, that there was a reduction in the overall grade point average in the Sansei generation (although it is still a respectable "B" average). The reduction in very high academic achievement was accompanied by an increased participation in school social activities.

Our data would tend to support Kitano but are of a more subjective nature. Instead of checking high school records we asked the Sansei the type of school activities in which they had been participants. Overall we discovered that 83 per cent of the boys and 83 per cent of the girls had participated in extracurricular school activities. The boys were generally involved in athletics (75 per cent); however, 25 per cent mentioned that they had held school offices such as class representative or treasurer, or they were active in one or more clubs. A higher percentage of girls held school offices (35 per cent), and these were usually that of class secretary or class representative. The remainder (65 per cent) mentioned a variety of clubs. Chief among these were the rally club, pep club, or cheerleading. Of interest here is that in the interviews there was little mention of membership in organizations that were exclusively meant for Japanese Americans, although the past year or so has seen the growth of ethnic organizations in many high schools and, of course, on the college campuses There was, however, more frequent mention of membership in broader-based ethnic organizations such as the Asian American Club.

With regard to their academic records, there was an interesting male-female difference. When asked how their high school academic records compared with that of their parents, 47 per cent of the males and 50 per cent of the females claimed theirs was better, 36 per cent of the males and 41 per cent of the females said that theirs was just as good as their parents', and 16 per cent of the males and 9 per cent of the females reported that it was poorer.

Although the above parent-offspring academic comparison is subjective, the Sansei male-female difference does occur, and it also agrees with the author's observations as a high school teacher. Based on personal experience, it could be said that the female consistently performed better academically, a conclusion that will be supported by our findings on the Sansei college grades to be given in a later chapter.

Again, my teaching experience further supports the degree to which the Sansei have engaged in school activities. Without question, there are still a number who are shy or reserved, but perhaps no more so than in any other group. An example that comes to mind is that of one young Sansei who was so active and so dependable as a class officer that he almost drove himself to exhaustion attempting to keep up his grades and meet all demands on his time.

In comparison with their parents, the number of Sansei who have attended Japanese language school has decreased dramatically. In all, only 12 per cent of the males and 19 per cent of the females indicated that they had gone to such a school. Of those who had attended, the overwhelming consensus was that the schools were very ineffective in teaching them the Japanese language. And indeed, from a pedagogical standpoint they probably are ineffective. Because of the dispersal of the Japanese community, difficulties in transportation, and other factors, most of the schools meet only once a week on Saturday—hardly the time needed for learning a language.

About the same percentage of Sansei (males, 60 per cent; females, 51 per cent) as Nisei (males, 58 per cent; females, 64 per cent) reportedly watch Japanese films. But again, although there is an apparent generation difference in the females, the figures are not too meaningful as an index of change or acculturation since both groups indicate that they watch the films on the average of only once every three or four months.

By the same token, the change in food habits was not too meaningful since over two-thirds of our Sansei were students with irregular eating habits and some were living away from home. Nevertheless 36 per cent of the males and 23 per cent of the females reported having some form of Japanese food every day, usually rice. The same number (28 per cent) of males and females indicated that they ate Japanese food at least three to four times a week, and the remainder listed once a week or less.

On the other hand, there was a clear generation difference in the reporting of Japanese food disliked. Whereas 39 per cent of the Nisei males and 40 per cent of the females indicated dislikes, this increased among the Sansei to 62 per cent of the males and 67 per cent of the females. Again, as with the Nisei, seafood, especially raw fish and octopus, accounted for most of the food disliked.

The direction of greater interaction with the larger community can be seen in the number of Sansei who report having non-Japanese friends. While 46 per cent of the Nisei females and 48 per cent of the males indicated that over half of their friends were Caucasian, in the Sansei generation the number rises to 75 per cent of the females and 66 per cent of the males. In other words, over two-thirds of the Sansei report that one-half or more of their friends are non-Japanese. Undoubtedly the higher percentage is due in part to the many who were students. However, this has not always been the case. Slightly over a decade ago, when I was an undergraduate on the same campus, the Japanese Americans had more of a reputation for keeping to themselves.

The occupational goal of most of the Sansei was in the professions. Law, business, accounting, engineering, and teaching were most frequently mentioned by the males, although almost one-fourth had no clear-cut goal and listed either that they wanted to be successful or, simply, "be happy." The females listed teaching most frequently. This was followed by career choices in nursing, clerical, business, pharmacy, laboratory technician, and working with children. Twelve per cent simply listed a happy marriage as their goal in life. The occupational goals and grade point average of the Sansei college students will be discussed in some detail in a subsequent chapter.

The occupations given for the fathers are in rough agreement with the information given by the Nisei. About 18 per cent were working as farmers and 17 per cent as gardeners. The Sansei, male and female, further report one-fifth of the fathers engaged in small business, one-fourth in skilled trades, and about 20 per cent each in clerical work or in the professions.

When asked what they admired most about the Issei generation, the most frequently mentioned characteristics were their perseverance, courage, hard work, and stubborn pride.

The characteristics least admired in the Issei were their clannishness, conservatism, narrow-mindedness, authoritarianism, and inability to speak English.

As indicated previously, the Sansei do not have much contact with the Issei generation. Most of their information about the Issei is secondhand, and much of it was obtained indirectly from what they had read and by hearsay from their parents. Undoubtedly, much of the lack of contact is a result of differences both in age and experience, but the inability to communicate is an even greater barrier. The marginal competence of many Issei in English is more than matched by the even poorer competence of the Sansei in Japanese.

The Sansei are aware of their lack of skill and feel somewhat guilty about it. On the other hand, many believe that the Issei should have acquired greater competence in English. Whereas a common complaint by the Issei with regard to the Sansei was that they could not speak to them, or did not understand them at all, the Sansei retaliated by stating that, among other things, one thing they disliked about the Issei was their inability to speak English.

This one aspect of the generation gap was poignantly expressed by a young Sansei girl who had taken part in the Japanese Community Study Class mentioned earlier. As part of the semester assignment she was required to interview representatives of all three generations, including six Issei. Following established procedure, she interviewed her own grandparents first and then those of close friends. With the last Issei interview she experienced some difficulty. In this instance the Issei female spoke no English and she asked the women's son, a Nisei with some ability in Japanese, to interpret for her. Apparently there was more than a simple reluctance on his part, for he refused, saying in part: "If you Sansei wanted to study the Issei, why didn't you learn Japanese?"

The girl was hurt by his comments. Indeed, as she later remarked: "I was about to answer, 'Well, if the Issei wanted to come to this country, why didn't they learn English?' But I didn't. I guess there is a part of me that's still Japanese."

The Sansei were next asked a series of questions pertaining to dating and marrying non-Japanese. They were first asked their attitude towards dating non-Japanese and then asked to predict the Nisei and Issei attitude to their dating non-Japanese. The same series of questions was then asked with relation to their marrying non-Japanese. Again, they were also asked to predict the Nisei and Issei response. The data on their replies, together with the previously presented data on the Issei and Nisei responses to similar questions, are given in Table 3.

Once again, as with the Nisei attitude towards dating non-Japanese, slightly more females than males indicated approval. The number who expressed outright disapproval was only 2 per cent of the males and 4 per cent of the females. On the other hand, more of the males (25 per cent) approved with reservations compared to only 12 per cent of the females. Usually those who expressed reservations indicated that approval depended upon the kind of person being dated. In both groups, however, the number who expressed approval was quite large. In all, 73 per cent of the males and 84 per cent of the females gave outright approval. The approval ranged all the way from such expressions as "It's O.K. by me" to "Great idea! I do it all the time." One Sansei girl who was interviewed by the writer on several occasions disclosed that, so far, she has dated only Caucasians and her parents are still waiting for her to bring home a Sansei date.

One aspect of the generation gap can be seen in the Sansei estimation of what their parents and grandparents would think of their dating non-Japanese. In both cases it can be seen that they greatly overestimated the degree to which the Issei and Nisei would express disapproval. When compared to the data presented in Tables 3 and 4, which list the response of the Issei and Nisei to the Sansei dating and marrying non-Japanese, it can be seen that the estimations of the Sansei were largely in error. For example, 50 per cent of both male and female Sansei thought that the Nisei would be definitely against dating non-Japanese when the number was really closer to 30 per cent. Another 45 per cent of the females and 38 per cent of the males felt that Nisei would approve with reservation while the percentage reported by the Nisei was really 25 per cent for the females and 32 per cent for the males. Again, while 43 per cent of the Nisei females and 37 per cent of the males indicated outright approval, only 4 per cent of the Sansei females and 11 per cent of the males thought they would.

Table 3
Percentage Distribution on Attitude Expressed Toward Sansei Dating Non-Japanese

Attitude expressed	Issei		Nisei		Sansei	
	M.	F.	M.	F.	M.	F.
Definite opposition	39	36	31	32	2	4
Assent with reservations	43	44	32	25	25	12
Definite approval	18	20	37	43	73	84
Total percentage	100	99	100	100	100	100
Number of respondents	124	110	101	131	177	195

The lack of contact with the Issei generation is easily seen in the Sansei estimation of their response. The data show that 39 per cent of the Issei males and 36 per cent of the females were definitely against dating non-Japanese, 43 per cent of the males and 44 per cent of the females approved with reservations, and 18 per cent of the males and 20 per cent of the females expressed approval. However, some 91 per cent of the Sansei, both male and female, felt that the Issei would be definitely against it, and only 9 per cent felt that they would approve with reservations.

As indicated in Table 4, the differences were even more pronounced when the Sansei were asked to give their attitudes toward marrying non-Japanese and also to estimate the responses of the Nisei and Issei generations.

With regard to marrying non-Japanese, more of the Sansei expressed disapproval. This time, however, the replies of males and females were identical, with 15 per cent of both males and females definitely against it. The number that approved with reservation was 18 per cent of the males and 8 per cent of the females, while 67 per cent of the males and 77 per cent of the females gave unqualified approval.

The estimates of the responses of the Nisei and Issei generations, however, indicated very little male-female difference.

Table 4

**Percentage Distribution on Attitude Expressed
Toward Sansei Marrying Non-Japanese**

	Issei		Nisei		Sansei	
Attitude expressed	M.	F.	M.	F.	M.	F.
Definite opposition	49	70	39	42	15	15
Assent with reservations	41	20	21	17	18	8
Definite approval	10	9	40	40	67	77
Total percentage	100	99	100	99	100	100
Number of respondents	123	110	101	131	177	195

While 53 per cent of the females felt that the Nisei would give outright disapproval, 58 per cent of the males felt they would disapprove. Again, 35 per cent of the females and 34 per cent of the males believed that the Nisei would approve with certain reservations, and only 12 per cent of the females and 1 per cent of the males believed that they would give outright approval.

The number of Nisei who actually did express disapproval was 42 per cent of the females and 39 per cent of the males. However, only 17 per cent of the females and 21 per cent of the males approved with reservations, and fully 40 per cent of both males and females gave outright approval.

The Sansei were perhaps a little closer in their assessment of the Issei response to their marrying non-Japanese. Fully 100 per cent of the males and 91 per cent of the female Sansei felt that they would be against it, while 9 per cent of the Sansei females believed that the Issei would approve with certain reservations.

In reality, 49 per cent of the Issei males and 70 per cent of the females were definitely against it, while 41 per cent of the males and 20 per cent of the females assented with reservations and only 10 per cent of the males and 9 per cent of the females gave approval.

Given the change in attitudes, the question might be asked if the changes really do eventuate in practice. That is, are the Sansei really marrying non-Japanese? Fortunately, access to the Sacramento County marriage records does provide us with some data. How conclusive or accurate a reflection of actual marriage practices it is, remains to be seen. From personal experience it can be said that some of the marriages involving Sansei and non-

Japanese do take place in Reno, Nevada, rather than in Sacramento County. Nonetheless, the data are readily available and they are revealing.

An examination of the Sacramento County marriage records was made by Atsushi Ikemoto, a graduate student in Social Science, who had participated in the Japanese American Research Course mentioned previously. Mr. Ikemoto graciously provided the data that are depicted in Table 5.

For purposes of comparison with the current Sansei population, it was decided to review the records for the past decade since this would roughly encompass the age span of the Sansei group we had interviewed. The Sansei were readily identifiable in the marriage records by means of simple definition. That is, the marriage data indicated both the place of birth of the married couple and that of their parents. If the parents were born in Japan and the offspring here, we could assume a Nisei couple. On the other hand, if both the parents and the offspring were born in the United States, we could assume a Sansei couple. It may be objected that, by the same logic and definition, one could assume a Yonsei or fourth-generation couple; however, although Yonsei do exist, by and large they have not yet arrived at a marriageable age.

One obvious drawback on the use of the records is that they do not indicate race or ethnicity. There is, therefore, no way of determining if the Sansei marriages to non-Japanese involved Caucasians or blacks. However, given the ratio of Caucasians to blacks in the larger society and the reports of the Sansei that most of their non-Japanese friends were Caucasian, we can reasonably assume that when we encounter the record of a marriage between two people, one of whom has a Japanese surname and the other a European surname, the marriage involved a Sansei and a Caucasian. By the same logic we were to determine Chinese and Spanish surnames although, as Table 5 indicates, they were not too numerous.

Within the last decade a total of 435 marriages involving individuals of Japanese surames have been recorded. Of the 435, 123 or 28.3 per cent were mixed marriages. The table further indicates that of these mixed marriages, a total of 48, or 39 per cent, were between males with European surnames and females with Japanese surnames, and 39 or 31 per cent were between

Table 5

Number of Recorded Marriages Involving Individuals of Japanese and Non-Japanese Surnames in Sacramento County for the Years 1961-1970

Type of marriage	1961	1962	1963	1964	1965	1966	1967	1968	1969	1970	Total for 1961-70
1. Japanese surname male, Japanese surname female	36	27	37	27	36	34	31	24	31	29	312
2. Japanese surname male, European surname female	2	0	2	3	5	2	3	5	9	8	39
3. European surname male, Japanese surname female	4	1	8	7	3	3	7	7	6	2	48
4. Japanese surname male, Chinese surname female	0	0	0	1	0	1	1	2	3	3	11
5. Chinese surname male, Japanese surname female	2	1	2	1	1	0	1	0	3	1	12
6. Japanese surname male, Spanish surname female	0	1	0	0	1	1	0	2	0	0	5
7. Spanish surname male, Japanese surname female	1	1	0	1	1	0	0	1	0	0	5
8. Filipino surname male, Japanese surname female	0	0	1	0	0	0	0	0	0	0	1
9. Japanese surname male, Filipino surname female	0	0	0	0	0	0	0	0	0	0	0
10. Korean surname male, Japanese surname female	0	0	1	0	0	0	0	0	0	0	1
11. Japanese surname male, Korean surname female	0	0	0	0	0	0	0	0	0	1	1
Total marriages each year	45	31	51	40	47	41	43	41	52	44	435

males with Japanese surnames and females with European surnames. In other words, the data indicate that both male and female Sansei are marrying non-Japanese in about equal numbers.

Furthermore, our data indicate that 18 per cent of the mixed marriages involved Japanese and Chinese, with approximately the same number (11 and 12) of males and females of both groups intermarrying.

Our data, then, would seem to indicate that there is considerable out-marriage, and the Sansei attitude of having little or no objection to such marriages does eventuate in practice.

An article appearing in the December 3, 1971, issue of the *Pacific Citizen* by Gene Kuhn indicated that Sansei intermarriages are even higher in Fresno, California. Kuhn reports that since 1964 the intermarriage rate rose to 50 per cent and has continued to about the same rate (1971). With those comments in mind, it is probable that our data do not reflect a true picture and it is very likely that the percentage of mixed marriages is actually higher. As was mentioned previously, I know of several mixed marriages involving Sacramento Sansei that took place in Reno, Nevada. The reason given was that they wanted to keep the information out of the local papers.

A further indication of the direction of change can be seen in the smaller number of Sansei who were raised in the Japanese community. Compared to 63 per cent of the Nisei females and 65 per cent of the males, only 31 per cent of the Sansei females and 30 per cent of the males state that they were brought up in a Japanese community. Both sexes agreed that the Japanese community has become much more dispersed since they were children. However, it should be emphasized that the millennium has not yet arrived for the Japanese Americans. Prejudice still exists, and over half of the Sansei report that they have experienced it. Again, however, as with the Nisei, there was a substantial difference according to sex. The males reported far more prejudice (75 per cent) than the females (62 per cent). As with their parents, more reported the prejudice to be in the form of name calling or denial of service. Some interesting comments were by several of the females who felt that, in their case, prejudice had been shown to them by their families when they brought home Caucasian dates. Others stated that prejudice had been a positive force, in that they knew they were given job preference as teachers or clerical workers because of the reputation Japanese Americans have for dependability. By way of personal comment it might be added that all of the above has been verified either in the author's own experience or in that of members of his family.

The degree of understanding the Sansei have for parental rules and codes of conduct can be seen in the answers they gave when asked what behavior would be most quickly punished by the Nisei. Some 14 per cent of the males and 11 per cent of the females answered that it would be a lack of respect. Breaking the law was given by 26 per cent of the females and 29 per cent of the males. Bringing shame to the family was reported by 24 per cent of the males and 19 per cent of the females. Other answers reported were using drugs, getting pregnant, or marrying a black, which was reported by 15 per cent of the females.

The emphasis placed on the avoidance of shame is easily seen in Table 6 and in the series of questions that were asked relating to that subject. When asked whether or not their parents stressed that they must behave properly to avoid bringing shame to the family, 83 per cent of the males and 84 per cent of the females said that it had been stressed, 15 per cent of the males and 12 per cent of the females said it had not, and 2 per cent of the males and 4 per cent of the females could not recall. In all, as Table 6 indicates, this marks a slight reduction from the 90 per cent of Nisei males and 95 per cent of the females who reported it stressed.

Again, only a slight reduction of 3 per cent in the Sansei females was reported for the principle that returns should be made for all kindness received. Of the Nisei males and females and the Sansei males, 90 per cent reported it stressed, while 87 per cent of the Sansei females, or some 3 per cent fewer, so indicated.

A rather significant reduction was seen in the number of Sansei who indicated that stress was placed on the principle that one must act so as not to bring shame to the Japanese community. As compared to 84 per cent of the Nisei males and 85 per cent of the females, only 61 per cent of the Sansei males and 62 per cent of the females reported that the principle was stressed. The reduction is probably due to the dispersal of the Japanese community and is reflected in part by the smaller number of Sansei who reported being raised in one.

Some change was also evident in the number of Sansei who report their religious faith as Buddhist. While almost 50 per cent of both male and female Sansei report being Buddhist, and the remaining 39 per cent of the females report Christianity as their faith, only 33 per cent of the males so indicated; the remainder gave agnostic or no religion as their response. Our data therefore disclose a gradual decline in the percentage of Japanese Americans who identify themselves as Buddhists. Our figures indicate a decline from over 70 per cent among the Issei, to some 60 per cent of the Nisei, then down to about 50 per cent of the Sansei.

Table 6

Percentage Distribution of Nisei and Sansei Reporting Parental Stress on Certain Principles

Principle reported stressed	Nisei		Sansei	
	M.	F.	M.	F.
1. Avoid bringing shame to the family				
A. Stressed	90	95	83	84
B. Not stressed	5	5	15	12
C. Don't recall	5	0	2	4
2. Make returns for all kindness received				
A. Stressed	90	92	90	87
B. Not stressed	7	10	10	12
C. Don't recall	1	0	0	1
3. Must not bring dishonor to the Japanese community				
A. Stressed	84	85	61	62
B. Not stressed	10	10	29	30
C. Don't recall	6	5	10	8
Number of respondents	101	131	177	195

Again, as is indicated in Table 1, the greatest change came in the identification of Japanese words. On (an obligation passively incurred) was identified by only 4 per cent of the males and 9 per cent of the females. Giri (a duty to pay back) was identified by only 4 per cent of the males and 9 per cent of the females. Gimu (an obligation to pay back) was identified by 2 per cent of the males and 5 per cent of the females. Chū (loyalty to one's superior) was not identified. Ninjō (human feelings) was identified by 3 per cent of the males and 2 per cent of the females.

Amaeru (a desire to be pampered) was identified by 10 per cent of the males and 25 per cent of the females. *Makenki* (a desire not to lose) was identified by only 9 per cent of the males and 14 per cent of the females. *Seikō* (success) was identified by 5 per cent of the males and 6 per cent of the females. Some indication of exposure to Japanese advertising is evident, however, in the fact that almost 40 per cent of the Sansei misidentified *seikō* as being the brand name of a watch. The word *gaman* (endurance or suppression of emotion) was correctly identified by 17 per cent of the males and 23 per cent of the females. *Enryo* (to be reserved) was identified by 25 per cent of the males and 36 per cent of the females.

It seems obvious that there has been a shift from such words as *on, giri, gimu, chū, ninjō, makenki,* and *seikō* and a partial retention of *amaeru, gaman,* and *enryo,* especially in the females. It should also be noted that the identification of *on, giri,* and *gimu* may not necessarily indicate the retention of concepts. Several of the Sansei being interviewed mentioned that they had read Benedict's *Chrysanthemum and the Sword* (1946) and had thus become familiar with the words.

On the other hand, fully one-fourth of the Sansei females recognized *amaeru, enryo,* and *gaman.* Once again, as in the case of the Nisei females, these words appear to suggest role differences. *Amaeru* was seen in relation to child rearing, *gaman* was usually defined as "putting up with it," and *enryo* was frequently seen to be a form of polite refusal or holding back.

The traditional female role requires the female to be more reserved, more passive, more deferent, and less self-assertive than the male. Moreover, the familiarity of the Sansei female with the concept of *amaeru* and its association with child rearing is not simply a coincidence. It will be demonstrated in the final chapter that, while the Sansei mother has adopted some of the American style of child caretaking, she has also retained a number of the Japanese caretaking practices.

Also, as with the Nisei generation, there was a dropping off in the observation of some of the Japanese holidays. As indicated in Table 2, the data for both males and females point in the same direction, although overall there was a tendency for a higher percentage of females than males to observe both the American and the Japanese holidays. The difference is apparent in the following compilation: Easter (males, 82 per cent; females, 85 per cent); Memorial Day (males, 55 per cent; females, 80 per cent); Fourth of July (males, 87 per cent; females, 95 per cent); Labor Day (males, 71 per cent; females, 74 per cent); Thanksgiving (males, 96 per cent; females, 96 per cent); Christmas (males, 96 per cent; females 100 per cent); O-Shōgatsu (males, 52 per cent; females, 63 per cent); O-Shōgatsu visiting (males, 27 per cent; females, 50 per cent); Hinamatsuri (males, 24 per cent; females, 38 per cent); Girls' Day (males, 15 per cent; females, 35 per cent); Boys' Day (males, 22 per cent; females, 25 per cent); O-Bon (males, 67 per cent; females, 72 per cent).

It seems obvious from the above that there has not been a precipitous decline in the observation of all Japanese holidays. Indeed, with respect to the observance of O-Bon, it is apparent that the Sansei responses of 67 and 72 per cent male and female observance is actually higher than the 62 per cent and 66 per cent reported for the Nisei. Of course, this should come as no surprise to someone who has attended an O-Bon ceremony. There are usually more young people who are actively involved than older ones. An additional factor is that the young people think of O-Bon primarily as a social activity while the older generations are more concerned with its religious aspects. This is in part supported by the findings that, while only one-half of the Sansei consider themselves Buddhist, over two-thirds take part in the O-Bon ceremony. On the other hand, the number of Nisei who participated was almost the same as those who reported themselves to be Buddhists. That is, 64 per cent of the males gave their religion as Buddhist and 62 per cent participated in O-Bon. Also, 66 per cent of the females stated they were Buddhists and 66 per cent participated in O-Bon. An elaboration on the above comment on the continuing observation of Japanese holidays by the Sansei has been suggested by Professor K. H. K. Chang formerly of the Department of Anthropology, University of California, Davis. He suggests that a large number of the Sansei are still living with their parents and are therefore under their influence. If the parents observe a particular holiday, the Sansei would almost certainly be involved. Moreover, in local Buddhist churches the religious ceremonies that are a part of the O-Bon festival are usually held for the congregation in the afternoon, while the dancing and social activity take place at night. It should be mentioned in this regard that the dancing and general festivities are open to all. Indeed, as Professor Chang has indicated, and as is immediately apparent to any observer, there are many non-Buddhist Sansei and even many non-Japanese Americans who are invited to participate in the festivities.

A final measure of Sansei acculturation is shown is Table 7. Again, asked to rank themselves on a scale from one to ten, ranging from a completely Japanese identity (1) to a completely American identity (10), the Sansei scores reflected their change. The mean score for the males was 6.7 and that of the females 6.6.

Table 7

Arithmetic Mean Distribution on Subjective Self-Evaluation of Degree of Acculturation

Generation	Japanese identity								American identity	
	1	2	3	4	5	6	7	8	9	10
Issei										
Male (N-123)			3.9							
Female (N-110)			3.3							
Nisei										
Male (N-101)					5.35					
Female (N-131)					5.2					
Sansei										
Male (N-177)						6.9				
Female (N-195)						6.6				

Like their parents and grandparents, the Sansei were asked if they believed the Japanese had been successful in the United States. In reply, 82 per cent of the males and 92 per cent of the females said yes. The reasons given for the success were much like those of their parents and grandparents. Emphasis was placed on the virtues of hard work, education, and perseverance. The replies of other Sansei would seem to indicate a belief that success would finally be realized in their own generation. Their answers emphasized success as a goal towards which they were still striving. Somewhat the same sort of belief was implicit in the responses made by those who did not think the Japanese had been successful. Their negative responses were usually phrased in such a way as to indicate that the definition of success which they were using implied access to the sources of power and the policy-making structure in American society.

In other words, what we are observing in the third generation is the beginning of an attempt to achieve structural assimilation. According to the model established by Gordon in *Assimilation in American Life* (1964), there are postulated two main types of assimilation—cultural and structural.

Gordon (1964:70-71) is using the term assimilation to include what anthropologists and others have called acculturation. However, Gordon makes a distinction between what he calls cultural or behavioral assimilation and structural assimilation.

Cultural or behavioral assimilation is also termed acculturation. It is marked by changes of the cultural patterns of the assimilating group to that of the host society, although a reciprocal influence on the host society is also recognized.

Structural assimilation, on the other hand, takes place when the assimilating group has entered fully into the social network of groups and institutions of the larger society. As Gordon (1964:71) indicates in Table 8, which follows, there are seven assimilation variables. Structural assimilation, then, includes such things as a large-scale entrance into cliques, clubs, and institutions of the host society on a primary-group level. Of the seven variables, Gordon believes that structural assimilation is the most impor-tant since, once structural assimilation has taken place, the other forms of assimilation naturally follow.

Kitano (1969:155) believes that the Nisei and Sansei have largely achieved cultural assimilation but he does not believe that structural assimilation has yet taken place. Unquestionably, almost all scholars on the Japanese American would agree with him. However, with the Sansei generation the goals have changed. The fact is that many of the Sansei are now beginning to define success in terms of access to the power structure and no longer see it solely in terms of achieving middle-class respectabil-ity by being home owners or having no one on welfare.

Again, while a number of previous observers (Burma 1953, Meredith 1966, Kitano 1969) have mentioned that for various reasons the Nisei generation had been somewhat unwilling to assume leadership roles, this appears to be changing. The recent election of a Nisei congressman from San Jose, and the election of a Sansei to the Sacramento City Council, plus the recent appointments of several Japanese Americans to high level state positions indicate that some profound changes have already taken place.

Table 8
The Assimilation Variables
(Table 5 in Gordon)

Subprocess or condition	Type of stage of assimilation	Special term
Change of cultural patterns to those of host society	Cultural or behavioral assimilation	Acculturation
Large-scale entrance into cliques, clubs, and institutions of host society, on primary group level	Structural assimilation	None
Large-scale intermarriage	Marital assimilation	Amalgamation
Development of sense of peoplehood based exclusively on host society	Identificational assimilation	None
Absence of prejudice	Attitude receptional assimilation	None
Absence of discrimination	Behavior receptional assimilation	None
Absence of value and power conflict	Civic assimilation	None

Indeed, even in the Sacramento Chapter of the Japanese American Citizens League a change is occurring. Within the past year a number of Sansei activists in their early thirties have emerged as leaders. Their changing attitude is nowhere better expressed than in the words of Frank Iwama, the new president, which were printed in the May, 1971, issue of the Sacramento JACL Newsletter:

After reading Bill Hosokawa's excellent book "Nisei—The Quiet Americans" and reflecting on the status of Japanese Americans today, I began to wonder if we can afford to continue to be characterized as "quiet Americans." At the outset, I don't want to give the impression that I advocate being vociferous just for the sake of making noise. However, I sincerely feel that we should make our position publicly known whenever and wherever the situation requires it.

Many Japanese Americans have fallen into the "middle class syndrome"—i.e., we feel that we have it made and that problems of discrimination are past history. This attitude, whether conscious or subconscious in nature, lulls us into accepting our present comfortable position as being a sign of total acceptance into the American society.

But why then, for example, are there so many Japanese Americans employed in the fields of education and government service and yet so few of them are serving in administrative capacities? This is particularly true in our state government where there are many Japanese American employees but too few Jerry Enomotos (our past National JACL President who was recently named as the Superintendent of the California Correctional Institution at Tehachapi). We have some of the most qualified employees in state government service, yet middle management is the zenith of their advancement. Like one state administrator recently told me, "I like Japanese employees because they are quiet, mind their own business and do their work." However, maybe these traits do not make the qualities of an administrator? My point is this: We have not eliminated all forms of discrimination against us! If it requires speaking out in order to make known the distinguished forms of discrimination being practiced today, then I advocate that we should speak out after carefully collecting the facts and studying the issues. How else can we rise above just being "good average citizens"? Our history shows that we are capable of being leaders as well as followers in the so-called white dominated society. Think about it!

Returning to our basic concern with acculturation rather than assimilation, however, we do see some very interesting changes in the Sansei generation with respect to the definition of success. As previously mentioned, the Sansei no longer see success solely in terms of middle-class respectability, and therein lies an interesting point. In our discussion of the Nisei generation, we emphasized the gap that separated the Nisei from their offspring. We further tried to indicate that a good part of the difference could be attributed to the ambition, the drive, the achievement, and the success of the Nisei themselves. The implications of this generation gap will be explored in some detail in the final chapters of this book. Perhaps in their own way, then, the Sansei are paying unconscious tribute to their parents and grandparents. For in a very real sense the mere fact that they are now in a position to ask an entirely new set of questions about the meaning of success serves only to emphasize the degree of success achieved by their forebears. Yet at the same time it will be premature to assume that the Sansei are "completely Americanized" as the Nisei and especially the Issei so easily assume. Indeed, as we will indicate in subsequent chapters, when the Sansei are administered various psychological tests and their scores matched with those of Caucasian Americans of comparable age and education, it becomes readily apparent that an appreciable residue of the more traditional Japanese culture still remains.

Chapter 9

The Incomplete Sentence Test*

The Incomplete Sentence Test was introduced by Payne in 1928 as a diagnostic technique. Since then, clinical psychologists and others have used it to evaluate attitudes and personality characteristics. The simplicity and effectiveness of the Incomplete Sentence Test are reported in the works of Burwen, Campbell, and Kidd (1956), Forer (1950), Holspopple and Miale (1954), Hanfman and Getzels (1953), Kline (1948), Rohde (1957), Rotter and Willerman (1947), and Sacks and Levy (1950).

In addition to the above, a number of writers have utilized the Incomplete Sentence Test in cross-cultural research. Chief among these are Phillips (1965) in his study of Thai personality, Aronoff (1967) in his study of the personality of cane cutters and fishermen in the West Indies, Rabin (1959), who compared Israeli and American children, and Rychlak, Mussen, and Bennett (1957), who studied the social adjustment of Japanese students in the United States.

The Incomplete Sentence Test was selected as a projective device in the study of changing attitudes in Japanese Americans in the Sacramento area for several reasons. At the beginning of the study the author had initially selected the Thematic Apperception Test as the most productive projective device that could be employed in a survey of this nature. Subsequent experience indicated that there were limitations in its use; chief of these limitations was time. The author and his wife soon discovered in

---

*Portions of this chapter were published under the title, "Persistence and Change in Japanese American Value Orientations," in *Ethos*, vol. 4, no. 1, Spring 1976. Reprinted by permission of the Regents of the University of California.

the Issei interviews that the completion of the basic interview form required between one and a half and two hours, after which there was insufficient time remaining to administer the Thematic Apperception Test. This necessitated returning at a subsequent date. It was at this time that another limitation became manifest—that is, the reluctance of many of the Issei to give full or complete stories of the pictures they saw displayed. Many complained of their lack of creativity and inability to make up stories. But perhaps even more important was the author's distinct impression that the Issei sensed that the test was more than simply one of story-telling aptitude. They knew it was personal and they knew they were revealing something of themselves, but they were never quite sure what it was.

It was at this time that the advantages of the Incomplete Sentence Test became apparent. Given the nature of the research problem and the desire to obtain a broad sample, it was felt that, although the Incomplete Sentence Test is a relatively superficial projective technique when compared to the Rorschach or TAT, it would nonetheless provide us with the information we desired on changing attitudes. Furthermore, it has the advantage of being easily administered and avoids the "pressure" component of many other projective tests in that one's response is open, obvious, and apparently innocuous. All that is required is that the individual complete the sentence in a manner that makes sense. That is, the second part should agree with the first. For example, if the incomplete sentence reads: "All children should . . .," the concluding part might be "be happy" or "be obedient." Frequently, when the hour was late, the test would be explained and then left with the person to be completed at his leisure.

In construction the test was designed to create situations in which the respondent would be able to read in answers which would reveal either the Japanese or American characteristics previously mentioned. The major Japanese characteristics are an emphasis on collectivity, duty and obligation, hierarchy, deference, and dependence. The major American characteristics are an emphasis on individualism, equality, a concern for rights and privileges, self-reliance, and self-assertion. Initially the test consisted of sixty incomplete sentences. It was soon apparent that this was far too many; the test itself frequently took more than an hour to complete. The list was then reduced to twenty-eight incomplete sentences which are discussed in subsequent pages. In order to measure both the Caucasian American response and the Japanese American response, the Incomplete Sentence Test was administered to a total of one hundred sixty-five persons. Of these, ninety-five were Japanese American and seventy were Caucasian Americans. The Japanese American sample consisted of ten male and ten female Issei, ten male and twenty female Nisei, and fifteen male and thirty female Sansei. The test was introduced and explained as a part of the interviewing of members of the Japanese community, and was given to those who expressed a willingness to cooperate.

The Caucasian American sample was composed of fifteen male and thirty female students in anthropology classes at Sacramento State College. In addition, ten male and fifteen female working-class adults in Western Pennsylvania were given the test. This was accomplished by mailing copies of the test to our relatives, who in turn distributed them to friends in the region.

The occupations of the majority of working-class males were mostly those associated with the steel industry, while almost all of the females were housewives. The mean age was 43 for the males and 40 for the females. As such, they provide a better age comparison group for the Nisei than do the Caucasian American students, who were in their mid-twenties. An additional purpose in utilizing the working-class group was to provide a basis for comparison in examining the stress placed on obedience, conformity, and authoritarianism in both the working class and among Japanese Americans. In this respect the Japanese Americans appear to have characteristics in common with both classes. When viewed from the perspective of the stress placed upon education, keeping up appearances, and a strong sense of duty and obligation, the Japanese Americans appear to be middle class. However, when seen in terms of the emphasis placed on conformity and obedience, the behavior seems to be more like that of the working class.

In his book, *Class and Conformity* (1969), Kohn has these observations:

Middle and working-class mothers share a common, but by
no means identical, set of values. There is considerable agreement in what is highly valued in the two social classes, happiness and such standards of conduct as honesty, consideration,
obedience, dependability, manners, and self-control are most
highly ranked for both boys and girls of this age. Standards of
conduct outrank all other requisites except happiness.

Although there is agreement on this broad level, middle-class
mothers differ from working-class mothers in which of these
values they emphasize. Middle-class mothers give higher priority to values that reflect *internal dynamics*—the child's own and
his emphatic concern for other people's. Specifically, they are
significantly more likely than are working-class mothers to
value happiness (in particular, for sons), consideration, self-
control, and curiosity. Working-class mothers, by contrast, give
higher priority to values that reflect *behavioral conformity*—
obedience and neatness.

It must be repeated that the class differences are variations on
a common theme, most of the highest rated values reflecting
respect for the rights of others. The middle-class variant focuses
on the internal processes of self-direction and emphatic understanding, while the working-class variant focuses on conformity
to externally defined standards. . . . Moreover, among fathers,
too, consideration and self-control are more highly valued in
the middle class, and obedience is more highly valued in the
working class. There are two additional class differences for
fathers: Dependability is more highly regarded in the middle
class, and the ability to defend oneself, in the working class.
(1969:21-22)

A further object in utilizing the working-class sample was to
provide a basis for comparison in examining the importance of
collectivity or collaterality in both the Japanese Americans and
Caucasian Americans. From personal experience with both
groups, it was obvious that there was a rather strong feeling of
familism they seemed to have in common. It was hoped that the
Incomplete Sentence Test would provide some insight into the
degree to which collectivity, collaterality, or familism was
emphasized in the two groups.

Because of the characteristics that the working-class sample
shared in common with the Japanese-American group, their
responses were also needed for another reason. That is, the author
felt that, if the Incomplete Sentence Test was a valid instrument
and if the sentences were carefully constructed and thereby

properly discriminated among the various groups, it should be possible to identify each group by means of a blind analysis. For that reason, the working-class sample was needed in order to have a group that resembled the Japanese Americans in a number of ways that the college students would not. In other words, an attempt was made to avoid making the blind analysis too easy.

Analysis of the
Incomplete Sentence Test

The initial step in conducting the blind analysis was to conceal any information that might reveal the identity of the respondent. This was done by placing a card over the biographical information at the top of the form. The forms were then very thoroughly mixed to prevent the possibility of their being identified as being a part of a series. That is, if one had correctly identified a Sansei, one might reasonably infer that the next form would also be that of a Sansei unless they were thoroughly mixed.

The next step was to read the response to each incomplete sentence and label it with a "J" for a Japanese response, an "A" for an American response, or an "E" for a neutral response that could be *either* Japanese or American. At the end of the form, the number of "J"'s, "A"'s, and "E"'s, was totaled and an attempt was made to deduce the identity of the respondent. In practice, the procedure gained in sophistication as the analysis continued. In order to discriminate the Sansei from the other groups, the "E" for *either* was modified to contain a small subscript "a" for American or "j" for Japanese. The purpose here was to indicate a response which, while it was not strictly either a Japanese or an American response, seemed to contain a little more of one component than of the other. On the basis of the various categories of responses, an attempt was then made to deduce whether the respondent was Issei, Nisei, Sansei, Caucasian working class, or Caucasian student. In order to add to the challenge, an attempt was also made to deduce the age and sex of the respondent. Usually the sex was apparent in both language usage and type of response. For example, females were more prone to emphasize feelings in interpersonal relations than males.

Overall, the results were most encouraging. Of the ninety-five Japanese Americans, only ten were mistaken for Caucasian

Americans. Of these ten, six were Sansei females who were mistaken for Caucasian students, three were Nisei females who were mistaken for working-class Caucasians, and one was an Issei male whose very brief responses led to his being mistaken for a Caucasian student.

In addition to the ten Japanese Americans mistaken for Caucasian Americans, another twenty-two were incorrectly identified as to their generation. Again, however, these were usually the older or younger members of their generation. In no case was a Sansei mistaken for an Issei or an Issei for a Sansei. Of the Sansei, seven males and five females were mistaken for Nisei. Among the Nisei, three older males and three older females were mistaken for Issei, while two younger females were mistaken for Sansei. Finally, among the Issei, two females were mistaken for Nisei.

With the Caucasian student sample the results were not so clear-cut. As a matter of fact, they were at first glance rather puzzling. In retrospect, the responses of the Caucasian students indicate more of an openness and consideration of the feelings of others, a dislike of overt competition, and more of a passive component with an emphasis on duty and obligation than had been expected. This was especially true of the females. Yet even the males displayed more of a concern for others than had been anticipated. This is not to imply that they favor only a passive conformity, but rather that there is a dislike in the exploitation of others for personal gain.

Nor does the increased concern for others imply a loss of personal autonomy. On the contrary, there was a realization that nonviolence and peace must first of all begin with oneself. It is a feeling that seems to be reflected in the youth culture in general, and in such sayings as "Let there be peace, and let it begin with me." One Caucasian female student expressed the importance of both individual autonomy and a concern for others in her answer to incompleté sentence 9: "A man's strongest obligation is to . . ." In her response she wrote:

> A man's strongest obligation is to realize when his attachments to any one group are fogging his responsibilities to all life on this planet. No one else is responsible for what he is when he dies except himself, his strongest obligation is to refine himself, for the benefit of others.

In all, of the seventy Caucasian Americans, a total of twenty-five were mistaken for Japanese Americans. Of the twenty-five, eighteen were students. In turn, twelve of the female students were mistaken for Sansei females, while four of the male Caucasian students were mistaken for Sansei males. The remaining two students were retired military and were mistaken for Nisei males largely on the basis of their emphasis on obedience, conformity, and duty that was apparent in their answers.

The seven other Caucasians mistaken for Japanese Americans were from the working class. Of these, three males and one female were mistaken for Nisei and one sixty-two-year-old female was mistaken for an Issei. In addition, two males were mistaken for Sansei.

In retrospect, it cannot be said that the final decision to categorize a given test as being Issei, Nisei, Sansei, Caucasian working class, or Caucasian student was made on the basis of a simple quantitative tabulation of responses. Frequently there would be a large number of "either" or neutral responses. In such a case, the other responses would have to be weighed one against the other.

For example, Table 9.1 indicates that a large percentage of both the Issei and the Caucasian working class believe that children should be obedient and respect parents and elders. Further, Table 9.6 indicates that both the Japanese Americans and the Caucasian working class place great importance on the family. On the other hand, however, there are considerable differences in the responses given in Table 9.5 It is here that the Japanese American emphasis on the repayment of a favor becomes manifest. The Caucasian Americans were much more prone to respond that a person should acknowledge the favor and thank the person, but there were far fewer who felt a compulsion to repay the favor. By the same token, considerable differences appear in Table 9.8, which reads, "When an elected official recommends a certain policy a good citizen should . . ." It is here that the Japanese emphasis on hierarchy and deference becomes apparent. Both the Issei and Nisei males were more disposed to assume that the official was correct, while the Sansei and Caucasian males indicated that the policy should be studied carefully before support was given.

The method used, then, was one of a process of elimination.

If a given test contained a large number of "either" responses, the test was carefully reviewed in order to determine those answers that provided the greatest contrast. For example, if the test contained a number of responses emphasizing obedience and familism, a check was made to see if there were also indications of both deference and an emphasis on duty and obligation. If the latter two characteristics were missing and there was instead an emphasis on individualism and rights and privileges, the assumption was made that there was more of an American working class component than a Japanese one. The differences were frequently very subtle. For example, in response to the incomplete sentence, "When someone does him a favor he . . . ," a working-class male completed it by adding" . . . is appreciative and should extend favors as freely as he takes them." This response was correctly identified as being Caucasian American for the major reason that, although appreciation is shown and reciprocity is implied, there is no indication whatsoever of a debt or compulsion to repay the favor.

Perhaps at this point the question might be raised as to the degree of involvement by the subject in the test. In other words, do the answers really reflect his own thoughts, attitudes, and values, or is he simply freely fabricating with someone else in mind. From a clinical point of view, the authorities cited at the beginning of the chapter appear to be satisfied as to its validity and believe that the individual really is involved.

For our purpose here it seems reasonable to assume that the respondents were indeed involved and the test does reflect the changes in attitudes and values we predicted it would. For example, Table 9.17 lists the answers to the incomplete sentence: "What he is really afraid of is . . ." A glance at the table indicates that the answers reflect both generational and cultural differences. These are especially evident in the Issei responses, which disclose a fear of illness and death.

Given the advanced age of the Issei, it is to be expected that there would be a concern for health. What is both surprising and revealing, however, was the reported fear of fire. For the purpose of identifying an Issei reply, the answer was an unmistakable disclosure and immediately revealed an Issei response. Here again is an example of an identification made on the basis of a broader familiarity with Japanese culture than is shown in the characteristics listed. By that is meant that even though it may be argued that the fear of fire is an understandable and perhaps even a justifiable fear in older people, the point to be made is that the fear of fire is especially pronounced in Japanese culture. Given the nature of Japanese housing construction, congested dwellings, and the traditional use of open braziers for cooking and heating, the fear is a realistic and everpresent one. It is a fear that is incorporated in both art form and folk sayings, such as, "The four things to fear are earthquake, thunder, fire, and father."

The author has frequently been struck by the realism with which fire scenes are portrayed in Japanese movies. Not only is there an attempt to convey the physical intensity of the heat and flames, both visually and audibly, there is often a portrayal of the emotional impact of the conflagration on the people involved. One additional observation is that the fire scenes in American and British films are more commonly presented as taking place at a distance, while Japanese films make frequent use of closeups and attempt to involve the audience in the actual experiencing of the fire itself.

Overall, then, the answers do seem to disclose a sufficient degree of involvement in the test to indicate that the respondents were in fact the subject of their replies and were not answering with another person in mind. While it may have been possible to give a response to an isolated question with someone else in mind, from a psychological point of view it is quite difficult to sustain such a role throughout. Further, as previously indicated, the incomplete sentences were so constructed that there were very few that necessitated a response that might be too personally revealing. Even here, however, when respondents were assured of anonymity, replies were frequently given that were more personal than were required by the question. For example, in reply to the incomplete sentence, "The deepest emotional relationship is between . . .," one married female Caucasian student responded, "The deepest emotional relationship is between a husband and wife and is best expressed by sexual intercourse."

Of the total number of twenty-eight incomplete sentences, it was anticipated that not all would be equally discriminating. Such, indeed, proved to be the case. Of the twenty-eight, seventeen were found to be the most discriminating and will be discussed in greater detail in subsequent pages. The remaining eleven, while not so highly discriminating as the others, frequently provided useful information during the blind analysis. For example, the incomplete sentence, "People who never show their feelings . . .," discriminated very poorly among all of the groups. Typical responses were such as: ". . . will probably get ulcers," and ". . . really have hang-ups." Nevertheless, there were two replies by Issei which were revealing and were correctly identified as being Japanese. One Issei male responded, ". . .are men, strong and respected." The other, an Issei female, answered, "Nobody likes to show their feelings."

The eleven incomplete sentences that discriminated poorly among the five groups are listed as follows:

1. The best way to treat someone working for you . . .
5. People who never show their feelings . . .
7. The ideal occupation or job . . .
10. It is always best to listen . . .
11. When a child brings home a note from school that he has been disobedient . . .
13. In times of personal trouble it is best to . . .
14. A child should be disciplined at once if he . . .
18. The worst way to treat a subordinate . . .
19. A really close friend is one who . . .
26. His greatest ambition is . . .
27. When his boss told him to get to work . . .

Again, it should be emphasized that, while the above sentences did not elicit replies that could be categorized as being more typical of one group than of another, they frequently provided clues as to the identity of the respondent. One final illustration of this is to be found in the answers given to incomplete sentence 27: "When his boss told him to get to work . . ." Here the typical answer was simply, ". . . he went to work." Occasionally, however, a qualifying word or phrase would be added, such as "he grumbled, and went to work," or "he sighed and went to work." These answers, while not in themselves sufficiently revealing to discriminate among Sansei, working class, or student groups, would nevertheless indicate that the respondent was probably not an Issei or Nisei.

Those incomplete sentences that provided a higher degree of discrimination among the five groups are as follows:

1. All children should . . .
2. The most important lesson that parents can teach a child . . .
3. The best time of life is . . .
6. In the long run a person is better off if he depends on . . .
8. When someone does him a favor he . . .
9. A man's strongest obligation is to . . .
12. When his boss asked him to work on a day he had planned to go fishing . . .
15. When an elected official recommends a certain policy, a good citizen should . . .
16. The deepest emotional relationship is between . . .
17. When a neighbor reported to her that her child was misbehaving, she . . .
20. When he thinks of his mother . . .
21. If a person finds himself in difficulty . . .
22. While seated on a crowded bus he noticed his boss standing nearby and . . .
23. When he heard that his child had been threatened by a neighborhood bully, he . . .
24. When he thinks of his father . . .
25. When his superior gave him an order that he thought was wrong . . .
28. What he is really afraid of is . . .

Following the blind analysis, each of the twenty-eight sentences was then independently analyzed to ascertain if there were discernible group differences. This was accomplished by first separating the tests into the five major groups and then recording each individual's response to every incomplete sentence for each separate group. The next step was to organize the answers into various categories. Usually this was not too difficult in any one group because there would be a certain amount of repetition in the answers. However, when an attempt was made to establish broad categories which would be applicable to all groups, it became immediately apparent that many of the intergroup subtleties would be lost. On the other hand, an attempt to preserve the subtleties led to an expansion of all categories and therefore a consequent reduction in meaningful percentages.

What is presented in Tables 9.1 through 9.17 is the result of numerous attempts at rephrasing to create categories of response that were both sufficiently broad and precise. The intention throughout has been to preserve those distinctions which appeared to discriminate one group from another. For example, in Table 9.6, in reply to the sentence, "A man's strongest obligation. . .," it would have been relatively simple to group most of the responses into four or five categories such as "his duty," "his family," "himself," "others," and "God." While these are not necessarily incorrect and are defensible, they do lack the discrimination and perhaps also the subtleties that are provided by the additional categories.

Incomplete sentence 1, "All children should . . ." The percentage distribution on incomplete sentence 1, "All children should . . .," is contained in Table 9.1. The table indicates that eleven categories were used. In turn, these categories are listed largely in the order they appeared during the analysis of data. The order of analysis was the same as appears below the table headings: Issei, Nisei, Sansei, Caucasian working class, and Caucasian students.

The table discloses a number of similarities among Japanese Americans and also some significant differences. All three generations reveal an emphasis placed on respect for parents and elders, although there is a progressive decline from Issei to Sansei. Likewise, as anticipated, there was a correspondingly high emphasis on obedience and respect in the working class sample.

Similarly, the Japanese American emphasis on achievement through education is reflected in the responses of all three generations. The importance of education was also indicated in the working class answers, but with a lesser frequency. Interestingly, there was no mention of education by the Caucasian students. This may be a reflection both of their present status as students and of a largely middle-class background. By that is meant that while education is seen as a necesary prerequisite for a career, its attainment is more often thought of as being an accepted and natural progression in the maturation process rather than an object of choice or something to be striven for.

A further distinction is to be found in the emergence of an interest among the Nisei and Sansei in the child as an individual with certain needs and even rights. While all groups stressed the need for love, that need was frequently seen in conjunction with an equally strong need for security in the Nisei, Sansei, and Caucasian groups. Both the Issei and working-class females, however, were more often disposed to see love tempered with discipline than were the other groups.

Table 9.1

**Percentage Distribution on Incomplete Sentence 1,
All Children Should . . ., for Total Sample**

Category of response	Issei		Nisei		Sansei		Caucasian working class		Caucasian students	
	M.	F.	M.	F.	M.	F.	M.	F.	M.	F.
Be obedient	20	20	10	10	10	10	20	20	12	3
Respect parents and elders	60	40	40	35	15	27	40	20	0	0
Receive a good education	10	0	20	15	15	3	0	3	0	0
Study hard	10	20	10	0	0	6	10	0	0	0
Be loved and disciplined	0	20	10	0	5	6	0	20	0	6
Be given love and security	0	0	0	15	5	16	10	20	20	30
Be happy	0	0	0	0	20	10	0	14	8	0
Develop own talents	0	0	10	5	25	6	10	0	20	20
Explore childhood	0	0	0	0	5	6	0	0	30	20
Be treated as individuals	0	0	0	5	0	3	10	0	0	6
Respect others' rights	0	0	0	15	0	6	0	0	9	14
Total percentage	100	100	100	100	100	99	100	100	99	99
Number of respondents	10	10	10	20	15	30	10	15	15	30

The emerging interest in the child as an individual becomes apparent in the emphasis the Nisei and Sansei place on the child's being given an opportunity to develop his own talents. At the same time there was a rather curious response of 20 per cent of the Sansei males and 10 per cent of the females that children should "be happy"—a response that was also indicated by 14 per cent of the working-class females and 8 per cent of the male students. On the face of it, the answer seems to indicate a lack of immediate goals for the child and is apparently a less precise formulation of the "explore childhood" category that was given by 10 per cent of the male and 20 per cent of the female students.

In reading these last responses, one receives the definite impression that there has been a change, or even a reaction to a forced achievement orientation. This was especially apparent in the replies given by the male students. This is not to imply that the students are without ambition or incapable of self-discipline, but rather there is more a respect for the child's autonomy and a belief that such achievement should be a result of the child's volition rather than being forced upon him. For example, a Caucasian male student, aged twenty-four, answered: "All children should have the opportunity of being a child and enjoying childhood, for we are only young once." Also a female Caucasian student, aged twenty-four, replied: "All children should be given the opportunity to express their individuality and not be labeled as an adult perceives them." Another student, a Caucasian male, aged twenty-one, answered, "All children should be allowed to feel and live the uninhibitive qualities which can only be felt and lived when one is a child." Finally, the above sentiments were shared by a more mature student, a Caucasian females, aged forty-three: "All children should be allowed the freedom to be children, to utilize their imagination, curiosity, and be encouraged, and guided (gently) into individualistic achievements."

Yet, for all the emphasis on autonomy and individualism, there was also an expression of the need to respect the rights of others. This is indicated in both the Nisei and the student groups, and can be seen in such responses as that given by a Caucasian male student, aged twenty-six: "All children should be given every opportunity to develop fully their respective potentials and individualities in such ways as to fulfill themselves without interference with the rights of others."

Incomplete sentence 2, "The most important lesson parents can teach a child . . ." The second incomplete sentence, "The most important lesson parents can teach a child . . .," in many ways supplements and complements the first. As Table 9.2

indicates, there was again an emphasis on obedience, respect, and proper behavior in the Japanese Americans. There were significant differences, however. When analyzed by each generation, it can be seen that the Issei are more apt to stress conformity. This is apparent in the emphasis placed on obedience, proper behavior, respect for authority, honesty and sincerity, and self-discipline.

The Nisei, while also emphasizing conformity, did not place so much stress on obedience, proper behavior, and respect for authority as they did on honesty and sincerity. There is also apparent in the Nisei response both a drive to do one's best and a concern for self-discipline and the rights of others.

The Sansei males were equally as concerned with obedience and respect as they were with self-reliance. The Sansei females, on the other hand, were apparently much less self-assertive. They were more apt to emphasize a respect for others and were more concerned with self-acceptance. Overall, they placed as much emphasis on conformity as did the males, but they stressed different aspects of it. While the male responses appeared to be more concerned with parental authority, the females were more diffuse in that they expected conformity to extend to outside authority as well.

The Caucasian working class also believe that children should conform and place about as much stress on it as do the Nisei and Sansei, but in different areas of conformity. Again, there is a male-female difference, with the males emphasizing obedience, respect for authority, and honesty and sincerity. The females stressed obedience and respect and proper behavior. The largest difference, however, came in the emphasis placed on a respect for others. Usually this was given in terms of obeying the Golden Rule and is apparently a reflection of the less assertive female role.

The male-female responses were different in other areas involving independence or self-assertiveness. Thus the males were more prone to emphasize self-reliance, self-acceptance, and self-respect than were the females.

With the Caucasian student sample there can be seen a continuation of the previously mentioned emphasis on an openness to others and a respect for the rights of others. At the same time, stress was placed on personal autonomy or self-reliance, which was expressed in self-fulfillment in the males and self-respect and self-acceptance in the females. Again, with the exception of 13 per cent of the males, there was little concern with conformity among the students.

Table 9.2
Percentage Distribution on Incomplete Sentence 2, The Most Important Lesson Parents Can Teach . . ., for Total Sample

Category of response	Issei		Nisei		Sansei		Caucasian working class		Caucasian students	
	M.	F.	M.	F.	M.	F.	M.	F.	M.	F.
Obedience and respect	20	10	0	10	28	12	10	16	13	0
Proper behavior	50	10	20	0	0	2	0	8	0	0
Be a good student	10	0	0	0	7	2	0	8	0	0
Always do your best	0	10	20	10	7	5	0	0	0	0
Respect for authority	0	30	10	0	0	11	10	0	0	0
Honesty and sincerity	10	30	30	45	8	8	20	0	0	0
Self-discipline	10	10	0	0	0	2	0	0	0	0
Self-reliance	0	0	10	20	28	5	30	17	13	24
Respect for others	0	0	10	5	14	31	10	50	33	34
Self-acceptance	0	0	0	0	7	17	10	0	0	13
Self-respect	0	0	0	0	0	2	10	0	7	7
Openness to others	0	0	0	5	0	2	0	0	20	12
Self-fulfillment	0	0	0	0	0	0	0	0	13	7
Personal happiness	0	0	0	5	0	0	0	0	0	0
Total percentage	100	100	99	99	99	99	100	99	99	100
Number of respondents	10	10	10	20	15	30	10	15	15	30

In all of the above responses, then, there is a perceptible change among the various groups. Whereas the Issei were almost unanimously concerned with the various aspects of conformity,.

we see a change emerging in the Nisei and Sansei generations in the direction of lessened concern with conformity and an increasing interest in personal autonomy and a respect for others. This is not to imply that such characteristics do not exist among the Issei but only that they did not receive the same emphasis. Furthermore, the Nisei are much more concerned with honesty and sincerity than are the other groups. The working class respondents also emphasize conformity, but this area is far outweighed by the greater stress placed on self-reliance and a respect for others.

Finally, the students appear to be little concerned with teaching their children to conform. They are more deeply interested in the child's self-fulfillment and in his openness and respect for others. In this regard they are perhaps a little closer to the Sansei than to the other groups.

Incomplete sentence 3, "The best time of life . . ." The third incomplete sentence was designed to provide insight into several areas. Given the previously cited importance on *amaeru* (Doi 1962:132), or the inculcation of dependency needs in the child by means of early pampering or gratification, it was hoped that the responses might reflect this in part by emphasizing early childhood as the best time of life. Further, it was hoped that the sentence might indicate the achievement drive of the Nisei and the orientation towards the present that is characteristic of the working class. To a certain extent, these expectations were met.

Table 9.3 discloses group and generational differences which, although not conclusive, are nevertheless revealing. In the Issei generation there are male-female differences in responses. The only reference to childhood is to be found in the 30 per cent of the males who mentioned school time and the 10 per cent of the females who mentioned early childhood. Among the females a great amount of satisfaction was derived from raising children—a satisfaction, moreover, that is to be found with almost the same frequency among working-class females.

In the Nisei generation, however, we do find some differences. Fully 40 per cent of the males gave school time as the best time of life, while 20 per cent of the males and 25 per cent of the females mentioned early childhood. Further, the achievement orientation of the Nisei is apparent in the 10 per cent of the males and 20 per cent of the females who mentioned that the best time of life is when one is accomplishing one's goals.

Given the comparative youth of the Sansei, it is to be expected that they would place a greater importance on youthful activities. And indeed this proved to be the case. However, there were a number of responses that indicate both an enjoyment of the present and a belief that there is no one "best" time of life. Still, 20 per cent of the Sansei females stated that early childhood was the best time in life. Similarly, 25 per cent of the Sansei males indicated that the more imprecise time of "youth" was the best time of life. It is possible that they were including childhood in this classification, but that cannot be said for certain.

The working-class group seemed to be concerned with the present and with their families. The latter is apparent in the number of males, and especially of females, who indicated that the best time of life was while raising children. In this regard they certainly differ from the student group, who resembled the Sansei in several respects. The student group was different, however, in the greater importance they placed on being truly alive. Like the Sansei, they were more apt to think of any time or all of life as being important rather than any one particular period. Some difference was seen in the phrasing. The Sansei would emphasize happiness, while the Caucasian student group emphasized being alive.

In classifying the above responses, it is difficult to reach conclusions that could not be almost as easily attributed to age rather than culture. Yet there are differences. For example, the Nisei and working-class groups are similar in age but differ markedly in what they emphasize. Again, in comparing the Caucasian with the Japanese American groups, it does seem that the Japanese Americans attach greater importance to the early childhood and youthful periods than do the Caucasians. Finally, although these differences are not exceptional, they are in the predicted direction.

Incomplete sentence 6, "A person is better off if he depends on . . ." The sixth incomplete sentence, the responses to which are classified in Table 9.4, was designed to measure collectivity and self-reliance. Based upon the previously cited importance of collectivity in Japanese society and the corresponding emphasis on self-reliance in American society, it was predicted that the Japanese Americans would place greater emphasis on depending on others especially the family, than the Caucasian sample. On the other hand, the Caucasians were expected to disclose a greater emphasis on self-reliance, although it was anticipated that the working-class sample would also emphasize a dependence on the family, but perhaps to a lesser extent than the Japanese American groups.

Table 9.3

Percentage Distribution on Incomplete Sentence 3, The Best Time of Life . . ., for Total Sample

Category of response	Issei		Nisei		Sansei		Caucasian working class		Caucasian students	
	M.	F.	M.	F.	M.	F.	M.	F.	M.	F.
School time	30	0	40	5	5	3	0	0	0	6
When raising children	10	50	0	10	0	6	20	42	0	3
Middle age	30	0	0	0	0	0	0	0	0	3
Retirement age	20	20	0	0	0	0	0	0	0	0
Present	0	10	10	5	10	17	40	33	12	16
Anytime	0	0	0	5	10	10	0	6	6	3
When you are happy	0	10	0	10	20	17	10	0	6	0
Early childhood	0	10	20	25	5	20	0	6	6	6
Youth	0	0	10	0	25	6	10	6	0	0
Young adult	10	0	10	10	15	17	0	0	26	10
When independent	0	0	0	0	5	3	0	0	6	10
When accomplishing goals	0	0	10	20	5	0	10	6	6	3
All of life	0	0	0	10	0	0	10	0	12	20
When truly alive	0	0	0	0	0	0	0	0	20	19
Total percentage	100	100	100	100	100	99	100	99	100	99
Number of respondents	10	10	10	20	15	30	10	15	15	30

Overall, the responses were in the predicted direction although there were surprises. Among the Issei, for example, Table 9.4 indicates that, while there was the predicted emphasis on the family, there was also a strong self-reliance theme in the males. Indeed, if one considers those responses in which primary reliance was placed on the *individual himself* first, and "others" or "family" second, then fully 70 per cent of the Issei males disclose some degree of emphasis on self-reliance. However, if one restricts se f-reliance to those responses in which sole reliance was placed on the individual, then this number is reduced to 40 per

Table 9.4

Percentage Distribution on Incomplete Sentence 6,
A Person Is Better Off if He Depends . . .,
for Total Sample

Category of response	Issei		Nisei		Sansei		Caucasian working class		Caucasian students	
	M.	F.	M.	F.	M.	F.	M.	F.	M.	F.
Religion	10	30	0	5	0	0	0	13	7	3
His children	10	0	0	0	0	0	0	0	0	0
Himself	30	10	50	35	46	50	30	53	27	42
His own ability	10	0	20	25	33	16	30	7	33	16
Those he respects	0	0	10	10	7	0	0	0	0	0
Himself and others	20	0	0	10	7	10	30	0	33	30
Friends and family	0	10	20	15	0	0	0	7	0	3
His family	10	10	0	0	0	7	0	13	0	0
Himself and family	10	40	0	0	7	15	0	0	0	6
Steady work	0	0	0	0	0	0	10	7	0	0
Total percentage	100	100	100	100	100	99	100	100	100	100
Number of respondents	10	15	10	20	15	30	10	15	15	30

cent. Of the remaining male responses, 50 per cent involve dependence on others, especially the family. Reliance on the family increases in the female Issei to 60 per cent, although even here there was an expression of *reliance on oneself* first and the family or others second.

While initially surprising, the emphasis on self-reliance and the family is in perfect accord with the earlier discussion in Chapter 3 on the *ie* ideal. It will be recalled that Johnson (1962) postulates that the differential socialization of the *jisannan,* or non-household successors, helped to produce in them an orientation toward achievement and self-reliance. Moreover, our biographical data indicate that the majority of the Issei we interviewed were indeed *jisannan* and not *chōnan,* or household successors, in Japan. Yet the continued emphasis on the family that appears repeatedly throughout their responses would also indicate that Issei would wish to preserve the *ie* ideal in this country.

In the Nisei generation there is an increase in the number of self-reliance responses, especially in the males. Table 9.4 discloses that fully 70 per cent of the males indicate that it would be best if they depended on themselves or on their own ability rather than on friends or the family. With the females this was only slightly reduced to 60 per cent: however, 10 per cent indicated that one should depend on oneself first and then on others.

The emphasis on self-reliance increases to 79 per cent in the Sansei males and 66 per cent in the females. Indeed, in an additional 14 per cent of the males and 26 per cent of the females the responses were so worded as to indicate that one should rely on oneself first and then on the family and others second.

In the working-class group, however, there are several differences. Sixty per cent of both males and females indicated that it would be best to depend on themselves or their own ability. Another 30 per cent of the males stated that they should depend on themselves and others, while 20 per cent of the females indicated that they should depend on friends and family. The working-class concern with economic security can be seen in the 10 per cent of the males and 7 per cent of the females who responded that a man is better off if he depends on steady work.

In the Caucasian student groups, approximately 60 per cent of males and females gave responses indicating self-reliance. Moreover, an additional 33 per cent of the male and 30 per cent of the female responses were so phrased as to indicate an awareness that, while self-reliance is important, a person should not let his self-reliance close him off from other people. As one thirty-year-old female stated:

In the long run a person is better off if he depends on himself as much as possible, but with the expectation and attitude that others will help and cooperate with him. It is better not to weigh heavily upon others, but if necessary to be dependent to be graceful about it. People who cannot accept help from other people are not showing love for other people.

In all, 93 per cent of the Caucasian student males and 88 per cent of the females gave responses indicating major self-reliance themes. This is to be contrasted to 70 per cent of the Issei males, 70 per cent of the Nisei males, 93 per cent of the Sansei males, and 90 per cent of the working-class males. With the exception of the Issei generation, the female percentages of the other groups were only slightly below those given for the males.

Finally, while it is unwise to generalize too broadly on the basis of one incomplete sentence, it was the distinct impression of the author, in analyzing the tests, that the Japanese American responses indicate a narrower range of affiliation or collectivity than do the working-class and especially the Caucasian student samples. By that is meant that the Japanese Americans were more apt to indicate that one should depend more on close friends and family rather than others when one was not being self-reliant. Some support for this is to be found in Tables 9.6, 9.9, 9.11, and especially 9.12, which indicates that the Japanese Americans were more prone to seek help from their families in time of difficulty than were the Caucasian groups.

Incomplete sentence 8, "When somebody does him a favor . . . ' The percentage distribution on the categories of response to incomplete sentence 8 is to be found in Table 9.5. This sentence was designed to measure the Japanese emphasis on obligation, or making returns for all favors received, that had been mentioned previously.

It was here, however, that one of the minor difficulties of the incomplete sentence test became manifest. That is the tendency of many individuals to give an abbreviated rather than a full response. For example, as Table 9.5 indicates, many Nisei simply answered that when someone does him a favor he gratefully appreciates it—thus leaving up in the air the question of reciprocity or an obligation to repay the favor. Implicit in the reply is the apparent understanding that one has an obligation to repay the favor. From personal experience the author can testify that it would be a most unusual Nisei who would not feel such an obligation to reciprocate. Indeed, it will be recalled that in Table 6, 90 per cent of the Nisei, male and female, reported that the principle that one must make returns for all kindness received was stressed by the Issei when the Nisei were growing up. Table 9.5 discloses that the Issei undoubtedly believed what they preached in that fully 80 per cent of the Issei males and 90 per cent of the females gave replies which included a definite obligation to repay a favor.

Table 9.5
Percentage Distribution on Incomplete Sentence 8,
When Someone Does Him a Favor . . ., for Total Sample

Category of response	Issei		Nisei		Sansei		Caucasian working class		Caucasian students	
	M.	F.	M.	F.	M.	F.	M.	F.	M.	F.
Should thank him	10	0	0	10	14	10	40	12	0	13
Obligation to repay	70	60	20	30	21	6	0	0	14	17
Gratefully appreciate it	10	10	60	30	8	16	30	48	14	23
Gratitude and obligation to repay	10	30	10	30	28	20	0	0	7	0
Reciprocates if possible	0	0	10	0	28	15	0	16	21	6
Appreciate and perhaps repay	0	0	0	0	0	10	30	24	7	3
Accept without obligation	0	0	0	0	0	0	0	0	16	27
Returns it	0	0	0	0	0	16	0	0	14	0
Passes it on	0	0	0	0	0	6	0	0	6	10
Total percentage	100	100	100	100	99	99	100	100	99	99
Number of respondents	10	10	11	20	15	30	10	15	15	30

The categories of responses were arranged in order to indicate the various degrees of response. These ranged from a simple expression of thanks through the various combinations and degrees of gratitude and obligation to a rather straightforward statement of reciprocity devoid of any sense of obligation.

Again, as can be seen in Table 9.5, there is a very strong feeling of an obligation to repay a favor in the three generations of Japanese Americans. There are also discernible differences. For example, whereas the Issei were rather forthright in their expressions of a need for repayment and a feeling of gratitude, the Nisei were more apt to stress gratitude first and then to mention repayment. This tendency continues in the Sansei generation, although the Sansei replies lack the more compulsive feeling of obligation that characterizes the Issei and Nisei responses. For example, the Sansei were more likely to add that a favor should be returned, if possible, or that the recipient should appreciate the favor and perhaps repay it when he could. Similarly, the number of replies devoid of either a deep sense of gratitude or obligation increased. More of the Sansei responses were simple expressions of thanks or reciprocity, as in the replies of several that when someone does him a favor he "thanks them"; others simply answered that he "returns it."

The responses of the two Caucasian groups were most interesting, especially those of the working class. While the working class indicated that appreciation should be shown to anyone who does a favor, there were no expressions of a deep obligation to repay the favor. Reciprocity, when implied, was usually expressed in such a way as to indicate that the other person had a favor coming if he ever needed it. There was none of the compulsion, or *giri,* with its precise equivalent repayments within a given time period, that Benedict (1946:116) found so characteristic of Japanese society.

The Caucasian student replies, on the other hand, disclose more of an obligation to repay a favor than those of the working class, but the total responses indicate less of an overall obligation to repay than any of the Japanese American groups. Indeed, approximately one-third of the students answered in such a way as to indicate that they had either no obligation to the one who had done the favor or that they should, in turn, pass the favor on to another. Typical responses here were as follows. The first, from a female, aged twenty-two: "When someone does him a favor he should accept it with grace and a 'thank you.' He should not feel obligated to run out and return the favor, but if a chance does arise it would be nice if you did."

Another response, also from a female, aged twenty-two, indicates that while there is an implied reciprocity there is little of a compulsive nature in it: "When someone does him a favor he thanks him formally but, more importantly, he shows his appreciation by appropriate nonverbal behavior, and does not constantly worry about repaying the favor, just naturally helps out when the time comes."

A final response, this time by a female, aged thirty, reveals not only the equality and openness to others that was mentioned previously as being a characteristic of the student group but also a lessening emphasis on the type of achievement that is attained at the expense of others: "When someone does him a favor he should accept gracefully with the attitude that it is all right for him as a person to be cherished and honored, just as it is a good thing for others to be treated in this way. There is the realization some people think of this as a barter, however this is one area where a person can prevail if they are persistent to have their own view of things made known. A favor should best be passed on in some form quickly so it can multiply love and not let it atrophy. A favor should never be refused, it might be like refusing the person his well being."

Finally, as Table 9.5 clearly indicates, when compared to the Caucasian groups the Japanese Americans still retain a strong sense of obligation to repay a favor. This sense of obligation, however, is undergoing a change in the three generations, and although still strong in the Sansei generation it lacks the compulsive quality that was found in the Issei and Nisei responses. Further, the attenuation of a compulsive need to repay is reflected in the answers given to question 41 on the Ethnic Identity Questionnaire, which will be discussed in a subsequent chapter. Question 41 reads, "I believe that, 'He who does not repay a debt of gratitude cannot claim to be noble.'" The replies are given on a five-point scale: Strongly agree (5), agree (4), undecided (3), disagree (2), and strongly disagree (1). The mean score of the three responses to this question was as follows: Issei, 4.27; Nisei, 3.58; and Sansei, 3.31.

Incomplete sentence 9, "A man's strongest obligation . . ."
The ninth incomplete sentence was designed to measure duty and
obligation collectivity, and individualism. Table 9.6 gives the
percentage distribution of the various categories of responses.
Again, it can be seen from the table that it would have been
possible to reduce these categories from twelve to perhaps four or
five. However, it was felt that such a consolidation would
subsequently blur the various and sometimes subtle differences by
which the various groups were distinguished during the blind
analysis. For example, the last category—"those depending on
him"—could with some justification be classified in the same
category as "his family" or even "his family and friends." Yet to
do so wou d be to distort the intent of the respondents, which was
to include a larger number of people or a broader category than
that implied by the family group alone.

Table 9.6 immediately reveals the emphasis placed on the
family or the group among Japanese Americans. Further, it
reveals the sense of duty previously mentioned. Both the Issei and
Nisei, but in particular one-half of the Issei males, replied that a
man's strongest obligation was to do his duty. This is not to
maintain that they were not equally concerned with family, but
only to suggest that family obligations could also be included in
the general emphasis on duty. Familial replies are quite strong in
all three generations of Japanese Americans, with fully 80 per
cent of Issei females, 70 per cent of the Nisei males and females,
and 56 per cent of the Sansei males and 67 per cent of the Sansei
females giving such replies.

In the Nisei and Sansei generations, however, there are
indications of an obligation to oneself or to an individual's own
inner convictions. This tendency is quite strong in the Sansei
generation, where 40 per cent of the males and 25 percent of the
females gave such replies.

The responses of the working class were as anticipated. Here
some 60 per cent of the males and 73 per cent of the females
indicated a strong feeling of obligation to the family. Another
characteristic of the working class became manifest—that is, the
religious orientation, or a reliance upon God.

In contrast to the other groups, the Caucasian students gave
fewer "family" responses and more "individual" responses. That

is, there was more stress placed on obligation that one had to oneself or one's inner convictions than to the family. Further, when obligations to others were stated these were not expressed in terms of the family alone but rather in terms of "his fellow man" or "those depending on him."

Table 9.6

Percentage Distribution on Incomplete Sentence 9, A Man's Strongest Obligation . . ., for Total Sample

Category of response	Issei M.	Issei F.	Nisei M.	Nisei F.	Sansei M.	Sansei F.	Caucasian working class M.	Caucasian working class F.	Caucasian students M.	Caucasian students F.
Do his duty	50	0	10	5	0	0	0	0	0	3
His family	30	30	30	30	49	47	40	40	7	20
His family and friends	10	10	20	5	0	7	0	7	0	0
His parents	0	30	10	25	0	0	0	0	0	0
Himself and his family	0	10	10	5	7	13	10	26	0	11
Himself and friends	10	0	0	0	0	8	0	0	13	0
His family and country	0	10	0	5	0	0	10	0	0	0
Himself	0	0	10	10	20	13	10	13	33	33
His inner convictions	0	10	10	10	20	12	10	0	13	8
Benefit his fellow man	0	0	0	5	4	0	0	0	7	10
God	0	0	0	0	0	0	20	13	5	6
Those depending on him	0	0	0	0	0	0	0	0	21	3
Total percentage	100	100	100	100	100	100	100	99	99	99
Number of respondents	10	10	10	20	15	30	10	15	15	30

The ninth incomplete sentence, then, does reflect both the Japanese American and working class concern with the family. Undoubtedly, part of the contrast with the Caucasian student group is a result of the larger percentage of married respondents in the Issei, Nisei, and working-class groups. However, in both the Sansei and student groups the proportion of married was about the same—that is, about one-third. Nevertheless, there were significant differences in the other instruments used, which corroborates the greater emphasis placed on the family in the Sansei group. For example, as will be discussed in detail later, statements 1 and 29 in the Contrasting Values Survey disclose that, while the Sansei do not place the same emphasis on the importance of the family as do the Issei and Nisei, the degree of importance is still greater than that of the Caucasian student group. Statement 1 read, "In the long run the greatest satisfaction comes from being with one's family." The possible responses were strongly agree (5), agree (4), undecided (3), disagree (2), and strongly disagree (1). The mean response for the total survey was: Issei, 4.33; Nisei, 4.38; Sansei, 3.69; and Caucasian students, 3.52. Statement 29 read, "A man can never let himself down without letting down his family at the same time." Again, for the total survey the mean response was as follows: Issei, 3.85; Nisei, 3.97; Sansei, 3.31; and Caucasian students, 2.87.

The above indicates both an overall progression in the direction of the Caucasian student response and a retention of an emphasis on the family group and a feeling of duty or obligation towards it.

Incomplete sentence 12, "When his boss asked him to work on a day he had planned to go fishing, he . . ." Incomplete sentence 12 was included to measure the conflict between duty and obligation and rights and privileges. Table 9.7 discloses rather clearly the gradation from a strong obligation to work to an equally strong desire to go fishing. Further, there is a discernible pattern of such responses in the three generations of Japanese Americans. The strong emphasis on duty and obligation and deference to one's superior is especially apparent in the Issei generation, in which 90 per cent of the males and 90 per cent of the females answered in such a way as to indicate that there was no alternative. "If the boss asks you to work, you work," was the reply one gave.

The Nisei were almost as strongly disposed to answer as though there was no choice. However, there was less of a feeling of compulsion and more a sense of helping the boss out in a tight situation. One Nisei male, aged fifty-seven, answered, "He should work to help out." Another Nisei, aged forty, answered in such a way as to suggest almost an *oyabun-kobun* relationship with his boss, "You should remember that another time will come to go fishing, and besides your boss will always stand by you in time of need."

Table 9.7

Percentage Distribution on Incomplete Sentence 12, When His Boss Asked Him to Work . . ., for Total Sample

Category of response	Issei		Nisei		Sansei		Caucasian working class		Caucasian students	
	M.	F.	M.	F.	M.	F.	M.	F.	M.	F.
He must work	20	30	30	15	0	10	0	0	0	0
He works	60	60	30	25	37	26	10	57	0	6
Work before pleasure	10	0	0	15	0	6	10	14	7	0
He should help out	0	10	20	25	14	6	0	0	0	6
He reluctantly worked	0	0	0	0	14	10	10	0	30	17
He grudgingly worked	0	0	0	0	0	6	0	7	0	3
Worked only if essential	0	0	0	0	0	12	20	14	13	10
Talk it over with boss	0	0	0	10	7	8	10	0	13	12
Weigh both sides	10	0	0	10	14	8	30	7	30	39
Help boss find replacement	0	0	10	0	0	4	0	0	0	3
He went fishing	0	0	10	0	14	4	10	0	7	3
Total percentage	100	100	100	100	100	100	100	99	100	99
Number of respondents	10	10	10	20	15	30	10	15	15	30

While the obligation to work remains strong in the Sansei generation, there are more expressions of both reluctance and a desire to talk it over with the boss to find out if it is really necessary to work. For example, a Sansei female, aged twenty-four, replied, "He said that he already had plans for that day but would work if it was absolutely necessary." A male Sansei, aged twenty-nine, responded, "You should explain your situation and he may let you off, if not, then do him a favor by working because he may help you out someday." A Sansei female, aged eighteen, answered, "He mentally promised himself a fishing trip at a later date and, hiding his reluctance as best he could, agreed to work."

In the working-class sample there were significant differences between the male and female responses. The females more frequently replied that he had to work, as though there were few other alternatives available. The males, however, felt less of a compulsion to work. Only 20 per cent indicated that they would work. The others responded that they would work only if essential or that they would talk it over with the boss or weigh both sides. One male, aged thirty-three, answered, "He reluctantly worked, but would have rather gone fishing." Another male, a steel worker, aged thirty-six, replied, "The work needing to be done should be evaluated against the satisfaction that can be gotten from a trip, and the decision to work be made accordingly." A locomotive engineer, aged thirty-seven, responded, "He should go fishing. There is always someone willing to work overtime for the extra money (assuming no emergency)." The Caucasian student group felt even less of a compulsion to work; only 7 per cent of the males and 12 per cent of the females responded that they would work without qualification. On the other hand, the number of those who went to work reluctantly or who would look into other alternatives increased greatly.

For example, a male, aged twenty-one, replied, "He worked, reluctantly." Another male, aged twenty-seven, answered, "The employee did not like it, but instead he did the work, because he was dedicated and knew the boss would not ask him unless it was important." A female, aged twenty-four, responded, "He should tell his boss he has already made other plans for that day—unless the work is extremely important." Another response from a female, aged twenty, reflects a little of the openness and willingness to help others that was discussed earlier. Yet at the same time there can be detected a strong note of personal autonomy: "A man should try to help his boss. Chances are the boss did not mean to interrupt his plans but something has come up. The employee should do a favor but not jump to help just because the man is his boss."

Based on the above discussion and the information contained in Table 9.7, it is apparent that there are obvious and easily discernible differences in the five groups. An obligation to one's work is quite strong in all three generations of Japanese Americans, although there are important changes occurring in the Sansei generation. This is not to imply that the Sansei do not feel an obligation to work but rather that one's own personal wishes more frequently need to be taken into account. Further, it could hardly be argued that, as a minority group, the Japanese Americans are under greater pressure to conform than the Caucasian groups. On the contrary, the working class has even less job security than the Japanese Americans, a fact easily substantiated in Table 9.17, which indicates that over 50 per cent of the working class respondents were afraid of the loss of their jobs and security. Despite the concern for the security, only 20 per cent of the males reported without qualification that they would work if the order to do so conflicted with their personal plans.

Incomplete sentence 15, "When an elected official recommends a certain policy, a good citizen should . . ." The intent of incomplete sentence 15 was to measure deference and, to a lesser extent, hierarchy. As can be seen in Table 9.8, there were eight categories of responses, ranging from an implied obedience to the policy and support for the official to a skepticism of elected officials.

It was predicted that the Issei would give a high proportion of replies indicating assent to the official's recommendations, and, indeed, this did prove to be the case. As Table 9.8 discloses, 80 per cent of the Issei responded that one should follow the recommendation or support the policy. The remaining 20 per cent gave replies indicating that a citizen's responsibility was also to study the policy carefully before committing himself. The responses of the Issei to this sentence were usually terse, such as ". . . a good citizen should obey it," ". . . a good citizen should obey the official," or ". . . a good citizen should obey the laws."

The Nisei, however, disclosed an interesting male-female difference in responses. Again, the males were more prone to give short replies, and these were also in somewhat the same form as the Issei's: ". . . a good citizen should support the official," ". . . a good citizen should follow the policy," or ". . . a good citizen should go along with it." In all, some 80 per cent of the Nisei males gave such assenting replies. There is, however, the possibility of a misreading or misinterpretation of the sentence and assuming that the elected official had formulated a law. Yet if that be the case, it was only the Issei of both sexes and the Nisei males who made such an assumption; the Nisei females, the Sansei, and the Caucasian groups apparently did not. Indeed, even when giving the same type of initial answer, the Nisei females were more prone to add qualifying phrases: ". . . a good citizen should follow the policy if it is a sound policy," or ". . . a good citizen should go along with it provided he believes in the certain policy."

The Sansei were much more apt to want to consider the official's recommendation carefully before committing themselves. For example, a Sansei male, aged twenty-nine, answered, ". . . a good citizen should analyze the problem and determine if this is what you consider a good policy. Elected officials should follow the dictates of the electors." Another Sansei, a male, aged twenty-six, replied, "a good citizen should carefully scrutinize the advantages and disadvantages before committing himself." A Sansei female, aged twenty-four answered, ". . . a good citizen should weigh the facts carefully to decide whether the policy is a good one."

The working-class respondents were also concerned with examining the policy before committing themselves, although 27 per cent of the females gave short replies indicating either a willingness to follow the policy without examination or a desire to support the official. The males, though, maintained a right to disagree and oppose the official's policy. A male, aged thirty-seven, stated, ". . . a good citizen should try to understand the reason for that policy and make up his own mind." Another male, aged thirty-six, replied: ". . . a good citizen should follow that policy unless it is completely foreign to his personal beliefs. The decision to obey or not to obey should be the individual's. His personal life is always his responsibility." A housewife, aged fifty-eight, responded, ". . . a good citizen should express his opinion, even if he doesn't agree with him."

As might be expected from the events on college campuses over the past few years, the responses of the college students were much more apt to be critical of an elected official's policy. For example, a female student, aged twenty-one, had this to say,

Table 9.8

Percentage Distribution on Incomplete Sentence 15, When an Elected Official Recommends a Policy . . ., for Total Sample

Category of response	Issei		Nisei		Sansei		Caucasian working class		Caucasian students	
	M.	F.	M.	F.	M.	F.	M.	F.	M.	F.
He should follow it	60	60	40	13	0	6	0	7	0	0
Support the official	20	20	40	13	0	0	0	20	0	0
Study the policy, then decide	0	10	20	40	20	16	20	14	14	16
Carefully consider it	10	10	0	0	33	23	10	12	40	23
Weigh all the facts	10	0	0	0	7	23	30	33	40	36
Go along if he believes it	0	0	0	33	7	3	0	0	0	8
Follow it, or try to change it	0	0	0	0	13	12	30	14	0	0
Be skeptical	0	0	0	0	20	6	10	0	6	16
Total percentage	100	100	100	99	100	99	100	100	100	99
Number of responses	10	10	10	20	15	30	10	15	15	30

". . . a good citizen should make his own decision. For many people are sheep, and do not take it upon themselves to investigate the goings on of government. Consequently, lobbyists have the upper hand and often determine the policies elected officials recommend." Another student, a female, aged twenty-four, stated, ". . . a good citizen should find out all the information possible about the policy and make up his own mind as to the worth of the policy, then let the official know what those attitudes are." A male, aged twenty-seven, had these remarks: "a good citizen should look at all the facts about the policy." And finally, a female, aged twenty-three, had this to say: ". . . a good citizen should consider whether or not that is indeed the best policy. There is even international agreement (Geneva accords) with the idea that there is no valid justification for delivering one's conscience to another."

Overall, the sentence responses do indicate a high degree of deference in the Issei and in the Nisei males. In the Sansei generation and in the other groups—with the exception of 27 per cent of the working-class females and 26 per cent of the Nisei females—the replies indicated a belief that a good citizen should not simply accept a policy because an official recommends it but should consider it carefully and even skeptically.

Incomplete sentence 16, "The deepest emotional relationship is between . . ." The purpose of the sixteenth incomplete sentence was to discover if the aforementioned traditional Japanese emphasis on the mother-child bond has remained strong in the Japanese American group. Table 9.9 indicates that, while the responses given do not specifically emphasize the mother-child bond as being more important than the husband-wife bond, they do indicate that the Japanese Americans were more apt to place a somewhat greater importance on the family than did the Caucasian groups.

The importance of the family is clearly brought out in the Issei and Nisei generations. If the four categories reporting emotional relationships among family members are grouped together, the total response indicates a rather strong emphasis on family relationships. In the Issei generation, 50 per cent of the males and 70 per cent of the females reported that the strongest emotional relationships were in those categories relating to family members. Further, among the Nisei, 50 per cent of the males and 60 per cent of the females also gave responses indicating the importance of family relationships.

The Sansei sample is somewhat different, as might be expected, in that approximately two-thirds of the respondents were unmarried. Nonetheless, 40 per cent of the male and 47 per cent of the female replies were in those categories emphasizing family relationships. In this regard the Sansei can be compared with the Caucasian student group and the working-class group.

The number of unmarried in the student group was about the same as the Sansei group—about two-thirds. Yet in the student group only 26 per cent of the males and 40 per cent of the females gave replies in the above categories. On the other hand, while all of the working class group were listed as being married, 40 per cent of the males and 27 per cent of the females emphasized family relationships. Moreover, from the perspective of the husband-wife, or man-woman, bond there would appear to be little difference between the Sansei and the Caucasian responses. In this respect the Sansei are about the same as the Caucasian groups.

Table 9.9
Percentage Distribution on Incomplete Sentence 16, The Deepest Emotional Relationship . . ., for Total Sample

Category of response	Issei		Nisei		Sansei		Caucasian working class		Caucasian students	
	M.	F.	M.	F.	M.	F.	M.	F.	M.	F.
Members of the family	20	20	20	40	33	20	20	7	0	8
Mother and child	20	20	0	13	0	4	20	0	6	24
Father and son	0	10	10	0	7	0	0	0	0	0
Parents and children	10	20	20	7	0	23	0	20	20	8
Husband and wife	40	20	50	40	20	33	50	42	20	20
Man and woman	0	0	0	0	33	6	10	14	6	12
Lovers	0	0	0	0	0	13	0	0	42	24
Friends	10	10	0	0	7	0	0	0	0	0
Man and God	0	0	0	0	0	0	0	14	6	4
Total percentage	100	100	100	100	100	99	100	100	100	100
Number of respondents	10	10	10	20	15	30	10	15	15	30

In retrospect, the greatest family emphasis appears to be among the Issei and Nisei females. Fully 70 per cent of Issei and 60 per cent of the Nisei females indicated strong emotional ties with family members. These responses, while by no means conclusive, are nonetheless in the predicted direction. In this regard, perhaps the best comparison would be with the working-class females who are similar to the Nisei in age and marital status. Indeed, as already established in Table 9.6, the emphasis on the family is quite strong in the working class. Nevertheless, when reporting emotional relationships, the strongest bond appears to be more between husband and wife and, to a lesser degree, among members of the family.

Support for the above assertion is found in the replies given to other incomplete sentences and in the other instruments used in the study. For example, in Tables 9.11 and 9.15, which relate the feelings of the respondent toward his mother or father, it is immediately apparent that there are far fewer expressions of love and affection in the Caucasian groups. In addition, in the Contrasting Values Survey Form (Chapter 11), statements 5 and 14 were included to complement and perhaps corroborate the information revealed by incomplete sentence 16. Statement 5 in the survey read, "The strongest emotional bond is between a mother and her child." Statement 14 reads, "In the family the strongest emotional tie is between the husband and the wife." The degrees of response were strongly agree (5), agree (4), undecided (3), disagree (2), and strongly disagree (1). The mean response for the total survey for statement 5 on the mother-child bond was: Issei, 4.13; Nisei, 3.85; Sansei, 3.15; and Caucasian, 2.76. The mean response for statement 14 on the husband-wife bond was: Issei, 4.18; Nisei, 3.90; Sansei, 3.49; and Caucasian 3.36.

It can be seen from the above that there was considerable agreement to both statements by the Japanese Americans, although the husband-wife bond was more strongly agreed to than the mother-child bond. It is also apparent that the difference in agreement between the two statements increases with each generation, with the greatest difference expressed in the Caucasian group. Again, based on the above discussion of emotionality in the family, the answers were largely as anticipated. Since the statements were not paired and a choice was not demanded, it was anticipated that there would be some agreement to both statements. What is important here, however, is the direction of change. In both cases the direction suggests a diminished degree of emotionality from the Issei to the Sansei and Caucasian groups. This is apparent in the Sansei and Caucasian groups, which are quite similar with regard to age and marital status.

Incomplete sentence 17, "When a neighbor reported her

child was misbehaving, she . . ." Incomplete sentence 17 was included for several reasons. One, to investigate further the principle that one should not bring shame to the family that was reported in Table 6. Two, to discover the extent to which respondents would assume the child's guilt or defend the child's behavior. The extremes of the latter are to be found in the range of responses given in Table 9.10.

In *The Chrysanthemum and the Sword* (1946:273-74), Benedict reports that once children have entered school they become in fact representatives of the family and their behavior, in turn, reflects upon the family. If a child has misbehaved, his family will turn against him. Benedict further quotes Geoffrey Gorer that whereas in most societies the extended family or other social group will rally to the support of its members, in Japan the reverse is true. If outsiders disapprove, one's own group will turn against one. Or, as Benedict states:

> By the time he is eight or nine his family may in sober truth reject him. If a teacher reports that he has been disobedient or disrespectful and gives him a black mark in deportment, his family turns against him. If he is criticized for some mischief by the storekeeper, "the family name has been disgraced." His family are a solid phalanx of accusation. Two Japanese I have known were told by their fathers before they were ten not to come home again and were too ashamed to go to relatives. They had been punished by their teachers in the schoolroom. In both cases they lived in outhouses, where their mothers found them and finally arranged for their return. (1946:273)

Table 9.10 discloses that the Issei males were much more apt to assume the child was wrong and initiate disciplinary action. Seventy per cent of the Issei males would take strong corrective action, while 30 per cent would investigate and ask the child to explain. The Issei female, however, would listen to the child's side first. These responses are in accord with what is known of the Issei family. The father was often a patriarch who was both respected and feared, while the mother was a gentle force who frequently interceded on behalf of the children. As one Nisei describes this relationship:

> As a mother she was kind, gentle, and patient . . . Without her warm gentle care over us, it would have been impossible to

endure the severity and strict discipline of our father . . . Whenever my father scolded us, she comforted us and told us to be patient. (Masuoka 1937:245)

With the Nisei generation, however, approximately the same percentage (60) of males and females agreed that something should be done at once to stop the misbehavior. Only 40 per cent of the males and 34 per cent of the females would investigate all sides or ask the child to explain.

The Sansei, on the other hand, were more disposed to investigate all sides or ask the child to explain before disciplining the child. As one Sansei male, aged twenty-six, stated, "She should first see if her neighbor is telling the truth. If the child was misbehaving he should be disciplined." A Sansei female, aged 18, answered, "She should pause long enough to determine how justified the neighbor was in making the accusation before taking any disciplinary action."

Both of the Caucasian groups were similar in their responses to the Sansei. Like the Sansei, they were less willing to assume that their child was automatically at fault and should be disciplined. More frequently, they wanted to investigate the report before taking action. There was nothing in their responses which would indicate that they believed the child's behavior would bring shame to the family. There were even a few who began with the assumption that their child had been in the right. One male Caucasian student, aged thirty-three, replied, "She probably wouldn't believe it because more than likely they believe their child can do no wrong." While there may be a note of cynicism in the above remark, it does touch upon the defensiveness of many American mothers. This tendency to support the child over the accusations of the neighbor can be found in the following response by a female student, aged twenty-one: "She inquired as to what he was doing. Mothers should give the child the benefit of trust and question the neighbor, as more than likely the child will behave in ways condoned by the mother. What the neighbor thought could be of no significance." Another student, female, aged twenty-one, replied in a manner that was poles apart from the Issei responses: "At first she became indignant and thought the neighbor must be mistaken, and then realized she must hear all sides and all facts before disciplining or not disciplining her child."

It would seem, then, that sentence 17 does bear out Benedict's contention that, at least in the Issei generation and to a lesser

Table 9.10

**Percentage Distribution on Incomplete Sentence 17,
When a Neighbor Reported Her Child Misbehaving . . .,
for Total Sample**

Category of response	Issei		Nisei		Sansei		Caucasian working class		Caucasian students	
	M.	F.	M.	F.	M.	F.	M.	F.	M.	F.
Discipline child at once	20	10	10	20	0	10	10	20	20	0
Apologize to neighbor	30	10	10	0	0	3	0	0	0	3
Thank the neighbor	10	0	0	0	0	0	0	6	0	10
Ask neighbor to discipline	0	0	0	6	0	6	0	0	0	0
Take care of it at once	0	0	40	26	21	17	10	14	0	0
Make certain it would stop	10	20	0	14	0	0	0	0	0	0
Investigate all sides	10	10	20	20	33	17	40	33	33	30
Ask child to apologize	0	0	0	0	0	0	0	6	0	3
Ask child to explain	20	50	20	14	33	33	30	20	20	20
Hear child's side first	0	0	0	0	6	17	0	0	7	17
Couldn't believe it	0	0	0	0	6	0	0	0	7	6
Became defensive	0	0	0	0	0	0	10	0	13	10
Total percentage	100	100	100	100	99	100	100	99	100	99
Number of respondents	10	10	10	20	15	30	10	15	15	30

extent in the Nisei generation, the child is seen more as a representative of the family whose behavior might reflect on or bring shame to the family. Some support for the continuing importance of the avoidance of bringing shame to the family is to be found in Table 6, which discloses that over 60 per cent of both male and female Sansei reported that the principle of not bringing shame to the family was stressed when they were growing up. Further, it will be recalled that almost 30 per cent of the Sansei reported that the behavior most likely to anger or upset the Nisei would be to bring shame to the family. There is, however, an attenuation of this principle in the Sansei generation and their replies were very close to those of the Caucasian groups.

Incomplete sentence 20, "When he thinks of his mother . . ." Incomplete sentence 20 was added to the test for a number of reasons. It was hoped that the answers would reveal something of the emotional bond between the mother and child that has been discussed in relation to sentence 16. In this sense the two are complementary. Table 9.11 reveals a rather broad spectrum of responses, ranging from an expression of love and respect to a feeling of ambivalence. Further, the table immediately reveals a most interesting difference between the Japanese American replies and those of the Caucasian groups; that is, the far fewer expressions of emotionality in the Caucasian replies, especially among the males.

This difference also becomes manifest in the Sansei males. When compared to 80 per cent of the Issei males and 60 per cent of the Nisei males who mentioned "love and respect" or "love and warmth," only 14 per cent of the Sansei males gave such replies. By contrast, only 7 per cent of the male students and none of the working-class males gave such a response.

A possible explanation of the above is offered by Caudill and Doi, who contrast patterns of emotionality in Japan and in the United States:

> One way, admittedly too shorthand a way, of summarizing this comparison between Japan and the United States, is to suggest that tenderness is handled well and adaptively in Japan, but that aggression is a source of great trouble since it has remained psychologically primitive, and is less utilized and reworked for adaptive purposes during the course of childhood development. Thus, when aggression comes out in Japan, as in student demonstrations (which to Americans appear as "riots") or in fist fights among members of the National Diet, its explosive and ego-syntonic qualities give evidence of its primi-

tiveness. On the other hand, aggression is handled more adaptively during childhood, and difficulties for Americans arise more in the adequate communication and expression of tenderness, which for them, in contrast to the Japanese, has remained on a psychologically primitive level. (1963:414-15)

Table 9.11

**Percentage Distribution on Incomplete Sentence 20,
When He Thinks of His Mother . . ., for Total Sample**

Category of response	Issei		Nisei		Sansei		Caucasian working class		Caucasian students	
	M.	F.	M.	F.	M.	F.	M.	F.	M.	F.
Love and respect	50	40	40	20	7	16	0	7	0	0
Love and warmth	30	20	20	25	7	25	0	20	7	19
Hardship and sacrifice	10	10	10	20	14	12	10	0	7	3
Sadness	10	10	20	5	0	4	0	13	0	3
He is grateful	0	0	0	10	0	0	10	7	7	3
He thinks of childhood	0	0	10	0	28	10	30	13	12	6
Respect	0	20	0	15	10	10	30	20	20	8
Strengths and weaknesses	0	0	0	0	7	0	10	0	20	12
Affection	0	0	0	0	0	10	0	0	0	3
Comfort and security	0	0	0	5	7	12	0	7	0	10
Tenderness	0	0	0	0	0	0	0	13	7	6
Wonders how she is	0	0	0	0	7	0	0	0	7	6
Someone who cares	0	0	0	0	7	0	0	0	7	6
He is ambivalent	0	0	0	0	12	0	0	0	7	10
Total percentage	100	100	100	100	99	99	100	100	99	99
Number of respondents	10	10	10	20	15	30	10	15	15	30

There is also a possibility, which is reflected in the female's apparently greater proclivity to indicate love and affection in their replies, that the unwillingness to express emotionality may be more of a male cultural trait than one that is characteristic of Americans in general. This would not negate what Caudill and Doi have stated and, indeed, is offered more as an addendum than as a criticism. Moreover, while Table 9.11 does indicate a pronounced male-female difference in the expression of emotionality it also discloses that, while the Caucasian females gave more responses expressive of emotionality than the males, the totality of such responses was still less than that of the Japanese Americans.

The replies of the various groups were illuminating and frequently poignant. One Issei male, aged sixty-eight, answered, "I would have gone home once before she died." Another Issei female, aged seventy-four, answered simply, ". . . he is sad." The Nisei responses frequently expressed a warmth and love. A male, aged fifty-seven, replied, ". . . he remembers how sweet and kind she was." A female, aged forty-three, stated, ". . . he remembers her as a real special person." Another Nisei, a male, aged forty, answered, ". . . he thinks of her love and understanding."

The Sansei responses were in the same vein although the tone was more objective than the answers given by the Issei or Nisei. For example, a female, aged twenty-four, replied, ". . . he thinks of the warm busy home of his childhood." Another female, aged eighteen, answered, ". . . he thinks of a plump matronly type who loves him unconditionally, who worries about him." A male, aged twenty-six, stated, ". . . he thinks of how hard she worked and how much she sacrificed."

In the working-class sample, there were no outright expressions of love by the males. When love was mentioned, it was the love the mother gave to the son. For example, a male, aged thirty-seven, answered, ". . . a person should remember the work and sacrifice she made for him, the love and hope she shared." Another male, aged forty-six, stated, ". . . he should think of someone who he owes an awful lot to." Frequently, even the expressions of emotion were more in the nature of sentimentality rather than an outright statement of love. As one housewife, aged fifty-eight, stated, ". . . he gets real sentimental. You only have one mother and you never really forget her."

In the student group there were a number of replies that

mentioned affection and love, but many times these were seen as something that one received from the mother rather than expressed toward her. A female, aged twenty-four, responded as follows: ". . . he thinks of good cooking and the gossiping she did with her friends, the clean house and clothes she provided and most of all the affection she gave him." Another female student, aged twenty-one, gave a similar reply: ". . . he thinks of a hard worker, a good mother, a good cook, a kind and loving person, a person he can turn to, and a person that's just a little bit old fashioned." A male, aged twenty-one, answered simply, ". . . he thinks of a hard worker." Another male, aged thirty-three, gave a rather laconic reply: ". . . he thinks of a woman who to him is his ideal."

When the total range of responses is examined for the various groups, the overall impression is one of the higher degree of emotionality toward the mother in the Japanese Americans than in the Caucasian groups. On the face of it, this is a paradox. Relationships in the Caucasian homes are frequently more open, relaxed, and uninhibited than those of the Japanese Americans, who are comparatively more reserved and formal. This last observation is based on both personal experience and interviews. Yet the tie with the mother in the Japanese American family appears to have more an emotional component than it does in the Caucasian groups. The extent and meaning of the emotionality is a point to which we will return later.

Incomplete sentence 21, "If a person finds himself in difficulty, he . . ." The object of sentence 21 was to indicate the importance of collaterality and self-reliance. In this regard it both complements and elaborates upon the reponses given in Tables 9.4 and 9.6. As can be seen in Table 9.12, the categories of responses were somewhat limited due to the nature of the sentence itself. The responses range from a reliance upon the family and friends to an attempt to seek help from others or even professional advice. Of the various categories, two recorded self-reliant responses. These were, "Rely on himself first" and "Try to reason a way out." The others involved reliance upon others in various degrees, although the last two categories, "Get help from others" and "Seek professional advice," were more diffuse than the others.

The emphasis on collaterality in the Japanese Americans is apparent in Table 9.12. Forty per cent of the Issei and Nisei gave replies that indicated that they would seek help from the family or from family and friends. Answers that were typical of the Issei were given by a husband and wife who both reported that they "would go to talk to the children." Another Issei male, aged eighty-one, replied, ". . . a real close friend will help you out."

Table 9.12
Percentage Distribution on Incomplete Sentence 21,
If a Person Finds Himself in Difficulty . . ., for Total Sample

Category of response	Issei		Nisei		Sansei		Caucasian working class		Caucasian students	
	M.	F.	M.	F.	M.	F.	M.	F.	M.	F.
Seek help from family	40	40	30	40	20	16	0	13	0	3
Ask family and friends	0	0	10	20	0	7	0	0	0	0
Ask close friends	10	0	0	5	7	7	0	0	20	7
Pray to God	10	10	10	0	0	0	0	20	0	0
Rely on himself first	20	10	20	15	20	16	20	13	13	22
Try to reason a way out	0	10	10	0	13	32	40	20	33	50
Get help from others	20	30	20	20	40	21	31	26	33	14
Seek professional advice	0	0	0	0	0	0	10	7	0	3
Total percentage	100	100	100	100	100	99	100	99	99	99
Number of respondents	10	10	10	20	15	30	10	15	15	30

A Nisei female, aged forty-three, stated, ". . . he should discuss it with his family." A Nisei male, aged forty, answered, ". . . it is best that you talk it over with your family or a trusted friend."

The Sansei, however, while still emphasizing the importance of receiving family help or help from others, were more likely than either the Issei or Nisei to answer that one should try to reason a way out or rely on oneself. For example, a Sansei male, aged thirty-three, replied, ". . . he should try his best to solve his problem before going to others for help." Another male, aged twenty-nine, said simply, ". . . he should try and find a solution." There was no implication of seeking help from others. The working-class sample was also more apt to try to solve the problem first than to ask others. It is perhaps significant that none of the males mentioned family or friends specifically but only the more general "others" when the difficulty could not be solved. Several even gave somewhat philosophical answers. One male, aged thirty-six, responded, ". . . he realizes that nothing is permanent, everything changes, through your own application you can get out of any difficulty." Another male, aged forty-five, answered simply, ". . . he should appraise the situation, then move in a philosophical manner."

The Caucasian students, especially the females, favored self-reliant solutions; there were very few references to the family. In most cases the students reported that they should first attempt to resolve the difficulty on their own and, failing that, turn to someone they could trust. A male, aged twenty, answered, ". . . he tries to solve the problem himself and if he can't he then goes to others close to him." The same solution was proposed by another male, aged twenty-one: ". . . he should try to work it out on his own; if he can't he should turn to someone he can trust."

It would seem, then, based on the above, that the emphasis on collaterality or a reliance upon the family is still rather strong in the Japanese American groups. This is not to imply that they are not self-reliant, or are reluctant or even incapable of solving their own difficulties, but rather, given the emphasis on the family, there will be more easily available assistance and aid that are apparently unavailable to the working-class or student groups except as a last resource.

Incomplete sentence 22, "When seated on a crowded bus, he noticed his boss standing nearby and . . ." Sentence 22, as with sentences 12 and 15, was included to measure deference. Table 9.13 reveals the various categories of response. These ranged from a simple statement that the respondent would offer his seat to the boss to several somewhat cynical remarks that one should offer his seat to the boss to impress him or for "political" reasons.

Table 9.13

**Percentage Distribution on Incomplete Sentence 22,
When Seated on a Crowded Bus . . ., for Total Sample**

Category of response	Issei		Nisei		Sansei		Caucasian working class		Caucasian students	
	M.	F.	M.	F.	M.	F.	M.	F.	M.	F.
Offers him the seat	50	50	50	50	27	33	20	20	7	3
Greets him	30	40	30	30	33	33	10	13	33	10
Greets, but remains seated	0	0	0	0	0	15	30	13	0	36
Offer seat if old or female	10	10	10	20	20	6	20	13	7	10
Stand up with him	0	0	0	0	13	3	0	0	20	17
Pretend not to see him	0	0	0	0	7	0	10	20	7	3
Remain seated	10	0	10	0	0	0	10	13	13	3
Make room for boss	0	0	0	0	0	3	0	7	0	0
Offer seat to impress boss	0	0	0	0	0	0	0	0	0	7
Total percentage	100	100	100	100	100	99	100	99	100	99
Number of respondents	10	10	10	20	15	30	10	15	15	30

Based upon prior research and the responses to sentences 12 and 15, it was anticipated that a fairly large number of Issei and Nisei would indicate that they would offer the boss their seat, and indeed such was the case. One-half of the Issei and Nisei respondents answered that they would offer the boss their seat. The proportion decreased to about one-third in the Sansei generation, while there was an increase in such answers as ". . . he greeted him but did not feel it necessary to offer his seat." Several Sansei males answered candidly that the best solution would be to pretend not to see the boss. This solution was arrived at by the same number of Caucasian male students and also by several of the working-class respondents. One interesting solution was to stand up with the boss and give the seat to someone else.

The working-class respondents were less willing to offer the boss their seat immediately. In fact, 30 per cent of the males made it a point to say that, while they would greet the boss, they would remain seated.

In all, 80 per cent of both working-class males and females gave replies indicating that they preferred not to give the boss their seat. This was obvious in the replies given by several that they would pretend not to see the boss. And one female, aged fifty-nine, even answered, "I paid for my seat, let him get his own."

The Caucasian students were apparently even less disposed immediately to offer the boss their seat. Only 7 per cent of the males and 3 per cent of the females gave such a response. On the contrary, 36 per cent of the females explicitly stated that, while they would greet the boss, it was not necessary to give him the seat.

Overall, in considering the five groups, there appears to be a rather clear trend from Issei to Nisei to Sansei in the percentage of Japanese Americans who stated that they would offer their seat to the boss. While the responses of the Nisei are almost identical to those of the Issei, there is an obvious change in the Sansei group. Fewer Sansei answered in such a fashion, although the percentage remains higher than for the Caucasian groups, and particularly the student group, which more closely resembles the Sansei in age, education, and economic status than does the working-class group.

From the above, one can deduce that deference is still rather strong in the Issei and Nisei generations and, to a lesser extent, in the Sansei generation. The sentence responses, therefore, both complement and confirm the data presented in Tables 9.7 and 9.8.

Incomplete sentence 23, "When he heard that his child had been threatened by a neighborhood bully, he . . ." Sentence 23 was included to determine both the extent of the American characteristic of self-defense or self-assertion and the retention of the Japanese prohibition or taboo against overt physical aggression. It will be recalled that in the earlier discussion of American characteristics it was stated that the Americans have a greater tolerance of aggressive attitudes in their children. Thus in their study on the behavior of American mothers, as compared to those in five other cultures, Minturn and Lambert reported:

As part of their child training they encourage children to "stand up for their rights" and if necessary, fight back when attacked by other children. (1964:198)

By contrast, the middle-class Japanese mother enforces a strong taboo against physical aggression:

When a child reaches the age of three or four, he is taught to withhold his aggression. When a child below that age hits an older sibling the mother may regard it as a form of play, but she may say that it will not do (*ikenai*) for the older child to hit the younger one. If she hears that her child has been in a fight with a neighbor, she will tell him that will not do, regardless of whether he started the fight or not. To hit in self-defense is considered about as bad as to start a fight. While the mother may sympathize with her child when he has been wronged by others, there is virtually no situation in which returning aggression is condoned. (Vogel: 1963:247)

Table 9.14 reveals a variety of responses ranging from avoiding the bully to investigating the matter or waiting until the child asks for assistance. It is immediately apparent from Table 9.14 that the majority of the Issei and Nisei wished to have their child avoid a confrontation with the bully. The most common response was to tell the child to stay away from the bully. Others favored talking to the bully or the bully's parents. Only 10 per cent of the Nisei males and 15 per cent of the females suggested that their son be taught to defend himself.

Approximately one-third of the Sansei still suggested that the child avoid the bully. At the same time, the same percentage as the Caucasian students replied that their sons should be taught self-defense. Further, the Sansei answered almost as frequently as the working class that they would speak to the bully's parents.

The working-class males, however, were almost as likely to answer that the child be taught self-defense as the Issei males were likely to suggest that the child avoid the bully. The responses of the working-class females were much like those of the Sansei and student female groups; however, more of the working-class females answered that they would speak to the bully, and a slightly higher percentage said that they would teach the son to defend himself.

More of the Caucasian students favored talking to the bully's parents over teaching the son to defend himself, but the difference was not a great one. The female students also answered that it would be better to investigate the matter more thoroughly, and a few thought that the proper thing to do would be to protect the child's autonomy by not meddling in his affairs until the child asked them to.

Table 9.14

Percentage Distribution on Incomplete Sentence 23, When He Heard That His Child Had Been Threatened . . ., for Total Sample

Category of response	Issei		Nisei		Sansei		Caucasian working class		Caucasian students	
	M.	F.	M.	F.	M.	F.	M.	F.	M.	F.
Avoid the bully	70	40	50	30	26	33	0	7	7	0
Spoke to the bully	10	20	30	15	0	0	0	20	13	0
Spoke to the bully's parents	10	0	10	25	26	33	30	33	40	38
Told his child to be friendly	0	30	0	0	0	0	0	0	0	3
Call the police	10	0	0	5	0	0	0	0	0	0
Taught his son self-defense	0	10	10	15	33	28	60	33	33	28
Investigate the matter	0	0	0	10	14	6	10	7	7	20
Wait until child asks	0	0	0	0	0	0	0	0	0	10
Total percentage	100	100	100	100	99	100	100	100	100	99
Number of respondents	10	10	10	20	15	30	15	15	15	30

In classifying the responses, it was obvious that there was a rather clear progression towards the Caucasian emphasis on self-defense or self-assertion in the three generations of Japanese Americans. In many respects the answers of both the Sansei and student groups were similar, with the exception that almost one-third of the Sansei replied that the son should avoid the bully while only 7 per cent of the student males and none of the females gave such a response.

Incomplete sentence 24, "When he thinks of his father . . ."
Sentence 24 was included to complement sentence 20 concerning

the mother It was anticipated that the Japanese Americans would more frequently include responses that mentioned respect and discipline. Table 9.15 indicates that such replies were more frequently given than in the Caucasian groups. Here again, however, as with sentence 20 relating to the mother, the Japanese Americans made more frequent use of such terms as love and affection than did the Caucasian groups.

Table 9.15

Percentage Distribution on Incomplete Sentence 24, When He Thinks of His Father . . ., for Total Sample

Category o response	Issei		Nisei		Sansei		Caucasian working class		Caucasian students	
	M.	F.	M.	F.	M.	F.	M.	F.	M.	F.
Love and respect	40	60	20	40	0	32	10	7	7	3
Gratitude	40	20	20	5	0	0	0	20	7	0
Admiration	10	10	10	0	0	0	0	13	0	3
Love and understanding	0	0	0	0	0	7	0	7	0	7
Hard work and sacrifice	0	0	0	25	13	16	20	20	13	7
His advice	0	0	30	10	7	7	10	0	0	3
His discipline	10	0	20	15	26	7	0	0	0	10
A good man	0	0	0	5	7	0	10	0	27	16
Remember the good times	0	0	0	0	33	14	20	13	0	13
Thinks of his childhood	0	10	0	0	7	16	10	13	20	13
His strengths and weaknesses	0	0	0	0	7	0	20	7	26	24
Total percentage	100	100	100	100	100	99	100	100	100	99
Number of respondents	10	10	10	20	15	30	10	15	15	30

Table 9.15 discloses that 90 per cent of the Issei gave emotionally positive responses in reference to the father. This tendency is continued in the Nisei generation to a somewhat lesser extent, with approximately one-half of the Nisei giving such replies. There were some male-female differences in response. The males were much more frequently inclined to remember the father's

advice and discipline, while the females reported the hard work and sacrifice of the father. What is most apparent in both the Issei and Nisei replies is the impression they convey of a very positive father figure. What emerges is the picture of a man who was hard-working, stern, and yet at times capable of displaying a warmth to his children.

The Sansei, however, were somewhat different in their replies. The more overt expressions of affection were given by the females while the males more frequently remembered the discipline, advice, hard work, and sacrifice of their fathers. Even the females included some feeling of discipline in their replies. The Sansei female student, aged eighteen, answered, ". . . he thinks of him with 'Yes, sir' respect, as well as with love." Again, as with the Issei and Nisei, the responses were almost entirely positive. There was the beginning of what might be called a neutral or perhaps "demystified" view of the father in the 7 per cent of the males who answered that they thought of both the father's strengths and weaknesses.

The working class also displayed much the same sexual differentiation in responses. Again it was the females who gave more of the emotionally positive answers. The replies of the males were more neutral in that there were far fewer expressions of affection.

The Caucasian student sample was interesting also in the lower incidence of overt expressions of affection in both males and females. The impression conveyed by the student answers is that, while the students are quite positive toward the father, they see the father on a more equal basis than do the other groups. The difference is one that is hard to define and is perhaps more apparent in the totality of the responses rather than in their categorization. For example, a male, aged twenty-seven, replied, ". . . he remembers a man he wishes to emulate, but still understands that he has his imperfections like everyone else." A female, aged twenty-one, answered, ". . . he is able to see that he is completely human, able to make mistakes." Another response by a female, aged twenty-four, reveals respect but there is no indication of awe or deference: ". . . he remembers the good times they had together and all the good things about him. The trust and respect he had for his father and the guidance his father gave him."

Sentence 20, then, does indicate progression from Issei and
Nisei through Sansei in emotionality, advice, and discipline. In
many respects the Sansei are closer to the Caucasian student
group than they are to the Nisei. There is more of a tendency to
remember experiences that were shared. At the same time, the
Sansei made more frequent reference to the father's discipline
than did the student group.

*Incomplete sentence 25, "When his superior gave him an
order he thought was wrong, he . . ."* The intent of sentence 25
was not so much to measure deference as it was to measure
independence. Table 9.16 reveals that the number of categories of
responses is relatively small; there were, obviously, narrow limits
in the range of answers. The table discloses both uniformities and
differences. For example, the percentage of Issei who said that
they would do it and not argue was the same as the percentage of
working-class respondents who answered that they would refuse
to do it. All the groups, however, reported that they would give
their opinion or explain their reluctance to the boss. Roughly
between 20 and 30 per cent of all respondents replied that they
would follow the order if the boss insisted.

While none of the Issei or Nisei specifically stated that they
would refuse to follow the order, there was the expression of a
reluctance and an assertion that the order would be questioned
and one's opinion would be given. For example, one Issei male,
aged eighty-seven, answered, ". . . he did it and didn't argue."
Another Issei male, aged eighty-one, however, replied, ". . . in
this country you could at least tell your boss he was wrong—not
so in Japan.' And one Issei commented, ". . . he gave his opinion, but did what he was told." The Nisei were often acutely
aware of the dilemma but found it difficult to openly express disobedience. As one Nisei male stated, ". . . I'd have a discussion
on the matter and if I'm wrong, I'd follow his order anyway." A
female Nisei, aged forty-three, expressed the difficulty of her position by remarking, ". . . he became very angry and wished he
had the nerve to tell him what he really thought of him."

The Sansei, however, were more outspoken in their expressions of disobedience, as one male, aged twenty-nine,
indicated: ". . . he must not follow the order unless it is lawful."
Another Sansei, a female, aged thirty-three, answered, ". . . he
should point it out without offending the superior."

The working-class respondents were equally willing to refuse to carry out the order, a fact which is most interesting in view of the responses of over 50 per cent of them, as indicated in Table 9.17, that they were most afraid of insecurity or the loss of a job. Nonetheless, 30 per cent of the males and 20 per cent of the females replied that the order should be disobeyed. As one steelworker, aged thirty-six, stated, ". . . if at all possible he should ignore the order until discussion can be made with the superior. If the order is not of major importance he should do as ordered. If the reaction would be of major importance he should not follow the order." Further, a railroad conductor, aged thirty-three, answered, ". . . he refused to carry out the order."

Table 9.16

Percentage Distribution on Incomplete Sentence 25, When His Superior Gave Him an Order . . ., for Total Sample

Category of response	Issei		Nisei		Sansei		Caucasian working class		Caucasian students	
	M.	F.	M.	F.	M.	F.	M.	F.	M.	F.
Did it and didn't argue	30	20	0	0	7	4	0	13	0	0
Did it if boss insisted	10	30	20	20	27	20	30	20	13	14
Explained his reluctance	20	30	20	40	13	16	10	0	7	20
Questioned the order	10	0	30	20	13	26	20	33	33	25
Gave his opinion	30	20	30	20	13	26	10	13	20	16
Refused to do it	0	0	0	0	27	7	30	20	27	24
Total percentage	100	100	100	100	100	99	100	99	100	99
Number of respondents	10	10	10	20	15	30	10	15	15	30

The students were also reluctant to carry out the order and the majority of them stated that they would explain their reluctance to the boss or let him know how they felt. Some believed that they should point out the error to the superior in a tactful way, but if that failed they would go ahead and then let the superior make the discovery. Others felt that they would try to find a better solution and then attempt to convince the superior to accept it. However, about the same percentage as in the working-class and Sansei males replied that they should disobey the order. For most it was a matter of conscience. As one female, aged twenty, answered, ". . . he did not obey it. A man has to live with himself and to lie destroys a man's faith in himself."

The responses for the five groups, then, were in many ways similar. Yet it does seem apparent that the Issei and Sansei were much more reluctant to express outright disobedience to the superior. In this respect, however, the Sansei, especially the males, were much closer to the Caucasian groups in their willingness to disobey or, perhaps better yet, to follow the dictates of their conscience.

Incomplete sentence 28, "What he is really afraid of is . . ." The last incomplete sentence is one of the most revealing. In it can be seen a range of responses that reflect both generational and cultural differences. As might be expected, the Issei and older Nisei would be concerned with problems of health, while the younger people would be more concerned with success and achievement. Table 9.17 indicates the various responses, some of which, such as fear of fire, have already been discussed.

Several characteristics that have been mentioned previously are given additional support in the replies. Chief among these is the aforementioned emphasis on the family that was seen to be of importance in the Issei and Nisei generations. Another characteristic that was not discussed but has been implicit in many of the other replies is the sensitivity to criticism by others that was given by 40 per cent of the Nisei males and 30 per cent of the females.

Some indication of the achievement orientation of both the Sansei and Caucasian student groups is the fear of failure that was reported by 50 per cent of the Sansei and by about one-third of the student group. Perhaps related to this is the lack of self-confidence that was indicated in about the same percentage for the Sansei and Caucasian groups.

Another characteristic of the younger groups, in particular the females, was the reported fear of loneliness—a fear that was confined to the single women. An additional fear, again one that was confined to the younger groups, was the fear of what might be called an inability to achieve an openness or spontaneity—a fear of being closed in or overregulated; what they would call a fear of not being alive and not being able to sample all that life has to offer. Needless to say, the very nature of such a fear presupposes a certain level of affluence.

Table 9.17

Percentage Distribution on Incomplete Sentence 28, What He Is Really Afraid of . . ., for Total Sample

Category of response	Issei		Nisei		Sansei		Caucasian working class		Caucasian students	
	M.	F.	M.	F.	M.	F.	M.	F.	M.	F.
Illness	30	20	20	15	0	6	0	0	0	0
Death	10	10	0	0	0	0	0	6	7	0
Fire	20	20	0	0	0	0	0	0	0	0
Criticism by others	20	20	40	30	20	12	20	6	7	10
Nothing	0	0	20	0	0	0	0	0	0	6
Welfare of family	20	30	10	35	6	3	10	7	0	0
Failure	0	0	10	15	50	50	10	13	36	27
Himself	0	0	0	5	0	0	0	7	13	3
Loneliness	0	0	0	0	0	28	0	0	0	20
Insecurity	0	0	0	0	0	0	20	28	0	0
Loss of job	0	0	0	0	0	0	30	33	0	3
Lack of self-confidence	0	0	0	0	12	0	10	0	13	10
Not really being alive	0	0	0	0	6	0	0	0	13	10
Being afraid of life	0	0	0	0	6	0	0	0	7	10
Total percentage	100	100	100	100	100	99	100	100	99	99
Number of respondents	10	10	10	20	15	30	10	15	15	30

Neither the affluence nor the fear of not being alive can be said to be characteristic of the working-class sample. Here the overriding concern is still with the bread-and-butter issues of making a living. Over one-half of them are afraid of insecurity and the loss of jobs—hardly the level of affluence needed to sample what life has to offer.

The sentence, then, does reflect the feelings of the various groups and does indicate a certain degree of involvement in the test itself. On the basis of these replies one might reasonably assume that the respondents were indeed talking about themselves in the answers they gave. As such, the final incomplete sentence serves not only to indicate the range of fears of the respondents, but perhaps more importantly, helps to verify the assumptions on which the test was constructed.

Summary

In conclusion, the Incomplete Sentence Test reveals a considerable retention of Japanese characteristics in the Issei and Nisei generations, although these are somewhat attenuated in the Sansei generation. The retention was especially pronounced in the areas of duty and obligation, deference, and hierarchy. Further, a consistent finding was the greater emphasis on the family and the greater expression of emotionality toward the family in the Japanese Americans than in the Caucasian-American groups. In addition, while the Sansei are unquestionably closer to the Caucasian-American students in their overall responses, nonetheless they are still much closer to the Nisei and Issei in their expressions of the importance of duty and obligation and family ties.

Finally, a somewhat surprising finding was the number of Caucasian student responses which indicated that the students were more open, more considerate and gregarious, and less overtly competitive than had been anticipated. During the blind analysis these responses, in turn, were responsible for approximately one-third of the Caucasian students being mistaken for Sansei. It might be added at this point that the above-mentioned changes in the Caucasian students were also measured by our other instruments. The implications of these findings are discussed in detail in the concluding chapter.

Chapter 10

The Ethnic Identity Questionnaire

The Ethnic Identity Questionnaire, or E.I.Q., was devised by Masuda, Matsumoto, and Meredith (1970:199-207) for the purpose of quantifying the extent of ethnic identification in three generations of Japanese Americans. The questionnaire is self-administered and consists of fifty sentences which were prefaced by five responses weighted on a five-point scale from which the individual could choose: strongly agree (5), agree (4), undecided (3), disagree (2), and strongly disagree (1). The wording of the items was so devised as to produce an equal number of "agree" and "disagree" responses. The items were keyed and scored so that the highest ethnicity score was "5." The total ethnic identity score of an individual, then, would be the sum of the scores of all fifty items; the higher the score, the greater the degree of ethnicity.

The items chosen for inclusion in the questionnaire consisted of a number of categories such as a preference for things Japanese (movies, food, etc.), family kinship, community relations, child-rearing practices, personality characteristics, sex roles, etc. Initially, this list was composed of over one hundred items but was reduced to the more manageable number of fifty (Masuda, Matsumoto, and Meredith 1970:200).

The questionnaire was then translated by an Issei professional translator at the University of Washington for use with the Issei population, many of whom have only marginal ability in English. The questionnaire was first administered to a group of Japanese Americans in Seattle, Washington. The method used was by means of mailings and church distribution. The rate of return for the entire sample was 24.3 per cent for the

Issei and 33.9 per cent for the Nisei and Sansei. The Seattle sample was composed of 125 Issei, 114 Nisei, and 94 Sansei (Masuda, Matsumoto, and Meredith 1970:201). An additional survey of the Honolulu population was carried out in the summer of 1968. Of the 700 questionnaires mailed, 287 were returned for an overall return rate of 41 per cent (1970:64). Results of the two population samples are available in the aforementioned articles.

I became aware of the E.I.Q. through the above articles and wrote to Minoru Masuda of the Department of Psychiatry, School of Medicine, University of Washington. Dr. Masuda very kindly supplied copies of both the English and Japanese versions of the E.I.Q. The next step in the study was to obtain a copy of a directory of Japanese Americans for the Sacramento area. The directory, published by the *Nichi Bei Times* of San Francisco, lists over two thousand Japanese American names for the Sacramento area. Further, the directory also indicates whether the person listed was born in the United States or in Japan. It should be added, however, that not all individuals are so identified and in many cases the listings are apparently out of date. Of the 600 E.I.Q. forms mailed out, 78 (12 per cent) were returned because the addressee had moved and had left no forwarding address. Further, as was expected, the majority of names listed in the directory were those of Nisei.

Mailings were done in two stages. The first mailing was made in January 1971, from a mailing list composed of 100 randomly picked Issei and 200 other randomly picked Japanese Americans. Of these, 14 forms addressed to Issei and 22 addressed to other Japanese Americans were returned to the sender by the Post Office as being undeliverable. The return rate for the remainder of the forms was very close to that reported for the Seattle survey. In all, 22 of the Issei returned the forms for a return rate of 25.5 per cent. The Nisei and Sansei response was higher, with a total of 62 forms returned for a return rate of 34.8 per cent.

A second mailing was made in March, 1971, to 100 randomly picked Issei and 200 randomly picked Nisei and Sansei. Once again, 16 of those addressed to the Issei and 26 addressed to the Nisei and Sansei were returned by the Post Office as being undeliverable. The return rate for the remainder of the forms was very close to that of the earlier mailing. The Issei returned 23 forms for a return rate of 27 per cent and the Nisei and Sansei returned 64 of the forms for a return rate of 36 per cent. The total return rate for both mailings was 26.5 per cent for the Issei and 35.8 per cent for the Nisei and Sansei.

Since the majority of the names listed in the directory were Nisei, some 93 of the 126 non-Issei-returned forms were from Nisei; the remainder consisted of 12 Kibei and 21 Sansei. In order to increase the size of the Sansei group, the students participating in the Japanese American community study project discussed earlier were asked to administer the form to those Japanese Americans they were interviewing. Fortunately, this was no problem. Some two-thirds of the students in the class were themselves Sansei and therefore had access not only to other Sansei but to the Nisei and Issei as well. The remaining sample of the Japanese Americans, then, was derived from personal contact by the students. In most cases those Sansei who were so contacted were themselves students and were often personally known to the interviewer. Similarly, the remaining sample of Issei and Nisei were in many instances relatives and friends of the interviewer. The total sample, then, consisted of 69 Issei, 149 Nisei, and 105 Sansei. In turn, these were composed of 37 male and 32 female Issei, 103 male and 46 female Nisei, and 59 male and 46 female Sansei. As indicated earlier, the larger Nisei male sample was a result of a far larger number of male listings in the directory. The Kibei were not included in the analysis of data because of the small size (12) of the sample.

The biographical information reported on the E.I.Q. indicates that the respondents in the three generations were very much like those we had interviewed. Thus the mean age of the Issei was 71 years, the Nisei 47 years, and the Sansei 23.71 years. The mean education reported was 9 years for the Issei, 13.8 for the Nisei, and 14.48 for the Sansei. The religious preference of the Issei was 69 per cent Buddhist, 25 per cent Protestant, and 5 per cent listed no religion. The Nisei reported 60 per cent Buddhist, 38 per cent Protestant, and 2 per cent listed no religion. The Sansei reported 45 per cent Buddhist, 38 per cent Protestant, 2 per cent Catholic, and 15 per cent gave no religion. Once more, the above figures are quite close to those given during the interviewing.

The marital status is also in accord with our previous

information. Thus 64 per cent of the Issei are married, 32 per cent widowed, and 3 per cent report having never married. The Nisei list 87 per cent married, 3 per cent widowed, 8 per cent never married, and 2 per cent divorced. The Sansei,'as was expected, reported 73 per cent never married, and 27 per cent married.

Overall, then, the biographical information substantiates our previous data and indicates that those who responded were not unusual or aberrant to any degree.

Once collected, the data were then transferred to data processing cards. A program was next written which would allow us to process our data in the same manner as was done in the Seattle and Honolulu studies, as ultimately we wished to share our data with those at the University of Washington. Essentially this amounted to obtaining an item analysis of each statement for the males and females in all three generations and then a total score for each generation. The statistical analysis was derived by means of the Mann-Whitney U test for pairs, the same test used in the Seattle and Honolulu surveys.

Analysis of Data

Following Masuda, Matsumoto, and Meredith (1970:202), the five-point scale ranging from strongly agree (5) to strongly disagree (1) was further categorized in terms of endorsement of an item on either side of neutrality. This score was on an equal distribution basis. That is, a strongly positive identification would be greater than 4.20; a positive identification would be greater than 3.40; a neutral identification or undecided would range from below 3.39 to 2.61; a negative identification would be below 1.80.

Table 10.1 indicates those items which show the significant differences between sexes within generations. It will be noted that Table 10.1 and subsequent tables contain abbreviated items for the sake of simplicity. The complete wording of each statement is to be found in the copy of the E.I.Q. included in the Appendix.

An analysis of the items revealing a significant difference in sex supports a number of previous studies and complements our other data. For example, the Issei interview forms disclosed that the males were more acculturated than the females in a number of areas, largely because they were in greater contact with other Americans than were the Issei females. Table 10.1 discloses that the Issei males scored higher on items 17, 29, 32, and 43, while the Issei females scored higher on items 3, 19, 22, 35, and 48. A glance at Table 10.1 indicates that a single item, item 32, "When in need of aid, it is best to rely mainly on relatives," was the only item scored higher by the Issei males that would indicate higher Japanese identity or ethnicity. The other items scored higher (17, 29, and 43) are all those which indicate a more American identity. On the other hand, all of the items (3, 19, 22, 35, and 48) scored higher by the Issei females indicate a greater Japanese identity or ethnicity. By the same logic, the lower score on items 17, 22, and 48 would also indicate more of a Japanese identity or ethnicity. In particular, two are most revealing. These are items 29 and 35.

Table 10.1
Significant Differences Between Sexes Within Generations†

Item no.	Item	Generation	Sex	Mean item score
1	A good child is an obedient child.	Sansei	M	3.20
			F	2.76
2	All right for personal desires to come before family.	Nisei	M	2.43
			F	2.83
3	Japanese Americans shouldn't disagree around Caucasians.	Nisei	M	2.30
			F	2.62
4	I especially like Japanese food.	Sansei	M	3.37
			F	3.76
9	It's the duty of the eldest son to care for the parents.	Nisei	M	2.83
			F	2.40
		Sansei	M	2.95
			F	2.57
17	Japanese Americans should identify completely as Americans.	Issei	M	3.97
			F	3.44
		Nisei	M	2.99
			F	2.40
18	I am apt to hide my feelings in some things.	Nisei	M	3.19
			F	3.65
		Sansei	M	3.25
			F	3.63
19	It's a shame for Japanese Americans not to know Japanese.	Issei	M	3.89
			F	4.27
		Sansei	M	3.32
			F	3.83

20	Japanese have a refinement and feeling for nature.	Sansei	M	3.19
			F	3.83
21	I would be disturbed if not treated as an equal.	Sansei	M	3.70
			F	4.13
22	Unrealistic of Japanese Americans to hope to be a leader.	Issei	M	2.38
			F	2.79
26	Older brother's decision is to be respected more than younger's.	Sansei	M	2.53
			F	2.15
29	I always think of myself as an American first.	Issei	M	3.73
			F	3.00
30	Children will appreciate Japanese schools later.	Nisei	M	3.66
			F	4.02
		Sansei	M	3.14
			F	3.70
32	When in need of aid, rely on relatives.	Issei	M	3.92
			F	3.59
		Nisei	M	3.44
			F	2.98
35	Once a Japanese always a Japanese.	Issei	M	3.38
			F	3.94
		Sansei	M	2.76
			F	3.20
37	Nice to learn Japanese culture but not necessary.	Sansei	M	3.59
			F	3.09
43	I usually participate in mixed group discussions.	Issei	M	2.76
			F	2.21
48	I prefer attending an all-Japanese church.	Issei	M	3.19
			F	3.65
50	Interracial marriages to Caucasians should be discouraged.	Sansei	M	2.12
			F	1.98

†Significant at the .05 level or better (Mann-Whitney U Test).

Item 29, "I always think of myself as an American first and a Japanese second," was scored 3.73 by the Issei males and 3.00 by the Issei females. Item 35, "Once a Japanese always a Japanese," was scored 3.38 by the Issei males and 3.94 by the females. These items and those just mentioned, then, do support our earlier contention that the Issei males are more acculturated than the females.

With respect to the Nisei and Sansei, the results are less clear-cut. There is some evidence (Caudill 1952, DeVos 1955, Arkoff, Meredith, and Iwahara 1962) that Nisei and Sansei females are acculturating more rapidly than the males. The results of the E.I.Q., however, do not permit a simple affirmation or denial. For example, the Nisei males scored higher on items 9, 17, and 32, while the females scored higher on items 2, 18, and 30. Table 10.1 reveals that items 9 and 32 indicated a more Japanese identity, while item 17 does not. Similarly, items 18 and 30 indicate a greater Japanese identity while item 2 does not. Again, the higher scores of the Sansei males on items 1, 9, 26, 37, and 50 would indicate that they have more of a Japanese identity on those items than do the females. Yet, on items 4, 18, 19, 20, 30, and 35 the females scored higher and therefore have a greater ethnic identity than the males. The E.I.Q., then, does not appear to offer a clear male-female pattern for the Nisei and Sansei.

Table 10.2 lists those items showing the hypothesized generation differences. Those items scored positively (above 3.40) and those scored negatively (below 2.60) by each generation will be discussed in greater detail in subsequent pages. By way of simple numerical analysis, certain generational differences became immediately apparent. Of the twenty-seven items in the table, 22 were scored positively, three neutrally, and two negatively by the Issei generation. In the Nisei generation, fifteen items were scored positively, ten neutrally, and two negatively. The Sansei generation scored nine items positively, eleven items neutrally, and seven items negatively.

For the most part, the implications of the progression of mean item scores through the three generations are fairly self-evident. However, there are several items that do require additional comment. In particular, while the majority of items support the retention of the Japanese identity in at least two of the three generations, there are a number of items that point toward acculturation. These are items 3, 17, 23, and 36. Item 3, "Japanese Americans should not disagree among themselves if there are Caucasians around," was disagreed to by all three generations. Item 17, "The best thing for the Japanese Americans to do is to associate more with Caucasians and identify completely as Americans," was agreed to by the Issei, scored neutrally by the Nisei, and disagreed to by the Sansei. Item 17 is interesting in that it indicates a higher degree of agreement in the Issei than might at first sight be expected. It is possible, however, that the Issei favor greater association with Caucasians for all Japanese Americans and not just themselves. That is to say, based upon all of our evidence, the Issei are the least acculturated of the three

gro⅃ps and, from their perspective, increased association may be a
goɔd thing. From the Sansei perspective and, to a lesser extent the
Niꞩi as well, there has already been considerable acculturation
and the effort now is more in the retention of an ethnic identity.

Table 10.2
Items Showing Hypothesized Generation Differences

Item no.	Item	Issei (N–69)	Nisei (N–147)	Sansei (N–105)
		Category group and mean item scores		
1	A good child is an obedient child.	3.97†	3.52.h	2.98
3	Japanese Americans shouldn't disagree around Caucasians.	2.46†	2.06	1.83
5	Japanese background helps prevent trouble.	3.80†	3.41†	2.90
7	More comfortable to live with Japanese Americans.	3.19	3.02	2.98
11	Japanese Americans should retain own culture.	4.18	4.12	3.95
13	Japanese Americans are deprived of opportunities.	3.45‡	3.12‡	2.66
17	Japanese Americans should identify completely as Americans.	3.71†	2.69‡	2.39
19	Shame for Japanese Americans not to know Japanese.	4.08‡	3.68	3.57
20	Japanese have a refinement and a feeling for nature.	3.10†	3.64	3.51
23	I don't have a strong attachment to Japan.	2.76†	3.49	3.59
26	Older brother's decision is to be respected more than younger's.	3.01‡	2.47	2.34
27	I feel less at ease with Caucasians than with Japanese Americans.	3.68†	2.82†	2.34
28	Japanese are no better or no worse than others.	3.68	3.69	4.04
30	Children will appreciate Japanese schools later.	3.94	3.84‡	3.41
31	Life in U.S. is ideal for Japanese Americans.	4.00‡	3.70	3.11
32	When in need of aid, rely on relatives.	3.75†	3.21	3.08
33	Better that Japanese Americans date Japanese Americans.	3.73†	2.91†	2.02
35	Once a Japanese always a Japanese.	3.66†	3.00	2.98

36	Good relations with Caucasians without organizations.	3.44	3.70	3.79
40	Those unfavorable to Japanese culture are wrong.	3.97	3.74	3.62
41	He who cannot repay gratitude cannot be noble.	4.27†	3.58	3.31
42	Best to avoid places where one is not welcome.	3.83‡	3.50†	2.77
43	I usually participate in mixed group discussions.	2.48†	3.36	3.44
45	I enjoy Japanese movies.	3.67	3.42	3.15
47	Person who raises questions interferes with the group.	3.64†	2.72	2.51
48	I prefer attending an all-Japanese church.	3.42†	2.98	2.60
49	A man cannot let himself down without letting family down.	3.89	3.67†	3.00

†Significant at the .01 level (Mann-Whitney U Test).
‡Significant at the .05 level (Mann-Whitney U Test).

Item 23, "I don't have a strong feeling of attachment to Japan," was scored neutrally by the Issei and positively by the Nisei and Sansei, thus revealing a more American identity. Item 26, "An older brother's decision is to be respected more than that of a younger one," was scored neutrally by the Issei and negatively by the Nisei and Sansei, again indicating a change from the more traditional Japanese response. Item 28, "The Japanese are no better or no worse than any other race," was scored positively by each generation and, as such, indicates an attenuation of a Japanese identity in each group. Item 31, "Life in the United States is quite ideal for Japanese Americans," was agreed to by the Issei and Nisei and scored neutrally by the Sansei. Again, however, given the totality of our evidence, the Sansei response does not necessarily indicate that they believe the United States to be a bad place for Japanese Americans, but rather that they want to better their position here, a conclusion supported by item 36. Item 36, "Good relations between Japanese and Caucasians can be maintained without the aid of traditional organizations," was scored positively by all three generations, with the Sansei scoring highest.

The items listed in Table 10.2 reveal both a considerable retention of a Japanese identity in the Issei generation and the

predicted attenuation of ethnicity in the Nisei and Sansei generations. However, neither the retention nor the divestment of
identity is clear-cut. Tables 10.2 and 10.3 disclose that there has
been both acculturation in the Issei generation and an attempt to
preserve a Japanese cultural heritage in the Nisei and Sansei
generations. The degree of retention and the form it has taken
will be a topic of discussion later in this chapter; for the moment,
suffice it to say that the Issei retain the more psychological and
behavioral Japanese characteristics while the Issei and Nisei
appear to be more interested in the artistic and aesthetic heritage.

Table 10.3 in a sense complements Table 10.2 in that it lists
those items not showing the hypothesized generation differences.
In several cases the differences were not too significant but were
included in the table in the interest of consistency. For example,
there is little significant difference between the Issei and Nisei
scores on items 4, 22, and 37, or between the Nisei and Sansei on
items 2, 4, 15, and 16.

Table 10.3
Items Not Showing Hypothesized Generation Differences

Item no.	Item	Category group and mean item scores		
		Issei (N–69)	Nisei (N–147)	Sansei (N–105)
2	All right for personal desires to come before family.	2.26‡	2.62	<u>2.59</u>
4	I especially like Japanese food.	3.57	3.54	3.57
6	It's unlucky to be born Japanese.	1.67	<u>1.85</u>	1.59
8	When I feel affectionate I show it.	<u>3.60‡</u>	3.17	3.70
9	It is the duty of the eldest son to care for parents.	3.34†	<u>2.61</u>	2.76
10	Japanese Americans without expectation of discrimination are naive.	3.00	<u>3.25</u>	2.94
12	A wife's career is just as important as the husband's.	<u>3.55</u>	3.26	3.62
14	It is all right for children to question decision of parents.	<u>4.09</u>	3.90‡	4.20
15	In Japanese community, relationships are more warm.	3.93†	3.03	<u>3.06</u>
16	I would not feel tendency to agree with Japanese government.	3.41‡	<u>3.78</u>	3.71

18	I am apt to hide my feelings in some things.	3.06‡	3.42	3.44
21	I would be disturbed if not treated as an equal.	3.62	3.56‡	3.91
22	It's unrealistic of Japanese Americans to hope to be a leader.	2.59	2.60‡	2.21
24	I am not too spontaneous and casual with people.	2.51	2.82	2.59
26	Not necessary for parents to preserve cultural heritage.	2.66	2.57	2.64
29	I always think of myself as an American first.	3.37	3.55	3.23
34	Parents who are companionable can still maintain respect.	4.12	3.93	4.19
37	Nice to learn more about Japanese culture, but not necessary.	3.34	3.36	3.34
38	Better if there were no all-Japanese communities.	2.84‡	2.44	2.45
39	Japan has art heritage and has contributed to civilization.	4.00	3.94	4.07
44	Many Japanese customs are no longer adequate.	3.23‡	2-85	3.13
46	It is a natural part of growing up to "wise off."	2.87‡	2.45‡	3.03
50	Interracial marriages to Caucasians should be discouraged.	2.64	2.79	1.95

Note: Underlining indicates discrepant group.
†Significant at the .01 level (Mann-Whitney U Test).
‡Significant at the .05 level (Mann-Whitney U Test).

The table does, however, reveal a number of differences in the generations. It appears that on several of the items the Issei emerge as more liberal while the Nisei, and occasionally even the Sansei, are more conservative than anticipated. For example, in items 8, 12, 14, 18, 25, 34, 37, 44, 46, and 50, the responses of the Issei are more liberal than would be expected when compared to the Nisei and Sansei. A possible explanation which is elaborated upon later is that the Issei are now largely retired and are therefore more easy going, relaxed, and spontaneous than are the Nisei, who are in their late forties and at the height of their responsibilities. Another possible explanation is that the Nisei, although inculcated with Japanese values in childhood, had a more direct confrontation with American society and were exposed to more prejudice than either the Issei or Sansei. They may be more guarded in the expression of their feelings and opinions than the others. Some indication of this can be seen in items 6, 10, 16, 21, 22, 29, and 44.

These items disclose that the Nisei are more predisposed to expect prejudice and perhaps a little more prone to demonstrate their Americanism than are the Issei or Sansei. On items 8, 12, 14, 15, 24, 25, 34, 44, 46, and 50, the Nisei are more conservative than either the Issei or Sansei. Again, this may be a reflection of their position as parents and their awareness of their responsibilities as mature adults. The Nisei are more reserved, more guarded, and less spontaneous than their parents or offspring in these areas. Once more, however, this behavior of the middle-aged Nisei in many respects resembles that of their contemporaries in Japan. As Benedict remarks:

> The arc of life in Japan is plotted in opposite fashion to that in the United States. It is a great shallow U-curve with maximum freedom and indulgence allowed to babies and to the old. Restrictions are slowly increased after babyhood till having one's own way reaches a low just before and after marriage. This low line continues many years during the prime of life, but the arc gradually ascends again until after the age of sixty men and women are almost as unhampered by shame as little children are. In the United States we stand this curve upside down. Firm disciplines are directed toward the infant and these are gradually relaxed as the child grows in strength until a man runs his own life when he gets a self-supporting job and when he sets up a household of his own. The prime of life is with us the high point of freedom and initiative. Restrictions begin to appear as men lose their grip or become dependent. (1946:253-54)

The responses of the Sansei reveal both a change toward American values and the retention of a Japanese identity. A more American response is seen in items 8, 12, 14, 16, 21, 22, 24, 34, and 50. The more Japanese responses are items 2, 4, 6, 18, 25, 29, 38, and 39. For the most part, the American items indicate a change toward American values such as a greater show of affection (8) and husband-wife equality (12). On the other hand, with the exception of items 2, 18, and 29, most of those that reveal a more Japanese response are items expressive of a more aesthetic and symbolic identification with Japan. Further, it is difficult to evaluate to what degree the responses were prompted by the current interest in "ethnic identity" among the Sansei. It is possible that such an interest may have influenced the scores on a number of items, such as item 29, "I always think of myself as an American first" (3.23), and item 38, "It would be better if there were no all-Japanese communities" (2.45).

The Issei Generation

Table 10.4 indicates those items scored positively by the Issei generation—that is, those with means of 3.40 or higher. The table discloses that there were thirty-one items to which the Issei gave a positive response. Of these thirty-one items, twenty-one were phrased so that they would indicate a more Japanese identification or ethnicity if scored positively. These were items 1, 4, 5, 11, 13, 15, 19, 20, 27, 30, 32, 33, 35, 39, 40, 41, 42, 45, 47, 48, and 49. Also included in the thirty-one positively scored responses were ten which indicated a more American identification. These were items 8, 12, 14, 16, 17, 21, 28, 31, 34, and 36.

In the above classification of positively scored Japanese responses are a number which directly relate to the five major Japanese characteristics of collectivity, duty and obligation, hierarchy, deference, and dependence discussed in detail earlier. Further, it will be recalled that implicit in these were some twenty subsidiary characteristics and that among these were such as "children are trained to be docile, obedient, and dependent." The positively scored Japanese responses, then, which directly relate to the major and subsidiary Japanese characteristics are items 1, 32, 41, 47, and 49. Of these, item 1, "A good child is an obedient child," illustrates the importance of hierarchy and deference. Item 32, "When in need of aid it is best to rely mainly on relatives," indicates the emphasis on collectivity. Item 41, "He who does not repay a debt of gratitude cannot claim to be noble," was given the highest positive response of all the items and most certainly indicates the importance of duty and obligation. The stress on the group and group unanimity or collectivity receives additional emphasis from item 47, "A person who raises too many questions interferes with the progress of the group." And again, duty and obligation and collectivity come together in item 49, "A man can never let himself down without letting the family down at the same time." This item further illustrates not only the importance of family ties but also the extent to which a person is seen less as an autonomous individual and more as a representative of the group, and one whose very actions reflect upon the group.

The ten American responses, on the other hand, may reveal several things. One, they might indicate a higher degree of acculturation than anticipated. Two, they may just possibly indicate behavior that is in reality quite Japanese. By that is meant that a number of items indicating a more open, less reserved attitude were scored positively by the Issei and lower by the Nisei, and occasionally even lower by the Sansei. For example, item 8, "When I feel affectionate I show it," was scored 3.60 by the Issei, 3.17 by the Nisei, and 3.70 by the Sansei. Likewise, item 18, "I am apt to hide my feelings in some things, to the point that people may hurt me without their knowing it," was agreed to by the Nisei (3.42) and Sansei (3.44) but not by the Issei (3.06). Further, item 34, "Parents who are very companionable with their children can still maintain respect and obedience," was scored positively by all groups: Issei (4.12), Nisei (3.93), and Sansei (4.19), although the Issei scored slightly higher than the Nisei.

Table 10.4
Items Scored Positively by the Issei Generation

Item no.	Item	Mean item score (N–69)
1	A good child is an obedient child.	3.97
4	I especially like Japanese food.	3.57
5	Japanese background helps prevent trouble.	3.80
8	When I feel affectionate I show it.	3.60
11	Japanese Americans should retain their own culture.	4.18
12	A wife's career is just as important as the husband's.	3.55
13	Japanese Americans are deprived of opportunities.	3.46
14	It's all right for children to question the decision of parents.	4.09
15	In Japanese community, relationships are more warm.	3.93
16	I would not feel a tendency to agree with Japanese government.	3.41
17	Japanese Americans should identify completely as Americans.	3.71
19	It's a shame for Japanese Americans not to know Japanese.	4.08

20	Japanese people have a refinement and feeling for nature.	4.11
21	I would be disturbed if I was not treated as an equal.	3.62
27	I feel less at ease with Caucasians than with Japanese Americans.	3.68
28	Japanese are no better or no worse than others.	3.68
30	Children will appreciate Japanese schools later.	3.94
31	Life in the United States is ideal for Japanese Americans.	4.00
32	When one is in need of aid, it is better to rely on relatives.	3.75
33	It's better that Japanese Americans date only Japanese Americans.	3.73
34	Parents who are companionable can still maintain respect.	4.12
35	Once a Japanese, always a Japanese.	3.66
36	Can have good relations with Caucasians without organizations.	3.43
39	Japan has a great art heritage and has contributed to civilization.	4.00
40	Those unfavorable to Japanese culture are wrong.	3.97
41	He who cannot repay a debt of gratitude cannot be noble.	4.27
42	It is best to avoid places where one is not welcome.	3.83
45	I enjoy Japanese movies.	3.67
47	A person who raises too many questions interferes with the group.	3.64
48	I prefer attending an all-Japanese church.	3.42
49	A man cannot let himself down without letting his family down.	3.92

Other items, although less indicative of personality, nonetheless disclose the Issei as being more relaxed and open on some issues than the Nisei. Item 12, for example, "A wife's career is just as important as the husband's," was agreed to by the Issei (3.55) and Sansei (3.62), while the Nisei were uncertain (3.26). Similarly, item 14, "It is all right for children to question the decisions of their parents once in a while," was agreed to by all groups: Issei (4.09), Nisei (3.90), and Sansei (4.20), although the Issei were slightly more positive than the Nisei.

The nature of the replies to the above items suggests that the relaxed attitude of the Issei may be a result of their looking at the behavior of their children and grandchildren more from the perspective of being grandparents and retired rather than as an indication of a higher degree of acculturation. Support for the changing perspective on behavior is found in much of the literature on Japan. Embree mentions that when a man reaches sixty-one he holds a party to celebrate reaching the last and oldest age group. He can now wear red, the traditional color of children. And, like children, old people may now say and do things without criticism. I they demand something, it should be given to them (Embree 1939:214).

Keene reports somewhat the same pattern for contemporary Japan. A Japanese who has spent most of the years of his adult life catering to the wishes of his superiors may look forward to old age, at which time his own cravings are indulged and his whims will be humored. Old men and old women enjoy a freedom of speech unknown to other than children. They may forget honorifics or present opinions quite bizarre to others. They can indulge themselves in outlandish Western clothes or even attend meetings of the Communist Party—Keene remarks that it is amazing how many old people show up (1960:78-79).

By way of personal experience in support of the above, a Japanese relative of the author who was visiting us in the summer of 1971 reported that her father, who is now retired, has become very demanding and does, in fact, wish to have his every whim catered to and his every desire satisfied. Yet it could be argued that, if retirement brings about a change in behavior, then those Issei in o her areas who are about the same age—and consequently also retired—should score about the same. Fortunately, the Seattle survey provides us with a basis for comparison (Masuda, Matsumoto, and Meredith 1970).

It will be recalled that the ten items which indicated a more American identification for the Issei were items 8, 12, 14, 16, 17, 21, 28, 31, 34, and 36. Table 10.5 below compares the scores of the Sacramento Issei with those of the Seattle Issei on the ten items.

From Table 10.5 it is at once apparent that, with the exception of items 21 and 31, the scores of the Sacramento Issei are much higher. These scores, then, do indicate a higher degree of acculturation than is apparent in the Seattle group.

There are, moreover, a number of other items scored positively by the Issei that do appear to indicate a degree of acculturation, although these are more in the direction of a change in attitude than a change in behavior. And, indeed, some of these are in fact contradicted by others. For example, item 17,

"Japanese Americans should identify completely as Americans,"
was scored 3.71 by the Issei, 2.69 by the Nisei, and 2.39 by the
Sansei. Likewise, item 31, "Life in the United States is ideal for
Japanese Americans," was scored 4.00 by the Issei, 3.70 by the
Nisei, and 3.11 by the Sansei.

Table 10.5
Comparison of Sacramento and Seattle Issei Scores on Ten Items

Item no.	Item	Sacramento (N–69)	Seattle (N–125)
8	When I feel affectionate I show it.	3.60	2.21
12	A wife's career is just as important as the husband's.	3.55	2.59
14	It's all right for children to question the decision of parents.	4.09	1.88
16	I would not feel a tendency to agree with the Japanese government.	3.41	2.50
17	Japanese Americans should identify completely as Americans.	3.71	1.98
21	I would be disturbed if I was not treated as an equal.	3.62	3.84
28	Japanese are no better or no worse than others.	3.68	2.62
31	Life in the United States is ideal for Japanese Americans.	4.00	4.20
34	Parents who are companionable can still maintain respect.	4.12	1.93
36	Can have good relations with Caucasians without organizations.	3.44	2.20

These figures are most interesting for what they reveal. On
item 17, the Issei are answering from the standpoint of being
marginally acculturated—a fact supported by the large number of
Japanese items they scored positively. Therefore, from their
perspective, additional acculturation is a desirable trend. The
Nisei, however, see themselves as combining the best of both
cultures and are especially worried about the erosion of Japanese
characteristics in the Sansei generation. They therefore believe
that the trend should be reversed. The Sansei, moreover, agree

with them but for different reasons. As Table 10.9 discloses—and our other data support—the Sansei are even more psychologically and behaviorally acculturated than the Nisei. They are interested now in retaining as much as possible of their Japanese heritage. Again, however, the retention is more in the form of a symbolic identification with the more artistic aspects of Japanese culture. In other words, the Sansei idea of what is important and worth preserving in Japanese culture comes more and more to resemble that of the Caucasian Japanophile. With respect to the Japanese psychological and behavioral characteristics mentioned previously, the Sansei are beginning to view these as a bit foreign— an observation frequently made by those Sansei who have traveled to Japan.

Item 51, "Life in the United States is ideal for Japanese Americans," also disclosed the expected change from Issei (4.00), to Nisei (3.70), to Sansei (3.11). Again, these responses very strongly parallel the answers given in the interview forms. It will be recalled that, while over 90 per cent of the Issei and Nisei believed that the Japanese Americans had been successful in the United States, a somewhat lesser number (82 per cent) of the Sansei males so believed. In turn, this is a reflection both of the different definitions of success that were discussed in the chapter on the Sansei interviews, and also of the greater satisfaction shown by the Issei—who are largely retired—and the Nisei, who are now in the prime of life.

In all, Table 10.4 indicates a rather high degree of retention of Japanese in the Issei generation. Those items classified as American in Table 10.5 and scored positively indicate a higher degree of acculturation than anticipated, although the retired status of the Issei is undoubtedly a factor. This latter conclusion gains support from Table 10.6, which indicated those items scored negatively by the Issei.

These negatively scored items disclose both Japanese and American replies. Items 2 and 43 reveal a more Japanese response, while item 24, "I am not too spontaneous and casual with people," probably indicates a retired status since it was scored lower by the Issei (2.51) than for the Nisei (2.82) or for the Sansei (2.59).

Items 3, 6, and 22, however, complement the positively scored item 17, "Japanese Americans should identify completely as

Americans," as does item 31, "Life in the United States is ideal for Japanese Americans." The Issei do not believe that it is impossible for Japanese Americans to be leaders and they strongly disagree that it is unlucky to be born Japanese. Further, they do not believe that it is necessary for the Japanese Americans to put up a "solid front" when around Caucasians.

The Nisei Generation

As might be expected from their middle position in the three-generation span and their self-evaluation rating of 5 on the ten-point scale as given in Table 7, ranging from a completely Japanese identity (1) to a completely American identity (10), the Nisei had more undecided responses than did either the Issei or Sansei.

As can be seen in Tables 10.7 and 10.8, there were twenty-three items scored positively by the Nisei and seven items scored negatively. This leaves twenty items which were scored neutrally. Of the twenty-three items scored positively, there were fourteen which indicated a more Japanese identification or ethnicity. These were items 1, 4, 5, 11, 18, 19, 20, 30, 39, 40, 41, 42, 45, and 49. The more American response items were 14, 16, 21, 23, 28, 29, 31, 34, and 36.

Of the Japanese ethnicity items there are several that correspond to the listing of major and subsidiary Japanese characteristics already given. These are items 1, 5, 18, 41, and 49. Item 1, "A good child is an obedient child," indicates the importance of deference and hierarchy. It further supports the contention of many of the Sansei that the Nisei are somewhat authoritarian and conservative. Item 5, "A good Japanese background helps prevent youth from getting into all kinds of trouble that other American youth have today," complements item 1 and perhaps provides the justification for it. As such, it supports the emphasis placed on duty and obligation, and the principle of not bringing shame to the family, both of which have been previously mentioned.

Item 18, "I am apt to hide my feelings in some things, to the point that people may hurt me without their knowing it," indirectly supports the emphasis on deference rather than self-assertiveness or dominance. Item 41, "He who cannot repay a debt of gra_itude cannot claim to be noble," indicates the continued importance of duty and obligation in the Nisei generation. Further, the stress on duty and obligation receives additional emphasis in item 49, "A man can never let himself down without letting his family down at the same time." Again, as was mentioned in the analysis of the Issei responses, item 49 also supports the stress placed on collectivity, family ties, and the resultant view of the person as being a representative of the family group.

Table 10.6
Items Scored Negatively by the Issei Generation

Item no.	Item	Mean item score (N–69)
2	t is all right for personal desires to come before family.	2.25
3	_apane_e Americans should not disagree around _aucasians.	2.46
6	t's unlucky to be born Japanese.	1.67
22	t's unrealistic for Japanese to hope to be leaders.	2.59
24	am not too spontaneous and casual with people.	2.48
43	usual y participate in mixed group discussions.	2.48

The remaining Japanese ethnicity items are 4, 11, 19, 20, 26, 30, 39, 40, 42, and 45. Item 4, "I especially like Japanese foods," was also scored positively by the Issei and Sansei and the answer was very much as anticipated. Item 11, "I think it is all right for Japanese Americans to become Americanized, but they should retain part of their own culture," was also scored positively by the Issei and Sansei, and again the replies of the Nisei were as anticipated Items 19, 20, 30, 40, 42, and 45 were also as anticipated. Again, as Table 10.2 indicates, the Nisei responses place them in the middle of the three generations. Item 39, "Japan has a great art heritage and has made contributions important to world civilization." although scored positively by all three groups, was scored somewhat higher by the Sansei than by the Nisei. Once more this appears to be a strong indication that the Sansei are interested in the artistic heritage of the Japanese as an important element in ethnic identification.

Table 10.7
Items Scored Positively by the Nisei Generation

Item no.	Item	Mean item score (N–149)
1	A good child is an obedient child.	3.52
4	I especially like Japanese food.	3.54
5	Japanese background helps prevent trouble.	3.41
11	Japanese Americans should retain their own culture.	4.12
14	It's all right for children to question the decisions of parents.	3.90
16	I would not feel a tendency to agree with the Japanese government.	3.78
18	I am apt to hide my feelings in some things.	3.42
19	It is a shame for Japanese Americans not to know Japanese.	3.68
20	Japanese have a refinement and feeling for nature.	3.64
21	I would be disturbed if not treated as an equal.	3.55
23	I don't have a strong attachment to Japan.	3.49
28	Japanese are no better or no worse than others.	3.69
29	I always think of myself as an American first.	3.55
30	Children will appreciate Japanese schools later.	3.84
31	Life in the United States is ideal for Japanese Americans.	3.71
34	Parents who are companionable can still maintain respect.	3.93
36	Good relations can be had with Caucasians without organizations.	3.70
39	Japan has a great art heritage and has contributed to civilization.	3.94
40	Those unfavorable to Japanese culture are wrong.	3.73
41	He who cannot repay a debt of gratitude cannot claim to be noble.	3.58
42	It is best to avoid places where one is not welcome.	3.50
45	I enjoy Japanese movies.	3.42
49	A man cannot let himself down without letting his family down.	3.74

The American responses scored positively by the Nisei were items 14, 16, 23, 28, 29, 34, and 36. While most of the scores place the Nisei between the Issei and Sansei, there are several items that are quite revealing. We have already given an explanation of the higher scores of the Issei on items 14 and 34; however, there remain items 16 and 29, in which the Nisei scored higher than either the Issei or Sansei. Both items directly or indirectly reflect on the Nisei loyalty to the United States. Item 16, "I would not feel any more tendency to agree with the policies of the Japanese government than any other American would," was scored 3.41 by the Issei, 3.78 by the Nisei, and 3.71 by the Sansei. Likewise item 29, "I always think of myself as an American first and as a Japanese second," was scored 3.37 by the Issei, 3.55 by the Nisei, and 3.23 by the Sansei. These two items would tend to indicate that the Nisei are more sensitive about their Americanism than are the Issei or Sansei. It is most interesting in that in every other measure of acculturation that we have used the Sansei are psychologically and behaviorally more American than are the Nisei. For example, Tables 10.9 and 10.10 reveal those items scored positively and negatively by the Sansei. Table 10.2, which records those items that showed the hypothesized generation difference, further indicates the extent to which the Sansei have acculturated. What remains for the Sansei is more of a symbolic, artistic, and aesthetic identity and less of the psychological and behavioral identity maintained by their parents and grandparents.

Table 10.8 indicates those items scored negatively by the Nisei generation. These seven items disclose both Japanese and American identity items. Four of the negatively scored items reveal a more American response. These are items 3, 6, 22, and 26. Item 3, "Japanese Americans should not disagree among themselves if there are Caucasians around," was also scored negatively by the Issei and the Sansei. The Nisei response, as predicted, was in the middle. Item 6, "It's unlucky to be born Japanese," was also scored negatively by the other two groups.

Interestingly, although the Nisei did score it negatively, their score of 1.85 was less negative than the 1.67 of the Issei and the 1.59 of the Sansei. Here again is a slight indication that, because of their greater experience of prejudice, there is a slightly greater tendency to agree with the statement than is seen in the responses of the other two groups. Item 22, "It is unrealistic for a Japanese American to hope that he can become a leader of an organization composed mainly of Caucasians because they will not let him,"

Table 10.8
Items Scored Negatively by the Nisei Generation

Item no.	Item	Mean item score (N–149)
3	Japanese Americans shouldn't disagree around Caucasians.	2.06
6	It's unlucky to be born Japanese.	1.85
22	It's unrealistic of Japanese Americans to hope to be a leader.	2.59
25	Not necessary for parents to preserve cultural heritage.	2.57
26	An elder brother's decision is to be respected more than that of a younger one.	2.47
38	Better if there were no all-Japanese communities.	2.44
46	It is a natural part of growing up to occasionally "wise off."	2.45

was scored almost the same by both the Issei (2.59) and Nisei (2.60) and lower by the Sansei (2.21). Once more, the answer is revealing. Although scored negatively it is barely so, and the closeness of the Issei and Nisei scores is interesting. For one thing, although more discriminatory legislation was passed against the Issei, it was the Nisei who more directly confronted the Caucasian organizations. Further, the interviews revealed higher percentages of prejudice experienced by the Nisei than among the Issei. The scores to item 22, however, do reveal a changed expectation in that the majority of Japanese Americans no longer feel that their Japanese background will be a cause for job discrimination. Item 26, "An older brother's decision is to be respected more than that of a younger one," although scored negatively (2.47), was in the middle of the Issei (3.01) and Sansei (2.34) scores.

The remaining three items scored negatively by the Nisei (25, 38, and 46) indicate more of a retention of Japanese identity. Here again, we find a higher degree of ethnicity in the Nisei than in the Issei or Sansei. In each of the three items, the Nisei scores reveal more of a Japanese identity than do the other two groups. In item 25, "It is not necessary for Japanese American parents to make it a duty to promote the preservation of Japanese cultural heritage in their children," was scored 2.66 by the Issei, 2.57 by the Nisei, and 2.64 by the Sansei. The scores of the Issei and Sansei are just barely in the uncertain range, while the Nisei gave a clearly negative response. The differences in the scores are not great, but they do point toward a greater awareness of the necessity for preserving a cultural heritage in the Nisei generation.

Item 38, "It would be better if there were no all-Japanese communities in the United States," was scored 2.84 by the Issei, 2.44 by the Nisei, and 2.45 by the Sansei. The difference between the Nisei and Sansei is not significant, although it does reveal that both Nisei and Sansei see a greater need for the Japanese community structure as a means for the preservation of their cultural heritage. The Issei, however, are a little more uncertain. The last item scored negatively by the Nisei was item 46, "It is a natural part of growing up to occasionally 'wise off' at teachers, policemen, and other grownups in authority." This item was scored 2.87 by the Issei, 2.45 by the Nisei, and 3.03 by the Sansei. The barely undecided score of the Issei may be a result of their retired status or their status as grandparents. If so, it may reveal an uncertainty about the proper role of children in American society. It will be recalled that one of the most frequent comments on the behavior of the Sansei by the Issei was that the Sansei were completely Americanized. The Nisei, however, appear to be rather certain that such behavior is not to be a natural part of growing up. In this regard, the Nisei responses corespond very closely to the replies of the Sansei during the interviews that a lack of respect would rather quickly anger or upset the Nisei. It is also revealing that the Sansei themselves were largely undecided on this item.

The scores recorded by the Nisei on the E.I.Q. reveal the retention of a number of Japanese characteristics and a rather high degree of ethnicity or Japanese identity. As a matter of fact, in several items their ethnicity scores were somewhat higher than those of the Issei. This is not surprising and, indeed, closely parallels our other data. For the most part, the Issei are retired and appear to be satisfied with their accomplishments. As a group, they are more relaxed than the Nisei, who are still greatly concerned and actively involved in their own careers, and especially those of their offspring. The Nisei are most anxious that the Sansei get started in the right direction. This anxiety in turn leads them to be more demanding of their offspring, and frequently this leads to their being called conservative and authoritarian by the Sansei.

The Sansei Generation

Tables 10.9 and 10.10 record those items scored positively or negatively by the Sansei. There were a total of eighteen items scored positively and thirteen items scored negatively, for a total of thirty-one out of fifty. The remaining nineteen items were scored neutrally.

Of the eighteen items scored positively by the Sansei, eight were Japanese identity items and ten were American identity items. The Japanese identity items were 4, 11, 18, 19, 20, 30, 40, and 49. Of these, only one could be said to indicate a more Japanese personality characteristic. This was item 18, "I am apt to hide my feelings in some things, to the point that people may hurt me without knowing it." This item also disclosed a strong male-female difference. The females' score was 3.63 and the males' 3.25. The total score of 3.44, then, is more reflective of the female influence and, as such, corresponds to the higher female scores on deference, abasement, and intraception that were recorded on the Edwards Personal Preference Schedule to be discussed in detail in another chapter.

The remainder of the items were those relating to such things as food preferences and the retention of the more aesthetic or artistic elements in Japanese culture. Even here, however, except for item 4 on food preference and item 39 on Japan's art heritage, all of the remaining Japanese identity items were scored lower than in either the Issei or Nisei groups. The ten positively scored items which reveal a more American identity were items 8, 12, 14, 16, 21, 23, 28, 34, 36, and 43. Whereas almost all of the Japanese identity items were scored lower by the Sansei than by the Issei or Nisei, all but one American identity item were scored higher by the Sansei than by the Issei or Nisei. The one item scored lower by the Sansei was item 16, "I would not feel any more tendency to agree with the policies of the Japanese government than any other American would." This item was scored 3.41 by the Issei, 3.78 by the Nisei, and 3.71 by the Sansei. The difference is not a great one and its importance has already been discussed in the analysis of the Nisei scores.

Table 10.9
Items Scored Positively by the Sansei Generation

Item no.	Item	Mean item score (N–105)
4	I especially like Japanese food.	3.57
8	When I feel affectionate I show it.	3.70
11	Japanese Americans should retain their own culture.	3.95
12	A wife's career is just as important as the husband's.	3.61
14	It's all right for children to question the decisions of parents.	4.21
16	I would not feel a tendency to agree with the Japanese government.	3.71
18	I am apt to hide my feelings in some things.	3.44
19	It's a shame for Japanese Americans not to know Japanese.	3.57
20	Japanese have a refinement and feeling for nature.	3.51
21	I would be disturbed if not treated as an equal.	3.91
23	I don't have a strong attachment to Japan.	3.59
28	Japanese are no better or no worse than others.	4.04
30	Children will appreciate Japanese schools later.	3.42
34	Parents who are companionable can still maintain respect.	4.19
36	Can have good relations with Caucasians without organizations.	3.79
39	Japan has a great art heritage and has contributed to civilization.	4.07
40	Those unfavorable to Japanese culture are wrong.	3.62
43	I usually participate in mixed group discussions.	3.44

Of the other nine items, five can be said to relate to the major American characteristics discussed in detail earlier. In particular, the five are directly concerned with equality. These are items 12, 14, 21, 34, and 43. Item 12, "A wife's career is just as important as the husband's career," is a direct statement of sexual equality. Item 4, "It is all right for children to question the decisions of their parents once in a while," was scored 4.20 by the Sansei and certainly indicates a very positive response in favor of a more egalitarian approach to child-rearing. Item 21, "I would be disturbed if Caucasians did not accept me as an equal," was also scored positively by the other groups, but the Sansei score of 3.91

is far higher than the Issei 3.62 or Nisei 3.55. Item 34, "Parents who are very companionable with their children can still maintain respect and obedience," was scored highest by the Sansei at 4.19 while the Issei scored 4.12 and the Nisei 3.93. Item 43, "I usually participate in mixed group discussions," was disagreed to by the Issei (2.48), scored neutrally by the Nisei (3.36), and agreed to by the Sansei (3.44). These five items, then, indicate an increase in a feeling of equality and a decreasing emphasis on hierarchy or authoritarianism in the Sansei generation. The more open, less reserved feeling of the Sansei is also apparent in their response of 3.70 to item 8, "When I feel affectionate I show it."

The remaining American identity items were 23, 28, and 36. Item 23, "I don't have a strong attachment to Japan," was scored 3.59 by the Sansei, 3.49 by the Nisei, and 2.76 by the Issei. Item 28, "The Japanese are no better or no worse than any other race," was scored 4.04 by the Sansei, 3.69 by the Nisei, and 3.68 by the Issei. The final item, item 36, "Good relations between Japanese and Caucasians can be maintained without the aid of traditional Japanese organizations," was scored 3.79 by the Sansei, 3.70 by the Nisei, and 3.43 by the Issei, These positively scored items, then, disclose that, while the Sansei are still very much interested in the preservation of their Japanese heritage, that heritage for the most part is an artistic or aesthetic heritage. With but few exceptions, the Sansei are becoming psychologically and behaviorally closer to the Caucasians than to the Issei or Nisei, an observation that is supported by Table 10.10, which lists those items scored negatively by the Sansei.

Table 10.10 contains thirteen items scored negatively. Of these, ten were Japanese ethnicity items and three were American identity items. The Japanese ethnicity items were numbers 3, 6, 22, 24, 26, 27, 33, 47, 48, and 50. Among these items were three that relate to the major Japanese psychological and behavioral characteristics. These were items 24, 26, and 47. Item 24, "I am not too spontaneous and casual with people," was scored 2.59 by the Sansei and indicates more of an openness and less of a rigid approach in dealing with people. Item 26, "An older brother's decision is to be respected more than that of a younger one," was scored 2.34 by the Sansei. This item reveals the lessening importance of hierarchy in the family as relates to the older brother.

Table 10.10
Items Scored Negatively by the Sansei Generation

Item no.	Item	Mean item score (N–105)
2	All right for personal desires to come before the family.	2.59
3	Japanese Americans shouldn't disagree around Caucasians.	1.83
6	It's unlucky to be born Japanese.	1.59
17	Japanese Americans should identify completely as Americans.	2.39
22	It's unrealistic of Japanese Americans to hope to be a leader.	2.21
24	I am not too spontaneous and casual with people.	2.59
26	An older brother's decision is to be respected more than that of a younger one.	2.34
27	I feel less at ease with Caucasians than with Japanese Americans.	2.34
33	Better that Japanese Americans date only Japanese Americans.	2.02
38	Better if there were no all-Japanese communities.	2.45
47	A person who raises too many questions interferes with the group.	2.51
48	I prefer attending an all-Japanese church.	2.60
50	Interracial marriages to Caucasians should be discouraged.	1.95

Item 47, "A person who raises too many questions interferes with the progress of the group," was scored 2.51 and reveals the lessening importance of the need for group unanimity. Further, this item perhaps also indicates the development of a more democratic attitude and a willingness to accommodate divergent viewpoints.

The remaining Japanese ethnicity items (3, 6, 22, 27, 33, 48, and 50) scored negatively reveal that the Sansei see themselves on an equal level with Caucasians. This is expecially true with reference to items 33 and 50, which relate to dating and interracial marriage. Once again, these scores corroborate the information given in the Sansei interviews. That is, there is a little inclination to restrict dating and marriage to other Japanese Americans.

The three American identity items which were scored negatively and thereby indicate a Japanese ethnicity response were items 2, 17, and 18. Item 2, "It is all right for personal desires to come before duty to one's family," was scored 2.60 by the Sansei. This item reveals the continued importance of the family and substantiates the information given in the incomplete sentence tests. Item 17, "The best thing for the Japanese Americans to do is to associate more with Caucasians and identify completely as Americans," was scored 2.39 by the Sansei, 2.69 by the Nisei, and 3.71 by the Issei. Once again, as discussed earlier, this item reveals the intent of the Sansei to preserve their cultural heritage. Whereas the Issei, from the viewpoint of their lower acculturation, approved of a greater identification with the Caucasians, the Sansei—and to a lesser extent the Nisei—believe that complete identification is undesirable and that an attempt should be made to preserve some of the Japanese cultural heritage. In this sense, then, item 38 is complementary. Item 38, "It would be better if there were no all-Japanese communities in the United States," was scored 2.45 by the Sansei, 2.44 by the Nisei, and 2.84 by the Issei. These two items, and those previously discussed, apparently indicate that, although the Sansei see themselves more and more on an equal basis with Caucasians and are desirous of participating fully in American life, they nevertheless wish to retain certain aspects of their Japanese cultural heritage. The dilemma, then, like that of the Jewish middle class mentioned in Chapter 1, is what to retain. Obviously, such things as food habits and art objects are relatively easy to preserve, while such characteristics as deference, dependence, and hierarchy are already disappearing.

Summary

The Ethnic Identity Questionnaire, then, reveals both a considerable attitudinal acculturation in the Issei generation and a considerable attitudinal ethnicity in the Sansei generation. The term "attitudinal" is deliberate in that, as has been repeatedly demonstrated, the Issei remain psychologically and behaviorally Japanese. Conversely, while the Sansei are psychologically and behaviorally closer to the Caucasians than are the Issei or Nisei, their attitude is also one of seeing a need for the preservation of a Japanese ethnic identity. However, as has been illustrated throughout, those aspects of a Japanese identity that the Sansei wish to preserve are more the artistic and aesthetic rather than the psychological and behavioral; and, indeed, it could hardly be otherwise. The E.I.Q. further supports our other data in the information it reveals on the Nisei generation. In many respects they emerge as being more conservative than the Issei. In part, this is a direct result of their age and responsibilities. They are less affectionate and more reserved than the Issei and Sansei, less willing to tolerate an offspring who would "wise off," and less willing to tolerate an interracial marriage. This latter item apparently conflicts with the information given in the interview forms, but not exactly. The question relating to interracial marriage was somewhat different on the interview forms. The questions there were less specific, asking only the respondent's opinion with reference to marriages to non-Japanese, rather than to Caucasians or others. In this regard, we have already seen that there were frequently comments made as to the acceptability of marriage to Caucasians, whereas there were strong reservations expressed as to marriages to blacks and to other minority groups.

In sum, it appears that the E.I.Q. is a useful instrument for the determination of ethnicity, particularly when it is used in conjunction with other instruments. All of our instruments indicate that there is a gradual attrition of a Japanese identity through the three generations, although, as we have seen, the pattern of attrition does not uniformly affect all the characteristics that make up the Japanese identity. This pattern of attrition is apparent in the E.I.Q. scores. It will be recalled that the E.I.Q. score was simply a sum of the scores for all fifty items; the higher the individual's score, the higher the degree of ethnicity. On this basis, the scores of the three generations on the E.I.Q. were: Issei 170.65, Nisei 160.41, and Sansei 153.88. There were no significant male-female differences in the scores.

Chapter 11

The Contrasting Values Survey

In addition to the Ethnic Identity Questionnaire another instrument, the Contrasting Values Survey, was developed to measure the change in the Japanese psychological and behavioral characteristics discussed earlier to the more American psychological and behavioral characteristics. In constructing the Contrasting Values Survey form, a number of limiting factors had to be taken into consideration. First of all, we intended to mail the survey and we knew from previous experience that, if the form were too long and required more than fifteen or twenty minutes to complete, the rate of return would be considerably reduced. We also knew that, if the wording of the items was too long or involved the use of excessive modifiers or compound complex sentence construction, the rate of return could also be reduced. Therefore, since the basic intention in utilizing the survey form was to increase the size of the sample by maximizing the return rate, we did not attempt to design items which would provide us with the type of information obtained from the Incomplete Sentence Test or the Edwards Personal Preference Schedule. The data that we thus obtained were therefore more superficial in many respects but nevertheless were most informative. We did attempt, however, to obtain some information of a more personal nature by incorporating into our form a twenty-item dominance-deference inventory which had previously been utilized in Hawaii and Japan and appears in an article by Arkoff, Meredith, and Iwahara (1962:61-66).

In construction, the survey form consisted of forty items, twenty of which were derived from the list of subsidiary Japanese characteristics given in Chapter 3, and twenty from the list of subsidiary American characteristics given in Chapter 4. These forty items were then arranged so that the Japanese items appeared as the odd numbers and the American items as the even numbers. Thus items 1, 3, 5, 7, 9, 11, etc., are Japanese items and items 2, 4, 6, 8, 10, etc., are American items.

Items 41 through 60 constitute the dominance-deference inventory mentioned above. Of these, those numbered 41, 43, 46, 47, 49, 52, 54, 55, 58, and 60 make up the dominance items and those numbered 42, 44, 45, 48, 50, 51, 53, 56, 57, and 59 make up the deference items. The dominance-deference scale was modified from the manner in which it was presented in Arkoff, Meredith, and Iwahara (1962). In their study the subject was asked to circle ten of the twenty items that applied to him. The score, then, was simply the number of dominance items selected. Our modification was necessary in order to make the scoring of the dominance-deference inventory compatible with the rest of the survey. The manner of scoring was identical to that of the Ethnic Identity Questionnaire discussed in the previous chapter. That is, there were five possible responses weighted from 1 to 5: strongly agree (5), agree (4), undecided (3), disagree (2), and strongly disagree (1). Again, the purpose of utilizing the same scoring system was based on several considerations. One, the five-point scale is superior to a simple "true-false" response in that it allows for a much wider range of choice. Two, we wished to utilize the same computer program for both the E.I.Q. and the Contrasting Values Survey.

Our method of scoring the dominance-deference inventory was to calculate the mean for each item for each group, then total the means for all dominance items, and next, total the means for all deference items in each group. The total dominance means were then divided by ten, the number of dominance items, to obtain the mean dominance score for the particular group. The same procedure was followed to obtain the mean deference score for the group.

The survey form was next translated into Japanese for use by the Issei by the writer's wife, who is a native speaker of Japanese. The translation was then checked by Dr. K. H. K. Chang of the Department of Anthropology, University of California, Davis, who suggested several modifications which were incorporated into the final Japanese version.

The English and Japanese versions of the Contrasting Values Survey were then mailed to a randomly picked sample of names taken from the same Japanese directory which had been used in the E.I.Q. mailings. The initial mailing was made in January, 1971, and consisted of 100 forms addressed to Issei and 200 forms addressed to Nisei and Sansei. The response was almost identical to that obtained for the E.I.Q. Of the 300 forms mailed, 16 addressed to Issei and 25 addressed to other Japanese Americans were returned by the Post Office as being undeliverable. The return rate for the remainder was very close to that for the E.I.Q. Again, 20 of the Issei returned the forms, for a return rate of 23.8 per cent. The Nisei and Sansei returned 65 forms for a return rate of 37 per cent.

The second mailing was made in March, 1971, to 200 randomly picked Issei and 300 randomly picked other Japanese Americans. Once more, 24 addressed to Issei and 33 addressed to the Nisei and Sansei were returned by the Post Office. The return rate for the second mailing was close to that of the first. That is, 44 forms were returned by the Issei and 82 by the Nisei and Sansei. The overall return rate for both mailings was 24.6 per cent for the Issei and 33 per cent for the Nisei and Sansei. In all, 64 forms were available for the Issei and 147 for the Nisei and Sansei. Once again, as with the E.I.Q. mail-out, the majority of these, or 112, were Nisei and most of these were male.

In order to increase the Sansei sample, the Sansei students in the Japanese community study class were asked to administer the survey forms to other Sansei and to their parents. Here again, there was no problem: the majority of the students in the class were themselves Sansei and they simply asked their friends and relatives, and those whom they were interviewing, to complete the form. In this manner we were able to increase the total sample to 46 male and 38 female Issei, 94 male and 61 female Nisei, and 70 male and 54 female Sansei.

Further, in order to compare the Sansei group with an American Caucasian group of approximately the same age, the survey form was also administered to 52 male and 102 female students in anthropology classes at Sacramento State College.

The biographical data obtained were almost identical to those obtained for the E.I.Q. The average age of the Issei was 71 years, the Nisei 47 years, the Sansei 23.14 years, and the Caucasian students 25.81 years. The number of years of education was nine for the Issei, 13 for the Nisei, 14.98 for the Sansei, and 14.58 for the Caucasian students.

The religious preference of the Issei was 68 per cent Buddhist, 26 per cent Protestant, and 5 per cent listed no religion. The Nisei reported 61 per cent Buddhist, 36 per cent Protestant, and 3 per cent gave no religion. The Sansei reported 43 per cent Buddhist, 39 per cent Protestant, 3 per cent Catholic and 15 per cent gave no religion. The question of religious affiliation was not asked of the Caucasian students.

The biographical information and the rate of returns would permit us to say that, while our population is not a strictly random sample, it is nevertheless representative and is not aberrant to any marked degree.

The evaluation of the scoring was identical to that of the E.I.Q. That is, the five-point scale ranging from strongly agree (5) to strongly disagree (1) was further categorized in terms of endorsement of an item on either side of neutrality. This score was on an equal distribution basis. Thus, a strongly positive identification would be greater than 4.20; a positive identification would be greater than 3.40; a neutral, or undecided, identification would range from below 3.39 to 2.61; a negative identification would be below 2.60; and a strongly negative identification would be below 1.80.

Analysis of the
Contrasting Values Survey

The initial analysis of the data was in the form of determining significant differences between the sexes in each group. This information is depicted in Table 11.1. For the most part, the differences between the sexes were much as anticipated on the basis of ordinary male-female role expectations. That is, the male role usually requires the male to be more dominant and self-assertive than the female, who, in turn, is usually expected to be more deferent and less self-assertive than the male. Nonetheless, there were surprises, and occasionally the females emerged as being more self-assertive and the males less dominant than we had anticipated. These differences will be discussed as they apply to the males and females within each group.

Table 11.1

Significant Differences Between Sexes Within Groups†

Item no.	Item	Group	Sex	Mean item score
1	The greatest satisfaction comes from being with one's family.	Sansei	M	3.56
			F	3.82
3	The best way to train children is to raise them to be quiet and obedient.	Nisei	M	2.99
			F	2.44
4	A real man can be on his own and not be dependent.	Sansei	M	3.37
			F	2.87
6	A person is better off if he doesn't have to worry about others.	Nisei	M	3.25
			F	2.59
9	A person given a job should never rest until it is finished.	Sansei	M	3.37
			F	3.70
10	Most people feel hampered because we have too many rules.	Sansei	M	3.14
			F	3.59
11	When a person is depressed he wants others to feel sorry.	Issei	M	3.35
			F	3.73
14	The strongest emotional tie is between husband and wife.	Caucasian	M	3.19
			F	3.53
15	If someone in authority pushes you around, you can do little.	Sansei	M	1.97
			F	2.37
19	A person is more likely to succeed if he listens to others.	Nisei	M	3.29
			F	2.98
		Caucasian	M	2.96
			F	2.69
22	Everyone has a right to live his life as he sees fit.	Caucasian	M	3.89
			F	3.52
24	A person's chief responsibility is to be true to himself.	Sansei	M	3.79
			F	4.04
25	Parents can never be repaid for what they have done.	Caucasian	M	3.02
			F	2.70
26	People in authority are no better than anyone else.	Issei	M	3.67
			F	3.20
		Caucasian	M	3.96
			F	3.45
27	It is better not to shout or fight in public even if provoked.	Sansei	M	3.06
			F	3.59
		Caucasian	M	2.79
			F	3.47
28	Most people today are basically optimistic about the future.	Sansei	M	3.32
			F	2.91

30	The only way to become a success is to take advantage of an opportunity before someone else.	Sansei	M 3.31
			F 2.94
32	A person can never be a success until he stops following advice.	Sansei	M 3.55
			F 3.06
34	If a person doesn't watch out for himself, no one will.	Caucasian	M 2.83
			F 3.13
35	True success can only come through will power and discipline.	Sansei	M 3.66
			F 4.00
41	I assert myself with energy when the occasion demands it.	Issei	M 3.78
			F 3.40
45	I am capable of putting myself in the background.	Issei	M 4.07
			F 3.75
		Caucasian	M 3.58
			F 3.96
46	I argue with zest for my point of view.	Nisei	M 3.27
			F 2.97
47	I find it rather easy to lead a group of younger people.	Caucasian	M 3.14
			F 3.53
53	I give praise rather freely when the occasion warrants it.	Caucasian	M 3.64
			F 4.01
57	I usually follow instructions and do what is expected.	Issei	M 3.72
			F 3.20
		Caucasian	M 3.21
			F 3.74
58	I would like to be a leader and sway others.	Sansei	M 3.11
			F 2.61
		Caucasian	M 3.08
			F 2.75
59	In matters of conduct, I conform to custom.	Caucasian	M 2.87
			F 3.34

†Significant at the .05 level or better (Mann-Whitney U Test).

The Issei male-female differences appeared in items 11, 26, 41, 45, and 57. For the most part, these were as anticipated and several provided corroborating evidence for previous findings. For example, item 11, "When a person is depressed he really wants others to feel sorry for him and comfort him," was included as a measure of *amaeru,* or the desire to be pampered, which has been mentioned earlier. It will be recalled that in the discussion of *amaeru* most Japanese associated the word with the behavior of females. Some support for this assumption is given in the different responses. The Issei males scored 3.35, which is not quite at the previously defined 3.5 level of positive response, while the females' score of 3.73 indicates a considerably higher level of agreement.

On item 26, "People in authority are really no better than anyone else," the Issei males scored 3.67 and the females scored 3.20. These figures reflect the more active male participation in American society and the somewhat more isolated or sheltered life of the female as housewife and mother. Item 41, "I assert myself with energy when the occasion demands it," was scored 3.78 by the males and 3.40 by the females. Again, this is probably a reflection of the male's more active role as the provider. Item 45, "I am capable of putting myself in the background and working with zest for a person I admire," was scored 4.07 by the males and 3.75 by the females. Again, while both scores were high and thus supportive of our previous discussion on the importance of deference in Japanese society, the higher score of the male is probably a result of his role as the provider of the family income. Further, it will be recalled that the majority of the Issei spent a large part of their adult lives working for someone else. Undoubtedly the same explanation could be offered to explain the male score of 3.77 in item 57, "I usually follow instructions and do what is expected of me."

The Nisei male-female differences are found in items 3, 6, 19, and 46. Again, for the most part, these differences reflect differences in role expectations. Item 3, "The best way to train children is to raise them to be quiet and obedient," was scored 2.99 by the males and 2.44 by the females. The higher score by the male, while in the uncertain range, is in keeping with the male role of authority figure and disciplinarian. Item 6, "Ideally a person is better off if he can do what he really wants to do and doesn't have to worry about others," was scored 3.25 by the males and 2.59 by the females. Again, while the male score of 3.25 is in the high undecided range, it is much higher than the female score of 2.59 and may be indicative of the heavier responsibilities faced by the male in his role of provider and family head.

Item 19, "A person is more likely to succeed if he listens to the advice of others," was scored 3.29 by the males and 2.98 by the females. The difference in scores is at first glance puzzling. However, upon reflection, it does correspond to the father-mother role as seen in many Nisei households. Usually it is the father who provides the discipline and the guidance, while the mother's role is often more supportive of her offspring. Item 19, therefore, may have been interpreted by the Nisei males on the basis of their own experience in listening to their father's advice or, more likely, their present experience with their own offspring.

Item 46, "I argue with zest for my point of view against others," was scored 3.27 by the males and 2.97 by the females. While both scores are in the undecided range, the higher score of the male is reflective of the more dominant and self-assertive male role.

The Sansei male-female differences are found in items 1, 4, 9, 10, 15, 24, 27, 28, 30, 32, 35, and 58. Once again, the males appear to be more constrained, introspective, and self-disciplined than the males. The male assertiveness is seen in item 4, "A real man is one who can be on his own and not be dependent on anyone else," which was scored 3.37 by the males and 2.87 by the females. The greater approval of self-discipline in the female can be seen in their score of 3.70 and the male score of 3.37 in response to item 9, "A person given a job to do should never rest or slacken until it is finished." Likewise, the greater constraint felt by the female is apparent in the female score of 3.59 and the male score of 3.14 on item 10, "Most people feel hampered and tied in because we have too many rules." Item 1, "The greatest satisfaction comes from being with one's family," was scored 3.82 by the females and 3.56 by the males. Again, this supports our other data on the importance of the family for the female.

While both males and females disagreed to item 15, "If someone in a position of authority tries to push you around, there is very little you can do about it," the female score of 2.37 compared to the male score of 1.97 indicates that the females were less certain than the males in this regard. However, the female emphasis on introspection is more pronounced in item 24, "A person's chief responsibility is to be true to himself," which was scored 3.79 by the males and 4.04 by the females. It was also to be expected that the more passive role of the female would influence the response on item 27, "It is better not to shout or fight in public even if provoked," which was scored 3.06 by the males and 3.59 by the females.

Perhaps somewhat more surprising was the response to item 28, "Most people today are basically optimistic about the future," which was scored 3.32 by the males and 2.91 by the females. It must be added that in all four groups the females scored lower than the males on this item. For the most part, the differences were small—only about .10—but the Sansei male-female difference was the greatest. Yet the Caucasian female score of 2.76 was even lower. It is difficult to evaluate this item. On the basis of historic experience, it was always the young who were the most optimistic about the future, although, given the events on college campuses in the past few years, the lack of optimism among the young is understandable. In this regard, the lower scores of the females may be because they are more deeply involved in contemporary issues than the males or because, on the basis of personal experience, they feel that they have less control over the course of events.

Item 30, "The only way to become a success is to take advantage of an opportunity before someone else does," was scored 3.31 by the males and 2.94 by the females. Once again, this item is indicative of the more self-assertive male role. The same reasoning would apply to item 32, "A person can never really be a success until he stops following other people's advice and does what he really wants to do," which was scored 3.55 by the males and 3.06 by the females.

However, item 35, "True success in life can only come through will power and self-discipline," which was scored 3.66 by the males and 4.00 by the females, does suggest more self-discipline and a more introspective nature in the females than in the males. The last item, item 58, "I would like to be a leader and sway others to my opinion," was scored 3.11 by the males and 2.61 by the females. Again, this item indicates the male-female difference in self-assertion.

The Caucasian student group disclosed even more male-female differences than the Sansei. In particular, significant differences were found in items 14, 19, 22, 25, 27, 34, 35, 45, 47, 53, 57, 58, and 59. However, only about one-half of these items (22, 27, 45, 53, 57, 58, and 59) could be attributed to the more self-assertive male role. With the exception of item 14, the remainder of the items (19, 25, 34, 35, and 47) indicate that the females are in some ways more self-reliant than the males. Item 14, "In the family the strongest emotional tie is between the husband and wife," was scored 3.19 by the males and 3.53 by the females. This item apparently indicates the greater importance of the emotional bond in marriage to the wife than to the husband.

Items 19, 25, 34, 35, and 47 reveal the Caucasian female as being more independent or self-reliant than the male. This does not mean that they are more aggressive or self-assertive, but only more self-disciplined and self-assured. Some indication of this is found particularly in items 35 and 47. Item 35, "True success in life can only come through will power and self-discipline," was scored 3.14 by the males and 3.60 by the females. Item 47, "I find it rather easy to lead a group of younger people and maintain order," was scored 3.14 by the males and 3.53 by the females.

Items Showing Hypothesized Group Differences

Table 11.2 depicts the hypothesized group differences. On the basis of the previous discussions disclosing the Japanese emphasis on duties and obligations, hierarchy, deference, dependence, and collectivity, and the American emphasis on rights and privileges, equality, self-reliance, self-assertion, and individualism, the simple progression of item scores should be relatively self-evident. Yet there are interesting differences. Throughout this chapter it will become increasingly apparent that, while the Issei have retained many Japanese characteristics, as had been predicted, they also disclose a much higher degree of self-reliance and individuation than had been anticipated. Indeed, on many of the items which purportedly indicated American characteristics their scores were higher than those of the Caucasian students.

At first glance, this may appear to be an anomaly, one that flies in the face of all previous experience. Yet, on closer examination, the discrepancies disappear and the Issei response is not only understandable and predictable, but the Caucasian student answers are also in the right direction. There are a number of tentative explanations for the higher Issei scores on a number of "American" items. One, the Issei were not serious when they filled out the form but only did so to be accomodating. Two, the

Issei who responded were not typical of the "average" Issei. The first objection might be countered by the fact that the majority of the Issei forms were obtained by mail-out and hence the respondent was under little pressure to complete the form. Additionally, the form contains a rough index of reliability apart from the fact that the majority of the responses to the Japanese items are in the predicted direction, and that is that 7 and 31 are the same. The differences between the scores of the two items were much the same for all four groups. That is, the Issei scored 3.69 on item 7 and 3.63 on item 31, the Nisei scored 3.03 on item 7 and 2.98 on item 31, the Sansei scored 2.41 on item 7 and 2.34 on item 31, while the Caucasian students scored 1.89 on item 7 and 1.82 on item 31. These scores, then, indicate that the answers were not given on the basis of chance alone. Further, the dominance-deference scores were almost exactly as predicted.

The second objection may be countered by the argument used in discussing the biographical data. That is, on the basis of our information, we do not believe the sample to be biased or aberrant to any marked degree.

Table 11.2 discloses that there are a number of items that indicate a more Japanese identity and a number that indicate a more American identity. The Japanese items are numbers 3, 5, 7, 13, 15, 17, 21, 23, 25, 27, 31, 35, 44, 45, 51, and 59. The American items are numbers 4, 14, 26, 30, 34, 36, 43, 47, 54, and 58. Items above 40 are a part of the dominance-deference scale mentioned previously. The Japanese items can be grouped into the major categories discussed in Chapter 2. That is, collectivity (5, 17), hierarchy (3, 7, 21, 31), duty and obligation (23, 25, 35), and deference (13, 15, 27, 44, 45, 51, 59). Dependence was not indicated explicitly in Table 11.2 and it is difficult to determine its extent. One might state that dependence is implicit in the Issei and in many of the Nisei responses because of the high agreement scores on those items indicating hierarchy and deference. Yet this is not necessarily the case. It will be recalled that in Chapter 5, in contrasting American and Japanese forms of individuation, it was shown that when individuation was coupled with an emphasis on hierarchy, deference, and achievement, the personality pattern thus produced would be the "privatized" rather than the "individualized" or "democratized" individual. That is, it would be one who is strongly oriented toward the achievement of personal goals and therefore more concerned with personal rather than public affairs.

Table 11.2
Items Showing Hypothesized Group Differences

Item no.	Item	Issei (N–84)	Nisei (N–155)	Sansei (N–124)	Cauc. (N–154)
		Category group and mean item scores			
3	The best way to train children is to raise them to be obedient.	3.90†	2.72†	2.14	1.93
4	A real man is one who is not dependent.	4.19†	3.39	3.12‡	2.74
5	Strongest bond is between mother and child.	4.19‡	3.85†	3.15‡	2.76
7	Those in authority are entitled to respect.	3.72†	3.03†	2.41†	1.89
13	It is better to give in than to cause a scene.	3.82†	2.89‡	2.53	2.36
14	Strongest tie is between husband and wife.	4.19	3.90†	3.49	3.36
15	If authority pushes, you can do little.	2.91†	2.28	2.17	1.96
17	It is best to rely on your own family.	3.97‡	3.66†	3.05	2.95
21	You can tell what kind of individual a person is if you know his family.	3.93†	2.95†	2.43	2.32
23	Best way to succeed is to have a detailed plan.	3.47†	2.62	2.48‡	2.14
25	Parents can never be repaid by children.	3.86†	3.25	2.99	2.86
26	People in authority are no better than others.	3.46	3.57	3.59	3.71
27	It is better not to shout or fight in public.	4.12†	3.85†	3.33	3.13
30	To become a success, take advantage of opportunity.	3.45	3.22	3.13	2.71
31	Anyone in authority is entitled to respect.	3.66†	2.98†	2.34‡	1.82

34	A person must watch out for himself.	4.03†	3.45	3.31‡	2.98
35	True success comes through will power.	4.09	3.95	3.83‡	3.37
36	No one should be entitled to privileges not earned.	3.88	3.86	3.78†	3.04
43	I enjoy organizing activities of a group.	2.95	3.12	3.20	3.21
44	I see the good points of the people above me.	3.87‡	3.42	3.18	3.00
45	I am capable of putting myself in the background.	3.91	3.85	3.84	3.77
47	I find it easy to lead younger people.	2.91	3.02‡	3.31	3.32
51	I often seek advice of older people.	3.66‡	3.21	3.03	2.90
54	I feel that I can dominate a situation.	2.45	2.62	2.84	2.92
58	I would like to be a leader.	2.45‡	2.72	2.86	2.91
59	In matters of conduct, I conform to custom.	3.75	3.60†	3.26	3.13

†Significant at the .01 level (Mann-Whitney U Test).
‡Significant at the .05 level (Mann-Whitney U Test).

Indeed, considerable support for this position can be found in the Issei responses to the American items. The American items can be grouped under the headings of self-reliance (4, 34, 36), equality (26), and self-assertion (30, 43, 47, 54, 58). From Table 11.2 it can be seen that the Issei scored higher than even the Caucasian group on items 4, 30, 34, and 36. As a matter of fact, all three Japanese American groups scored higher on these items than did the American group. At first glance, this was puzzling and even a little disconcerting, although the high self-reliance scores of the Issei are in accord with Johnson's (1962) discussion as given in Chapter 3. When we first became aware of this difference, we readministered the survey form to some thirty Caucasian students in an anthropology class at Sacramento State College. In addition to completing the form, they were asked to indicate on the back of the form the reason why they disagreed with any particular item. The replies were most illuminating and parallel the responses made by many of the Caucasian students on the Incomplete Sentence Test. That is, there is an apparent moving away from rugged individualism and the type of self-reliance that walls off a person from others. Furthermore, self-assertion at the expense of others is frowned upon. On the other hand, the ethic of equality is quite strong, as can be seen in item 26 and as is elaborated below. In terms of Maruyama's (1965) formulation, which was discussed in detail in Chapter 5, there is more a movement away from the "individualized" type to the "democratized" type of person. Or, in terms of Lipset's (1967) formulation, there has been a shift from the ethic of individualism, with its emphasis on achievement and competition, to the ethic of equality, with its emphasis on civil rights and broadening the franchise. If one considers the Democratic Party to be more concerned with broadening the franchise and with civil liberties, then additional support for this is to be found in recently reported polls which indicate that the newly enfranchised eighteen- to twenty-one-year-old voters are registering almost 90 per cent Democratic in some areas of the state and as much as two to one Democratic in largely conservative Orange County.

Typical explanations of the Caucasian students to their negative responses on items 4, 30, 34, and 36 were as follows. Item 4, "A real man is one who can be on his own and not be dependent on anyone else," elicited such replies as "A real man does not let false pride rule him—no man is an island", or "A real man doesn't have to be independent all the time", or even, "There should be a two-way relationship. A man can depend on others and still be an extremely capable person." Item 30, "The only way to become a success is to take advantage of an opportunity before someone else does," received such comments as, "There are other ways of becoming a success"; or "You don't have to beat someone out to be a success." Item 34, "In this world, if a person doesn't watch out for himself, no one else will," received a large number of uncertain replies, but several who disagreed made such comments as, "I feel I have friends who will stand by me"; or, "Not everyone is out to get you." Item 36, "No one should be entitled to privileges he himself has not earned," likewise received a large number of uncertain replies. Here again, however, part of the difficulty might be with the phrasing. For example, one student apparently objected to the word "earned" and replied, "Privileges need not always be *earned*, they can be freely given, based on emotions."

The difference in the responses of the Japanese Americans on items 4, 30, 34, and 36 would seem to indicate a more competitive nature or a higher drive for achievement, a subject that will be explored in greater detail in subsequent pages.

One final discrepancy noted in Table 11.2 is item 14, "In the family, the strongest emotional tie is between the husband and the wife." This item was intended to be in opposition to item 5, "The strongest emotional bond is between a mother and her child." However, no forced choice was made and the Issei scored 'the same on both items. With the other groups, item 14 was scored higher, but not so high by the Sansei and Caucasian students as by the Nisei and Issei. Their higher scores are probably a result of their being married while the majority of the Sansei and Caucasion students are still single.

All in all, Table 11.2 does show a considerable retention of the Japanese characteristics of deference, duty and obligation, hierarchy, and collectivity in the Issei generation and their attenuation in the Nisei and Sansei generations. Further, those American characteristics agreed to by the Japanese Americans could be interpreted as indicating both a strong sense of competition and a drive for achievement. This apparent paradox between the high scores recorded in the areas of deference, duty and obligation, and hierarchy and the almost equally high scores in self-reliance or achievement is, according to Nakane (1970:92-93), the result of the great emphasis on hierarchy or ranking which, in turn, leads to competition:

> This ever-present consciousness of ranking contributes to the encouragement of competition among peers . . . The ranking order among institutions is likewise of immediate concern to individuals, in that individual status and prestige go according to this ranking as well as according to the individual's rank within the institution. Even typists and drivers take a pride in belonging to a company with a high ranking, for they are able to feel superior to typists and drivers employed by lesser-ranked companies, even though they receive the same pay. (1970:92-93)

Furthermore, if one thinks of equality as being the antithesis of hierarchy, then, with the use of negative evidence, one could build a rather strong case for the Caucasian students' belief in equality. That is, their greatest disagreement was expressed on those same items which indicated hierarchy (3, 7, 21, 31) and deference (13, 15).

Items Not Showing Hypothesized Group Differences

Table 11.3 contains those items not showing the hypothesized group differences. It will be noted that in several cases the differences in group scores were not statistically significant; however, they were included in the table in the interest of consistency. In other words, if, on the basis of chance, the scores had been a little higher or lower, the item could have been placed just as easily in Table 11.2.

Of the thirty-four items in Table 11.3, twelve (1, 9, 11, 19, 29, 37, 39, 48, 50, 56, and 57) could be considered Japanese items and eighteen (2, 6, 8, 10, 12, 16, 18, 20, 22, 24, 28, 32, 38, 40, 46, 49, 52, and 55) could be considered to be the more American items. Items 41, 42, 53, and 60, which are part of the dominance-deference inventory, are difficult to classify since they are not clearly in one category or the other. Further, items 16 and 24 were given a high score by all and did not discriminate in any one direction.

Table 11.3
Items Not Showing Hypothesized Group Differences

Item no.	Item	Category group and mean item scores			
		Issei (N–84)	Nisei (N–155)	Sansei (N–124)	Cauc. (N–154)
1	The greatest satisfaction comes from being with one's family.	4.33	4.38‡	3.69	3.52
2	If you don't speak out for yourself, no one else will.	3.73‡	4.06	3.96	3.84
6	A person is better off if he does what he really wants to do.	3.24‡	2.92	3.06	2.90
8	A moral person stands up for his convictions no matter what.	3.76†	3.16‡	3.57	3.70

9	A person given a job should never rest until it is finished.	3.95‡	_3.39_	3.54‡	2.93
10	Most people feel hampered because we have too many rules.	_3.46_	3.14	3.37	3.36
11	When a person is depressed, he wants others to feel sorry.	3.57†	3.03	_2.91_	2.95
12.	A person's greatest obligation is to be true to himself.	4.22	_3.99_	4.03	3.83
16	A person should treat his subordinates with mutual respect.	4.20	4.47	4.42	4.42
18	Parents should raise their children to be on their own.	4.20	4.13	_3.98_	4.22
19	A person will be likely to succeed if he listens to others.	3.41‡	3.14	2.80	_2.82_
20	People should all be given the same basic opportunities.	4.08	_3.89_	4.11	4.11
22	Every person has a right to live his life as he sees fit.	3.85‡	_3.55_	3.81	3.70
24	A person's chief responsibility is to be true to himself.	3.91	3.92	3.91	3.93
28	Most people are basically optimistic about the future.	3.36	3.54‡	_3.12_	_2.81_
29	A man can never let himself down without letting down his family.	_3.85_	3.97†	3.31‡	2.87
32	A person can never be a success until he stops following others.	3.29	_3.16_	_3.30_‡	3.00
33	Makes no difference what a man does since it all passes away.	3.17†	2.11	1.93	2.08
37	A wise man knows how to compromise by changing his moral position.	3.44†	_3.92_†	_3.60_‡	3.30
38	Better to rely on yourself than depend on others.	3.96	3.87	3.64	3.66
39	No one can be a success unless helped a lot by others.	3.63‡	3.34†	2.84	_2.90_
40	A man can never be a success until he breaks away from others.	_3.26_‡	2.84‡	3.14‡	_2.79_
41	I assert myself with energy when the occasion demands it.	3.56†	_4.05_‡	3.87	3.93
42	I express my enthusiasm and respect for those I admire.	4.09	4.08	3.91	_4.08_

46	I argue with zest for my point of view against others.	3.09	3.12‡	<u>3.50</u>	3.48
48	I accept suggestions rather than insist on my own way.	<u>3.44</u>	3.57	3.42	3.54
49	I usually influence others more than they influence me.	2.88	2.97	2.99	<u>2.90</u>
50	I am considered compliant and obliging by my friends.	<u>3.37</u>	3.49	<u>3.54</u>	3.28
52	I am usually the one to make the necessary decisions.	2.89	2.90	3.18	<u>3.12</u>
53	I give praise rather freely when the occasion warrants it.	3.32	3.73	3.71	<u>3.82</u>
55	I enjoy the sense of power when I control others.	2.53	2.69	2.81	<u>2.61</u>
56	I often find myself imitating or agreeing with a superior.	3.37	<u>2.56</u>	2.98	3.01
57	I usually follow instructions and do what is expected.	<u>3.44</u>†	3.91	3.72‡	3.47
60	I feel that I am driven by an underlying desire of power.	<u>2.51</u>	3.30	2.37	<u>2.22</u>

Note: Underlining = discrepant group.
†Significant at the .01 level (Mann-Whitney U Test).
†Significant at the .05 level (Mann-Whitney U Test).

With respect to the Japanese items, there are a number which are clearly in the hypothesized direction but which have one group slightly higher or lower than anticipated. These are items 1, 9, 11, 19, 29, 33, 37, and 39.

The higher score of the Nisei on item 1, "In the long run the greatest satisfaction comes from being with one's family," was not significantly higher than the Issei score. However, both are significantly higher than the Sansei and Caucasian student responses. While it cannot be said to be a strictly Japanese item, this item, nonetheless, does reinforce our other data as to the continued importance of the family for both the Issei and Nisei groups. Item 9, "A person given a job to do should never rest or slacken until it is finished," was scored higher by the Sansei than by the Nisei generation. Again, however, this discrepancy is due to the higher scores of the Sansei female (3.70) than the male (3.37), which were discussed in relation to Table 11.1. When the male-female difference is corrected, this item does follow the hypothesized direction for the males. That is, Issei (3.83), Nisei

(3.50), Sansei (3.37), and Caucasian males (2.87). As such, it provides additional evidence for the continued, though attenuated, importance of duty and obligation. Item 11, "When a person is depressed he really wants others to feel sorry for him and comfort him," was discussed in relation to Table 11.1 and was included as a rough measure of the concept of *amaeru*, a desire to be pampered by others. In this instance, the anomaly arises from the slightly higher Caucasian student score; the attenuation of scores in the Japanese American groups is as predicted. Again, however, the difference in the Sansei-Caucasian scores is not statistically significant.

The same reasoning could be used for item 19, "A person will be more likely to succeed if he listens to the advice of others." Here again, the scores of the Japanese Americans are in the predicted direction, while the slight difference in the Sansei-Caucasian scores is not statistically significant.

Item 29, "A man can never let himself down without letting down his family at the same time," was scored higher by the Nisei than by the Issei. Although both scores are high, the higher score of the Nisei is probably a reflection of their more active responsibility for their families in comparison with the Issei, who are now largely retired.

Item 33, "In the long run it probably doesn't make much difference what a person does since in the end it all passes away anyhow," was included as a rough measure of pessimism or futility that would be in opposition to item 28, "Most people are basically optimistic about the future." From Table 11.3 it can be seen that there are some surprises. In item 28, the Issei and Nisei are more optimistic about the future than are the Sansei or Caucasian students. Indeed, the Sansei, while uncertain, are much more optimistic than the Caucasian students. Further, on item 33 they are less pessimistic and see their lives as perhaps being less futile than the Caucasian students. Although the differences are not great, and while both groups gave negative responses, the more optimistic response of the Sansei does correspond with their higher dominance scores recorded in Table 11.14. These scores reveal the Sansei males as being slightly more self-assertive than the Caucasian students. The higher score of the Issei on item 33 is undoubtedly influenced by their advanced age.

Item 37, "Although there are precise rules of conduct, a truly wise man knows how to compromise by changing his moral position and adapting to new situations," was agreed to by all of the Japanese American groups, although the Nisei and Sansei scored higher than the Issei. While at first glance it would seem that since this item is derived from the Japanese "situational ethic" discussed in Chapter 3, it should be the Issei who would score higher, it must be remembered that the Issei were more insulated than the Sansei and especially the Nisei, who had to make many adjustments to the larger American society.

Item 39, "Despite all the talk, no one can really be a success unless he is helped a lot by others," was intended as a measure of collectivity or dependence. The responses of the groups are largely as predicted, although the Caucasian students reported a slightly higher score than the Sansei. Once more this is in keeping with our other data, which indicated either a greater competitive sense in the Sansei or a playing down of competition by the Caucasian students.

The remaining Japanese items indicating a more deferent position on the dominance-deference inventory were items 48, 50, 56, and 57. Of these, item 48, "I accept suggestions rather than insist on working things out my own way," was agreed to by all groups although the Issei scored lower than the other groups. One possible explanation of this may be in the phrasing of the item. It will be recalled that one of the most common criticisms of the Issei by the Sansei was that they were stubborn. Further, on item 23, Table 11.2, "The best way to succeed is to have a detailed plan and stick to it," the Issei agreed while the three other groups disagreed. Item 50, "I am considered compliant and obliging by my friends," was scored lower by the Issei than by the Nisei or Sansei. Again, this item is related to the discussion on item 48 and to the discussion on item 37 relative to Issei inflexibility and Nisei compromise. The higher score of the Sansei on item 50 is in keeping with their higher scores on deference and abasement, as reported in the Edwards Personal Preference Schedule scores given in the next chapter.

Item 56, "I often find myself imitating or agreeing with a superior," was scored lower by the Nisei than by the Sansei or Caucasian groups. The higher score of the Sansei and Caucasian students may be a result of their age and status as students, although this is not entirely clear.

Item 57, "I always follow instructions and do what is expected of me," was scored lower by the Issei than by the other groups. Here again, however, we have another example of the rigidity or stubbornness discussed above, although the retired status of the Issei may have had an influence.

The American items were 2, 6, 8, 10, 12, 18, 20, 22, 28, 32, 38, 40, 46, 49, 52, and 55. By and large, the explanation of these apparent anomalies parallels that just given for the Japanese items. That is, the Issei are more unyielding or tenacious in their established behavior patterns than are the Nisei or Sansei, who, because of their greater participation in the dominant American society, found it necessary to be more flexible in their responses. Further, in comparison with the Sansei, the Caucasian students appear to be less competitive and less self-assertive. These differences will be discussed in detail in subsequent pages.

On the remaining items, the Issei had the discrepancy on items 2, 8, 12, 20, 22, 32, and 41. The Sansei scores were not as hypothesized on items 2, 6, 18, 28, 32, and 38. The Caucasian student scores were divergent on items 12, 28, 38, 40, 42, 49, 52, and 55.

The discrepant scores of the Issei support our previous contention that the Issei can best be understood in terms of Maruyama's (1965) formulation of a "privatized" personality type. They are thus slightly more independent on item 6, more adamant in their convictions than the Nisei on item 8, more hampered by rules they may not understand on item 10, and more independent than others on item 40.

The Nisei scores indicate that they and the Sansei have a greater need to speak out for themselves than do the Caucasian students on item 2. However, in item 8 they are uncertain that a person should listen to his inner conscience and stand up for his convictions no matter how many say he is wrong. This item may indicate the continued importance of collectivity in the Nisei or it may be a reflection of their own experience in adapting to the larger American society. On items 12 and 20, all groups agreed and the small difference between the scores is not significant. On items 22 and 32, the lower Nisei score is most likely an indication of the greater responsibility felt by the Nisei in comparison with the Issei, who are retired, and the Sansei, who are just starting their careers. The higher score of the Nisei on item 41 is undoubtedly an indication of their drive for achievement.

The Sansei scores not in the hypothesized direction are generally different when compared with the Caucasian students. Usually the difference can be attributed to the greater self-assertion or competitive drive of the Sansei. Thus, on items 2 and 6, their scores were higher than those of the Caucasian students, while on item 18 it was somewhat lower, although not significantly so. The lower score does not indicate disagreement, only that there were fewer strongly agree responses. Item 28 has already been discussed. Of the remaining two items, item 32 supports the slightly more competitive and self-assertive drive of the Sansei mentioned above. The last item, item 38, while agreed to by all groups, was scored lower by the Sansei and the Caucasian students than by the Issei and Nisei. The lower scores may be a result of the more equalitarian feelings of the younger groups. Conversely, the higher scores of the Issei and Nisei may be due to their greater "privatization" and disinclination to be indebted to someone else, hence they would rather do things themselves.

On those items where the Caucasian student scores were not in the hypothesized direction, it is apparent that the discrepancy was due either to the greater self-assertiveness and competitiveness of the Sansei or to the change toward a more equalitarian, less dominant or less overtly competitive ethic among the Caucasian students. For these reasons, then, the scores were discrepant on items 12, 28, 38, 40, 42, 49, 52, and 55. Of these, item 28 has already been discussed. Overall, the Caucasian students were less self-centered than the other groups on item 12 and a little more prone to rely on the help of others than the Issei or Nisei, but slightly less so than the Sansei on item 38. One indication of the increased awareness for others is seen in the Caucasian student response to item 40, "A man can never be a success in life until he breaks away from others and does what he wants to do." This item was scored lowest by the Caucasian students, although all groups were in the uncertain range. Another possible explanation is that "success" for the middle-class Caucasian students involves less of a need to make oneself over into a new image, since "success" is already largely defined in middle-class terms. Items

42, 49, 52, and 55 are part of the dominance-deference inventory. As will be elaborated upon later, the Caucasian students were slightly less dominant, less self-assertive, and less competitive than the Sansei on a large number of these items. To sum up, while Table 11.3 discloses a number of apparent discrepancies, the discrepancies can be resolved by relating them to other items and by resorting to our other data. Once again, it may be noted that, while the type of data obtained by such a form is relatively superficial, nonetheless, when used in conjunction with other instruments, the data do serve to resolve inconsistencies appearing in the other forms and thereby provide a more coherent picture of the changes taking place.

Items Scored Positively
by the Issei Group

Table 11.4 consists of those items scored positively by the Issei generation. Of these thirty-nine items, twenty-three were Japanese items, fourteen were American items, and two (41 and 42) were from the dominance-deference inventory and could be classified as either.

The Japanese items scored positively by the Issei were items 1, 3, 5, 7, 9, 11, 13, 17, 21, 23, 25, 27, 29, 31, 35, 37, 39, 44, 45, 48, 51, 57, and 59. In turn, these twenty-three items can be grouped under the major headings of collectivity (1, 17, 29, 39), duty and obligation (9, 23, 25, 35), hierarchy (3, 7, 21, 31), dependence (5, 11), and deference (13, 27, 37, 44, 45, 48, 51, 57, and 59).

The collectivity items (1, 17, 29, 39) reinforce our previous data on the importance of the family for the Issei. Given the importance of the ie ideal discussed in Chapter 3 and the Japanese predilection for devoting their energies to a small number of groups, usually only one or two (Beardsley 1965a:361-65, Vogel 1967:118), it would seem most reasonable to assume that, of the possible groups that the Issei would have contact with in this country, the family group would be the most important and the longest enduring. This conclusion is supported by the data from Chapters 6, 7, and 8, which record not only the sizable percentage of Issei living with their children but also the frequency of the visits their offspring make.

Table 11.4

Items Scored Positively by the Issei Group

Item no.	Item	Mean item score (N–84)
1	The greatest satisfaction comes from being with one's family.	4.33
2	If you don't watch out for yourself, no one else will.	3.72
3	The best way to raise children is to train them to be quiet and obedient.	3.90
4	A real man is one who can be on his own and not be dependent.	4.19
5	The strongest emotional bond is between a mother and her child.	4.19
7	Those in authority are automatically entitled to respect.	3.72
8	A truly moral person stands up for his convictions no matter what.	3.76
9	A person given a job should never rest until it is finished.	3.95
10	Most people feel hampered because we have too many rules.	3.40
11	When a person is depressed, he wants others to feel sorry.	3.57
12	A person's greatest obligation is to be true to himself.	4.22
13	If someone starts an argument, it is better to give in.	3.82
14	In the family, the strongest tie is between husband and wife.	4.19
17	In times of difficulty it is best to rely on your own family.	3.97
18	Parents should raise their children to be on their own.	4.20
20	People should all be given the same basic opportunities.	4.08
21	You can tell what kind of a person an individual is if you know the family background.	3.93
22	Every person has a right to live his life as he sees fit.	3.85
23	The best way to succeed is to have a detailed plan and stick to it.	3.47
25	Parents can never be repaid for what they have done.	3.86
26	People in authority are no better than anyone else.	3.46
27	It is better not to shout or fight in public even if provoked.	4.12
29	A man can never let himself down without letting down his family.	3.85
30	The only way to become a success is to take advantage of an opportunity before someone else does.	3.45

31	Anyone in authority is automatically entitled to respect.	3.66
34	If a person doesn't watch out for himself, no one else will.	4.03
35	True success can only come through will power and self-discipline.	4.09
36	No one should be entitled to privileges he has not himself earned.	3.88
37	A wise man knows how to compromise by changing his moral position.	3.44
38	It is better to rely on yourself rather than depend on others.	3.96
39	No one can be a success unless helped a lot by others.	3.63
41	I assert myself with energy when the occasion demands it.	3.56
42	I express my enthusiasm and respect for the people I admire.	4.09
44	I see the good points rather than the bad points of the people above me.	3.81
45	I am capable of putting myself in the background.	3.91
48	I accept suggestions rather than insist on my own way.	3.44
51	I often seek the advice of people older than myself.	3.66
57	I usually follow instructions and do what is expected.	3.44
59	In matters of conduct, I conform to custom.	3.75

The items indicating duty and obligation (9, 23, 25, 35) testify to the drive, endurance, and competitive spirit of the Issei. Indirectly they also provide supporting evidence for the alleged "stubbornness" of the Issei and for the strength of the family. For example, item 9, "A person given a job should never rest or slacken until it is finished"; item 23, "The best way to succeed is to have a detailed plan and to stick with it no matter what happens"; and item 35, "True success in life can only come through will power and self-discipline," when taken together, form a profile that is rigid and tenacious. When such characteristics are coupled with a duty to repay one's parents for what they have done, it seems likely that the drive to succeed would indeed be intense.

The emphasis on hierarchy can be seen in items 3, 7, 21, and 31. As has been previously discussed, items 7 and 31 are the same and were included as a reliability check. Item 3, "The best way to raise children is to raise them to be quiet and obedient," testifies to the hierarchical nature of the family. Similarly, item 21, "You can usually tell what kind of a person an individual is if you know his family background," indicates more of a feeling for hierarchy than it does of equality. It is significant that this item was scored neutrally by the Nisei (2.95) and disagreed to by the Sansei (2.42) and the Caucasian students (2.32).

There were only two items (5, 11) that indicated dependence. Both of these were intended to provide some indication of the importance of *amaeru*, a desire to be pampered, which is fostered by the strong mother-child bond. Although the existence of *amaeru* or dependency cannot be deduced from these two items alone, they do serve to corroborate the evidence given in the interview forms, the Incomplete Sentence Tests, and the higher scores obtained by the Japanese Americans in nurturance, affiliation, and succorance, in the Edwards Personal Preference Schedule discussed in the next chapter.

Deference is the one characteristic supported by the largest number of items (13, 27, 37, 44, 45, 48, 51, 57, and 58). In turn, the large number of deference items supports the emphasis on hierarchy. The majority of the deference items listed, however, are those obtained from the dominance-deference inventory to be discussed later. For the moment, suffice it to say that, as Table 11.13 discloses, the Issei were more deferent than the other groups.

The American items scored positively by the Issei were items 2, 4, 8, 10, 12, 14, 18, 20, 22, 26, 30, 34, 36, and 38. These in turn could be grouped under the headings of individuation (2, 8, 10, 12, 18, 22), self-reliance (4, 30, 34, 38), and equality (20, 26, 36). Item 14 was intended to be in opposition to item 5. However, given the lesser number of married persons in the Sansei and Caucasian groups, the scores on item 14 were not so high as we had anticipated. Table 11.2 does show that there were higher scores on item 14 than on item 5 in the Nisei and Sansei groups. Further, the Issei scores were the same on both items. These high scores reinforce the importance of the family in the Issei group.

The individuation items (2, 8, 10, 12, 18, 22) have already been commented upon in the discussion of Table 11.3. At that time it was stated that, when seen in conjunction with the positively scored Japanese items, the resultant pattern of individuation was that of the "privatized" rather than the "democratized" or "individualized" person. Some support for this can be found in Table 11.10, wherein the Caucasian students scored positively a large number of the same American items and none from the list of twenty Japanese items. Indeed, in Table 11.11 the only items scored negatively are the Japanese items emphasizing hierarchy and deference. By and large, the individuation items are those that complement the items indicating duty and obligation (9, 23, 25, 35). That is, if the best way to succeed is to have a detailed plan and stick to it (23), and if one should never rest or slacken until a job is finished (9), then it follows that one should follow through on his plan (22) and stick up for it (2, 8, 10, 12) no matter what. Further, if true success can only come through will power and self-discipline (35), then one should be able to do it alone (4, 34) by taking advantage of every opportunity (30) and relying on oneself (38).

Item 18, "Parents should raise their children so that they can leave the family and be on their own," was agreed to by all groups. This item was obviously too imprecise to be selective. For example, even in Japan, daughters will be married and junior sons are expected to leave the household in rural areas where primogeniture is common.

The emphasis on equality recorded in the responses to items 20, 26, and 36 appears to be that of equality of opportunity and, as such, complements the competitive drive described above. Given the equally strong emphasis on hierarchy and deference, it does not seem to correspond to the egalitarianism described in Chapter 4.

Items Scored Negatively by the Issei Group

Table 11.5 lists those items scored negatively by the Issei group. All of the items are from the dominance scale of the dominance-deference inventory that will be discussed in greater detail later. For the moment, suffice it to say that the disagreement expressed on the dominance items is supportive of our other data relative to the style of competition in Japan, which is not overt. Further, the negative scoring of the dominance items and the positive scoring of the deference items is in keeping with previous studies which picture the Issei as being more deferent and self-effacing than the Nisei or Caucasian groups.

Table 11.5
Items Scored Negatively by the Issei Group

Item no.	Item	Mean item score (N–84)
54	I feel that I can dominate a social situation.	2.45
55	I enjoy the sense of power when I control the actions of others.	2.53
58	I would like to be a leader and sway others to my opinion.	2.45
60	I feel that I am driven by an underlying desire for power.	2.51

Items Scored Positively
by the Nisei Group

Table 11.6 records those items scored positively by the Nisei group. Of the twenty-nine items listed in the table, fourteen could be considered to be Japanese items and twelve American items. Three items (41, 42, 53) could not be clearly classified as being more in one area than in another.

The Japanese items were numbers 1, 5, 9, 17, 27, 29, 35, 37, 44, 45, 48, 50, 57, and 59. The American items were numbers 2, 4, 12, 14, 18, 20, 22, 26, 28, 34, 36, and 38.

The Japanese items can be grouped into the major headings of collectivity (1, 17, 29), duty and obligation (9, 35), and deference (27, 37, 44, 45, 48, 50, 57, and 59). Hierarchy is not explicitly indicated in the responses but its presence may be deduced from the number of deference scores. If one is deferent, there must be someone to whom one is deferential and therefore, by extension, one who is dominant. Further, dependence also was not explicitly indicated, although item 5 may possibly lead in that direction.

In the above groupings it can be seen that the family is of continued importance to the Nisei. Again, this is supported in the information obtained from the E.I.Q. and the Incomplete Sentence Test, as was the emphasis placed on duty and obligation.

The deference and, to a certain extent, the alleged conservatism, of the Nisei can be seen in items 45, 48, 50, 57, and especially in item 59.

The American items can be placed in the categories of individuation (2, 12, 18, 28), self-reliance (4, 34, 38), and equality (20, 26, 36). Item 14, as was mentioned earlier, was intended to be in opposition to item 5. However, the items were not paired and a choice was not required. Nevertheless, the high score of the Nisei on the item testifies to the importance of the family among the Nisei.

Table 11.6
Items Scored Positively by the Nisei Group

Item no.	Item	Mean item score (N–155)
1	The greatest satisfaction comes from being with one's family.	4.38
2	If you don't watch out for yourself, no one else will.	4.06
4	A real man is one who can be on his own and not be dependent on others.	3.40
5	The strongest emotional bond is between a mother and her child.	3.85
9	A person given a job should never rest until it is finished.	3.40
12	A person's greatest obligation is to be true to himself.	3.99
14	In the family, the strongest tie is between husband and wife.	3.90
17	In times of difficulty it is best to rely on your own family.	3.66
18	Parents should raise their children to be on their own.	4.13
20	People should all be given the same basic opportunities.	3.89
22	Every person has a right to live his life as he sees fit.	3.55
26	People in authority are no better than anyone else.	3.57
27	It is better not to shout or fight in public even if provoked.	3.85
28	Most people today are basically optimistic about the future.	3.54
29	A man cannot let himself down without letting down his family.	3.97
34	If a person doesn't watch out for himself, no one else will.	3.45

35	True success can only come through will power and self-discipline.	3.95
36	No one should be entitled to privileges he has not himself earned.	3.86
37	A wise man knows how to compromise by changing his moral position.	3.92
38	It is better to rely on yourself rather than depend on others.	3.87
41	I assert myself with energy when the occasion demands it.	4.05
42	I express my enthusiasm and respect for the people I admire.	4.08
44	I see the good points rather than bad points of those above me.	3.42
45	I am capable of putting myself in the background.	3.85
48	I accept suggestions rather than insist on my own way.	3.57
50	I am considered compliant and obliging by my friends.	3.49
53	I give praise rather freely when the occasion warrants it.	3.73
57	I usually follow instructions and do what is expected.	3.91
59	In matters of conduct, I conform to custom.	3.60

The individuation items disclose that the Nisei scored higher than any other group on item 2. Once again, it appears that the high positive response to this item is a result of the historical experience of the Nisei. They, more than the other groups, were placed in situations where they experienced more direct confrontation with the larger American society. The individuation items they agreed to reveal an interest in developing one's talents (12), training children to be on their own (18), and a belief that everyone has a right to live his life as he sees fit (22). However, it must be noted that, while the Nisei agreed to this item, the degree of agreement was lower than that of the other groups.

The self-reliance items (4, 34, 38) were largely the same as those agreed to by the Issei, as were the items on equality (20, 26, 36). Two of the items on equality (20, 36) refer to equality of opportunity. These in turn, when seen in relation to the items on self-reliance and the high degree of agreement to item 41, give some insight into the drive for achievement and competitiveness of the Nisei.

Items Scored Negatively by the Nisei Group

Table 11.7 lists those items scored negatively by the Nisei

group. Of the five items listed, two (54, 60) are from the dominance-deference inventory. Both of these items are dominance items; however, the low score on item 60 is not too significant as all groups disagreed to it. The score on item 54 is just barely in the disagree range and supports our other data which indicate that the Nisei are less self-confident, more deferent, and less dominant than the Sansei or Caucasian groups.

Table 11.7
Items Scored Negatively by the Nisei Group

Item no.	Item	Mean item score (N–155)
15	If someone in authority pushes you around, you can do little.	2.28
23	The best way to succeed is to have a detailed plan and stick to it.	2.60
33	In the long run it doesn't matter what a man does since in the end it all passes away.	2.11
54	I feel that I can dominate a social situation.	2.60
60	I feel that I am driven by an underlying desire for power.	2.30

The other items scored negatively (15, 23, 33) reflect the Nisei sensitivity to arbitrary force by a person in authority (15) and their greater flexibility as compared to the Issei (23). Item 33 discriminated poorly among all groups. The higher score of the Issei was perhaps more a result of their advanced age than an indication of a fundamental pessimism.

Items Scored Positively by the Sansei Group

Table 11.8 contains those items scored positively by the Sansei group. Of the 22 items, eight (1, 9, 35, 37, 45, 48, 50, 57) are the more Japanese items, and 11 (2, 8, 12, 14, 18, 20, 22, 26, 36, 38, 46) are the more American items. Items 41, 42, and 53 are from the dominance-deference inventory and are difficult to classify since they are clearly related to self-assertion or to deference as we have defined them.

Of the eight Japanese items, three (9, 35, 37) provide clues to the achievement motivation and aspiration of the Sansei. Item 9 indicates the value placed on perseverance, item 35 stresses the importance of will power, and item 37 testifies to the need for flexibility.

Moreover, if one takes Whyte's *The Organization Man* (1956) seriously, then three cardinal principles for success in a modern organization are "belongingness," "togetherness," and "conformity." These, in turn, are closely related to items 45, 48, 50, and 57, on which the Sansei expressed agreement. On item 50, however, the agreement score of 3.54 was due to the influence of the much higher female score of 3.69 as opposed to the male score of 3.39.

The remaining Japanese item (1), as was mentioned previously, cannot be said to be a strictly Japanese item because it was agreed to by all groups. However, the higher scores of the Japanese American groups do serve to support all of our other data on the greater importance of the family group among the Japanese.

The American items can be classified under the headings of individuation (2, 8, 12, 22), equality (20, 26, 36), self-reliance (38), and self-assertiveness (46). Once again, item 14 refers to the emotional tie between the husband and wife in the family. This item was scored neutrally by the Caucasian students. The higher score by the Sansei again reinforces the above material on the continued importance of the family in the Sansei group.

Taken as a whole, Table 11.8 corresponds rather closely with the responses given by the Caucasian students, as depicted in Table 11.10, the principal difference being that, with the exception of three deference items, there were no Japanese items agreed to by the Caucasian students. The Sansei responses differ in the agreement expressed on items indicating persistence (9), will power and self-discipline (35), flexibility (37), in being slightly more capable of putting themselves in the background (45), and in being more compliant and obliging (50) than the Caucasian students.

In comparison with the Nisei and Issei groups, the Sansei have less of a need to rely on the family, less of a feeling of duty and obligation, less of sense of hierarchy, and are far less deferent

than their parents or grandparents. On the other hand, they are
more self-assertive, more independent, and more egalitarian than

Table 11.8

Items Scored Positively by the Sansei Group

Item no.	Item	Mean item score (N–124)
1	The greatest satisfaction comes from being with one's family.	3.69
2	If you don't watch out for yourself, no one else will.	3.96
8	A truly moral person stands up for his convictions no matter what.	3.57
9	A person given a job should never rest until it is finished.	3.54
12	A person's greatest obligation is to be true to himself.	4.03
14	In the family, the strongest tie is between husband and wife.	3.49
18	Parents should raise their children to be on their own.	3.98
20	People should all be given the same basic opportunities.	4.11
22	Every person has the right to live his life as he sees fit.	3.81
26	People in authority are no better than anyone else.	3.59
35	True success can only come through will power and self-discipline.	3.83
36	No one should be entitled to privileges he has not himself earned.	3.78
37	A wise man knows how to compromise by changing his moral position.	3.60
38	It is better to rely on yourself than to depend on others.	3.64
41	I assert myself with energy when the occasion demands it.	3.87
42	I express my enthusiasm and respect for the people I admire.	3.91
45	I am capable of putting myself in the background.	3.84
46	I argue with zest for my point of view against others.	3.50
48	I accept suggestions rather than insist on my own way.	3.52
50	I am considered compliant and obliging by friends.	3.54
53	I give praise rather freely when the occasion warrants it.	3.71
57	I usually follow instructions and do what is expected.	3.72

the Issei or Nisei, as can be seen by the items scored negatively in
Table 11.9.

Items Scored Negatively
by the Sansei Group

Table 11.9 includes those items scored negatively by the Sansei group. These nine items reveal that the Sansei are less authoritarian (3), more egalitarian or less hierarchical (7, 21, 31), less deferent (15), less rigid (23), and perhaps less self-defeating (33) than their forebears.

What is also of interest in Table 11.9 is that, with the exception of item 60, which was scored negatively by all groups, the items listed are all Japanese items. As a point of interest, it might also be noted that the Caucasian students scored the same items negatively. Further, the Caucasian students scored lower than the Sansei on every item but one (33). Thus, although the Sansei scored the items negatively, their somewhat higher scores can be interpreted as being intermediate between the Nisei and Caucasian groups. While small, the difference could be interpreted to mean that there is a slight retention of the Japanese characteristics measured by those items.

Table 11.9
Items Scored Negatively by the Sansei Group

Item no.	Item	Mean item score (N–124)
3	The best way to raise children is to train them to be quiet and obedient.	2.14
7	Those in authority are automatically entitled to respect.	2.41
13	If someone starts an argument, it is better to give in.	2.53
15	If someone in authority pushes you around, you can do little.	2.17
21	You can tell what kind of a person an individual is if you know his family background.	2.43
23	The best way to succeed is to have a detailed plan and stick to it.	2.48
31	Anyone in authority is automatically entitled to respect.	2.34
33	It makes no difference what a man does since it all passes away.	1.93
60	I feel that I am driven by an underlying desire for power.	2.37

The information contained in Tables 11.8 and 11.9 reveals that the Sansei have become more self-assertive, more concerned with their rights, and in general more like the Caucasian students in their responses than are the Issei and Nisei. Indeed, their slightly higher score on item 60 might be interpreted to indicate that in some areas they may be more self-assertive. Yet a number of Japanese characteristics have been retained. The Sansei are somewhat more rigid and tenacious in pursuing a goal than the Caucasian students. In their interactions with others they are still likely to be more relaxed and self-assured.

Items Scored Positively
by the Caucasian Group

Table 11.10 indicates those items scored positively by the Caucasian group. Of the sixteen items, four could be considered Japanese items. These are items 1, 45, 48, and 57. The agreement score of 3.54 on item 57 is a result of the influence of the much higher female score of 3.74 as opposed to the lower male score of 3.21. Items 45, 48, and 57 are part of the dominance-deference inventory. Items 41, 42, and 53 are also a part of the inventory; however, these items are so phrased as to make it difficult to classify them as Japanese or American.

The agreement expressed on items 45, 48, and 57 is in keeping with the information obtained by the Incomplete Sentence Test, in which it was found that the Caucasian students were less overtly competitive, less self-assertive, less dominant, more cooperative, more willing to help others, and more open to others than we had anticipated. Also, as was mentioned in the discussion of the Japanese American groups, item 1 cannot be said to be a strictly Japanese item although it was included in that category because of the very positive response given. It will be recalled that the Issei and Nisei had scores of 4.33 and 4.38 respectively, while the Sansei response of 3.69 was significantly higher than the Caucasian student response of 3.52. Further, both the Sansei and the Caucasian student scores on this item were influenced by the higher female scores. The Sansei males scored 3.56 and the females 3.82. The scores of the Caucasian males and females were 3.44 and 3.60 respectively.

Table 11.10
Items Scored Positively by the Caucasian Group

Item no.	Item	Mean item score (N–154)
1	The greatest satisfaction comes from being with one's family.	3.52
2	If you don't watch out for yourself, no one else will.	3.84
8	A truly moral person stands up for his convictions no matter what.	3.70
12	A person's greatest obligation is to be true to himself.	3.83
18	Parents should raise their children to be on their own.	4.22
20	People should all be given the same basic opportunities.	4.11
22	Every person has a right to live his life as he sees fit.	3.70
26	People in authority are no better than anyone else.	3.71
38	It is better to rely on yourself than to depend on others.	3.66
41	I assert myself with energy when the occasion demands it.	3.93
42	I express my enthusiasm and respect for people I admire.	4.08
45	I am capable of putting myself in the background.	3.77
46	I argue with zest for my point of view against others.	3.48
48	I accept suggestions rather than insist on my own way.	3.54
53	I give praise rather freely when the occasion warrants it.	3.82
57	I usually follow instructions and do what is expected.	3.47

The remainder of the items scored positively on Table 11.10 are the more American items. These are items 2, 8, 12, 18, 20, 22, 26, 38, and 46. These items, in turn, can be grouped into the categories of individuation (2, 8, 12, 18, 22), equality (20, 26), self-reliance (38), and self-assertiveness (46). These categories and numbers are almost identical to those given by the Sansei. The only difference was on item 36, "No one should be entitled to privileges he has not himself earned," which was scored positively by the Sansei (3.78) and neutrally (3.04) by the Caucasian students and was therefore not included in Table 11.10.

Items Scored Negatively
by the Caucasian Group

Table 11.11 includes those items scored negatively by the Caucasian group. These items, it will be recalled, were the same as those scored negatively by the Sansei, the only difference being that, with the exception of item 33, every item was scored lower by the Caucasian group. In many respects Table 11.11 complements Table 11.10, for again, with the exception of item 60, every item scored negatively is a Japanese item. Thus we have evidence in support of equality, rights and privileges, individualism, and self-assertiveness by having such strong negative evidence against hierarchy (7, 21, 31), deference (3, 13, 15), and rigidity (23).

Table 11.11

Items Scored Negatively by the Caucasian Group

Item no.	Item	Mean item score (N–154)
3	The best way to raise children is to train them to be quiet and obedient.	1.93
7	Those in authority are automatically entitled to respect.	1.83
13	If someone starts an argument, it is better to give in.	2.36
15	If someone in authority pushes you around, you can do little.	1.96
21	You can tell what kind of person an individual is if you know his family background.	2.32
23	The best way to succeed is to have a detailed plan and stick to it.	2.14
31	Anyone in authority is automatically entitled to respect.	1.82
33	It makes no difference what a man does since it all passes away.	2.08
60	I feel that I am driven by an underlying desire for power.	2.22

Of the remaining two items scored negatively (33, 60), item 33 reveals that the Caucasian students, while not wholly optimistic about the future, as was indicated by the neutral response of 2.81 on item 28 in Table 11.3, are not quite ready to throw in the towel and abandon hope. The low score on item 60 is in keeping with our other data, which reveal that the students associate this item with a personal dominance or the imposition of the self on others.

Taken together, Tables 11.10 and 11.11 reveal that the Caucasian students are less rank conscious or hierarchical, less deferent, less concerned with duties and obligations, more egalitarian, more autonomous, more independent, and therefore perhaps more relaxed than the other groups. The latter remark is supported in part by the larger number of neutrally scored items in the Caucasian group. Of the sixty items in the form, the Issei scored fourteen neutrally, the Nisei twenty-six, the Sansei twenty-six, and the Caucasian students thirty-two. In other words, the Caucasian students scored over one-half of the items neutrally. Once more, as can be seen in Tables 11.2 and 11.3, the neutrally scored items were either the odd-numbered Japanese items or those American items (4, 6, 10, 30, 32, 34, 40) which emphasized what seemed to be a self-centered or too egocentric individualism. These items suggest that one imposes oneself on others or imply that success is achieved at the expense of others. This is not to suggest that the Caucasian students are not individualistic, but only that they are likely to reject the more aggressive forms of rugged individualism in which one's own desires are gratified at the expense of others.

The Dominance-Deference Inventory

As was stated at the beginning of this chapter, the dominance-deference inventory was adapted from the work of Arkoff, Meredith, and Iwahara (1962). Our method was to calculate the mean for each item in each group and then total the means for all items in each group. Tables 11.12 through 11.17 record the total dominance and deference scores for the total sample and for the males and females.

Table 11.12 lists the total mean dominance scores for all groups. Since it contains the composite score of both males and females, the mean scores are somewhat reduced by the lower female scores. This is readily apparent when the male dominance scores in Table 11.14 are compared with the female dominance scores in Table 11.15. Nevertheless, Table 11.12 is most informative. For example, there is a gradual progression in the total mean dominance score from the Issei to the Nisei and Sansei. As a matter of fact, the Sansei appear to be more dominant than the Caucasian students. Here again, however, there is an interesting male-female difference. Table 11.14 indicates that the Sansei males are indeed more dominant in their total score than the males, while Table 11.15 shows that the Caucasian females are more dominant than the Sansei females. The higher Sansei scores, then, are more a result of the higher male score.

Table 11.12
Total Mean Dominance Scores

Item no.	Item	Issei (N–84)	Nisei (N–155)	Sansei (N–124)	Cauc. (N–154)
		Category group and mean item scores			
41	I assert myself with energy.	3.56†	4.05	3.87	3.93
43	I enjoy organizing or directing a group.	2.95	3.12	3.20	3.21
46	I argue with zest for my point of view.	3.09	3.12‡	3.50	3.48
47	I find it easy to lead a group of younger people.	2.92	3.02‡	3.31	3.33
49	I influence others more than they influence me.	2.88	2.97	2.99	2.90
52	I usually make the decisions when with another.	2.89	2.90	3.18	3.12
54	I feel that I can dominate a social situation.	2.45	2.62	2.84	2.92
55	I enjoy the sense of power when I can control others.	2.53	2.69	2.81	2.62
58	I would like to be a leader and sway others.	2.45‡	2.72	2.86	2.91
60	I feel that I am driven by a desire for power.	2.51	2.30	2.37	2.22
	Total mean dominance score	2.78	2.89	3.05	3.04

†Significant at the .01 level (Mann-Whitney U Test).
‡Significant at the .05 level (Mann-Whitney U Test).

Table 11.12 is most interesting in the pattern of dominance items. The drive and ambition of the Nisei and Sansei are apparent in items 41, 49, 55, and 60, although item 54 discloses that they do not yet believe that they can dominate a social situation. The implications of the higher Sansei scores will be considered in greater detail when Table 11.14 is discussed.

Table 11.13, which lists the total mean deference scores, is also a composite of male and female scores. Once again, as Tables 11.16 and 11.17 disclose, the score on many of the items has been slightly increased because of the higher female scores.

Table 11.13 records a rather clear progression in the decreasing amount of agreement expressed on the total mean deference scores. There are, however, a few anomalies, most of which have already been considered in the discussion of Tables 11.2 and 11.3. For example, it does not appear that items 42 or 53 discriminate properly. In particular, item 53 seems to be ill-suited

Table 11.13
Total Mean Deference Scores

Item no.	Item	Category group and mean item scores			
		Issei (N–84)	Nisei (N–155)	Sansei (N–124)	Cauc. (N–154)
42	I express my enthusiasm and respect for people I admire.	4.09	4.08	3.91	4.08
44	I see the good points rather than bad points of those above me.	3.86†	3.42‡	3.18	3.00
45	I am capable of putting myself in the background.	3.91	3.85	3.84	3.77
48	I accept suggestions rather than insist on my own way.	3.44	3.57	3.52	3.54
50	I am considered compliant and obliging by my friends.	3.37	3.49	3.54‡	3.28
51	I often seek the advice of people older than myself.	3.66†	3.21	3.03	2.90
53	I give praise freely when the occasion warrants it.	3.32‡	3.73	3.71	3.82
56	I often find myself imitating or agreeing with a superior.	3.37†	2.76	2.98	3.01
57	I usually follow instructions and do what is expected.	3.44†	3.91	3.72‡	3.47
59	In matters of conduct I conform to custom.	3.75	3.56	3.26	3.13
	Total mean deference score	3.72	3.56	3.47	3.39

†Significant at the .01 level (Mann-Whitney U Test).
‡Significant at the .05 level (Mann-Whitney U Test).

for cross-cultural comparison with the Issei. It may well be that because of their age and retired status they do not often find themselves in a position where praise is called for. Further, the Caucasian student score on this item is inflated by the much higher female (4.01) than male (3.64) score.

Table 11.13 is also most useful for the information it provides on the importance of ranking or hierarchy. Two items in particular (44, 51) testify to the high value placed on hierarchy in the Issei group and its gradual attenuation in the Nisei and Sansei groups. Again, however, these differences are more clearly seen when the male and female dominance and deference scores are considered separately.

Table 11.14 contains the male mean dominance scores. This table provides a better understanding of the higher Sansei dominance score given in Table 11.12. From the data presented in Table 11.14, it is clear that the Sansei scored higher on every item but one—item 54. Item 54, "I feel that I can dominate a social situation," was also scored in the same manner by the females. That is, there was a progression from the lowest score obtained by the Issei to the highest score obtained by the Caucasian students.

The higher scores of the Sansei are largely the result of the higher scores obtained on items 46, 47, 55, and 60. These items, together with the others, suggest that the Sansei are more energetic, more anxious to succeed, and perhaps more competitive than the Caucasian male students. At the same time there has been a playing down of overt competition in the Caucasian student group, which may have served to deflate their scores somewhat. These considerations are to be kept in mind when an examination is made of Table 11.16, in which it is shown that the Sansei males are also much more deferent than the Caucasian student males. At the moment, suffice it to say that the differences among all groups recorded in Table 11.14 are not so great as those recorded in Table 11.16. In other words, while there is comparatively little difference between the Sansei and Caucasian student scores on each of the dominance items, there is a much greater difference with regard to the individual deference items; indeed, on one-half of these items there are significant differences. Further, all of the total mean dominance scores are in the neutral range.

Table 11.14

Male Mean Dominance Scores

Item no.	Item	Category group and mean item scores			
		Issei (N–46)	Nisei (N–94)	Sansei (N–70)	Cauc. (N–52)
41	I assert myself with energy.	3.78†	4.04	3.92	3.85
43	I enjoy organizing or directing a group.	2.98	3.22	3.21	3.27
46	I argue with zest for my point of view.	3.24	3.27†	3.63	3.44
47	I find it easy to lead a group of younger people.	3.00	3.22	3.31	3.14
49	I influence others more than they influence me.	2.89	3.11	3.13	3.08
52	I usually make the decisions when with another.	3.02	3.05	3.27	3.19
54	I feel that I can dominate a social situation.	2.48	2.60†	2.94	3.00
55	I enjoy the sense of power when I can control others.	2.50†	2.81	2.89	2.63
58	I would like to be a leader and sway others.	2.57†	2.88	3.11	3.08
60	I feel that I am driven by a desire for power.	2.54	2.39	2.49	2.35
	Total mean dominance score	2.10	3.06	3.19	3.10

†Significant at the .05 level (Mann-Whitney U Test).

The female mean dominance scores are depicted in Table 11.15. This table more clearly shows the progression in dominance scores from the Issei through the Nisei and Sansei to the Caucasian student females. Although the total mean dominance score for the Caucasian student females is higher than the others, the Sansei females scored slightly higher on items 49, 55, and 60. However, it is difficult to determine the significance of the difference; and, again, all of the total mean dominance scores are in the neutral range.

In comparing the total mean male-female dominance scores as given in Tables 11.14 and 11.15, it can be seen that in every case the male scores are higher than the female scores, but there are interesting differences. For example, on items 41, 43, 46, and 47, the Caucasian female scores are higher than those of the males. This difference does not occur in the Japanese American groups. Indeed, an item-by-item comparison discloses that in every case the male scores are higher than those of the females.

The higher Caucasian female scores suggest that they are more energetic and perhaps even slightly more outspoken than the males. It is also possible that, because of baby-sitting, playground supervision, or other activities, the females may have had more experience in organizing groups or caring for younger people (47).

Table 11.15
Female Mean Dominance Scores

| Item no. | Item | Category group and mean item scores | | | |
		Issei (N–38)	Nisei (N–61)	Sansei (N–70)	Cauc. (N–102)
41	I assert myself with energy.	3.34†	4.05	3.82	4.02
43	I enjoy organizing or directing a group.	2.92	3.02	3.19	3.26
46	I argue with zest for my point of view.	2.95	2.97‡	3.37	3.52
47	I find it easy to lead a group of younger people.	2.84	2.82‡	3.30	3.53
49	I influence others more than they influence me.	2.87	2.84	2.85	2.72
52	I usually make the decisions when with another.	2.76	2.75‡	3.03	3.05
54	I feel that I can dominate a social situation.	2.42	2.64	2.74	2.83
55	I enjoy the sense of power when I can control others.	2.55	2.57	2.74	2.57
58	I would like to be a leader and sway others.	2.34	2.56	2.61	2.75
60	I feel that I am driven by a desire for power.	2.47‡	2.84†	2.24	2.16
	Total mean dominance score	2.75	2.84	2.99	3.04

†Significant at the .01 level (Mann-Whitney U Test).
‡Significant at the .05 level (Mann-Whitney U Test).

Table 11.16 contains the male mean deference scores. This table reveals a very clear progression in the decreasing emphasis on deference in the three generations of Japanese Americans. The total mean scores indicate a much higher level of agreement on the deference items than on the dominance items, which were scored neutrally. For the most part, these items have been discussed in detail previously and the material presented in the table is largely self-evident. In particular, items 44, 45, 50, 51, 59, and 60 are most illuminating. These items suggest that, while the Sansei may be more energetic and even more competitive than the

Table 11.16
Male Mean Deference Scores

Item no.	Item	Category group and mean item scores			
		Issei (N–46)	Nisei (N–94)	Sansei (N–70)	Cauc. (N–52)
42	I express my enthusiasm and respect for people I admire.	4.02	4.01	3.79	3.98
44	I see the good points rather than bad points of those above me.	3.87†	3.26	3.09	2.87
45	I am capable of putting myself in the background.	4.07	3.85	3.79‡	3.58
48	I accept suggestions rather than insist on my own way.	3.35‡	3.66	3.47	3.48
50	I am considered compliant and obliging by my friends.	3.48	3.48	3.39‡	3.19
51	I often seek the advice of people older than myself.	3.57†	3.32	3.11‡	2.73
53	I give praise freely when the occasion warrants it.	3.35‡	3.72	3.66	3.64
56	I often find myself imitating or agreeing with a superior.	3.46†	2.78	3.00	3.00
57	I usually follow instructions and do what is expected.	3.72	3.96‡	3.63†	3.21
59	In matters of conduct, I conform to custom.	3.74	3.68†	3.14‡	2.87
Total mean deference score		3.84	3.53	3.29	3.28

†Significant at the .01 level (Mann-Whitney U Test).
‡Significant at the .05 level (Mann-Whitney U Test).

Caucasian male students, they are at the same time more deferent (45), more compliant (50), more prone to follow instructions (57) than are the Caucasian males. However, in all of these characteristics their scores are closer to those of the Caucasian males than are the scores of their parents or grandparents.

The scores of the females also indicate the reduction in agreement on deference items. Table 11.17 records the female mean deference scores. Here we find some interesting differences. The Caucasian females are somewhat less deferent than the Sansei females. The Caucasian females' lower total mean deference score was obtained in spite of their higher scores on items 42 and 53. These items refer to the expression of enthusiasm for an admired person and to the exhibition of praise. On the other hand, the Sansei females scored appreciably higher on items 44 and 50. These items refer to the tendency to see the good points rather than bad points in a superior and the belief that the respondent is considered compliant and obliging by friends. Table 11.17 does provide a clear indication of the decreasing need for deference in the Japanese American groups. The progression of scores is unmistakable.

When compared with the male total mean deference scores, the Sansei and Caucasian female scores are higher, the Nisei male and female scores are the same, and the Issei female scores are higher. The Issei male scores are significantly higher on items 45, 50, 56, and 57. These items, in turn, refer to the ability to put oneself in the background (45), to be considered compliant and obliging by friends (50), to imitate or agree with a superior (56), and to follow instructions and do what is expected (57). Taken together, these items undoubtedly reflect the employment history and role experience of the Issei males. It will be recalled that the Issei interview forms disclosed that the females had a more sheltered life, while the males had more direct occupational contact with the larger American society. Inevitably, the jobs they worked at required a more deferent attitude, the majority being employed as farm labor.

From the dominance-deference inventory we have rather clear evidence supportive of our other findings. Based upon our listing of Japanese and American characteristics, we had predicted that there would be a gradual attrition of the Japanese characteristics of deference in the Nisei and Sansei generations and an increase in the more American characteristic of dominance or self-assertion. Tables 11.14 through 11.17 indicate that the scores are as predicted. Moreover, the Sansei total mean dominance score is even slightly above that of the Caucasian male. The difference is not a great one and should not be taken as evidence that the Sansei are, as the Issei believe, completely Americanized. On the contrary, their higher scores on the deference items would indicate that there still remains at least a verbalization of the Japanese characteristic of deference.

Table 11.17
Female Mean Deference Scores

Item no.	Item	Category group and mean item scores			
		Issei (N–38)	Nisei (N–61)	Sansei (N–54)	Cauc. (N–102)
42	I express my enthusiasm and respect for people I admire.	4.16	4.15	4.04	4.18
44	I see the good points rather than bad points of those above me.	3.84‡	3.57‡	3.28	3.13
45	I am capable of putting myself in the background.	3.76	3.85	3.89	3.96
48	I accept suggestions rather than insist on my own way.	3.53	3.48	3.57	3.58
50	I am considered compliant and obliging by my friends.	3.26‡	3.51	3.69‡	3.37
51	I often seek the advice of people older than myself.	3.76†	3.18	2.94	3.07
53	I give praise freely when the occasion warrants it.	3.29‡	3.74	3.76	4.01
56	I often find myself imitating or agreeing with a superior.	3.29†	2.74	2.96	3.02
57	I usually follow instructions and do what is expected.	3.16†	3.85	3.82	3.74
59	In matters of conduct, I conform to custom.	3.76‡	3.53	3.37	3.39
	Total mean deference score	3.87	3.56	3.43	3.32

†Significant at the .01 level (Mann-Whitney U Test).
‡Significant at the .05 level (Mann-Whitney U Test).

Summary

Considered as a whole, the results obtained from the Contrasting Values Survey were most enlightening. The data indicate that the Issei are more self-reliant, competitive, and individuated than we had suspected. We also discovered that the Caucasian students are less dominant and less overtly competitive than we had anticipated. Although the Sansei still retain a number of Japanese characteristics, their overall responses were, on the whole, closer to those of the Caucasian students than they were to those of the Issei and the Nisei. And finally, as both the E.I.Q. and the Incomplete Sentence Test disclose, the Nisei replies place them right in the middle. Indeed, in many respects they are even more Japanese in their responses than are the Issei. This intensification of certain Japanese characteristics in the Nisei will be discussed in greater detail in the concluding chapter.

Chapter 12

The Edwards Personal Preference Schedule*

The Edwards Personal Preference Schedule (EPPS) was chosen as a useful instrument for several reasons. First, it had been used in Hawaii with a large sample of Japanese Americans (Arkoff 1959; Berrien, Arkoff, and Iwahara 1967; Fenz and Arkoff 1962) and in Japan among college students by Berrien (1964). Second, the form is relatively easy to administer and hand score. Third, the instrument was designed to measure the personal preference of respondents on fifteen needs that were originally defined by Murray et al. (1938). The fifteen needs are achievement, deference, order, exhibition, autonomy, affiliation, succorance, intraception, dominance, abasement, nurturance, change, endurance, heterosexuality, and aggression. Further, it can be seen that several of these variables, such as dominance, deference, order, achievement, and abasement, are similar to the Japanese values given earlier.

The EPPS attempts to minimize the role of "social desirability" in response items by forcing the subject to choose between equally desirable or undesirable alternatives. Yet, despite the attempt to control for social desirability, one of the chief criticisms of the EPPS is that it fails to distinguish between the individual's own preference and what he perceives to be socially desirable (Edwards 1959). For our purpose here, however, such criticism is largely irrelevant. Since the object of the study is one

---

*An earlier version of this chapter, based on a smaller sample, was published under the title, "Value Continuities and Change in Three Generations of Japanese Americans," in *Ethos*, vol. 2, No. 3, Fall 1974. Reprinted by permission of the Regents of the University of California.

of acculturation and changing values in the three generations of Japanese Americans, the EPPS should reveal the social values of a particular generation as perceived by the respondents. Yet if one agrees that EPPS does indeed measure the individual's own preference, then one can also assume from current learning theory, as reported by Goodman (1968:175-193), that the average response of a group of such individuals would represent the social values of that group as internalized.

An additional feature of the EPPS is that it contains a measure of test consistency. Of the 225 items in the EPPS, fifteen are repeated at various places throughout. There are, then, two sets of the fifteen items. In two appearances of one of these items, the possible response patterns are AB, BA, AA, and BB. If the subject marks the items by chance alone, each of these possible patterns of response is likely. Therefore, the probability of any of these patterns occurring by chance is 25 per cent. Since AA and BB represent identical choices in the set, however, the probability of an identical choice is 50 per cent for one item. For two sets of fifteen items, the expected number of identical choices on the basis of chance is 7.5 (Edwards 1959:15).

The consistency score, then, enables us to determine if the subject has indeed made personal choices or is simply filling in the form on the basis of chance alone. The probability of nine or more identical choices appearing by chance is approximately 30 per cent. The probability of ten or more identical choices occurring by chance is approximately 15 per cent, while the probability of eleven or more identical choices occurring by chance is approximately .06 per cent. Eleven or more identical choices may be considered as a significant departure from chance expectancy. Therefore, if a consistency score is eleven or higher, it can be assumed that the respondent is not making his choices on the basis of chance alone. A more lenient standard of ten or more identical choices could be used (Edwards 1959:15).

The EPPS was administered to a total of 1,235 individuals. Of these, 722 were Caucasian Americans and 513 were Japanese Americans. Since the intent of the study was to measure value changes associated with acculturation, it was first necessary to obtain samples of the three generations of Japanese Americans, and then find similar groups of Caucasian Americans of compatible age and education with whom the Japanese Americans could be compared.

Table 12.1 discloses that we were able to obtain a sample of 84 Issei (first generation, born in Japan), 163 Nisei (second generation, born of Issei parents), 276 Sansei (third generation, born of Nisei parents). The Issei sample consisted of 34 males and 50 females. The mean age and level of education of the males was 72.85 and 8.76 years. The mean age and level of education for the females was 70.72 and 7.48. The Nisei sample consisted of 68 males and 95 females. The mean age and level of education was 48.79 males and 13.40 for the males, and 46.68 and 12.15 for the females. The mean age and level of education for the Sansei was 23.35 and 13.83 for the males and 23.54 and 14.09 for the females.

The Issei were administered the Japanese Language version of the EPPS which was obtained from Dr. Iwahara of the Tokyo University of Education. The Nisei and Sansei were given the standard English language version of the EPPS.

The Caucasian sample was composed of 139 Caucasian senior adults (62 males and 77 females), 247 Caucasian adults (113 males and 134 females), and 346 Caucasian students (136 males, 210 females). The mean age and education of the senior Caucasian adults was 67.82 and 9.48 for the males, and 68.03 and 9.79 for the females. The mean age and education for the Caucasian students was 25.24 and 14.13 for the males, and 22.77 and 14.63 for the females. As can be seen in Table 12.1, the mean ages and levels of the education for each of the three Caucasian groups agree rather closely with the three generations of Japanese Americans.

With respect to methodology, I contacted nearly one hundred Japanese Americans. Some were students, some were neighbors, and some were personal friends of the family. Further contact with the Japanese Americans was made by the Sansei students in the Japanese Community Study Class mentioned above. One Sansei graduate student was successful in administering the EPPS to a Sansei convocation held in Sacramento in the summer of 1971. The Caucasian students were all students in anthropology classes at California State University, Sacramento. To avoid having other Sansei students or Chinese American student scores mixed in with the sample, only Caucasian student scores were used. Again, the purpose of having the Caucasian sample was to provide control groups with which we could compare the Issei, Nisei, and Sansei responses. It may be objected that the use of a control group for the Sansei was unnecessary since norms have already been established by Edwards based on 1,509 (760 men and 749 women) college students. But the norms were established more than two decades ago. I believe that if there has indeed been a change in college students toward a more open, less overtly competitive but still highly individualistic personality, as other data indicated (Connor 1972), then the norms may have changed significantly in such areas as nurturance, dominance, change, achievement, and succorance.

My students and I obtained the Caucasian senior adult and adult samples by administering the EPPS to neighbors, relatives, and friends. As with the Japanese Americans, selection was based on availability and willingness to cooperate. Moreover, our Caucasian adult sample was limited to those between the ages of forty and fifty-five, to match the Nisei sample, while our senior Caucasian group was composed of those over sixty-five.

The scoring of the EPPS is rather simple. Each need variable may range from zero to twenty-eight; the higher the score, the greater the expression of the particular need. In addition, to determine the significance of paired responses such as male-female or Nisei-Sansei, the t test was employed. The EPPS data were then transferred to computer cards and the arithmetic means and tests of significance were derived by the use of a computer.

From Edwards's (1959) description of the fifteen needs, it can be seen that several of them can be associated with the five major Japanese-American value orientations we have been utilizing in this study. Given the Japanese emphasis on hierarchy, collectivity, duty and obligation, deference, and dependence, we should be able to predict that the retention of these Japanese characteristics would result in higher scores on the variables of deference, order, affiliation, succorance, abasement, nurturance, and endurance in the Japanese Americans. Likewise, given the American emphasis on equality, individualism, self-reliance, self-assertion, and rights and privileges, we can predict that the Caucasian students should score higher on the variables of exhibition, autonomy, dominance, change, and aggression.

The remaining variables of achievement, intraception, and heterosexuality cannot be immediately determined from the

Japanese or American characteristics. Based upon the description given of these three variables, however, we can predict that the Japanese Americans would score about the same or higher on achievement and intraception, and the Caucasian students higher on heterosexuality. The lower Japanese American score on heterosexuality could be predicted on the basis of the literature. Kitano (1961) reports the Issei mother as being sexually repressive of her offspring. Further, we can also expect that there will be significant differences in the male-female scores. Again, we should be able to predict that the Japanese American females will score higher on the variables associated with the Japanese characteristics than will the males. We can also predict that the Caucasian females will score lower on the variables associated with the American characteristics than will the males. These predictions are based upon observed male-female role expectations that require the female to be more deferent, less dominant, and less aggressive than the male.

Research in Hawaii conducted by Arkoff (1959) supports these general predictions. He found that, in comparison with the normative college sample, the Japanese Americans have a higher need for deference, abasement, nurturance, order, and change and a lower need for dominance, achievement, exhibition, and heterosexuality. Furthermore, the EPPS has been administered in Japan to a rather large college population of 458 males and 504 females. In the report on his findings, Berrien (1964) notes that the Japanese college students scored lower than the normative American college group in their need for achievement, dominance, exhibition, and deference and higher in their scores on abasement, endurance, and change. These differences are depicted in Table 12.2. With the exception of the differing scores on change, achievement, and deference, the Japanese college student's lower scores on exhibition and dominance, and their higher scores on abasement and endurance, are in keeping with the major Japanese characteristics listed above. The lower scores on achievement and especially deference are at first glance most puzzling. One would expect achievement to be of high value. Berrien explained the lower achievement scores as follows:

> Both the college men and women score lower on the achievement category than their counterparts in America. This

is perhaps also a special feature of the college population which may not be generally true of the adult Japanese. There is a common saying in Japan that it is difficult to get into a university but easy to graduate. By American standards Japanese professors are notoriously easy graders giving 50 to 75 per cent of the students A grades. University attendance regulations are extremely liberal. Course final examinations are almost the sole measures of achievement and these do not require the same degree of work which characterizes most American college courses. (1964:16-17)

There are however, other explanations for the lower achievement score and these are discussed in detail below. The lower deference scores are explained by Berrien as being a result of student rebellion against tradition:

> The different results are therefore understandable in the context of the social changes going on in Japan. Moreover, in supporting the hypothesis only partially the results suggest that Japanese college students are not tradition-bound. This conforms with the observation that Japanese students have adopted a faddish verbal antipathy for many things traditional. Deference to the past or to the remnants of feudal customs is uncollegiate. (1964:16)

Berrien might also have mentioned the rise of radical student groups on college campuses and the widespread student disorder that accompanied the signing of the American-Japanese security treaty in 1960. Furthermore, the decade of the 1960s has been marked by student disorders in many parts of the world—not just in Japan. Moreover, when the data are updated and the Japanese college students are compared with the state university students, we find that with the exception of achievement, all of the scores are in the direction that would be predictable on the basis of the major Japanese and American value orientations. Thus, as Table 12.2 indicates, Japanese male college students have a higher need for order, affiliation, succorance, abasement, and endurance. The state university males have a higher need for achievement, exhibition, autonomy, intraception, dominance, nurturance, change, heterosexuality, and aggression.

Japanese college females, as shown in Table 12.3, have a higher need for deference, order, succorance, abasement, and endurance, while the state university females have a higher need

TABLE 12.1 MEAN SCORES OF EPPS VARIABLES FOR ALL GROUPS

Variables	Issei Male	Nisei Male	Sansei Male	Cauc. Senior Adult Male	CSUS Student Male	Cauc. Adult Male	Issei Female	Nisei Female	Sansei Female	Cauc. Senior Adult Female	Cauc. Adult Female	CSUS Student Female
Achievement	14.97	15.28*	14.56	14.92*	15.63	15.89	13.92	14.48*	13.69	14.01*	14.65*	14.07
Deference	14.91†	12.54†	9.91	13.97‡	9.98	11.81†	15.56*	14.77†	11.68	13.62*	12.91†	9.79
Order	19.79†	15.31†	10.65	14.40*	9.26	13.33†	19.18†	16.41†	12.11	16.12†	13.46†	9.01
Exhibition	9.32†	12.18†	13.84	13.00§	14.52	14.12	10.06§	11.15†	12.45	12.39§	13.00†	14.08
Autonomy	14.32*	15.27	15.83	14.68*	16.63	15.49‡	12.52*	13.61	13.56	14.91†	12.96†	14.63
Affiliation	17.38†	14.09‡	15.38	14.73§	13.99	13.45*	18.78†	15.87‡	17.23	17.32§	16.29	16.72
Intraception	12.68*	14.15*	15.01	14.40†	16.70	12.85†	12.60†	15.66‡	17.10	15.13‡	16.64†	17.80
Succorance	13.32‡	10.93*	12.13	10.87	10.98	11.13	15.00§	13.55	14.07	13.61	13.05	12.87
Dominance	12.27‡	14.56*	13.14	13.79†	13.69	16.66†	10.40	9.99*	9.28	10.71	11.21	11.55
Abasement	17.21‡	14.72*	13.73	13.93†	10.98	11.14	18.56*	17.45†	15.66	15.91‡	14.32*	13.45
Nurturance	19.68†	15.68	16.33	15.66‡	14.86	13.84§	20.64†	17.52	17.31	17.79§	16.55	17.01
Change	11.03†	14.85	15.17	14.37*	17.49	15.47†	11.42†	15.25†	17.45	15.07‡	16.81†	18.33
Endurance	17.27‡	15.46†	13.15	16.50*	12.02	15.03†	17.52§	16.35†	12.86	17.00†	14.57†	10.93
Heterosexuality	5.82†	12.15†	17.07	11.47†	19.64	14.53†	3.12†	7.42†	14.60	5.92†	12.77†	17.51
Aggression	9.09†	12.53§	13.86	12.34§	13.68	14.24	9.82	10.39	11.00	10.56	10.66†	11.97
Confidence Score	11.88	11.74	12.14	11.95	12.11	12.16	11.98	11.93	12.21	11.64	11.97	12.33
Number of Respondents	34	68	101	62	136	113	50	95	166	77	134	210

* = Significant at the .10 level or better
§ = Significant at the .05 level or better
‡ = Significant at the .01 level or better
† = Significant at the .001 level or better

Mean Age	Male	Female
Issei	72.85	70.72
Nisei	48.79	46.68
Sansei	23.35	23.54
Cauc. Senior Adult	67.82	68.03
Cauc. Adult	48.21	46.59
CSUS Student	25.24	22.77

Mean Education	Male	Female
Issei	8.76	7.48
Nisei	13.40	12.15
Sansei	13.83	14.09
Cauc. Senior Adult	9.48	9.79
Cauc. Adult	13.01	13.01
CSUS Student	14.13	14.63

for achievement, exhibition, nurturance, change, and heterosexuality.

From the information depicted in Table 12.1 it can be seen that in all three generations of Japanese Americans there is a decline of scores on deference, order, abasement, and endurance. Likewise there is a corresponding increase in the scores on such variables as exhibition, intraception, change, heterosexuality, and aggression (although the increased scores on aggression are not significant in the females). On the basis of this information alone it would appear that there have been some rather marked changes toward acculturation in the three generations of Japanese Americans. When we look at the scores of the three generations of Caucasian Americans, however, we find that with the exceptions of intraception and aggression, all of the scores of the same variables are in the same direction as in the three generations of Japanese Americans. That is, there is a similar decline of scores on deference, order, abasement, and endurance; and an increase on the scores of the variables of exhibition, change, and heterosexuality.

It does appear, then, that generational differences are important and must be taken into consideration in any diachronic study of acculturation. One can no longer assume that the differential responses of the immigrant and subsequent generations are due solely to their varying degrees of acculturation.

Does this mean, then, that there are no differences between generations that can be clearly seen to result from differing degrees of acculturation rather than to purely maturation factors? A glance at Tables 12.2 and 12.3 discloses that an appreciable number of differences remain. Tables 12.2 and 12.3 compare the responses of similar generations of Japanese Americans and Caucasian Americans, male and female, respectively. These tables show that when three generations of Japanese Americans are matched with comparable generations of Caucasian Americans, significant differences are found. For example, Table 12.2 discloses that the Japanese American males of all three generations score significantly higher than their Caucasian counterparts on order, abasement and nurturance, and lower on exhibition, dominance, change, and heterosexuality.

The Japanese American female scores are in the same direction as the Japanese American males with two exceptions.

TABLE 12.2 MEAN SCORES OF EPPS VARIABLES FOR MALE GROUPS

Variables	Issei Males	Cauc. Senior Adult Males	Nisei Males	Cauc. Adult Males	Sansei Males	CSUS Student Males	Norm-ative College Males	Sansei Males	Jpnse. College Males	CSUS Student Males
Achievement	14.97	14.92	15.28	15.89	14.56‡	15.63	15.66‡	14.56†	12.65†	15.63
Deference	14.91†	13.97	12.54*	11.81	9.91	9.98†	11.21†	9.91	10.08	9.98
Order	19.79†	14.40	15.31†	13.33	10.65‡	9.26‡	10.23	10.65	10.75†	9.26
Exhibition	9.39	13.00	12.18†	14.12	13.84*	14.52	14.40*	13.84†	10.17†	14.52
Autonomy	14.32*	14.68	15.27	15.49	15.83*	16.63†	14.34†	15.83*	15.23‡	16.63
Affiliation	17.38†	14.73	14.09	13.45	15.38†	13.99†	15.00	15.38	15.08†	13.99
Intraception	12.68§	14.40	14.15§	12.85	15.01‡	16.70*	16.12‡	15.01§	16.05*	16.90
Succorance	13.32‡	10.87	10.93	11.13	12.13§	10.98	10.74†	12.13§	15.09†	10.98
Dominance	12.27†	13.79	14.56†	16.66	13.14	13.69†	17.44†	13.14*	12.49†	13.69
Abasement	17.21†	13.93	14.72†	11.14	13.73†	10.98†	12.44†	13.73‡	16.31‡	10.98
Nurturance	19.68†	15.66	15.68‡	13.84	16.33‡	14.86*	14.04†	16.33†	13.04‡	14.86
Change	11.03†	14.37	14.85*	15.47	15.17†	17.49†	15.51	15.17§	16.19†	17.49
Endurance	17.27‡	16.50	15.46	15.03	13.15*	12.02*	12.66	13.15†	16.49‡	12.02
Heterosexuality	5.82†	11.47	12.15†	15.53	17.07†	19.64†	17.65	17.07	17.35†	19.64
Aggression	9.09†	12.34	12.53†	14.24	13.86	13.68‡	12.79‡	13.86*	13.05‡	13.68
Confidence Score	11.79	11.95	11.74	12.16	12.14	12.11	11.53	12.14		12.11
Number of Respondents	34	62	68	113	101	136	760	101	458	136

* = Significant at the .10 level (or better)
§ = Significant at the .05 level (or better)
‡ = Significant at the .01 level (or better)
† = Significant at the .001 level (or better)

Males Mean Age		Males Mean Education	
Issei	72.85	Issei	8.76
Cauc. Senior Adults	67.82	Cauc. Senior Adults	9.48
Nisei	48.79	Nisei	13.40
Cauc. Adult	48.21	Cauc. Adult	13.01
Sansei	23.35	Sansei	13.83
CSUS Student	25.24	CSUS Student	14.13

That is, like the males they score higher on order and abasement, and lower on exhibition, dominance, change, and heterosexuality. In addition, the females score higher on deference, while nurturance is no longer a significantly higher variable among the Sansei. In this regard, however, the lack of significance in the variable does not appear to be the result of a lower need for nurturance in the Sansei female. Rather, as Table 12.3 clearly indicates, there has been a corresponding increase in the nurturance score of the Caucasian female student. A close examination of Tables 12.2 and 12.3 also indicates that there are several variables significant in the Issei and Nisei groups but no longer significant in the Sansei. Likewise, some variables that are significant in the Issei disappear in the Nisei and reappear in the Sansei. The implications of these changing variables are discussed in detail below.

The Issei

Above I predicted that the retention of Japanese personality characteristics or values would result in the Japanese Americans attaining a higher score on the variables of deference, order, affiliation, succorance, abasement, nurturance, and endurance. I also predicted that the Caucasian Americans would score higher on the variables of exhibition, autonomy, dominance, change, and aggression. Moreover, I expected the Japanese Americans to score higher on achievement and intraception and lower on heterosexuality. Tables 12.2 and 12.3 largely bear out these predictions. The Issei males score higher in deference order, affiliation, succorance, endurance, and nurturance. They score lower in exhibition, dominance, change, heterosexuality, and aggression. There is, however, one puzzling exception: The Issei males show no significant differences in achievement. Furthermore, the intraception score is not in the predicted direction. That the achievement variable as described by Edwards (1959) does not accurately reflect the means or goals of Japanese American achievement may partly answer this discrepancy. This point is elaborated in some detail in the discussion of the lower Sansei achievement scores. Furthermore, with respect to the other variables not in the predicted direction, it must be remembered that each of the fifteen variables is paired twice with each of the other variables. This means, of course, that high scores on some

TABLE 12.3 MEAN SCORE OF EPPS VARIABLES FOR FEMALE GROUPS

Variables	Issei Females	Cauc. Senior Adult Females	Nisei Females	Cauc. Adult Females	Sansei Females	CSUS Student Females	Normative College Females	Sansei Females	Jpnse. College Females	CSUS Student Females
Achievement	13.92	14.08	14.48	14.65	13.69	14.07‡	13.08*	13.09†	12.23†	14.07
Deference	15.56†	13.62	14.77†	12.91	11.68†	9.79†	12.40‡	11.68*	11.24†	9.79
Order	19.18†	16.12	16.41†	13.46	12.11†	9.01†	10.24†	12.11†	10.53†	9.01
Exhibition	10.06†	12.39	11.15†	13.00	12.45†	14.08	14.28†	12.45†	10.03†	14.08
Autonomy	12.52‡	14.91	13.61*	12.96	13.56‡	14.63†	12.29†	13.56†	14.97	14.63
Affiliation	18.78§	17.32	15.87	16.29	17.23*	16.72‡	17.40	17.23‡	16.31	16.72
Intraception	12.60†	15.13	15.66§	16.64	17.10*	17.80*	17.32	17.10‡	18.15	17.80
Succorance	15.00*	13.61	13.55	13.05	14.02‡	12.87	12.53†	14.02‡	15.71†	12.87
Dominance	10.40	10.71	9.99‡	11.21	9.28†	11.55†	14.18†	9.28†	11.56	11.55
Abasement	18.56†	15.91	17.45†	14.32	15.66†	13.45‡	15.11*	15.66†	17.67†	13.45
Nurturance	20.64‡	17.79	17.52§	16.55	17.31	17.01*	16.42‡	17.31†	13.43†	17.01
Change	11.42†	15.01	15.25‡	16.81	17.45§	18.33†	17.20	17.45	17.08†	18.33
Endurance	17.52	17.00	16.35†	14.57	12.86†	10.93†	12.63	12.86†	16.63†	10.93
Heterosexuality	3.12†	5.92	7.42†	12.77	14.60†	17.51†	14.34	14.60†	12.48†	17.51
Aggression	9.82	10.56	10.39	10.66	11.00§	11.97†	10.59	11.00‡	11.93	11.97
Confidence Score	11.98	11.64	11.93	11.99	12.21	12.33		12.25		12.33
Number of Respondents	50	77	95	134	166	210	749	166	504	210

* = Significant at the .10 level or better
§ = Significant at the .05 level or better
‡ = Significant at the .01 level or better
† = Significant at the .001 level or better

Mean Age of Females	
Issei	70.42
Cauc. Senior Adult	68.03
Nisei	46.68
Cauc. Adult	46.59
Sansei	23.54
CSUS Student	22.77

Mean Education of Females	
Issei	7.48
Cauc. Senior Adult	9.79
Nisei	12.15
Cauc. Adult	13.01
Sansei	14.09
CSUS Student	14.63

variables will necessarily depress scores on other variables. Therefore, a lower score on a given variable does not necessarily mean that the variable or need is *not* valued, but only that some of the other variables with which it was paired were *more* highly valued.

It is also apparent from Table 12.2 that the deference variable does not discriminate in all of the male groups, while autonomy discriminates only slightly in the Sansei males. In these variables, at least, there do not appear to be appreciable differences between the Japanese American and Caucasian American groups. Table 12.2 indicates that the deference variable is also not significant between Berrien's (1964) Japanese student sample and our Caucasian students.

The Issei females, as indicated by Table 12.3, disclose a much greater retention of the variables associated with the Japanese than did the males. This would appear to be a result of their more sheltered existence as indicated earlier. Once again, I do not find the achievement variable to be significant. The aggression variable is not significant. With regard to aggression among the females, however, the response appears to be about the same in all three groups with the exception of the Caucasian student—a point to which I return later.

The Nisei

The male and female Nisei scores shown on Tables 12.2 and 12.3 indicate the expected higher scores for deference, order, abasement, and nurturance, and the anticipated lower scores on exhibition, dominance, change, and heterosexuality. In addition, the females have higher scores in deference, autonomy, and endurance. But with the exception of the slightly higher score on autonomy, the scores on deference and endurance are as anticipated. The higher score on autonomy, while not highly significant is in line with Caudill's (1952) and DeVos's (1955) findings that the Nisei female appeared to be considerably self-reliant and somewhat independent.

The Nisei male, in contrast, is more intraceptive than the Caucasian. The higher Nisei male score on this variable might be an expression of what Caudill and DeVos (1956:1117) stated: "In psychoanalytic terminology, this means that the Japanese Americans have an ego structure that is very sensitive and vulnerable to stimuli coming from the outer world, and a superego structure that depends greatly upon external sanction."

It was the Nisei males who were more exposed to both the prejudice and acculturation stress associated with earning a living in the larger American community. Of the 101 Nisei males and 131 Nisei females we interviewed at length, 90 per cent of the males and 75 per cent of the females reported that they had experienced moderate to severe prejudice.

Also curious in both the male and female Nisei responses is that their scores on affiliation and succorance are not only not significant when compared with the Caucasians, but are also lower than either the Issei or Sansei scores. However, the difference between the male Nisei and Sansei scores on succorance is not significant.

As a tentative explanation I would suggest that the higher Sansei scores are the product of other influences. For example, in other studies (Connor 1972, 1974a), I have reported that within the family the Sansei youth is considerably more subordinate, has stronger family ties, and has greater dependency needs than his Caucasian counterpart. In addition, a study of child-rearing practices in the Sacramento area (Caudill and Frost, 1972) reveals that the Sansei mother still retains certain aspects of the Japanese mother's child-rearing style. These child-rearing practices are of the sort that would lead to the inculcation of dependency needs and a close tie to the family, which in turn would be reflected in the higher succorance and affiliation scores. Of equal importance, of course, as Tables 12.2 and 12.3 so clearly indicate, is the marked decrease in the affiliation scores of the Caucasian students. In this regard, then, the higher Sansei scores are more a result of the decline in the Caucasian scores. When compared with Edwards's normative group of 1952, there are no significant differences in either the male or female Sansei affiliation scores.

The Sansei and Caucasian Students

Based upon a comparison of Sansei scores with those of Edwards's 1952 normative group, it could easily be said that rapid acculturation has taken place and the Sansei are now where Edwards's normative group was in 1952 in the expression of the variables of change, endurance, affiliation, and heterosexuality.

They have exceeded the normative group in autonomy and are much less deferent. In addition, the males are significantly more aggressive. Enormous changes, however, have taken place in the Caucasian students during the past two decades. Both males and females are less deferent, have less need for order, are significantly more autonomous, are less affiliative, slightly more introspective, considerably less dominant, far less abasive, slightly more nurturant (more apparent in females than males), and far more concerned with change, heterosexuality, and aggression (telling it like it is) than were the students of the early 1950s. Additionally, the females have a significantly less need for endurance than the normative group of twenty years ago, but this variable is not significant in the males. In all, it can be seen that there have been considerable changes in today's college students when compared with Edwards's normative group of two decades ago. These differences are especially marked in the Caucasian female. While the female scores may be the result of the woman's movement, it seems more than likely that they reflect in part a certain alienation. Indeed, the alienation is clearly evident in both the male and female lower affiliation scores.

The lower Sansei scores on achievement (both male and female) are puzzling, but are not unique. Arkoff (1959) found that his sample of Hawaiian Japanese Americans also scored lower than Edwards's normative groups in achievement. Perhaps a clue to this anomaly can be found in Edwards's (1959) description of the achievement variables: "To do one's best, to be successful, to accomplish tasks requiring skill and effort, to be a recognized authority, to accomplish something of great significance, to do a difficult job well, to solve difficult problems and puzzles, to be able to do things better than others, to write a great novel or play."

A careful look at the description of the achievement variable discloses that it contains many items indicating individual achievement in the sense that one will stand out above others. Numerous studies of Japanese achievement patterns (Benedict 1946; DeVos 1968; Nakane 1970; Berrien 1964; Goodman 1957) indicate that achievement is seen as a matter of achieving group rather than individual goals. Studies of Japanese Americans

(Caudill 1952; Schwartz 1971) indicate that Japanese American achievement is frequently seen in terms of goals laid down by others. Additionally, the achievement variable phrases achievement in terms expressive of dominance and self-assertion. It would seem that there is still a general unwillingness by the Sansei to accept such highly visible forms of achievement, although the emerging Sansei generation is well aware of a need for greater self-assertion (Connor 1972). I might add that Berrien (1964) also found lower achievement scores on the EPPS he administered to the Japanese college students and which is depicted in Table 12.2. In this regard, it is most revealing to compare the Sansei male scores on dominance with those of the Caucasian students. What is clear in Table 12.2 is not that the Sansei have become significantly more dominant—their scores on this variable are about the same as the Japanese students—but that the Caucasian students have become significantly less dominant than their counterparts of the early 1950s.

I might add that I do not believe that the lower Sansei scores are reflective of a lower drive for achievement. By all available evidence the Sansei males are still achievement oriented. What is important here, however, is the pattern of achievement.

To obtain information on the academic achievement of Sansei students, I went through the list of some 18,000 enrolled students at California State University, Sacramento. From this list, I was able to identify 275 Sansei undergraduates (158 males and 117 females). These individuals were next classified as to major and overall grade point averages (g.p.a.). The Sansei were then grouped by their majors and their g.p.a.'s were compared with those of all other students having the same major. The results were most informative.

The results disclose that the largest number of Sansei males (58 or 37 per cent) were majoring in business. The next largest group (40 or 26 per cent) were majoring in the sciences. The third largest were undeclared (18 or 11 per cent), and the remainder were majoring in criminal justice, park and recreation, social sciences, and others. The overall g.p.a. for the Sansei males majoring in business was 2.63 on a four-point scale, while that of all other males with the same major was 2.70. The g.p.a. of those majoring in the sciences was 2.78, while that of all other male students was 2.80. The g.p.a. for all male Sansei undeclared majors was 2.60 while that of all other males with an undeclared major was 2.79. The remainder of the male Sansei were scattered among other majors in numbers too small to obtain valid results.

The academic achievement pattern of the female Sansei was somewhat different. Of the 117 Sansei females only 56 were clustered in major areas in numbers sufficiently large to permit comparisons. Their g.p.a.'s in these majors were about the same as those of the other females with the same major. For example, the largest concentration of Sansei females (19) was in an undeclared major. In the undeclared major the overall g.p.a. of the Sansei females was 2.87, while that of all other female students with an undeclared major was 3.01. The next largest major (15) was in business. In this area the overall Sansei female g.p.a. of 2.90 was somewhat above that of other female g.p.a. of 2.83. The third largest clustering (11) was in nursing. In this major the g.p.a.'s of the Sansei females (2.90) and the other females (2.94) were about the same. The final grouping was the biological sciences where the Sansei g.p.a. of 3.02 was above that of the other females g.p.a. of 2.93. The remainder of the Sansei females were enrolled in such public service majors as special education, speech, speech pathology, child development, home economics, and social welfare.

From the above information several conclusions may be reached. First, Sansei academic achievement is no longer above the average as was frequently reported (Caudill 1952; Kitano 1962) as being a characteristic of their parental generation, the Nisei. Second, the overall g.p.a. of Sansei females—and indeed, of other females as well—is clearly above that of their male counterparts. For example, the Sansei male g.p.a. for an undeclared major was 2.50, while that of all other male undeclared majors was 2.69. This may be compared with the Sansei female g.p.a. of 2.87, and an overall female g.p.a. of 3.01 for an undeclared major. A final conclusion from the above would be that the Sansei—male and female—are still very much interested in what might be termed the "secure" or less "adventurous" professions. Of the 275 students, there were only 3 (2 males, 1 female) with an ethnic studies major.

In discussing the implications of the above conclusions several facts emerge. First, the achievement variable on the EPPS does not accurately reflect academic achievement, since the females—Sansei and others—have higher g.p.a.'s than the males, even though their achievement scores as depicted in Table 12.4 are significantly below the males. Second, as indicated previously, Japanese American achievement—and indeed, achievement in Japan itself, as indicated so clearly by DeVos (1968)—is a result of a distinctively different set of reinforcements. These reinforcements operate by first establishing in the individual strong dependency and affiliative needs. In turn, these needs create an ego structure that is quite sensitive to the opinions of significant others. Achievement, then, is often seen in terms of goals laid down by others. This point was first brought out in the work of Caudill and DeVos (1956) and has been amplified by Goodman (1957), DeVos (1968), Schwartz (1971), and others. The evidence for just such an ego structure in the Sansei can be seen in their significantly higher affiliation, succorance, nurturance, and abasement scores, and their lower scores on exhibition, autonomy, and change. Perhaps a better understanding of this essential point may be had when we examine Edwards's (1959) description of these variables.

In his manual (1959:11), Edwards provides a description of the fifteen variables. These decriptions are essentially paraphrases of the original statements appearing in the test booklet. The description of affiliation reads as follows:

> To be loyal to friends, to participate in friendly groups, to do things for friends, to form new friendships, to make as many friends as possible, to share things with friends, to do things with friends rather than alone, to form strong attachments, to write letters to friends. (Edwards 1959:11)

The higher Sansei scores on the above variable would certainly appear to emphasize the importance of belonging to a group and being influenced by group pressure. The need to belong to a group, or, better yet, what has been described as a dependency need (and a need stated by Doi [1962] to be of vital importance in understanding the Japanese personality structure),

TABLE 12.4 MEAN SCORES OF EPPS VARIABLES FOR MALES AND FEMALES IN SIX GROUPS

Variables	Issei Male	Issei Female	Nisei Male	Nisei Female	Sansei Male	Sansei Female	Cauc. Senior Adult Male	Cauc. Senior Adult Female	Cauc. Adult Male	Cauc. Adult Female	CSUS Student Male	CSUS Student Female
Achievement	14.97*	13.92	15.28*	14.48	14.56*	13.69	14.92*	14.08	15.89‡	14.65	15.63†	14.07
Deference	14.91	15.56	12.54‡	14.77	9.91†	11.08	13.97	13.62	11.81†	12.91	9.98	9.79
Order	19.79	19.18	15.31*	16.41	19.65‡	12.11	14.40†	16.12	13.33	13.46	9.26	9.01
Exhibition	9.32	10.06	12.18§	11.15	13.84†	12.45	13.00	12.39	14.12‡	13.00	14.52*	14.08
Autonomy	14.32‡	12.52	15.27‡	13.61	15.83†	13.56	14.68	14.91	15.49†	12.96	16.63†	14.63
Affiliation	17.38*	18.78	14.09†	15.87	15.38†	17.23	14.73†	17.32	13.45†	16.29	13.97†	16.72
Intraception	12.68	12.60	14.15‡	15.66	15.01†	17.10	14.40	15.13	12.85†	16.64	16.70‡	17.80
Succorance	13.32*	15.00	10.93†	13.55	12.13†	14.02	10.87†	13.61	11.13†	13.05	10.98†	12.87
Dominance	12.27‡	10.40	14.56†	9.99	13.14†	9.28	13.79†	10.71	16.66†	11.21	13.69†	11.55
Abasement	17.21§	18.56	14.72†	17.45	13.73†	15.66	13.93‡	15.91	11.14†	14.32	10.98†	13.45
Nurturance	19.68*	20.64	15.68‡	17.52	16.33§	17.31	15.66†	17.79	13.84†	16.55	14.86†	17.01
Change	11.03	11.42	14.85	15.25	15.17†	17.45	14.37	15.01	15.47‡	16.81	17.49*	18.33
Endurance	17.27	17.52	15.46*	16.35	13.15	12.86	16.50	17.00	15.03	14.57	12.02‡	10.93
Heterosexuality	5.82†	3.02	12.15‡	7.42	17.07†	14.60	11.47†	5.92	15.53†	12.77	19.04‡	17.51
Aggression	9.09	9.82	12.53‡	10.39	13.86†	11.00	12.34‡	10.56	14.24†	10.66	13.68†	11.97
Confidence Score	11.88	11.96	11.74	11.93	12.14	12.21	11.95	11.64	12.16	11.99	12.11	12.33
Number of Respondents	34	50	68	95	101	166	62	77	113	134	136	210

* = Significant at the .10 level or better
§ = Significant at the .05 level or better
‡ = Significant at the .01 level or better
† = Significant at the .001 level or better

Mean Age

	Male	Female
Issei	72.85	70.72
Nisei	48.79	46.68
Sansei	23.35	23.54
Cauc. Senior Adult	67.82	68.03
Cauc. Adult	48.21	46.59
CSUS Student	25.24	22.77

Mean Education

	Male	Female
Issei	8.76	7.48
Nisei	13.40	12.15
Sansei	13.83	14.09
Cauc. Senior Adult	9.48	9.79
Cauc. Adult	13.01	13.01
CSUS Student	14.13	14.63

is clearly evident in the higher Sansei scores on succorance. Edwards (1959:11) defines succorance as follows:

> To have others provide help when in trouble, to seek encouragement from others, to have others be kindly, to have others be sympathetic and understanding about personal problems, to receive a great deal of affection from others, to have others do favors cheerfully, to be helped by others when depressed, to have others feel sorry when one is sick, to have a fuss made over one when hurt.

Given the strong affiliation and succorance, or dependency needs, it would also be reasonable to expect that an individual with such needs would also have an ego structure quite sensitive to the opinions of significant others. Such an ego structure is reflected in Edwards's (1959:11) description of abasement:

> To feel guilty when one does something wrong, to accept blame when things do not go right, to feel that personal pain and misery suffered do more good than harm, to feel the need for punishment for wrong doing, to feel better when giving in and avoiding a fight than when having one's own way, to feel the need for confession of errors, to feel depressed by inability to handle situations, to feel timid in the presence of superiors, to feel inferior to others in most respects.

The remaining variables of nurturance, exhibition, autonomy, and changes are largely self-explanatory from their titles. For example, nurturance is in many ways a reciprocal of succorance. That is, it consists of such statements as a need to help friends, or to assist others, to be generous and sympathetic, and to show affection to others. Likewise, exhibition refers to such statements as to be the center of attraction, to talk about oneself, and to have others notice and comment on oneself. As such, exhibition is associated somewhat with autonomy, which is defined as being independent of others, to be able to come and go as one wishes, to be able to do what one wants, to be able to do things regardless of the opinions of others. Finally, as its name implies, change consists of wanting to do new things, changing one's routine, and taking part in fads and fashions (Edwards 1959:11).

When one observes the higher Sansei scores on affiliation, succorance, nurturance, and abasement, and their lower scores on exhibition, autonomy, and change, it seems obvious that there is an emphasis on the importance of the group or on group ties over that of individualism or independence. Other data on the Sacramento Japanese Americans are clearly supportive of this. In an earlier paper (Connor 1974a), I reported that there was a considerable retention of what might be called traditional Japanese family characteristics in all three generations of Japanese Americans. These characteristics emphasize a much closer bond with the family than is true of Caucasian Americans. Like the Japanese household or *ie*, the Japanese American family also creates in its members strong affiliative and dependency needs. It is in such a family milieu, then, that the high Sansei needs of affiliation, succorance, nurturance, and abasement are inculcated.

Given such needs, it is also reasonable to expect that the nature of Japanese American achievement would be somewhat different. With a lesser emphasis on individualism and independence as is reflected in the lower scores on autonomy, exhibition, and change, it would seem that achievement would be seen more in terms of the achievement of goals laid down by others—especially those goals established by the parents because of the strong family ties. This appears to be so. For example, a special report issued by the U.S. Bureau of the Census on Japanese, Chinese, and Filipinos in the United States (U.S. Bureau of the Census 1973:50) discloses that in the Sacramento metropolitan area in 1970, a total of 74.3 per cent of Sansei males, and 58.4 per cent of the Sansei females in the eighteen to twenty-four year age range were in school. While it was not possible to obtain a comparable percentage breakdown for the remainder of the Sacramento metropolitan area, the census figures do reveal that in the eighteen to nineteen age group, 63.4 per cent of the youth were in school. This figure declines to 32.9 per cent in the twenty to twenty-one age group, and further declines to 22.1 per cent in the twenty-two to twenty-four age group (U.S. Bureau of the Census 1972:6-1040). From local school officials, I was able to determine that slightly more males than females go on, but that the male dropout rate is higher. If this is so, it would appear that those males who do go on are a more select group than the Japanese Americans, and therefore the competition would be keener than in a more unselect group.

It appears, ironically, that the Japanese Americans are becoming victims of their own success. Perhaps because of parental pressure they are now sending more of their offspring on to higher education than did the Nisei generation. But, with three out of every four Sansei males in college, it is to be expected that a large number would be of only mediocre ability, and these students would find the competition keener.

It would also appear that the parental pressure is itself a reflection of the more traditional family structure. Remember that there was a significantly larger percentage of Sansei males (74.3 per cent) than females (58.4 per cent) in higher education. This difference indicates the greater pressure to enter college placed on the Sansei male. Again, this appears to be a reflection of the traditional Japanese family emphasis on providing a good education for the male offspring, especially the *chōnan,* or successor son. This point was repeatedly emphasized by Sansei females in the course of our interviewing. The Sansei females would often complain of the differential treatment accorded them within the family. They noted that frequently the son, especially a first son, would be treated better. He would be the one who received a bike, while the girl did not. He would be given a car, or use of the family car, and the girl would not; and he would be sent to a university, while the girl had to enter a junior college.

In this respect, then, the extraordinarily high percentage of Sansei males enrolled in higher education, and their concentration in business, the sciences, and the other "secure" professional majors, does appear to be most supportive of the conclusions reached by DeVos (1968) and others, that the achievement motivation of the Japanese—and indeed, that of the Japanese Americans also as indicated by Caudill and DeVos (1956)—is in response to a different set of reinforcements. These reinforcements operate by first creating in the individual strong dependency and affiliative needs that manifest themselves in stronger emotional ties to, and a dependency upon, the family. In turn, these affiliative and dependency needs give rise to guilt feelings when the individual has failed to meet the expectations of the family or group. As such, the nature of achievement differs from what is commonly thought to be the normal pattern in the larger American society. This conclusion is given ample support in the study conducted by

Schwartz (1971) on the achievement motivation of Japanese American high school students in the Los Angeles area:

> The point to be made here is that *Japanese-American pupils seem to reject the notion of individual autonomy. Not only are they oriented toward the "collectivity" and acceptance of its authority structure* (which is lineal for the family and school and collateral for the peer social system), *they, in comparison with Anglos, express little personal mastery over the future.* Whereas Japanese-American pupils indicate exceedingly high educational and mobility aspirations and express significantly greater desire than Anglos for extrinsic rewards . . . their mode of ascent is one of group cooperation rather than individual pursuit. *What is more, the presence or absence of the belief that individual action can modify a person's destiny has little relationship to the achievement of Japanese Americans,* in spite of the fact that it is significant and positive for the achievement of comparable Anglos, Mexican-Americans, and Negroes. (Schwartz 1971:349; italics added)

From the above discussion several major conclusions may be reached. One, it appears obvious that the distinctively Japanese values of collectivity, hierarchy, dependence, deference, and a strong sense of duty and obligation are closely related to the Japanese family structure. Indeed, exactly this point has been made by several authors (Benedict 1946, Caudill 1969, DeVos 1965, 1967, 1968). And in an earlier paper (Connor 1974a) I indicated that there were definite continuities in the retention of the *ie* ideal or traditional Japanese household in all three generations of Japanese Americans. Second, it seems equally evident that acculturation is not a unitary process. In certain domains such as language usage, the celebration of traditional holidays, and the retention of certain food habits, considerable change has taken place in the third generation (Connor 1972). But, as our data here so clearly indicate, many of the values associated with the more traditional family system have been retained.

Finally, the pattern of Japanese American achievement is distinctively different from the commonly accepted belief that achievement is solely associated with autonomy, independence, and a highly individualistically motivated self-assertion. By all available evidence, not only have the Japanese Americans succeeded in achieving a respected position in American society, but even the third generation still displays the adaptive measure and achievement techniques reflective of the more traditional Japanese modes of achievement and achievement reinforcement.

Summary and Conclusions

On the basis of an understanding of the Japanese and American value orientations, I predicted that the Japanese Americans would score higher on the variables of deference, order affiliation, succorance, abasement, nurturance, and endurance. In contrast, the Caucasian Americans should score higher on the variables of exhibition, autonomy, dominance, change, and aggression. I further predicted that the Japanese Americans would be about the same or higher on the variables of achievement and intraception, and lower on heterosexuality.

The research on the whole supports these predictions, although there were some exceptions. Japanese Americans consistently scored higher on order, abasement, and nurturance, and lower on exhibition, change, dominance, and heterosexuality. These characteristics, in turn, were found to be associated with the more traditional Japanese family system. Yet the predictions on autonomy, deference, affiliation, succorance, endurance, achievement, intraception, and aggression did not consistently hold true for both sexes of all three generations. These discrepancies were largely explainable in terms of both maturation and the acculturation experience. It was also demonstrated that the mode of Japanese American achievement was in many ways distinctively different from that of the larger American society.

Of equal importance was the finding that there were generational differences in both the Caucasian American and Japanese American groups in the decline of scores on deference, order, abasement, and endurance, and an increase in scores on exhibition, change, and heterosexuality as one went from the older to the younger generations. These changes can be seen to be largely a result of the normal maturation process. We expect youth to be more interested in change, heterosexuality, and exhibition, and less interested in order, endurance, and the like than the older adults.

Significant changes were also found in the contemporary

Caucasian student scores. Today's students are in many ways remarkably different from those of Edwards's normative group of 1952. They are far less deferent, have less of a need for order, are more autonomous, less affiliative, less dominant, less abasive, and have a higher need for nurturance, change, heterosexuality, and aggression. These changes are even more marked in the females than in the males.

When the Sansei are compared with the contemporary Caucasian student group, both continuities and changes are clear. The Sansei have retained some Japanese values in that they still express a higher need for order, affiliation, succorance, abasement, and endurance and have a lower need for autonomy, exhibition, dominance, and heterosexuality. These scores were largely explainable in terms of the retention of values clearly associated with the traditional Japanese family system. For the Sansei males, the deference and aggression scores are no longer significant, while their scores on exhibition, autonomy, dominance, and endurance are very close to the Caucasian scores.

On the basis of these changes, it can be said that the Sansei are moving in the direction of greater self-assertion. But these changes are more typical of the male than the female. When compared with her contemporary Caucasian counterpart, the Sansei female retains many Japanese value orientations.

Finally, it should be emphasized that the available evidence indicates that the higher Sansei scores on order, affiliation, succorance, abasement, and endurance and their low scores on autonomy, exhibition, dominance, and heterosexuality cannot be construed to be a result of their inferior position as a highly visible minority group in the larger American society. All of the available evidence would indicate that comparable results have been obtained from Hawaii (Arkoff 1959), where the Japanese Americans are hardly in the minority, and perhaps more important, from college students in Japan itself (Berrien 1964).

Chapter 13

Summary
and Conclusions

The problem of this investigation as originally stated, was to investigate certain psychological and behavioral characteristics in three generations of Japanese Americans in the Sacramento area in order to determine the degree to which the various generations have retained certain characteristics which are distinctively Japanese or have replaced them with those which are distinctively American. The distinctively Japanese characteristics were grouped under the major headings of hierarchy, collectivity, duty and obligation, deference, and dependence. The distinctively American characteristics were grouped under the major headings of equality, individualism, rights and privileges, self-assertion, and self-reliance.

Several subsidiary questions were also to be considered in the study. One, if the Japanese Americans have indeed arrived at middle-class status, is the next step to be complete assimilation into American society, with the concomitant loss of ethnic identity, or will there be the retention of the Japanese identity? The second question was also related to the retention of Japanese characteristics. That is, if the success of the Japanese Americans is due to the utilization of adaptive mechanisms and values that are essentially Japanese in nature, as Caudill maintains (1952), will there then be a tendency to retain those characteristics and inculcate them in the oncoming generation or will they ultimately be replaced with values that are more characteristic of the larger American society?

In organizing this study we relied upon two main categories of instruments. The first category was a biographical form which recorded essential biographic information and data on the more overt forms of acculturation such as changes in food habits, language use, celebration of holidays, and attitudes toward intermarriage.

The second category contained those instruments designed to measure the more covert forms of acculturation, such as changes in values, belief systems, and personality characteristics. Four instruments were employed in the second category: (1) an Incomplete Sentence Test, (2) the Ethnic Identity Questionnaire, (3) the Contrasting Values Survey, and (4) the Edwards Personal Preference Schedule. In the discussion which follows, the major findings of the study will be reviewed as they apply to each of the three generations.

The Issei

As was anticipated, all of our instruments indicated a rather high retention of Japanese characteristics among the Issei. Of these characteristics, the instruments most frequently disclosed the emphasis on deference, duty and obligation, hierarchy, and collectivity, which was apparent in the importance placed on the group, especially the family. Dependence was not always directly indicated and, for the most part, was inferred from the answers, which disclosed a reliance upon the family or others, as given in the Incomplete Sentence Test. It may well be that, although the Issei arrived with dependency needs, the nature of their experience in this country placed them more on their own resources and they thus had fewer opportunities to have their dependency needs met. On the other hand, one might argue that the Japanese community, with its various services, did provide a feeling of collectivity and solidarity which may have met certain dependency needs.

Moreover, in this regard, it will be remembered from the discussion in Chapter 3 on the Japanese psychological and behavioral characteristics that the *ie* ideal is the central concept in understanding those characteristics, and we have every reason to believe that the Issei brought the *ie* concept with them and attempted to preserve the *ie* ideal while in this country. While the evidence for the preservation of the *ie* ideal is indirect, it is nonetheless quite strong. Our biographical information discloses that 40 per cent of the Issei are living with their offspring—in most cases with the son and his family—and that even those who do not live with their children see them frequently.

Furthermore, all of our testing protocols disclose that the Issei rank high on those items that refer to the family, such as duty to the family, the importance of not bringing shame to the family, the strength of the emotional ties to the family, and the reliance upon the family in time of need. This is not to say that the Issei were completely successful in their attempt to maintain the *ie* ideal. Unquestionably, they realized that they were not in Japan and that adaptations had to be made. Nevertheless, an attempt was made to preserve the *ie* ideal, and overall it must be said that not only were they successful but that they also succeeded in passing at least a feeling for the *ie* concept to their children and even to their grandchildren. It will be recalled that four-fifths of the Nisei and two-thirds of the Sansei reported in Table 6 that it had been stressed that they should not act in any way that would bring shame to the family. Moreover, both the Nisei and Sansei consistently scored higher on the "family" items in all our instruments than did the Caucasian groups.

We also have considerable evidence, especially from the E.I.Q. and Contrasting Values Survey, that a certain amount of acculturation has taken place among the Issei. The E.I.Q. in particular indicates that the Issei are in many ways more relaxed, open, and permissive than are the Nisei. Undoubtedly this is in part due to their retired status; however, they do believe that Japanese Americans should identify completely as Americans, and appear to be more acculturated in some aspects when compared with the Seattle Issei. The phrase "in some aspects" is important because all of our other data show that the Issei are behaviorally and psychologically much more Japanese than American. While their basic internalized values are Japanese, their external attitudes have become more American.

At the same time, both the Incomplete Sentence Test and the Contrasting Values Survey reveal that the Issei expressed considerable agreement on the American characteristics of individuation and self-reliance. The use of "individuation" rather than individualism is important here. Based on the formulation by

Maruyama (1965), as given in Chapter 5, when individuation is accompanied by deference and the lack of concern with political goals, the personality type that is produced is the "privatized" rather than the "democratized" or "individualized" personality. That is, one who is concerned with the accomplishment of personal rather than public goals. Both "privatization" and self-reliance are understandable in the light of the Issei experience in this country. It will be remembered from the biographical information on the Issei that the great majority of them did not intend to reside in the United States permanently. Most reported that they came to the United States for economic reasons. That is, to make their fortunes and then return. We also know that almost all of them maintained some type of contact with relatives and friends in Japan and that well over 80 per cent have gone back to Japan to visit—some have made as many as five trips.

Given this continued tie to Japan, it is easy to see that the reference group for the Issei would be their relatives and friends in Japan. Success for them was seen in terms of what they had accomplished in comparison with those they had left behind in Japan. When the concept of the reference group is combined with the Japanese emphasis on hierarchy, we are also able to understand the surprisingly low incidence of reported prejudice. The emphasis on hierarchy enabled those Issei from agricultural backgrounds to accept low-status jobs and weather the overt discrimination practiced against them. As one Issei reported during an interview, "We were the foreigners here, you had to accept it." The fact that their reference group was in Japan meant that they did not interpret the discrimination against them as being extreme. The discrimination, we might add, was of a type that would strike most Sansei as being both outrageous and intolerable because their reference group is now middle-class American society. Of course, as previously mentioned, one other important consideration in the low incidence of reported prejudice was the insulating effect of the Japanese community.

For most Issei, however, the great change came after World War II. It was then that a choice had to be made to go back to their communities and salvage what they could or to return to Japan. A few did return to Japan to retire. Between 1 and 2 per cent of the

Sansei report their grandparents as having retired in Japan. For those who stayed, many changes were now possible. They were able to own land and obtain American citizenship. They had even stronger ties when their children married and the grandchildren were born. Almost all are now retired. Of these, almost one-half are living with their children, and even those who do not live with them see them frequently.

These changes, together with the observed success of their offspring, which the Issei feel that they had made possible, have brought about an attitudinal change. Obviously with deeper roots, and after a lifetime of toil, most of the Issei have a greater identification with American society, an identification that is reflected in their self-evaluation of almost 4 on the ten-point scale, ranging from a completely Japanese identity (1) to a completely American identity (10).

The Nisei

In many ways the Nisei are truly in between the two cultures. All of our instruments reveal that, when compared with the Sansei, the Nisei are more deferent, more abasive, have a greater need for order, endurance, and achievement, are more authoritarian, place a greater emphasis on emotionality in the family bond, and are more predisposed to think in hierarchical terms. On the other hand, when compared with the Issei they are more likely to be concerned with their rights and less likely to submit to arbitrary authority.

If one agreed with current acculturation theory (Goodman 1968, Caudill and Weinstein 1969) that the basic values or personality characteristics are inculcated in childhood and then maintained in social interaction with others, one is able to understand both the high degree of retention of Japanese characteristics among the Nisei and their oft-observed rise to middle-class status in American society. We may begin by remembering the insularity and low acculturation of the Issei, especially the Issei female. The insularity and low acculturation, in turn, made it most likely that the Issei mother would rear her Nisei children on the basis of her own background. That is, the child-rearing practices would be much the same as those in Japan. Some support for this is to be found in a study conducted by Kitano (1961) in which he administered the Parental Attitude Research Inventory to a group of Issei and Nisei females. The results indicated that the Issei ranked higher in every category. The higher scores indicated a more restrictive or "pathogenic" response. The scores were significantly higher in such areas as "fostering dependency," "martyrdom," and "suppression of sex." The values thus inculcated were essentially Japanese. We have some evidence of this in the large number of Nisei who reported the use of shame when they were growing up. Moreover, given the Japanese emphasis on the importance of the family and the emotional bond that accompanies it (the Nisei scored higher on family items than did the Issei), it is understandable that one way of disciplining a child would be to exclude him from the family group. When the subject of excluding the child from the family was brought up in the course of interviewing, one Nisei male said that to do such a thing to the child was worse than beating him. Another Nisei female confessed that her father would lock her in the closet when she was bad. Furthermore, the Nisei had to face this discipline alone. There were no soft-hearted grandparents or kindly aunts from whom they could seek sympathy and comfort.

The values were also continually reinforced as the children grew older. Not only did the majority of Nisei attend Japanese language school, with its prewar emphasis on *shūshin* or ethics, but the majority of them also resided in the Japanese community. It was the community that was most responsible for the low level of delinquency among the Nisei. As one Nisei who had lived in Sacramento's Japanese community before the war remarked, "You didn't dare step out of line. The first time you did your parents would be sure to hear about it."

However, the Nisei also went to American schools, and it was through the American schools that they became aware of what was to become for them a new reference group—the middle-class American society. There were a number of reasons why this came to be. First would be the Nisei themselves. As a group, they were quiet, shy, docile, eager to learn, and eager to please. In many ways they were the ideal students for the middle-class teacher.

Even today many teachers believe the ideal class would be one composed entirely of Japanese Americans.

The second reason would be the Issei. As we have seen in Table 9.10, when a child did something wrong he could expect little sympathy from his parents. As Benedict remarks, ". . . the family name has been disgraced. His family are a solid phalanx of accusation." (1946:273)

The pressure from the Issei and the eagerness of the Nisei to do well contributed to their success in school and their higher rate of academic achievement. It is one of the many peculiarities of the Japanese American experience that they were often praised by some of the groups that damned them the most. If one remembers the rabid anti-Japanese activities of the American Legion, it is most interesting to note the ironic touch in the large number of prewar Japanese American recipients of the American Legion Citizenship Award which are listed on a bronze plaque in the foyer of the Lincoln Elementary School in Sacramento.

These characteristics, then, as Caudill (1952) has shown, were similar to middle-class values. Though similar, they were not identical. Indeed, as we have indicated, if they were to exist in isolation, they would in fact be antithetical to the larger American values of individualism, self-assertion, equality, rights and privileges, and self-reliance. Nonetheless, the Japanese characteristics of hierarchy, duty and obligation, and deference were most adaptive to middle-class goals and were therefore reinforced. Indeed, in several of our testing protocols, the Nisei scored even higher in these characteristics than did the Issei.

The Japanese emphasis on hierarchy led to ranking. If a person thinks in hierarchical terms, it is likely he will want to know where he ranks in relation to another. It is interesting to see that the Nisei have preserved this characteristic and that it often comes out in unexpected behavior. For example, some time ago I was conversing with a Nisei businessman who had heard that I had met my wife in Japan. For some reason he had assumed that I was retired from the military. When another Nisei mentioned that I was on the faculty of the California State University his behavior immediately changed and he became quite deferent. In this regard, the following newspaper article is most informative.

A Nisei I know told me that when he thinks in Japanese, he begins to think, unless he guards himself, in hierarchical terms, that is—when he sees another Japanese that he knows he will unconsciously rank him as a superior or as an inferior, looking down, say, at a restaurant man and looking definitely up at a college professor, but when he thinks as an American the importance of rank diminishes. The Japanese place an almost exaggerated importance on a "Sensei" (teacher) even if he is a ping-pong teacher. (Oyama 1969)

The emphasis on hierarchy, then, leads to ranking. The ranking, in turn, leads to competition. The competition always takes place between parallel groups and is especially fierce in Japan, where the prize in the race is the rating of one's group over that of another. Undoubtedly this tremendous competitive drive has had a direct influence in the rapid economic recovery of Japan after World War II.

As Nakane states:

Because competition takes place between parallel groups of the same kind, the enemy is always to be found among those in the same category. (In other societies such groups could be linked by cooperative ties which would represent a totally opposite kind of strength in relations.) To illustrate this, competition arises among the various steel companies, or among import-export firms. Among schools it is just the same; university against university, high school against high school. In rural areas competition develops among neighboring villages and also among households within a village. . . . (1970:87)

This competitive drive is very much in evidence among the Nisei. By way of personal experience, I can think of several examples similar to those cited by Nakane. One Nisei couple who have been personal friends for some time remarked that when they and other Nisei were working in the Chicago area they frequently had difficulty with the Caucasian employees. In this instance the difficulty was not due to racial antipathy but was rather the result of their hypercompetition. The Nisei were such strivers that they soon earned the reputation of being "rate-busters." That is, they were those whose output increases the average rate of production and therefore increases the demands made on the other employees.

The competitive drive of the Nisei has also been noticed by others. A somewhat amusing verification of it appeared in a statement once made by a neighbor. He stated that he did not want to live next to a Japanese family. He then hastened to add that it had nothing to do with prejudice; it was simply that they maintained their homes and lawns so well that his would look shabby by comparison.

One final example, also from personal experience, involved a Nisei couple we had known for some time. When we moved from a duplex into a new house, the wife confessed that she had been really very hesitant about visiting us in our new home because it would make her feel bad.

The competitive drive of the Nisei, then, is derived from the system of ranking, which, in turn, is due to the Japanese emphasis on hierarchy. The emphasis on hierarchy leads to an acute awareness of status, or the tendency to think in terms of superior-inferior relationships. Given their awareness of status and their adoption of the middle class as a reference group, it is interesting to speculate that the discrimination against the Nisei may have been interpreted by them as a rather extreme external sanction and, as such, may have increased their competitive drive and motivation to achieve. Perhaps, ironically, the Nisei were outwardly becoming more American by behaving more intensely as Japanese.

The thesis is an intriguing one, but there are problems. The experience of the Japanese in Brazil and Peru indicates that acculturation need not be the goal even in the face of large-scale discrimination. Smith et al. (1967a) report two major outbreaks of anti-Japanese sentiment in Brazil in 1923-24 and in 1933-34. Far from creating a desire to acculturate, the Japanese continued to remain isolated from the rest of society and some became ultranationalistic—so much so that it led to the rise of terrorist secret societies which would not admit that Japan had lost the war. Titiev mentions somewhat the same desire of prewar Japanese in Peru to remain aloof (1951:246).

When I first became aware of the South American Japanese population remaining isolated from the rest of society, I wrote to Robert Smith of Cornell University, who did a study of the Japanese in Brazil in the mid-1960s. As to the question of the

Japanese remaining aloof from the population, he replied as follows:

> The Japanese communities in the interior of Brazil were indeed quite isolated from contact with Brazilian society in large part because the Japanese believed themselves to be superior to the Brazilians. (1967b)

The concept of hierarchy or superior-inferior relationships would help to explain the failure of ultranationalistic elements to become as established in North America as they did in South America. It would also explain the haste of many Japanese Americans to prove their loyalty during World War II.

With the middle class as a reference group and their need to prove their loyalty, the Nisei formed the 442 R.C.T. and the 100th Battalion, units that for their size won more citations and decorations than any comparable units in American military history. Here again we encounter another deep irony in the Japanese American experience. That is, their success in combat required exactly those characteristics of duty and obligation, collectivity, hierarchy, deference, and dependence that had been emphasized since their childhood by the Issei. In other words, the Nisei finally proved their Americanism by utilizing behavior patterns that were essentially Japanese in nature.

The Sansei

It is to the Sansei that we must look for an answer to the subsidiary questions posed at the beginning of this chapter. The first question stated that if one assumed that the Japanese Americans have indeed arrived at middle-class status, is the next step to be complete assimilation into American society or will there be a retention of ethnic identity? The second question related to the statement that if the success of the Japanese Americans was due to adaptive mechanisms and values that are essentially Japanese in nature, will there then be a tendency to retain those characteristics and inculcate them in the oncoming generation, or will they be replaced with values that are more characteristic of the larger American society?

We may begin discussing the Sansei by attempting to answer the second question first. As measured on our various instruments, there is no question but that there is a considerable retention of Japanese characteristics. As measured by the EPPS, the Sansei are more deferent, more abasive, less dominant, more affiliative, less aggressive, and have a greater need for succorance and order than do the Sacramento State University Caucasian students.

Our other instruments indicate that the Sansei have closer family ties, a greater sense of duty and obligation, and a greater fear of failure than do the Caucasian students. Further, Kitano (1967:253-63) reports that the delinquency rate for Japanese Americans is lower than that of any American group and is even lower than the rate in Japan.

Additional evidence for the retention of Japanese characteristics can be seen in the retention of Japanese patterns of child care in Sansei mothers in the Sacramento area. This information is available in a study done by Lois Frost (1970) under the author's supervision in the spring of 1970. This study was a replication of one conducted by Caudill and Weinstein (1969). The Caudill and Weinstein study consisted of a series of two-day observations made in the homes of thirty Japanese and thirty American first-born, three-to four-months-old infants, who were equally divided by sex and who were living in middle-class urban families. Information was obtained on the behavior of the mother and the child by means of time-sampling. One observation was made every fifteenth second over a ten-minute period on a predetermined set of categories. This resulted in a sheet containing 40 equally spaced observations. Ten sheets were completed for each of the two days, giving a total of 800 observations for each case.

Mrs. Frost's sample consisted of twenty-one infants, seven males and fourteen females. When she was completing the study, I advised her to write to Caudill and inform him of her findings. This she did. He in return was most interested in her study and flew out to see her. Together they carried out observations in the homes of four infants in order to have a reliability check for observer bias.

Mrs. Frost's data were next compared and analyzed with Caudill's Japanese and American samples. In a recently published paper, Caudill and Frost (1972) conclude that the Sansei mother is a kind of super caretaker who is attempting to combine both the Japanese and American styles of caretaking. She seems to have taken on much of the American mother's behavior while at the same time retaining much of the Japanese mother's style of caretaking. Somehow, after two generations, the Sansei mother is still behaving in some respects like a Japanese mother while also acting like an American.

Mrs. Frost's findings are very much in accord with ours. On the basis of the EPPS, the Incomplete Sentence Test, and the Contrasting Values Survey, we have been able to demonstrate that there is a considerable retention of Japanese characteristics in the Sansei. Furthermore, Mrs. Frost's study discloses that the Sansei mother does more vocal lulling, more breast and bottle feeding, more carrying, and more playing with the baby than the American mother. In these practices she is more like the Japanese mother. Moreover, her baby is also more like the Japanese baby in that he does less finger sucking than the American baby and spends less time playing by himself.

If Mrs. Frost's findings on the the caretaking style of the Sansei mother are seen in conjunction with the higher Sansei needs for succorance, affiliation, nurturance, deference, abasement, and the greater emphasis they place on the family, it is easy to suspect a continuation of dependency needs. Although difficult to demonstrate empirically, all of the above data are clearly supportive of the concept of *amaeru*, a dependency need or a desire to be pampered. While not so pronounced as in the Japanese mother, the Sansei mother has retained enough of the Japanese caretaking style so that we are already able to detect discernible differences in her child's behavior at the age of three to four months. Moreover, these differences are exactly the sort of differences we would expect if we were looking for evidence which would indicate inculcation of dependency needs.

Again, given the response of the majority of the Nisei that the type of behavior by the Sansei most likely to anger or upset them would be a lack of respect for parents or elders, we can see that the Sansei were indeed imbued with a sense of hierarchy and a feeling of dependency.

And once more we can see a reason for the continuation of the Japanese characteristics in the Sansei in the behavior of the Nisei themselves. It was not until after World War II that the success story of the Nisei began. They had to prove themselves by their dependability, skill, and citizenship, which resulted in widened job opportunities. Their success, in turn, as we have already seen, was due to their utilization of psychological and behavioral patterns that were essentially Japanese in nature. It is to be expected, then, that these patterns would be reinforced and inculcated into the Sansei, who were at that time in their formative years of childhood. Moreover, this continuity is apparent in the responses of over two-thirds of the Sansei that they were told when young not to bring shame to the family.

Keeping these characteristics in mind, we are beginning to see some of the reasons for the generation gap now separating the Nisei and Sansei. With the break-up of the Japanese community, the disappearance of the language schools, and the greater affluence of their parents came a greater freedom and a more direct and sustained exposure to the larger American society. With the greater freedom and interaction came behavior that the Nisei did not always consider proper.

In attempting to control their offspring, the Nisei have used a variety of methods. To my knowledge, one of the most common is the real or symbolic rejection of the offending person from the group. When one keeps in mind the higher Sansei need for nurturance, succorance, deference, and abasement, it is easy to see that such rejection can often be traumatic. In fact, one Sansei female student admitted somewhat bitterly that it was indeed quite effective.

Yet, the use of rejection is a two-edged sword and one that must be carefully employed. For, while the Sansei are more deferent and abasive than the Caucasians, they are at the same time closer to them in autonomy, self-reliance, and individualism. Therefore, one occasionally hears of instances wherein the Nisei have overreacted and their offspring have rebelled.

One such case is known to us personally. A Nisei neighbor had given his son an ultimatum: he would either conform to the wishes of the father—or he would get out. In this instance, the son left and the father very sheepishly came knocking on our door after midnight to find out if his boy was staying with ours. He was not. Instead, he had gone to a nearby church and had remained there all night while the police were out looking for him.

In this regard, by constantly stressing the principle that one should never bring shame to the family, the Nisei have given their potentially rebellious younsters an effective weapon for retaliation. Further, when one recalls the opposition that the Issei and Nisei expressed to the idea of the Sansei marrying a black, it is not at all surprising that the most shameful thing a daughter could do would be to allow herself to become pregnant by a black. And, in fact, this has occurred. The author is aware of at least three cases where this has happened.

Yet we can also argue from our evidence that considerable acculturation has taken place. On all of our instruments the Sansei scores are clearly closer to the Caucasian students than they are to their parents or grandparents. Indeed, a number of changes have already taken place that should hasten the process of acculturation. For one thing, proficiency in the Japanese language has largely disappeared and is therefore no longer available as a means of promoting a common identity. Another reason is the disappearance of the closely knit Japanese communities that served to reinforce the Japanese identity so well before the war. As a result, over two-thirds of the Sansei now have more non-Japanese than Japanese friends. Additionally, marrying-out is occurring at an unexpectedly high rate. Our data on the Sansei revealed that well over 28 per cent of the Japanese American marriages in the Sacramento area in the last decade involved non-Japanese, and this has been increasing in recent years. Finally, the Sansei have continued the drive for education and we are already finding that they are overrepresented in the professions. One possible result of the increased education and consequent specialization of interests will be that it may become increasingly more difficult for a highly educated Sansei to find a suitable Sansei mate with the same interests. Here again, we will find pressure for marrying non-Japanese.

At the same time, two counteracting elements have emerged in recent years. One is the economic success of Japan itself and the somewhat faddish preoccupation with things Japanese in intellectual and upper middle-class society. To their dismay, many Sansei find they are expected to be instant experts on everything from Zen Buddhism to the films of Kurosawa. Needless to say, this drives them to the books and to courses on their Japanese heritage.

The other element is the emphasis on cultural pluralism or ethnic identity that has received so much attention on college campuses. Here again, however, the Japanese Americans have come a little late. While the Japanese Americans can count as many scars as can the other groups, they are too much like the middle class in outlook to be much moved by discussions on the degradations of poverty.

Yet a problem does exist. For the Sansei, it is becoming a problem of identity. In speaking with a Sansei recently, I asked him what was the biggest problem facing Japanese Americans today. He answered simply, "Are we Japanese Americans, or Americans of Japanese ancestry?" On college campuses many young Sansei are trying to establish a new identity. When one rather militant Sansei objected to the term "Oriental American" and stated that he preferred to called an "Asian American," I asked him to define the difference. He said that they were trying to break away from the stereotype of the shy, submissive, and docile Oriental. The Asian American would be one who would stand up for his rights.

And to a certain extent this is true. While all of our instruments disclose a retention of Japanese characteristics in the Sansei, we can also demonstrate that they are in many ways closer to the Caucasian group than they are to their parents and grandparents. Indeed, on the basis of the E.I.Q., it is clear that, while the Sansei are most desirous of retaining their heritage, they express far more interest in retaining the symbolic, artistic, or aesthetic aspects of their heritage than they do in retaining the psychological or behavioral aspects.

Paradoxically, additional evidence for this is often supplied by those same Sansei who are not only highly critical of American society but are also the most anxious to preserve their Japanese heritage. When these Sansei do have the opportunity to go to Japan, they are more often than not disappointed. Frequently the disappointment stems from their having overidealized Japanese society. Yet to a large extent it is also the result of their viewing Japanese society with completely foreign eyes—and it is at this point that the degree of their acculturation becomes manifest. One Sansei student who visited Japan recently was surprised by what he termed the arrogance of those in authority and the submissiveness of the people. In particular, he was struck by the behavior of a policeman to a taxicab driver. The driver had apparently been guilty of a minor traffic violation. The driver was very submissive. With his hat in his hands, he kept bowing while the officer continued to admonish him.

The above comments are echoed by the impressions of another Japanese American visitor to Japan which appeared in the February 12, 1971, issue of the *Pacific Citizen*, the membership publication of the Japanese American Citizens' League:

> A Japanese American, born while his parents were being interned in World War II, says the United States is deeply racist but he prefers it to Japan. . . . In Japan, he asserts, "strong undercurrents of irrationalism, and outright anti-rationalism, flow beneath a good deal of contemporary thinking." He found much to admire in his mother country, but says: "Having been brought up in America, where informality and individuality are emphasized, I find Japan far too restrictive, group-oriented, and coercive."

Finally, in any discussion of the Sansei it must be kept in mind that over two-thirds of them are now students, and undoubtedly their behavior and responses are influenced by the other students and the youth subculture of which they are a part. To a certain extent this is true. Yet, at the same time, all of our instruments disclose significant differences between the Sansei and the Caucasian students. Despite the influence of the youth subculture, the Sansei still retain many of the Japanese characteristics. It is possible, then, that once they leave the campuses, their behavior and attitudes may become more like the Nisei.

While this is possible, it is not likely. If anything, their education, achievement motivation, and especially their desire to move into positions of leadership and full equality will have the effect of further incorporating them into the mainstream of American society. Moreover, the reputation of their parents and grandparents for hard work, perseverance, diligence, and dependability will have preceded them. In this regard, far from being excluded from full participation in American society, the Sansei may find that they will be in a process of continually reassessing their ethnicity and periodically redefining the elements that are essential in maintaining a distinct ethnic identity.

The Caucasian Students

Since the principal focus of the study was one of acculturation, it was necessary not only to determine the major American
characteristics, which were then contrasted with those of the
Japanese, but also to obtain a sample of Caucasian American
students to be used as a control group with whom the acculturation of the Japanese Americans and especially the Sansei could be
compared. Further, it was assumed that, by restricting our sample
to middle-class Caucasian students, we would have a control
group that would also reflect the major American characteristics
of individualism, equality, a concern for rights and privileges,
self-reliance, and self-assertion. This assumption, however, did
not prove to be entirely correct. Indeed, as we have seen, there has
been a change away from what might be called the more traditional form of "rugged" or ego-centered individualism, wherein a
person is preoccupied with his own self-interest, to a less dominant and more open form of individualism which still retains an
emphasis on personal autonomy but is marked by an increased
respect for the individualism of others.

Partly as a result of this redefinition of individualism, there
has been an intensification of interest in or value placed upon
equality. Moreover, the traditional concern for rights and privileges has been redefined to include a much broader interest in the
rights and privileges of others as well as with one's own. By
extension, that aspect of self-assertion that assumes the right to
impose one's ideas, beliefs, or self upon others has been subordi-
nated to a concern for respecting the autonomy or rights of
another. Likewise, self-reliance has been reinterpreted largely in
terms of personal and social maturity. A self-reliant person is one
who would be sufficiently mature to participate actively in social
interaction with others without either being overly dependent on
others or in continual need of self-assurance. Self-reliance is not
thought of favorably if it entails such a degree of self-sufficiency
that it isolates an individual from others.

With respect to the above findings, it was most interesting to
discover in the last stage of this study that Spindler had come to
almost identically the same conclusions. Spindler's report was
based upon the use of an incomplete sentence test on several

hundred lower and upper middle-class students, mainly in professional education courses (1963:133). When asked to describe the "ideal American boy" the answers ranged, from the highest number of responses to the lowest, as follows:

> He should be *sociable*, like people, and get along well with them; he must be *popular*, be liked by others; he is to be *well-rounded*, he can do many things quite well, but is not an expert in anything in particular; he should be *athletic* (but not a star), and healthy (no qualifications); he should be acceptable within limited norms; he must be *considerate of others*, ever sensitive to their feelings about him and about events. . . . (1963:134-35, italics as in the original)

Spindler then goes on to list what he believes to be the traditional American values, as contrasted with what he believes to be the values that have been emerging in recent years. These values are listed as follows (1963:136-37):

Traditional Values	Emergent Values
Puritan morality (Respectability, thrift, self-denial sexual constraint; a puritan is someone who can have anything he wants, as long as he doesn't enjoy it!)	Sociability (As described above. One should like people and get along well with them. Suspicion of solitary activities is characteristic.)
Work-Success Ethic (Successful people worked hard to become so. Anyone can get to the top if he tries hard enough. So people who are not successful are lazy, or stupid, or both. People must work desperately and continuously to convince themselves of their worth.)	Relativistic moral attitude (Absolutes in right and wrong are questionable. Morality is what the group thinks is right. Shame, rather than guilt is appropriate.)
Individualism (The individual is sacred, and always more important than the group. In one extreme form, the value sanctions egocentricity,	Consideration for others (Everything one does should be done with regard for others and their feelings. The individual has a built-in radar that alerts him to others'

expediency, and disregard for other people's rights. In its healthier form the value sanctions independence and originality.)

feelings. Tolerance for the other person's point of view and behavior is regarded as desirable, so long as the harmony of the group is not disrupted.)

Achievement orientation (Success is a constant goal. There is no resting on past glories. If one makes $9,000 this year he must make $10,000 next year. Coupled with the work-success ethic, this value keeps people moving, and tense.)

Hedonistic, present-time orientation (No one can tell what the future will hold, therefore one should enjoy the present— but within the limits of the well-rounded, balanced personality and group.)

Future-time orientation (The future, not past, or even the present, is most important. Time is valuable, and cannot be wasted. Present needs must be denied for satisfactions to be gained in the future.)

Conformity to the group (Implied in the other emergent values. Everything is relative to the group. Group harmony is the ultimate goal. Leadership consists of group-machinery lubrication.)

If Spindler is correct in his formulation—and our data strongly suggest that, in general, he is—we can then understand the rapid acculturation of the Sansei in a new light. What appears to have happened in recent years is more of a merging of the two value systems. The American middle-class students have moved more toward some of the Japanese characteristics and the Sansei have adopted more of the American characteristics. However, a number of differences remain. The Sansei are still closer to the Japanese norms in such areas as affiliation, succorance, abasement, and nurturance. Yet, from the point of view of the middle-class Caucasians, these differences are more of degree rather than kind. Indeed, the major Japanese characteristic of collectivity, with its emphasis on closer family ties and warmer interpersonal relations, appears to be the one characteristic many of the American students wish most to emulate. Moreover, the value the Caucasian students place on an openness and concern for others leads also to a reciprocal emphasis on duty and obligation. If one recognizes that others have a claim on one's time and resources, then one has an obligation to honor those claims. However, with regard to the remaining major Japanese characteristics of hierarchy, deference, and dependence, it would appear that both the Caucasian students and, to a somewhat lesser extent, the Sansei prefer the contrasting American characteristics of equality, self-assertiveness, and self-reliance.

In this respect it can be seen that, while the Caucasians as representatives of the larger American society are the controlling group towards which the Japanese Americans must acculturate, there has been nevertheless a merging of the two sets of characteristics. The Caucasian students are becoming more open and considerate of others, more interested in collectivity, and more conscious of a sense of duty and obligation to others. The Sansei, on the other hand, are becoming somewhat less dependent, more individualistic, more self-reliant, and more self-assertive than their parents or grandparents.

Parenthetically, it might be added that the above discussion provides supporting evidence for the validity of our instruments. It will be recalled that the changing emphasis in the American characteristics was first discovered in the Incomplete Sentence Test. Additional verification was obtained in the Caucasian student responses to the Contrasting Values Survey, and final confirmation came with the student responses to the EPPS in which it was demonstrated that changes had indeed occurred in the two decades since the EPPS was first standardized. These changes were especially marked in the following areas: When compared with Edwards' normative group the Sacramento State University Caucasian students were less deferent, more autonomous, less dominant, less abasive, and had a greater need for heterosexuality. In general, these findings support those obtained by our other instruments and agree with the conclusions reached by Spindler (1963:136-37) that there has indeed been a change toward a more open, less overtly competitive personality in contemporary American students. Finally, one might add that this change is also in accord with Lipset's (1967:144) contention that there have been periodic changes in the emphasis Americans place on equality or on achievement:

> Complete commitment to equality involves rejecting some of
> the implications of valuing achievement; and the opposite is

also true. Thus when the equalitarianism of left or liberal politics is dominant, there is a reaction against achievement, and when the values of achievement prevail in a conservative political and economic atmosphere, men tend to depreciate some of the consequences of equality, such as the influence of popular taste on culture. (1967:144)

Conclusions

In summary, then, we can list a number of items which can be seen to be leading toward greater acculturation and assimilation:
1. The dispersal of the Japanese community.
2. The almost complete disappearance of Japanese language facility in the young.
3. The continued strong emphasis on higher education.
4. The relatively high degree of marrying-out among the young.
5. The greater participation of the young in school activities.
6. The number of non-Japanese friends reported by the young.

On the other hand, we can list a number of items which are serving to preserve a Japanese identity:
1. The physical distinctiveness of the Japanese in a race-conscious society.
2. The continuance of a form of prejudice against orientals in general.
3. The success of post-war Japan, which is a source of pride for Japanese Americans. (Again, paradoxically, the economic success of Japan may increase hostility against Japanese Americans because of the fear that American workers may lose their jobs because of Japanese competition.)
4. The contemporary emphasis on ethnic identity and cultural pluralism.
5. The retention of such characteristics as duty and obligation, deference, strong family ties, and the inculcation of dependency needs in the young, as measured by our instruments and the child-rearing study by Caudill and Frost (1972).
6. The fact that most Japanese Americans still prefer to marry other Japanese Americans.

When the two sets of items are considered together, we can arrive at the following conclusions or predictions:

1. There will be a continuance of a Japanese ethnic group with a sense of a common identity for the next several generations.
2. Increasingly, this common identity will rest upon such attributes as a Japanese surname and, to a lesser extent, on physical appearance. The identity will be maintained symbolically by eating Japanese food, the possession of family heirlooms and art objects from Japan, and will be reinforced by religious practices and occasional trips to Japan.
3. Psychologically and behaviorally, the fourth generation will be almost indistinguishable from their middle-class Caucasian counterparts. They should continue to be slightly more deferent, have a stronger tie with their families, and have a slightly greater need for succorance, abasement, and nurturance. These characteristics will be more pronounced in the females than in the males. In all the other variables and in those characteristics such as equality, self-assertion, self-reliance, and individualism, they should be indistinguishable from their middle-class Caucasian counterparts.

Problems for Future Consideration

One of the advantages of utilizing the type of instruments that we have in this study is their replicability. The Sansei are just beginning their child-bearing years. In a little more than two decades, we will have the opportunity to study the same characteristics in the Yonsei (fourth generation). At that time we will have the opportunity of discovering the extent of the changes that have occurred. We will also have an opportunity to observe the changes that will have taken place in the next generation of Caucasian students.

A further problem for consideration is to challenge one of the principal assumptions of McClelland's *The Achieving Society* (1961). In this book, McClelland contrasts "need achievement" with "need affiliation," that is, individual motivation is contrasted with dependent behavior or a concern for family and interpersonal relationships. It was discovered at the time of this study that those who were rated high on "need achievement" tended to rate low on "need affiliation."

With the data we now have on the Japanese Americans, we can demonstrate that the study does not appear to be cross-culturally valid. By any measure of achievement, it seems obvious that the Japanese Americans have indeed displayed a "need achievement." Yet we can demonstrate empirically that they also have a correspondingly high "need affiliation" in that they are very much concerned with interpersonal relations and family matters. It is equally apparent, as Chapter 12 makes so abundantly clear, that the Japanese American's achievement motivation rests upon a different set of reinforcements. Far from being trained for independence and individualism, the socialization of the Sansei is more in the form of establishing in the child strong affiliative and dependency needs. These needs create an ego structure that is highly sensitive to the opinions of significant others. Achievement, then, is often seen in terms of fulfilling goals laid down by others.

A final problem for consideration must involve a deeper, more probing search to discover the means whereby these traditional cultural patterns, beliefs, values, and traits are transmitted from one generation to the next. It is not enough to stress the importance of the *ie* ideal and family continuities, or to simply state that the patterns, beliefs, values, and traits are functionally adaptive; more must be known as to how it is that some traits, values, and practices are continued over generations and others are not. It would appear that, more often than not, these are transmitted out of the level of conscious awareness. It does not appear, for example, that the caretaking style of the Sansei mother as reported by Caudill and Frost (1972) was the result of formal teaching or explicit instruction in child-rearing techniques. A recent article by Kaku and Matsumoto (1975) indicates that there was a significant decrease in the birth rate of Sansei mothers in California and Hawaii during 1966, the Year of the Elder Fire Horse, and a year considered most inauspicious for the birth of a female child according to traditional Japanese folk superstition. It would be somewhat difficult to establish the functional utility of such a folk superstition other than as a crude device to lower the birth rate in third generation Japanese Americans, let alone explain why it had endured for three generations when other beliefs and practices had been discontinued. In other words, we do not yet know the emotional intensity with which these beliefs and practices are transmitted. Perhaps, in one sense, the psychological dimension is of even greater importance than previously realized. It is a recurrent theme in all of Freud's work, for example, that one generation could never conceal its major psychological concerns or "hang ups" from the next.

There is an additional dimension that is worthy of discussion: the adaptability and even functional utility of many of these beliefs, values, and customs in the preservation of an ethnic identity. Throughout this study there has emerged the finding that acculturation is by no means a unilateral process. By this is meant that the preservation of an ethnic identity is functionally adaptive for a highly visible racial minority, especially for the Japanese Americans who have become the victims of two contrasting stereotypes. On the one hand they were once the victims of severe racial prejudice which has continued with diminished intensity down to the present; on the other, they have been praised as a "model minority" and congratulated on the speed, success, and thoroughness of their acculturation.

As we have seen, both stereotypes are erroneous. Despite the advancements, even the Sansei do not as yet feel completely comfortable or "at home" in the larger American society. There is, therefore, an adaptive need for what might be called a periodic retreat into ethnicity to escape the stresses of encounters with the larger society. In this respect many Nisei and Sansei resemble the Japanese businessman who, upon arriving home, slips out of his Western clothing into a kimono and the more traditional life style. Similarly, a conscientious Japanese American, with a heightened sense of achievement, more intense abasiveness, and more extreme sensitivity to the opinions of others, many experience a much greater need to exchange the stresses of the "outer" world for the warmer security of "familism" and ethnicity. As with the Jews mentioned by Gordon (1964:194), the ingredients of this ethnic identity are more likely than not to be composed of unrelated and imperfectly understood bits and pieces of the older culture. Thus, many Sansei have already put together an "Asian American" identity that would almost certainly mystify their grandparents. Yet the grandparents themselves subtly transformed many aspects of their traditional culture. Quite frequently, upon arriving back in their native villages for a visit, Issei were surprised to find that they had already incorporated so many American words and phrases into their vocabulary that friends and relatives found it difficult to understand them. Performances of traditional dances, festivities, and even religious practices have also been slowly modified over the years so that visiting Japanese are often quite surprised at what they find here.

These findings are, of course, no major revelation. Social scientists here have long maintained that change is endemic in the human condition. Yet there is no agreement on or even a clear understanding of the processes involved. Certainly, it appears obvious that the preservation of an ethnic identity is functionally adaptive if for no other reason than as a palliative for such widespread social maladies as deracination, alienation, and anomie. And, of course, the Japanese Americans are not alone in expressing this need. In my own experience, I have observed rather flamboyant reproductions of coats of arms hanging on the walls of poor third and fourth generation Irish Americans. The message conveyed by these emblems would in all cases appear to be about the same: "We ain't much now, but you should've seen us then." This retreat into ethnicity, then, should not obscure the major problems arising from the need to understand the acculturation process more clearly. Perhaps when this is done we will have made a major advancement towards clarifying what some have termed the major problem of the twentieth century, that is, how to understand the process of change itself.

Appendix A

Issei Interview Questionnaire

Interviewer _____   Male _____
Female _____
Age _____
Occupation _____
Marital Status __

1. When were you born? _____
2. Where were you born in Japan? (prefecture and city) _____
   _____
3. (a) What was the occupation of your father? _____
   (b) Your brother? _____
   (c) If male, were you the first, second, or third son? _____
4. (a) How much schooling did you have in Japan? _____
   (b) Of your early schooling, what subjects do you remember
       most? _____
   (c) What part of your early schooling or training do you believe
       has been of the most value to you? _____
5. When did you leave for the U.S.? _____
6. (a) Why did you decide to leave Japan? _____
   (b) Did you expect to leave Japan permanently? _____
7. Why did you decide to emigrate to the U.S. rather than to another
   area? _____
8. What had you heard of the U.S. before you left Japan? _____
   _____
9. Did you have a job promised before you left Japan? _____
10. Who paid for the journey? _____
11. (a) What were your experiences in leaving Japan? _____
    _____
    (b) The journey itself? _____
    _____
    (c) On first arriving in the U.S.? _____
    _____

12. What were your first impressions of the U.S.?
    (a) The land itself? _____

    (b) The people? _____

    (c) The customs? _____

13. What was your first job? _____
14. What were your later occupations? _____

15. Did you ideas or ambitions change in any way after you had arrived in the U.S.? _____
16. What were your relationships with:
    (a) Caucasians? _____
    (b) Chinese? _____
    (c) Other minority groups? (Filipino, Mexican-American, Negro) _____
17. Did you maintain contact with relatives or others in Japan? ___

    If so, which ones, and how often? _____
18. Have you been back to Japan?
    (a) If so, when? _____
    (b) When did you decide to live permanently in the U.S.? ___

19. Where did you live in the U.S.? _____
20. What were your experiences during the Great Depression? ___

21. Did you live in a Japanese community before the war? ___
22. What services did the Japanese community provide? ___

23. Was there a Japanese association in your community? ___
    If so, what did it do? _____
24. Did the Japanese community change in any way before World War II? _____

25. How did you meet your spouse? _____
26. Was your courtship and marriage different from your parents'? _____

27. Were the courtship and marriage of your son or daughter different from yours? _____
28. Did you raise your children in any way different from the way you were raised in Japan? _____
29. Do you think your children are raising their children in any way different from the way you were raised? _____

30. (a) What is your religious faith? _____
    (b) When did you adopt it? _____

(c) What church do you belong to? _____
31. What do these Japanese words mean to you?:
    (a) *On* _____
    (b) *Giri* _____
    (c) *Gimu* _____
    (d) *Chū* _____
    (e) *Ninjō* _____
    (f) *Amaeru* _____
    (g) *Makanki* _____
    (h) *Seikō* _____
32. Some Issei state that they experienced a great deal of prejudice; others state that it wasn't too bad. What do you think? _____

33. In what language do you speak to the Nisei? _____
    To the Sansei? _____
34. In what language do you count? _____
35. How often do you see relatives in this country? _____
36. Do you live with relatives? _____
    If so, which ones? _____
37. Some say that the Japanese-Americans are being rapidly assimilated into American culture and are losing their Japanese identity. On a scale from one to ten, ranging from a completely Japanese identity to a completely American identity, how would you rate yourself?

Japanese [| | | | | | | | |] American
38. What were your most vivid experiences during relocation? ____

    (a) What effect did relocation have on you and your family? _

    (b) What effect did relocation have on Japanese Americans in general? _____
39. How did the Japanese community change in the postwar years?

40. (a) Do you have non-Japanese friends? _____
    (b) If so, what group do they belong to? (Chinese, Caucasian, etc.) _____
    (c) Are they neighbors, co-workers, or what? _____
41. (a) In what ways are the Sansei different from the Issei? _____

    (b) In what ways are the Sansei different from the Nisei? _____

42. (a) What do you think of Sansei dating Chinese? _____
    Caucasians? _____
    Mexican Americans? _____
    Blacks? _____
    (b) What do you think of Sansei marriage to Chinese? _____

Caucasians? _____

Mexican Americans? _____

Blacks? _____

43. What do you think of Japan today? _____
44. What Japanese characteristics would you like to see retained by the Sansei? _____
45. Do you think the Japanese Americans have been successful in the U.S.? _____
    If so, why? _____
46. When was the last year you celebrated the following?:
    (a) Easter _____   (i) *Hinamatsuri* _____
    (b) Memorial Day _____ (j) Girls' Day _____
    (c) Fourth of July _____ (k) Boys' Day _____
    (d) Labor Day _____   (l) *O-Bon* _____
    (e) Thanksgiving _____ (m) *Kigensetsu* _____
    (f) Christmas _____   (n) *O-Higan* _____
    (g) *O-Shōgatsu* _____ (o) *Kikkunosekku* _____
    (h) *O-Shōgatsu* Visiting _____ (p) *Tenchōsetsu* _____
47. Do you observe *Yakudoshi?* _____
48. When your children misbehaved, how did you discipline them? For example, did you tell them they would bring shame to the family; did you isolate or threaten to isolate them from the family; did you use physical punishment; or what? _____
    _____
    _____
49. What advice would you give the Sansei? _____
50. What is the biggest problem facing Japanese Americans today? _
    _____

Appendix B

Nisei Interview Schedule

Interviewer _____   Male _____
                                        Female _____
                                        Age _____
                                        Marital Status __

1. What is your occupation? _____
2. What was the occupation of your father? _____
2. A. Do your parents live with you? _____
3. How much schooling have you had? _____
4. Did you attend Japanese school? _____
4. A. How often do you see your parents? _____
5. Do you watch Japanese movies? _____
   If so, how often? _____
6. How often do you have Japanese food? _____
7. Are there any Japanese foods that you dislike? _____
   If so, what? _____
8. What proportion of your friends are Caucasian? _____
   Chinese? _____
   Other minority groups (Filipino, Mexican American, Black)? __
   _____
9. Did you live in a Japanese community before the war? _____
   If so, what services did it provide? _____
10. Was your courtship and marriage different from your parents? _
    _____
11. What organizations do you belong to? _____
12. How often do you see your parents? _____
13. What is your religious faith? _____
14. When did you adopt it? _____
15. In what ways are the Nisei different from the Issei? _____
    _____
16. In what ways are the Sansei different from the Issei and Nisei? _
    _____

16. A. How often do you get together with other Japanese Americans?
17. What behavior by the Sansei would be most likely to anger or upset you? _____
18. What do you think of Sansei dating Chinese?_____
    Caucasians? _____
    Mexican Americans? _____
    Blacks? _____
19. What do you think of Sansei marrying Chinese? _____
    Caucasians? _____
    Mexican Americans? _____
    Blacks? _____
20. What Japanese characteristics would you like to see retained by the Sansei? _____
21. Have you ever experienced any acts of prejudice? _____
    If so, what kind? _____
22. Some say that the Japanese Americans are being rapidly assimilated into American culture and are losing their Japanese identity. On a scale from one to ten, ranging from a completely Japanese identity to a completely American identity, how would you rate yourself?

    Japanese | | | | | | | | | | | American

23. Do you think the Japanese have been successful in the United States? _____
    If so, why? _____
24. What do these Japanese words mean to you?
    a. *On* _____ g. *Maken-ki* _____
    b. *Giri* _____ h. *Seikō* _____
    c. *Gimu* _____ i. *Gaman* _____
    d. *Chū* _____ j. *Shūshin* _____
    e. *Ninjō* _____ k. *Enryo* _____
    f. *Amaeru* _____
25. When was the last time you celebrated the following:
    a. Easter _____ g. *O-Shōgatsu* _____
    b. Memorial Day _____ h. *O-Shōgatsu* Visiting _____
    c. Fourth of July _____ i. *Hinamatsuri* _____
    d. Labor Day _____ j. Girls' Day _____
    e. Thanksgiving _____ k. Boys' Day _____
    f. Christmas _____ l. *O-Bon* _____
26. Do you observe *Yakudoshi?* _____
27. What was your experience during relocation? _____
    _____
28. What advice would you give to the Sansei? _____
    _____
29. What is the biggest problem facing Japanese Americans today? _
    _____

30. When you were growing up did your family stress the following principles?
- (a) One must make returns for all kindness received.
  - (1) _____ stressed (2) ___ not stressed (3) ____ don't recall
- (b) One must act so as not to bring shame to the family.
  - (1) _____ stressed (2) ___ not stressed (3) ____ don't recall
- (c) One must act so as not to bring shame to the Japanese community.
  - (1) _____ stressed (2) ___ not stressed (3) ____ don't recall

Appendix C

Sansei Interview Schedule

Interviewer _____   Male _____
                                              Female _____

1. When were you born? _____
2. In high school did you participate in extracurricular activities?
   _____
   If so, what kind (athletics, school offices, yearbook, etc.)? _____
3. Would you say your high school academic record was as good as, better than, or poorer than your parents? _____
4. Did you attend a Japanese language school while you were going to high school? _____ If so, how effective was it in teaching you Japanese? _____
5. Do you watch Japanese movies? _____
   If so, how often? _____
6. How often do you have Japanese food? _____
7. Is there any Japanese food that you dislike? _____
   If so, what? _____
8. What proportion of your friends are non-Japanese? _____
   What is their ethnic background? _____
9. What is your occupational desire or life goal? _____
   _____
10. What is the occupation of your father? _____
    Grandfather? _____
11. How often do you see your grandparents? _____
11. A. Do you live with your grandparents? _____
12. In what language do you communicate with your grandparents?
    _____
13. What do you admire most about the Issei generation? _____
    _____

14. What characteristics do you admire least about the Issei generation? _____

15. What organizations do you belong to? _____

16. What is your attitude toward dating non-Japanese? _____

17. What do you feel would be the Nisei attitude toward dating Chinese? _____ Caucasians? _____ Mexican Americans? _____ Blacks? _____

18. How would the Issei feel about dating Chinese? _____ Caucasians? _____ Mexican Americans? _____ Blacks? _____

19. What is your attitude toward marrying a Chinese? _____ Caucasian? _____ Mexican American? _____ Black? _____

20. What would the Nisei attitude be toward marriage to Chinese? _____ Caucasians? _____ Mexican Americans? _____ Blacks? _____

21. What would the Issei attitude be toward marriage to Chinese? _____ Caucasians? _____ Mexican Americans? _____ Blacks? _____

22. Were you brought up in a Japanese community? _____ If so, how has it changed? _____

23. Have you experienced any acts of prejudice? _____ If so, what kind? _____

24. What is your religious faith? _____

25. On a scale from one to ten, ranging from completely Japanese to completely American, how would you rate yourself?

Japanese | | | | | | | | | | | American

26. What offense by a Sansei would be most rapidly punished by the Issei? _____

27. What do these Japanese words mean to you?
    (a) *On* _____(g) *Maken-ki* _____
    (b) *Giri* _____ (h) *Seikō* _____
    (c) *Gimu* _____ (i) *Gaman* _____
    (d) *Chū* _____ (j) *Shūshin* _____
    (e) *Ninjō* _____ (k) *Enryo* _____
    (f) *Amaeru* _____

28. When was the last year you celebrated the following?:
    a. Easter _____ g. *O-Shōgatsu* _____
    b. Memorial Day _____ h. *O-Shōgatsu* Visiting _____
    c. Fourth of July _____ i. *Hinamatsuri* _____
    d. Labor Day _____ j. Girls' Day _____
    e. Thanksgiving _____ k. Boys' Day _____
    f. Christmas _____ l. *O-Bon* _____

29. How frequently do you get together with other Japanese Americans? _____
    What do you share in common with them? For example, common

occupation, common interests or background, relatives from the same prefecture (Kenjin Kai), or parents who were relatives or friends. _____

30. What is the biggest problem facing Japanese Americans today?
_____

31. When you were growing up, did your family stress the following principles?
   (a) One must make returns for all kindness received.
       (1) _____ stressed (2) ___ not stressed (3) ___ don't recall
   (b) One must act so as not to bring shame to the family.
       (1) _____ stressed (2) ___ not stressed (3) ___ don't recall
   (c) One must act so as not to bring shame to the Japanese community.
       (1) _____ stressed (2) ___ not stressed (3) ___ don't recall

Appendix D

The Ethnic Identity Questionnaire

Date of Birth _____ Age _____ Date today _____
        (month) (day) (year)

Sex _____ Years of education _____ Generation: Issei _____
                              (number) (Check one) Nisei _____
                                               Sansei _____

Occupation _____ Kibei _____

Marital status: Never married _____ Religious preference:
(Check one)   Married _____ Protestant _____
               Separated _____ Catholic _____
               Divorced _____ Buddhist _____
               Widowed _____ Other _____
                                                (specify)

Instructions. Below are a number of statements about which people often have different opinions. You will discover that you agree with some, that you disagree with others. Please read each statement carefully, then circle the letter that indicates the extent to which you agree or disagree with it. **Answer every statement,** even if you have to guess at some. There is no right or wrong answer. This information will be treated as confidential.

Strongly agree | Agree | Undecided | Disagree | Strongly disagree

SA A U D SD 1. A good child is an obedient child.

SA A U D SD 2. It is all right for personal desires to come before duty to one's family.

SA A U D SD 3. Japanese Americans should not disagree among themselves if there are Caucasians around.

SA A U D SD 4. I especially like Japanese foods.

SA A U D SD 5. A good Japanese background helps prevent youth from getting into all kinds of trouble that other American youth have today.

SA A U D SD   6. It's unlucky to be born Japanese.

SA A U D SD   7. It would be more comfortable to live in a neighborhood which has at least a few Japanese Americans than in one which has none.

SA A U D SD   8. When I feel affectionate I show it.

SA A U D SD   9. It is a duty of the oldest son to take care of his parents in their old age.

SA A U D SD 10. Japanese Americans who enter into new places without any expectations of discrimination from Caucasians are naive.

SA A U D SD 11. I think it is all right for Japanese Americans to become Americanized, but they should retain part of their own culture.

SA A U D SD 12. A wife's career is just as important as the husband's career.

SA A U D SD 13. In regard to opportunities that other Americans enjoy, Japanese Americans are deprived of many of them because of their ancestry.

SA A U D SD 14. It is all right for children to question the decisions of their parents once in a while.

SA A U D SD 15. In the Japanese community, human relationships are generally more warm and comfortable than outside in American society.

SA A U D SD 16. I would not feel any more tendency to agree with the policies of the Japanese government than any other American would.

SA A U D SD 17. The best thing for the Japanese Americans to do is to associate more with Caucasians and identify themselves completely as Americans.

SA A U D SD 18. I am apt to hide my feelings in some things, to the point that people may hurt me without their knowing it.

SA A U D SD 19. It is a shame for a Japanese American not to be able to understand Japanese.

SA A U D SD 20. Japanese people have an unusual refinement and depth of feeling for nature.

SA A U D SD 21. I would be disturbed if Caucasians did not accept me as an equal.

SA A U D SD 22. It is unrealistic for a Japanese American to hope that he can become a leader of an organization composed mainly of Caucasians because they will not let him.

SA A U D SD 23. I don't have a strong feeling of attachment to Japan.

SA A U D SD 24. I am too spontaneous and casual with people.

SA A U D SD 25. It is not necessary for Japanese-American parents to make it a duty to promote the preservation of Japanese cultural heritage in their children.

SA A U D SD 26. An older brother's decision is to be respected more than that of a younger one.

SA A U D SD 27. Socially, I feel less at ease with Caucasians than with Japanese Americans.

SA A U D SD 28. The Japanese are no better or no worse than any other race.

SA A U D SD 29. I always think of myself as an American first and as a Japanese second.

SA A U D SD 30. Although children may not appreciate Japanese schools at the time, they will later when they grow up.

SA A U D SD 31. Life in the United States is quite ideal for Japanese Americans.

SA A U D SD 32. When in need of aid, it is best to rely mainly on relatives.

SA A U D SD 33. It is better that Japanese Americans date only Japanese Americans.

SA A U D SD 34. Parents who are very companionable with their children can still maintain respect and obedience.

SA A U D SD 35. Once a Japanese always a Japanese.

SA A U D SD 36. Good relations between Japanese and Caucasians can be maintained without the aid of traditional Japanese organizations.

SA A U D SD 37. It is nice if a Japanese American learns more about Japanese culture, but it is really not necessary.

SA A U D SD 38. It would be better if there were no all-Japanese communities in the United States.

SA A U D SD 39. Japan has a great art heritage and has made contributions important to world civilization.

SA A U D SD 40. Those Japanese Americans who are unfavorable toward Japanese culture have the wrong attitude.

SA A U D SD 41. I believe that "He who does not repay a debt of gratitude cannot claim to be noble."

SA A U D SD 42. To avoid being embarrassed by discrimination, the best procedure is to avoid places where a person is not totally welcomed.

SA A U D SD 43. I usually participate in mixed group discussions.

SA A U D SD 44. Many of the Japanese customs, traditions, and attitudes are no longer adequate for the problems of the modern world.

SA A U D SD 45. I enjoy Japanese movies.
SA A U D SD 46. It is a natural part of growing up to occasionally "wise off" to teachers, policemen, and other grownups in authority.
SA A U D SD 47. A person who raises too many questions interferes with the progress of a group.
SA A U D SD 48. I prefer attending an. all-Japanese church.
SA A U D SD 49. One can never let oneself down without letting the family down at the same time.
SA A U D SD 50. Interracial marriages between Japanese Americans and Caucasians should be discouraged.

Appendix E

The Contrasting Values Opinion Survey

Age _____
Male _____
Female _____
Education _____
Occupation _____
Marital
Status _____

This is not a test. There are no correct answers. It is simply a means of finding out how people feel about things. The number 5 means strongly agree, 4 means agree, 3 means undecided, 2 means disagree, and 1 means strongly disagree. For example, if you strongly agree with a statement, simply circle the 5; if you disagree, circle the 2, etc. *Please answer every statement,* even if you have to guess at some.

Strongly agree	Agree	Undecided	Disagree	Strongly disagree	
5	4	3	2	1	1. In the long run, the greatest satisfaction comes from being with one's family.
5	4	3	2	1	2. In this world, if you don't speak out for yourself, no one else will.
5	4	3	2	1	3. The best way to train children is to raise them to be quiet and obedient.
5	4	3	2	1	4. A real man is one who can be on his own and not be dependent on anyone else.
5	4	3	2	1	5. The strongest emotional bond is between a mother and her child.
5	4	3	2	1	6. Ideally, a person is better off if he can do what he really wants to do and doesn't have to worry about others.
5	4	3	2	1	7. Those in positions of authority are automatically entitled to respect.

5 4 3 2 1 8. A truly moral person is one who listens to his own inner conscience and stands up for his convictions no matter how many people say he is wrong.

5 4 3 2 1 9. A person given a job to do should never rest or slacken until it is finished.

5 4 3 2 1 10. Most people feel hampered and tied in because we have too many rules.

5 4 3 2 1 11. When a person is depressed he really wants others to feel worry for him and comfort him.

5 4 3 2 1 12. A person's greatest obligation is to be true to himself and develop his own talents.

5 4 3 2 1 13. If someone starts an argument and raises his voice, it is better to give in than to cause a scene and be embarrassed.

5 4 3 2 1 14. In the family, the strongest emotional tie is between the husband and the wife.

5 4 3 2 1 15. If someone in a position of authority tries to push you around, there is very little you can do about it.

5 4 3 2 1 16. Even though a person may have authority, he should not use his authority openly but should treat his subordinates with mutual respect.

5 4 3 2 1 17. In times of difficulty, it is best to rely on your own family for assistance rather than to seek help from others or to depend entirely on yourself.

5 4 3 2 1 18. Parents should raise their children so that they can leave the family and be on their own.

5 4 3 2 1 19. A person will be more likely to succeed if he listens to the advice of others.

5 4 3 2 1 20. People are essentially the same in that they should all be given the same basic opportunities.

5 4 3 2 1 21. You can usually tell what kind of a person an individual is if you know his family background.

5 4 3 2 1 22. Every person has a right to live his own life as he sees fit.

5 4 3 2 1 23. The best way to succeed is to have a detailed plan and to stick to it no matter what happens.

5 4 3 2 1 24. A person's chief responsibility is to be true to himself.

5 4 3 2 1 25. Parents can never be repaid for what they have done for their children.

5 4 3 2 1 26. People in authority are really no better than anyone else.

5 4 3 2 1 27. It is better not to shout or fight in public even if provoked.

5 4 3 2 1 28. Most people today are probably basically optimistic about the future.

5 4 3 2 1 29. A man can never let himself down without letting down his family at the same time.

5 4 3 2 1 30. The only way to become a success is to take advantage of an opportunity before someone else does.

5 4 3 2 1 31. Anyone in a position of authority is automatically entitled to respect.

5 4 3 2 1 32. A person can never really be a success until he stops following other people's advice and does what he really wants to do.

5 4 3 2 1 33. In the long run it probably doesn't make much difference what a person does, since in the end it all passes away anyhow.

5 4 3 2 1 34. In this world, a person must watch out for himself because no one else will.

5 4 3 2 1 35. True success in life can only come through will power and self-discipline.

5 4 3 2 1 36. No one should be entitled to privileges he has not himself earned.

5 4 3 2 1 37. Although there are precise rules of conduct, a truly wise man knows how to compromise by changing his moral position and adapting to new situations.

5 4 3 2 1 38. It is better to rely on yourself than depend on the help of others.

5 4 3 2 1 39. Despite all the talk, no one can really be a success unless he is helped a lot by others.

5 4 3 2 1 40. A man can never be a success in life until he finally breaks away from others and does what he wants to do.

5 4 3 2 1 41. I assert myself with energy when the occasion demands it.

5 4 3 2 1 42. I express my enthusiasm and respect for the people I admire.

5 4 3 2 1 43. I enjoy organizing or directing the activities of a group.

5 4 3 2 1 44. I see the good points rather than the bad points of the people who are above me.

5 4 3 2 1 45. I am capable of putting myself in the background and working with zest for a person I admire.

5 4 3 2 1 46. I argue with zest for my point of view against others.

5 4 3 2 1 47. I find it rather easy to lead a group of younger people and maintain order.

5 4 3 2 1 48. I accept suggestions rather than insist on working things out my own way.

5 4 3 2 1 49. I usually influence others more than they influence me.

5 4 3 2 1 50. I am considered compliant and obliging by my friends.
5 4 3 2 1 51. I often seek the advice of people older than myself and follow it.
5 4 3 2 1 52. I am usually the one to make the necessary decisions when I am with another person.
5 4 3 2 1 53. I give praise rather freely when the occasion warrants it.
5 4 3 2 1 54. I feel that I can dominate a social situation.
5 4 3 2 1 55. I enjoy the sense of power that comes when I am able to control the actions of others.
5 4 3 2 1 56. I often find myself imitating or agreeing with somebody I consider superior.
5 4 3 2 1 57. I usually follow instructions and do what is expected of me.
5 4 3 2 1 58. I would like to be a leader and sway others to my opinion.
5 4 3 2 1 59. In matters of conduct I conform to custom.
5 4 3 2 1 60. I feel that I am driven by an underlying desire for power.

References

Arkoff, Abe. "Need Patterns in Two Generations of Japanese Americans in Hawaii." *Journal of Social Psychology*, 1959, 50:75-79.

Arkoff, Abe; Gerald Meredith; and Janice Dong. "Attitudes of Japanese American and Caucasian American Students Toward Marriage Roles." *Journal of Social Psychology*, 1963, 59:11-15.

Arkoff, Abe; Gerald Meredith; and Shinkuro Iwahara. "Dominance-Deference Patterning in Motherland Japanese, Japanese American, and Caucasian American Students." *Journal of Social Psychology*, 1962. 58:61-66.

Aronoff, Joel. *Psychological Needs and Cultural Systems: A Case Study*. New Jersey: D. Van Nostrand Company, Inc., 1967.

Asch, Solomon E. "Opinions and Social Pressure." *Scientific American*, November, 1955. Reprint Number 451. San Francisco: W. H. Freeman Co.

Bales, Robert F. "How People Interact in Conferences." *Scientific American*, Match, 1955. Reprint Number 451. San Francisco: W. H. Freeman Co.

Beals, Ralph. "Acculturation." In *Anthropology Today: Selection*, Sol Tax, ed. Chicago: University of Chicago Press, 1962.

Beardsley, R. K.; J. W. Hall; and R. Ward. *Village Japan*. Chicago: University of Chicago Press, 1959.

Beardsley, Richard K. "Cultural Anthropology: Prehistoric and Contemporary Aspects." In *Twelve Doors to Japan*, by John W. Hall and Richard K. Beardsley. New York: McGraw-Hill Book Co., 1965. (a)

_____. "Personality Psychology." In *Twelve Doors to Japan*, by John W. Hall and Richard K. Beardsley. New York: McGraw-Hill Book Co., 1965. (b)

Becker, Carl. *Modern Democracy*. New Haven: Yale University Press, 1946.

Befu, Harumi. "Corporate Emphasis and Patterns of Descent in the Japanese Family. In *Japanese Culture: Its Development and*

Characteristics, Robert J. Smith and Richard K. Beardsley eds. Chicago: Aldine Publishing Co., 1962.

Benedict, Ruth. *The Chrysanthemum and the Sword.* New York: Houghton Mifflin Co., 1946.

Berrien, F. K. *Values of Japanese and American Students.* Technical Report 14, Contract Nonr-404(10). Group Psychology Branch, Office of Naval Research, Department of Defense, Washington, D.C., 1966.

_____."Japanese vs. American Values." *Journal of Social Psychology,* 1965, 65:131-91.

_____."Generational Differences in Values: Americans, Japanese Americans, and Japanese." *Journal of Social Psychology,* 1967, 71:169:75.

Broom, L.; B. J. Siegel; E. Z. Vogt; and J. B. Watson. "Acculturation: An Exploratory Formulation. In *Beyond the Frontier,* Paul Bohannon and Fred Plog, eds. Garden City, Natural History Press., 1967. (Originally published in *American Anthropologist,* Vol. 56 [1954], 973-1000.)

Burwen, Leroy S.; Donald T. Campbell; and Jerry Kidd. "The Use of a Sentence Completion Test in Measuring Attitudes Toward Superiors and Inferiors." *Journal of Applied Psychology,* 1956, 40:248-50.

California, State of; Department of Industrial Relations; Division of Fair Employment Practices. *Californians of Japanese, Chinese, and Filipino Ancestry.* San Francisco.

Caudill, William "Japanese-American Personality and Acculturation." *Genetic Psychology Monographs,* 1952, 45:3-102.

_____. "The Influence of Social Structure and Culture on Human Behavior in Modern Japan." Unpublished manuscript, 1969.

Caudill, William, and George DeVos. "Achievement, Culture and Personality: The Case of the Japanese-Americans." *American Anthropologist,* 1956, 56:1102-26.

Caudill, William and Harry Scarr. "Japanese Value Orientations and Culture Change." *Ethnology,* 1962, 1:53-91.

Caudill, William, and Takeo Doi. "Interrelations of Psychiatry, Culture and Emotion in Japan." In *Man's Image in Medicine and Anthropology,* Iago K. Goldston, ed. New York: International Universities Press, 1963.

Caudill, William, and Helen Weinstein. "Maternal Care and Infant Behavior in Japan and America." *Psychiatry,* 1969, 32:12-43.

Caudill, William, and Lois Frost. "A Comparison of Maternal Care and Infant Behavior in Japanese-American, American, and Japanese Families." *In Influences on Human Development,* Urie Bronfenbremmer, ed. New York: Dryden Press, 1972.

Coleman, Lee. "What is American?" In *The Character of Americans,* Michael McGiffert, ed. Homewood, Ill.: The Dorsey Press, 1964.

Connor, John W., *A Study of Changing Psychological and Behavioral Characteristics in Three Generations of Japanese Americans in the Sacramento Area.* Unpublished Ph.D. dissertation, U.C. Davis, 1972. Xerox University Microfilm No. 72-24, 590, 433 pp.

_____. "Acculturation and Family Continuities in Three Generations of Japanese Americans." *Journal of Marriage and the Family,* February, 1974. (a)

_____. "Acculturation and Changing Need Patterns in Japanese American and Caucasian American Students." *Journal of Social Psychology,* August, 1974. (b)

_____. "Value Continuities and Change in Three Generations of Japanese Americans." *Ethos,* 1974, 2:No. 3: 232-64 (c)

Daniels, Roger. *The Politics of Prejudice.* Berkeley and Los Angeles: University of California Press, 1963.

de Tocqueville, Alexis. "Democracy in America." In *The Character of Americans,* Michael McGiffert, ed. Homewood, Ill.: The Dorsey Press, 1964.

DeVos, George. "A Quantitative Rorschach Assessment of Maladjustment and Rigidity in Acculturating Japanese Americans." *Genetic Psychology Monographs,* 1955, 52:51-87.

_____. "Social Values and Personal Attitudes in Primary Human Relations in Niiike." Center for Japanese and Korean Studies, Institute of International Studies, University of California, 1965. Reprint No. 26.

_____. "The Relation of Guilt Towards Parents to Achievement and Arranged Marriage Among the Japanese." In *Personalities and Cultures,* Robert Hunt, ed. New York: Natural History Press, 1967.

_____. "Achievement and Innovation in Culture and Personality." In *The Study of Personality: An Interdisciplinary Appraisal,* Edward Norbeck, Douglas Price-Williams, and William McCord, eds. New York: Holt, Rinehart and Winston, 1968.

_____. *Socialization for Achievement: Essays on the Cultural Psychology of the Japanese.* Berkeley and Los Angeles: University of California Press, 1973.

Doi, Takeo L. "Amae: A Key Concept for Understanding Japanese Personality Structure." In *Japanese Culture: Its Development and Characteristics,* Robert J. Smith and Richard K. Beardsley, eds. Chicago: Aldine Publishing Co., 1962.

Dore, Ronald P., ed. *Aspects of Social Change in Modern Japan.* Princeton: Princeton University Press, 1967.

Dozier, Edward P. "Resistance to Acculturation and Assimilation in an Indian Pueblo." *American Anthropologist,* 1951, 53:56-66.

DuBois, Cora. "The Dominant Value Profile of American Culture." In *The Character of Americans,* Michael McGiffert, ed. Homewood, Ill.: The Dorsey Press, 1964.

Edwards, Allen L. *Edwards Personal Preference Schedule Manual.* New York: The Psychological Corporation, 1959.

Embree, John. *Suye Mura.* Chicago: University of Chicago Press, 1939.

Emerson, Ralph Waldo. "Self-Reliance." In *Selections From Ralph Waldo Emerson,* Stephen E. Whicher, ed. New York: Houghton Mifflin Co. (Riverside Edition No. A-13), 1960.

Fenz, Walter D., and Abe Arkoff. "Comparative Need Patterns of Five Ancestry Groups in Hawaii." *Journal of Social Psychology,* 1962, 58:67-89.

Fischer, Anne, and John L. Fischer. *The New Englanders of Orchard Town U.S.A.: Six Cultures Series.* Vol. 5. New York: John Wiley and Sons, 1966.

Forer, Bertram R. "A Structured Sentence Completion Test." *Journal of Projective Techniques,* 1950, 14:15-29.

Frost, Lois. *Child Raising Techniques as Related to Acculturation Among Japanese Americans.* Unpublished Master's thesis, Sacramento State College, 1970.

Gillespie, James M., and Gordon W. Allport. *Youth's Outlook on the Future: A Cross-National Study.* Garden City, N.Y.: Doubleday and Co., 1955.

Gillin, John. "National and Regional Values." In *The Character of Americans,* Michael McGiffert, ed. Homewood, Ill.: The Dorsey Press, 1967.

Goodman, Mary Ellen. "Values, Attitudes and Social Concepts of Japanese and American Children." *American Anthropologist,* 1957, 59:979-99.

———. "Influences of Childhood and Adolescence." In *The Study of Personality: An Interdisciplinary Appraisal,* Douglas Price-Williams and William M. McCord, eds. New York: Holt, Rinehart and Winston, 1968.

Gordon, Milton. *Assimilation in American Life.* New York: Oxford University Press, 1964.

Hall, John Whitney. "Education and Modern National Development." In *Twelve Doors to Japan,* John W. Hall and Richard K. Beardsley, eds. New York: McGraw-Hill Book Co., 1965.

Hallowell, A. Irving. "Objibwa Personality and Acculturation." In *Beyond the Frontier,* Paul Bohannon and Fred Plog, eds. Garden City, N.Y.: Natural History Press, 1967.

Hanfman, Eugenia, and J. W. Getzels. "Studies of the Sentence Completion Test." *Journal of Projective Techniques,* 1953, 17:280-94.

Haring, Douglas G. "Japanese Character in the Twentieth Century." *Annals of the American Academy of Political and Social Science,* March 1967, 370:133-42.

Holspopple, James D., and Florence R. Miale. *Sentence Completion: A Projective Method for the Study of Personality.* Springfield, Ill.: Charles C. Thomas, 1954.

References

Hsu, Francis L. K. "American Core Values and National Character." In *Psychological Anthropology*, Francis L. K. Hsu, ed. Homewood, Ill.: The Dorsey Press, 1961.

Hulse, Fredrick S. "Convention and Reality in Japanese Culture." In *Japanese Character and Culture*, Bernard S. Silberman, ed. Tucson: University of Arizona Press, 1962.

Iga, Mamoru. "Changes in Value Orientations of Japanese Americans." Quoted in *Japanese Americans: The Evolution of a Subculture*, by Harry Kitano. Englewood Cliffs, N.J.: Prentice-Hall, 1969.

Iwama, Frank. "Why—The Quiet American?" *Sacramento J.A.C.L. News Letter* Number 5, May 1971, Sacramento, California.

Jessor, Richard D. Graves; Robert C. Hanson; and Shirley L. Graves. *Society, Personality, and Deviant Behavior: A Study of A Tri-Ethnic Community.* New York: Holt, Rinehart, and Winston, 1968.

Johnson, Erwin. "The Emergence of a Self-Conscious Entrepreneurial Class in Rural Japan." In *Japanese Culture: Its Development and Characteristics*, Robert J. Smith and Richard K. Beardsley, eds. Chicago: Aldine Publishing Co., 1962.

Kaku, Kanae, and Y. Scott Matsumoto. "Influence of a Folk Superstitition on Fertility of Japanese in California and Hawaii, 1966." *American Journal of Public Health*, 1975, 65:No.2: 170-74.

Kawashima, Takeyeshi. "The Status of the Individual in the Notion of Law, Right, and Social Order in Japan." In *The Japanese Mind*, Charles A. Moore, ed. Honolulu: East-West Center Press, 1967.

Keene, Donald. *Living Japan.* Garden City, N.Y.: Doubleday and Company, 1960.

Kitano, Harry H. L. "Differential Child-Rearing Attitudes Between First and Second Generation Japanese in the United States." *Journal of Social Psychology*, 1961, 53:13-19.

_____ "Changing Achievement Patterns of the Japanese in the United States." *Journal of Social Psychology*, 1962, 58:257-64.

_____ *Japanese Americans: The Evolution of a Subculture.* Englewood Cliffs, N.J.: Prentice-Hall, 1969.

Kline, Milton. "A Short Form Sentence Projection Technique." *Journal of General Psychology*, 1948, 38:273-87.

Kluckhohn, Clyde. "Have There Been Discernible Shifts in American Values in the Past Generation?" In *The American Style*, Elting E. Morison, ed. New York: Harper and Row, 1958.

_____ *Mirror for Man.* Greenwich, Conn.: Fawcett Publications (A Premier Reprint), 1960.

Kohn, Melvin L. *Class and Conformity: A Study in Values.* Homewood, Ill.: The Dorsey Press, 1969.

Kuhn, Gene. "Hirabayashi Challenges Nisei to Fight All Inequalities." *Pacific Citizen*, December 3, 1971.

Lee, Dorothy. *Freedom and Culture.* Englewood Cliffs, N.J.: Prentice-Hall, 1959.

Lerner, Max. "A Changing American Character?" In *The Character of Americans*, Michael McGiffert, ed. Homewood, Ill.: The Dorsey Press, 1964.

Lipset, Seymour Martin. *The First New Nation*. Garden City, N.Y.: Doubleday and Co., (An Anchor Book), 1967.

Maruyama, Masao. "Patterns of Individuation and the Case of Japan: A Conceptual Scheme." In *Changing Japanese Attitudes Toward Modernization*, Marius B. Jansen, ed. Princeton: Princeton University Press, 1965.

Masuda, Minoru; Gary H. Matsumoto; and G. M. Meredith. "Ethnic Identity in Three Generations of Japanese Americans." *Journal of Social Psychology*, 1970, 81:199-207.

Masuoka, Jitsuichi. "The Japanese Patriarch in Hawaii." *Social Forces*, 1937, 17:241-48.

Matsumoto, Yoshiharu Scott. "Contemporary Japan: The Individual and the Group." *Transactions of the American Philosophical Society*, 1960, 50:Part I.

McClelland, D. C. *The Achieving Society*. Princeton: D. Van Nostrand Company, 1961.

McWilliams, Carel. *Prejudice: Japanese Americans: Symbol of Racial Intolerance*. Boston: Little, Brown and Co., 1944.

Mead, Margaret. "We Are All Third Generation." In *The Character of Americans*, Michael McGiffert, ed. Homewood, Ill.: The Dorsey Press, 1964.

Minami, Hiroshi *Nihonjin no Shinri* (Psychology of the Japanese People). Tokyo: Iwanami-Shoten, 1953.

Minturn, Leigh, and William W. Lambert. *Mothers of Six Cultures: Antecedents of Child Rearing*. New York: John Wiley and Sons, 1964.

Modell, John. "Japanese American Family: A Perspective for Future Investigation." *Pacific Historical Review*, 1968, 36:No. 1: 67-81.

Moloney, James Clark. *Understanding the Japanese Mind*. New York: Philosophical Library, 1954.

Moore, Charles A., ed. *The Japanese Mind*. Honolulu: East-West Center Press, 1967.

Murray, Henry Alexander, et al. *Exploration in Personality*. New York: Oxford University Press, 1938.

Nakamura, Hajime. *Ways of Thinking of Eastern People*, Philip P. Weiner, ed. Honolulu: East-West Center Press, 1964.

Nakane, Chie. *Kinship and Economic Organization in Rural Japan*. New York: Humanities Press, 1967.

————. *Japanese Society*. Berkeley and Los Angeles: University of California Press, 1970.

Norbeck, Edward. "Age-Grading in Japan." *American Anthropologist*, 1953, 55:373-84.

Norbeck, Edward, and DeVos, George. "Japan." In *Psychological*

Anthropology, Francis L.K. Hsu, ed. Homewood, Ill.: The Dorsey Press, 1961.

Oyama, Joe. "An A.J.A. vs Japanese." *Pacific Citizen*, January 3, 1969.

Parkes, Henry Bamford. *The American Experience*. New York: Alfred A. Knopf and Random House (Vintage Books), 1955.

Passin, Herbert. "Japanese Society." In *The International Encyclopedia of the Social Sciences*. Vol. 8:236-49. New York: Macmillan, 1968.

Payne, A. F. *Sentence Completions*. New York: New York Guidance Clinic, 1928.

Peterson, William. "Success Story: Japanese American Style." *New York Times*, January 9, 1966, p. 20.

Phillips, Herbert P. *Thai Peasant Personality: The Patterning of Inter-Personal Behavior in the Village of Bang Chan*. Berkeley and Los Angeles: University of California Press, 1965.

Plath, David. *The After Hours: Modern Japan and the Search for Enjoyment*. Berkeley and Los Angeles: University of California Press, 1964.

Potter, David M. "Economic Abundance and the Formation of American Character." In *The Character of Americans*, Michael McGiffert, ed. Homewood, Ill.: The Dorsey Press, 1964.

Rabin, A. I. "Comparison of American and Israeli Children by Means of a Sentence Completion Technique." *Journal of Social Psychology*, 1959, 59:3-12.

Reischauer, Edwin O. *The United States and Japan*. 3rd ed. New York: The Viking Press, 1965.

Reischauer, Edwin O., and John K. Fairbank. *East Asia: The Great Tradition*. Boston: Houghton-Mifflin, 1960.

Reisman, David. "The Saving Remnant." In *The Character of Americans*, Michael McGiffert, ed. Homewood, Ill.: The Dorsey Press, 1964.

Rieff, Philip. *Freud: The Mind of a Moralist*. New York: Doubleday and Co., (An Anchor Book), 1961.

Rohde, A. R. "Explorations in Personality by the Sentence Completion Method." *Journal of Applied Psychology*, 1946, 30:169-81.

Rotter, Julian B., and B. Willerman. "The Incomplete Sentence Test as a Method of Studying Personality." *Journal of Consulting Psychology*, 11:43-48.

Rychlak, Joseph F.: Paul H. Mussen; and John W. Bennet. "An Example of the Use of the Incomplete Sentence Test in Applied Anthropological Research." *Human Organization*, 1957, 16:No. 1:25-29.

Sacks, Joseph M., and Sidney Levy. "The Sentence Completion Test." In *Projective Psychology* by L. E. Abt and L. Bellak. New York: Alfred A. Knopf Co., 1950.

Sansom, George B. *Japan: A Short Cultural History*. New York: Appleton-Century Crofts, 1943.

————. *The Western World and Japan.* New York: Random House (Vintage Books), 1973.

————. "Santa Anita—Born Nisei Author of New Book: *American in Disguise.*" *Pacific Citizen,* February 12, 1971.

Sears, Robert R.; Eleanor E. Maccoby; and Harry Levin. *Patterns of Child Rearing.* Evanston, Ill.: Row, Peterson & Co., 1957.

Schwartz, Audrey James. "The Culturally Advantaged: A Study of Japanese-American Pupils." *Sociology and Social Research,* 1971, 59:341-53.

Silberman, Bernard S. *Japanese Character and Culture.* Tucson: University of Arizona Press, 1962.

Smith, Elmer. "Japanese in the Americas, Pioneering Work of Nikkei on This Hemisphere Retold: The Japanese in Brazil." *Pacific Citizen,* December 21-28, 1973, 77: No. 25 (originally published in *Pacific Citizen* in 1951).

Smith, Robert. Personal communication, October 25, 1967.

Smith, Robert J.; J. B. Cornell; H. Saito; and To Maeyama. *The Japanese and Their Descendants in Brazil: An Annotated Bibliography.* Sao Paulo, Brazil: Centro De Estudos, Nipo-Brasileiros, 1967.

Smith, Thomas C. *The Agrarian Origins of Modern Japan.* Stanford: Stanford University Press, 1959.

Spindler, George D. "Education in a Transforming American Culture." In *Education and Culture.* New York: Holt, Rinehart and Winston, 1963.

Tax, Sol. "Acculturation." In *Selected Papers of the Fifth International Congress of Anthropological and Ethnological Sciences: Men and Cultures.* Anthony F. C. Wallace, ed. University of Pennsylvania Press, 1960.

Titiev, Mischa. "The Japanese Colony in Peru." *Far Eastern Quarterly,* 1951, 10:227-47.

Tunnard, Christopher, and Henry Hope Reed. *American Skyline.* New York: The New American Library, 1956.

Turner, Frederick Jackson. "The Significance of the Frontier in American History." *American Historical Association Report* for 1893. Washington: U.S. Government Printing Office, 1894.

U.S. Bureau of the Census. *1970 Census of the Population: General Social and Economic Characteristics: California.* Washington: U.S. Government Printing Office, 1972.

————. *1970 Census of The Population: Final Report PC(2)-1G, Japanese, Chinese, and Filipinos in The United States.* Washington: U.S. Government Printing Office, 1973.

Vogel, Ezra. *Japan's New Middle Class.* Berkeley and Los Angeles: University of California Press, 1967.

Watts, Alan. *Psychotherapy East and West.* New York: The New American Library (A Mentor Book), 1963.

Whyte, William H., Jr. *The Organization Man.* Garden City, N.Y.: Doubleday and Company (A Doubleday Anchor Book), 1956.

Williams, Robin M., Jr. *American Society.* 3rd ed. New York: Alfred A. Knopf, 1970.

Yamamoto, Tatsuro. "Japanese National Character." In *Cross Cultural Understanding: Epistemology in Anthropology,* F. S. C. Northrup and Helen H. Livingston, eds. New York: Harper and Row, 1964.

Index

Acculturation
  failure of, in Brazil, 303-4
  of female Issei, 99-100
  of Issei, 89-91, 93-94, 297-98
  of Japanese Americans, 271-94
  levels of, compared, 198-222
  of Nisei, 104-7, 300-310
  of Sansei, 133-36, 308
"Acculturation" (Beals), quoted, 8
Achievement levels, 283-92
Achieving Society, The (McClelland),
  316
Adaptation, 242
Aggression, 183-85
Aichi, Japan, 83, 95
Allport, Gordon W., on rights, 57
American characteristics, 43-65
American values, study of, 311-13
Anthropology Today, 8
Arkoff, Abe, 2, 198, 223, 224, 260, 271,
  284, 294
Asch, Solomon E., on conformity, 78
Assimilation in American Life
  (Gordon), 133

Bales, Robert F., 78
Beals, Ralph, 8
Beardsley, Richard K., 10, 18, 25, 26,
  78, 245
  on antagonistic cooperation, 76-77
  on conformity, 77
  on dependency, 41-42
  on group affiliation, 29-30

  on social structure, 21-22
Becker, Carl, on individual self-
  direction, 48
Befu, Harumi, 23
  on family ties, 24
Behavioral characteristics, Japanese
  American, compared to
  Caucasian American, 223-69
Benedict, Ruth, 10, 32, 37, 38, 41, 130,
  284, 292
  on family discipline, 173
  on Japanese life, 204
  on meaning of On, 92-93
  on obedience to authority, 38
  on social hierarchy, 34
Berrien, F. K., 2, 10, 37, 271, 282, 284,
  285, 294
  on authority, 38
  on test results, 276
"Best-time-of-life" question, 153-54
Brazil, social isolation of Japanese in,
  303-4
Broom, L., on acculturation, 7
Buddhism, relation of Sansei to, 129
Bureau of the Census, 13
  report on Chinese, Japanese and
  Filipinos, 290

California Fair Employment Practices
  Commission, 1
California State University
  (Sacramento), 11, 117, 285
Cather, Willa, 47

Caucasian Americans
  characteristics of, 257-60
  compared to Sansei, 283-93
  values of, 3-15
Caudill, William, xiii, 1, 4, 8, 10, 81,
  82, 83, 105, 173, 198, 282, 283,
  285, 286, 287, 292, 299, 301, 305,
  315, 317
  on collaterality, 40
  on dependency, 39-40
  on group affiliation, 40-41
  on Japanese emotionality, 176-77
  on self-assertion, 63
Chang, K. H. L., 141, 224
"Changing American Character"
  (Lipset), 55
Characteristics, determining specific
  Japanese, 7-44
Chiba, Japan, 23
Chicago, middle class status of
  Japanese in, xiii-xiv
Child-rearing practices, 89, 299-300,
  305-6
Children, duties of, 148-50
Chōnan (household successors), 157
Chrysanthemum and the Sword
  (Benedict), 12, 30, 173
Citizenship, duties of, 167-70
Class and Conformity (Kohn), 139
Coleman, Lee, 2, 45
Collectivity, Japanese reliance on,
  29-32, 245
Competitiveness, 302-3
Conformity
  American pressure toward, 54-56
  patterns of, 76-80
Connor, John W., 283, 285, 290, 292
Contemporary Japan: The Individual
  and the Group (Matsumoto),
  30-31
Contrasting Values Survey, 164, 172
Cooper, James Fenimore, 47
Culture patterns, transmission of,
  317-18

Daimyos, Japanese ruling, 16-17
Daniels, Roger, 2, 83, 84
  on Issei males, 2

Deference, social, 37-42, 181-83,
  242-43, 248, 301-2
Dependency, social, 39-42
DeVos, George, 1, 4, 10, 26, 27, 41, 81,
  198, 282, 284, 287, 292
Division of Fair Employment
  Practices, 102
Doi, Takeo L., 10, 178
  on dependency, 39-40
  on emotionalism, 176-77
  on self-assertion, 63
Dominance-deference inventory,
  260-68
Dong, Janice, 2
Dozier, Edward P., 2
DuBois, Cora, 10
Duty and obligation, 20-21, 32-34,
  164-67, 247

Education
  of Nisei generation, 102-3
  of Sansei generation, 118-19,
  291-92
Educational achievement of Japanese
  Americans, 284-87, 301
Edwards, Allen L., 279, 280, 283, 284
  on group affiliation, 287, 289
  on self-abasement, 289
Edwards Personal Preference
  Schedule, 10, 12, 271-94
Embree, John, 208
Emerson, Ralph Waldo, on self-
  reliance, 59-60
Emotional ties, 170-72
Emotionality, patterns of, 176-79
English, expelling of from Japan, 15
Enomotos, Jerry, 135
Equality, American, 52-57
Ethnic identity, of Japanese in the
  U.S., 193-222, 232-45, 309,
  318-19
Ethnic Identity Questionnaire, 10, 12

Fairbank, John K., 17
Family ties, Japanese, 21-28, 89-90,
  128, 172-76, 240-41, 297
Father-child relationship, 185-88
Fear, measures of, 190-92

Fenz, Walter D., 271
Fire, fear of in Issei generation,
    144-45
Fischer, Anne & John L., 10
    on self-realization, 61
Food habits
    Nisei, 103-4
    Sansei, 120
442nd Regimental Combat Team
    (World War II), 112, 304
Franklin, Benjamin, maxims of, 19
Fresno, California, 127
Freud, Sigmund, and individualism,
    50-51
Frontier heritage, American, 45-46
Frost, Lois, 283, 305, 306, 315, 317
Fujinkai (women's associations), 88

Gans, Herbert, 3
Generation gap, Japanese American,
    307-8
Generations
    average age of, xiv
    differences among the, 89-92, 98,
        105-7, 112-14, 121, 141-92
        passim, 193-222 passim, 223-69
    social values of the Japanese
        American, 271-94
Gillespie, James M., on rights, 57
Goodman, Mary Ellen, 284, 287, 299
Gordon, Milton, 133, 318
    on assimilation, 2-4
Gratitude and obligation, 158-61
Group affiliation, 29-32, 287-89

Hall, John W., 10, 19
Haring, Douglas, on social status, 35
Hawaiian Japanese Americans, 284
Hideyoshi, leadership of in Japan, 15
Hierarchy, social, 34-37, 247-48
Higher education, Japanese
    Americans in, 291-92
Hiroshima, Japan, 83, 95
Holidays, Japanese American
    observance of, 93, 98-99, 110-11,
    131-32
Hopi Tewa Indians, 2
Hosokawa, Bill, 135

Household structure, Japanese, 21-28
Hsu, Francis, L. K., 10
    on self-reliance, 60, 61
Hulse, Frederick, on mother-son
    bond, 41
100th Batalion (World War II), 304
Hypothesized group differences,
    232-45

Ie (household), Japanese concept of,
    21-28, 296
Iga, Mamoru, 1
Ikemoto, Atsushi, 125
Immigration, Japanese, to the U.S.,
    84-86, 95-96
Incomplete Sentence Test, 10, 12,
    137-92, 235
Independence
    versus collectivity, 242
    versus deference, 188-90
Individual, the Japanese, and the
    household structure, 21-28
Individualism, American, 48-52
Individuation, patterns of, 67-75,
    297-98
Issei
    acculturation of, 2, 89-91, 93-94,
        297-98
    characteristics of, 205-11, 245-50,
        280-82
    females, 95-100
    interviews with, 81-100
    males, 83-94
    retention of Japanese characteristics
        by, 296-99
Iwahara, Shinkuro, 2, 198, 223, 224,
    260, 271, 273
Iwama, Frank, on acculturation,
    134-35

Japan, isolation of from the outside
    world, 15
Japanese
    characteristics that are, 7-44
    individual and household, 21-28
Japanese American Citizens League
    (JACL), 134, 310
Japanese Americans

Japanese American (continued)
  compared with Caucasian
    Americans, 141-92
  low crime rate among, xiii
  middle class status of, xiii-xiv, 1
  as a "model minority," 4
  testing of, to determine
    characteristics, 10-11
Japanese Language School, 103
Japanese Mind (Moore), 30
"Japanese vs. American Values"
    (Berrien), 37
Japanese words, familiarity with,
    91-93, 107-8, 129-30
Jews, acculturation of American, 2-4
Jisannan (non-successor sons), 83, 157
Johnson, Erwin, 157, 235
  on family structure, 27-28

Kagawa, Japan, 83
Kaku, Kanae, 317
Kanagawa, Japan, 95
Kawashima, Takeyeshi, on social
    obligations, 32-33
Keene, Donald, 208
Kenjinkai (prefectural associations),
    87-88
Kitano, Harry H. L. xiii, 1, 81, 82,
    102, 118, 133, 286, 300, 305
  on assimilation, 2
  on Japanese Language School, 103
Kluckhohn, Clyde, 10, 65
  on conformity in America, 56
  on personal rights, 58-59
Kochi, Japan, 83
Kohn, Melvin L.
  on middle class attitudes, 139, 140
  on parental values, 65
Kuhn, Gene, 127
Kumamoto, Japan, 83, 95

Lambert, William W., 10
  on child-rearing, 59
  on self-assertion, 62, 183-89
Land, availability of in early
    America, 45-48
Lee, Dorothy, on individualism, 50
Lerner, Max, 10
Levin, Harry, 62

Lincoln, Abraham, 19
Lipset, Seymour M., 10, 236
  on equality, 53-54, 72-73, 314-15
Literature, American and European,
    compared, 51-52
Locke, John, and the English liberal
    tradition, 58
Loyalty, need to prove, 304

McClelland, D. C., 316
Maccoby, Eleanor E., 62
McWilliams, Carel, 83
Mair, Lucy, 8
Male-female attitudes, differences
    between in Nisei, 106-11
Male-female behavioral characteristics
    compared, 271-94
Marriages, attitudes of Sansei toward
    mixed, 122-27
Maruyama, Masao, 74, 76, 236, 298
  on individualism, 71-72
  on modernization, 68
Masuda, Minoru, 2, 193, 194, 196, 208
Matsumoto, Gary H., 2, 193, 194, 196,
    208
Matsumoto, Yoshiharu Scott, 317
  on collectivity, 30-31
Meredith, Gerald, M., 2, 193, 196, 198,
    208, 223, 224, 260
Mie, Japan, 95
Minority groups, relations with other,
    88, 90
Minturn, Leigh, 10
  on child-rearing, 59
  on self-assertion, 62, 183-84
Mirror for Man (Kluckhohn), 58
Miyagi, Japan, 95
Modell, John, 81, 82, 83, 89, 90, 95
"Model minority," Japanese
    Americans as a, 4
Moloney, James C., on Japanese
    psychoanalysis, 51
Moore, Charles, A., on status of the
    individual, 30
Mother-child relationships, 176-79

Nagasaki Harbor, Dutch traders in,
  · 15
Nakamura, Hajime, 10

on social relationships, 31
Nakane, Chie, 21, 284
  on competition, 302
  on democracy, 78-79
  on household structure, 22-23, 24,
    25
  on ranking order, 237
  on social relationships, 36-37
Nichi Bei Times (San Francisco), 194
Nihonjin kai (Japanese association),
    88
Nippon-ichi, 35-36
Nisei
  characteristics of, 101-15, 211-17,
    250-53, 282-83
  intermediate status of, 299-304
Nisei: The Quiet Americans
    (Hosokawa), 134
Nobunaga, leadership of in Japan, 15
Norbeck, Edward, 10, 112

Obligation, the individual's strongest,
    162-64
Occupational goals, Sansei, 120-21
Ojibwa Indians, 2
Okayama, Japan, 83, 95
On (obligation), concept of, 32,
    92-93, 107
"Opinions and Social Pressure"
    (Asch), 78
Optimism, 241
Organization Man (Whyte), 254
Osaka, Japan, 95
Oyabun-kobun relationship, 36
Oyama, Joe, on hierarchical thinking,
    302

Pacific Citizen, 127, 310
Parental Attitude Research Inventory,
    300
Parent-child relationship, 39-41,
    150-53
Parkes, Henry Bamford
  on individual rights, 58
  on literature, 51-52
Passin, Herbert, on social
    relationships, 36
Patterns of Child Rearing (Sears,
    Maccoby, & Levin), 62

Payne, A. F., 137
Peru, Japanese in, 303
Peterson, William, on assimilation, 4
Plath, David, on individualism, 31
Portuguese, expelling of from Japan,
    15
Potter, David M., 10
  on American character, 52-53
  on equality, 56-57
Psychoanalysis, American versus
    Japanese, 50-51
"Psychological lag," 4

Rainwater, Lee, 1
Ranking, social, 301-2
Reischauer, Edwin, O., 10, 17, 38
  on duty, 33-34
  on group affiliation, 31-32
  on the Japanese soldier, 43-44
  on obedience to authority, 35-36
Reisman, David, 53, 71, 77
Reno, Nevada, 125, 127
Rieff, Philip, on Freud, 50-51
Rights and privileges, 57-59, 164-67
Rural life, early American, 47-48

Sacramento (Calif.), 290
  Japanese community in, 87-88
  testing of Japanese community in,
    12-13
Sacramento State College, 139, 235
Samurai class, 16, 20
Sankin kotai, system, 17
Sansei
  acculturation of, 2, 133-36, 308
  characteristics, 117-36, 217-21,
    253-57, 283-93
  relation of, to Nisei, 113-14
  status in American society, 304-10
Sansom, Goerge B., 10
  on popular rights, 20
  on social ethics, 34
Schwartz, A. J., 285, 287
  on achievement motivation, 292
Sears, Robert R., 62
Seattle, Washington, testing of
    Japanese in, 193
Seicho no ie (religious sect), 89
Sekigahara, battle of (1600), 15, 16

Self-assertion, 62-63, 183-85
Self-reliance 59-61, 154-58, 179-81
Sexes, differences between, analyzed,
    226-32
Shimabara rebellion of 1638, 15
Shizuoka, Japan, 83
Silberman, Bernard S., 10
Situational ethic, 43-44
Smith, Thomas C.
    on Ishikawa Takuboku, 32
    on Japanese in Brazil, 303-4
Social isolation, 303-4
Social Science Research Council
    Summer Seminar on
    Acculturation (1953), 7
Social values of Japanese Americans,
    compared to Caucasian
    Americans, 271-94
Sontaku, Niromiya, 20
Spindler, George D., on American
    values, 3 1-12, 314
Survey of Contrasting Values, 10, 12
"Symbolic Judaism," 3

Takuboku, Isnikawa, 32
Tax, Sol, 4
Thematic Apperception Test, 137, 138
Titiev, Misch:, 303
Tocqueville, Alexis de, 10, 53
    on conformity in America, 54-55
    on frontier America, 46
Tokugawa Ieyasu, unification of
    Japan by, 15-21, 45
Tokyo, Japan 83
Tokyo University of Education, 273
Turner, Frederick Jackson, frontier
    thesis of, 5
Twelve Doors to Japan (Beardsley),
    29

U.S. Bureau of the Census report on
    Japanese, Chinese, and Filipinos,
    290
University of Washington, 193

Vogel, Ezra, 10, 38, 245
    on child rearing, 38
    on dependency, 40

    on group affiliation, 31
    on obedience to authority, 37

Wakayama, Japan, 83, 95
Ward, R., 10
Watts, Alan, on individuality, 49
Weinstein, Helen, 30, 299, 305
    on group affiliation, 40-41
Whyte, William H., 254
Williams, Robin M., 10, 65
    on conformity, 55
    on equality and conformity, 76
    on freedom, 58
    on individualism, 48-49
    on self-assertion, 63
    on self-reliance, 60
    on valuations, 57

Yamaguchi, Japan, 83, 95
Yamamoto, Tatsuro, on social
    relationships, 34-35
Yamanashi, Japan, 83, 95
Yamato damashii (Japanese spirit),
    100
Yobiyose (summoned immigrants),
    84, 85
Yukichi, Fukuzawa, 20

Zen Buddhism, ascetic practices of, 35